PROGRAMMING WITH

R

base® 5000

No. 2666
$28.95

PROGRAMMING WITH

base® 5000

CARY N. PRAGUE AND JAMES E. HAMMITT

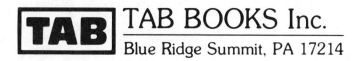

TAB BOOKS Inc.
Blue Ridge Summit, PA 17214

Dedication

This book is dedicated to the Nowacki Family of Feeding Hills, Massachusetts. To Bob, Cis, Mark, and Chris whose support and enthusiasm for our work keeps us going.

FIRST EDITION
FIRST PRINTING

Copyright © 1986 by TAB BOOKS Inc.
Printed in the United States of America

Library of Congress Cataloging in Publication Data

Prague, Cary N.
Programming with R:base 5000.

Includes index.
1. Data base management.   2. R:base 5000
(Computer program)   I. Hammitt, James E.   II. Title.
III. Title: Programming with R:base five thousand.
QA76.9.D3P72927   1986   005.75′65   86-5841
ISBN 0-8306-0366-2
ISBN 0-8306-0466-9 (pbk.)

Contents

Acknowledgments

We wish to thank Bob Nowacki for getting us an advanced copy (a real one) of R:base 5000. Also, Michael Sherwood of Microcrim for providing us support when we needed it and for providing a copy of R:base for ourselves and TAB BOOKS. We also wish to thank the support people at Microcrim for answering all our questions every time we called.

Introduction

R:base 5000 is a very powerful database language. It features user-friendly commands to create database structures and to add, change, and delete data items. R:base 5000 also allows you to search, select, and display records in the database. Reports can easily be designed and printed. For many users, these commands are sufficient to provide them with simple database queries and reports. Other users, however, would like to unlock the power of R:base 5000 as a programming language.

In the ever-expanding world of microcomputers, R:base 5000 is quickly gaining popularity as a programming language. For many people it has replaced BASIC or Pascal. In big business it is even used as a replacement for COBOL, FORTRAN, and PL/I. R:base 5000 has a "full" programming language that is capable of solving almost any data processing problem.

Because of its use of database techniques, R:base 5000 makes programming easier than with traditional languages. All normal programming techniques can be used with R:base 5000—decision making, looping, sorting, searching, selecting, displaying, data manipulating, and custom reporting. Full-screen selection and data entry menus are simple to design and implement. Many database programming commands can also be integrated into R:base 5000 programs. You can set the programming environment or do housekeeping with very simple commands. If a record description needs to be changed after the program is substantially complete, it is a simple task to change the program. It would not be a complicated task as it is with non-database languages. Database query commands used to sort, search, and select records are also used as programming commands to replace many programming statements found in traditional languages.

R:base 5000 also features a complete application generator that can create complete programs or be used as a stepping stone to create your own programs. The application generator also creates menus for inclusion into your own custom systems. Reports are simplified by a very powerful report generator, and creating data entry screens is just as simple with the R:base form generator. Add this to R:base's own word processor for creating your program code and you can program faster than you ever thought possible.

R:base 5000 is truly the fourth-generation programming generator for the eighties. This book is written for the computer novice as well as the experienced programmer who wishes to add a new language to his toolbox. The book will help both the weekend hacker and the businessman.

It is expected that you are somewhat familiar with R:base 5000 and have at least created a database and produced simple reports. If you are a novice, you will find this book a good introduction to programming concepts and database techniques. The use of R:base 5000 is explained in-depth with each of these topics. If you are an experienced programmer, you will find the book a complete guide to making the transition from whatever languages you already know to R:base 5000.

The book is organized into three main sections: Programming Fundamentals, Database Fundamentals, and Programming with R:base 5000. In each section, you will meet Fred. Fred owns a fish market and will help teach you to program. Fred will help you learn in each of the three sections. Programming Fundamentals covers a complete introduction to programming, along with comparisons of how R:base 5000 differs from traditional programming languages. Database Fundamentals explains what a database is and how you can efficiently and effectively design and use the databases. The final section, Programming with R:base 5000, is subdivided into several chapters. Each shows how to use a particular R:base 5000 command. Each chapter presents the topic as a stand-alone subject and also integrates it with the previously discussed topics, allowing you to break down the programming topics into individual subjects and understand how they come together to form the complete program.

After reading this book, both novice and expert will be prepared to design, code, and implement any problem with the R:base 5000 solution.

Section I

PROGRAMMING
FUNDAMENTALS

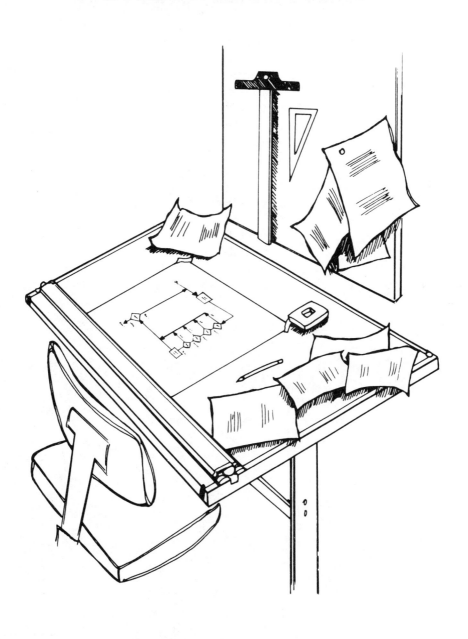

Chapter 1

The Basics
of Programming

Database programming is the use of specialized language statements to manipulate items of information. The purpose of this manipulation is to produce a desired result that is presented in the form of reports, graphs, or tables of information. The name that programmers give to unprocessed information is *data*.

DATA VERSUS INFORMATION

Simply stated, data is the raw form of information; that is, facts and figures that alone have very little or no meaning. The purpose of computer programs is to arrange data into more meaningful or useful forms.

For example, if you saw a list of numbers **199462482010454**, the numbers appear totally meaningless. The list could be anything. However, when it is broken up slightly, the result is **199462482-010454**. The list is still data; that is, no new information has resulted from that division. If the number is broken into its smallest components, **199-46-2482-01-04-54**, it appears, and I mean *appears*, to be a social security number and a date. If the data is now labeled

SSN   DATE
199-46-2482/01-04-54

you know something that was not known before; the meaningless data has become *information*. This example explains the difference between data and information.

DATA TYPES

Computer programming is the manipulation of data to form information. The data items that are manipulated can take two basic forms: character and numeric.

Character data includes things like names, addresses, telephone numbers, and any other items that are later reported in the same form in which they are stored. Character data items can be manipulated in some ways but cannot be used in mathematical calculations. For example, names can be stored in a last, first, middle order, but appear on a report in a first, middle, last format. The manipulation, in this case, involved the rearrangement of the characters that make up the data item. Any attempt to add, subtract, multiply, divide, or perform any other type of mathematical calculation using the name information would not only be meaningless, but would quite probably cause an error.

Character data can also surprise you. Usually social security numbers, zip codes, and telephone numbers are character data. Why? Because they are merely character strings that happen to be all numbers. You would rarely multiply a zip code by 35 or add 15 to a social security number. Since they are never used in calculations, they are character data.

Throughout this book you will see other examples of character data that are all numbers. Codes are a good example. In most computer systems, every item has a code number. This number can range from a few digits to many tens of characters in a Federal parts file. These code numbers can be all alphabetical characters (a-z), all numeric characters (0-9) or a combination of both. No matter which way they are used, codes will usually be considered text data. Character data is referred to in R:base 5000 as *text*.

Numeric data is stored in a slightly different manner. This type of data can be reported as is, or can take part in mathematical calculations. Numeric data items include dollar amounts, dates, counts of anything, or any data item that is to be used in a calculation. Numeric information can be added to totals, averaged, or calculated with to provide still another data item. R:base 5000 numeric data types include *integer, real*, and *dollar*.

When character or numeric data items appear in computer programs they are called *expressions*, whether they are used alone or in combination with other data items. Expressions contain items of only one type. Using character data in a numeric expression is called *mixing modes*, and is illegal in a program.

There are also special types of data called *date* and *time* data. These consist of dates or times that may need to be used. Often, the advantage of using date and time data is the ability to perform date or time arithmetic on these types of data. For example,

15 hours + 15 hours = 1 day 6 hours.

Another example is:

2:00 + 90 minutes = 3:30.

VARIABLES

Variables are areas of storage used in a program to hold data items. The use of variables is what gives the computer program its basic flexibility. Because of variables, computer programs can be written to work for any value that the variable can contain.

Variables can be thought of as buckets that hold the values the program will use. In this manner, a program might refer to a variable called Name, which can hold any value. Without knowing the exact contents, the Name variable can be positioned on an output report, displayed as a title of a section, or used for whatever function is needed. If the maximum length of the Name variable is 25 characters, the program must allow for 25 characters in the *output* (the printed report or screen display in most cases).

As an example, a *record* may contain a Name (25 characters) and a Phone number (10 characters). The first record on the file might read:

Cary Prague   2035557685

The second record might read:

Jim Hammitt   2035556281

Now, if the first record is requested, the value of Name will be **Cary Prague** and the value of Phone will be **2035557685**. If the purpose of the program is to print a name and phone number list, the program would first read a record, print the values of the variables Name and (possibly with some modifications) Phone, and then loop back to read the next record. By referring to Name and Phone, the program becomes general; that is, it works for any record that is set up in the same format with the same variable names (Name and Phone).

The ability to work with variables is the most useful feature of computers in general. Computers work with the values, but you, in your programming, do not.

The manipulation of variables is the most important function of computer programs, and the concept of variables is important to an understanding of the way programs work. When a variable is assigned a certain value, the value stays in that variable until it is either replaced with a new value or the program ends, whichever comes first. The only way to change the value of a variable is to place a new value into it. So, if you create a variable called Title to use as the title of your output report and never change it, you may use it throughout your program, and it will retain its value.

LITERALS

Another way a value can enter an expression is by the value itself appearing in the statement. This type of value is called a *literal*, and cannot be manipulated by the program. A literal is inserted directly into the expression in which it is to be used. Let's look at an example of an expression. The calculation that is necessary to calculate the simple interest on an amount left in a bank for 1 year at 7 1/2 percent is:

```
INTEREST = PRINCIPL X .075
```

In this expression, Interest and the Principl are variables; that is, they can have varying values. The .075 is a literal, because the value doesn't change. In a mathematical expression like the one just used, the equal sign (=) is used to show equality between the left and right halves of the equation. In a computer language, such an equation is called an *assignment statement* and does not express equality. It tells the computer to take the value expressed on the right side of the statement and place it into the variable on the left side.

STATEMENTS

Computer languages are comprised of statements like the one mentioned in the previous paragraph. That statement is an assignment statement because it assigns a new value to the variable Interest. No matter what value Principl has when that particular statement is executed, the calculation is performed with that value and the literal values, to result in the interest being placed into the variable Interest. This does not change the value of Principl, nor are the literals changed. Only the variable that is on the left side of the equal sign is changed. Most of the statements in a computer program are assignment statements.

The assignment statement in R:base 5000 is written in a slightly different manner. The assignment statement is:

```
SET VARIABLE variablename TO expression
```

The computation of interest would then appear as:

```
SET VARIABLE INTEREST TO PRINCIPL X .075
```

There are generally four types of statements in a computer language. Apart from the assignment statement, there are decision statements, loop control statements, and input/output statements.

Computer language statements are used to cause action. Assignment statements cause new values to be assigned to variables; those new values can be the result of calculations. *Decision statements* cause a section of statements to be executed or skipped over, depending on the value of variables. *Loop statements* cause a series of statements to be executed repeatedly until some condition occurs, such as a count exceeding a target value. *Input/output statements* cause the computer to copy information to or from some external device. Computer language statements always cause action of some type.

Chapter 2

Developing Programs

The result of all the actions taken in a computer program is the *output*. It was the need for the output that caused the program to be written in the first place. To ensure that a computer program is written properly, every item of information required from that program must be defined before the program can be written. As with all problem-solving methods, including the scientific method, the first step in finding the solution is to have an accurate definition of the problem. This is the first step in the seven-step problem-solving method that will be used in creating a computer program. The seven steps are:

- ☐ Define the problem.
- ☐ Define the output.
- ☐ Define the input.
- ☐ Determine the process.
- ☐ Code the program.
- ☐ Test the program.
- ☐ Evaluate the program.

THE BUSINESS PROBLEM

A business problem occurs when the current way of performing some business-oriented activity can no longer produce acceptable results. This can happen for a variety of reasons: a reduction in staff, an increase in the workload, a need for instantaneous retrieval of information, or a need for a change in the way of doing things.

In a company where the entire payroll is 4 persons, including the president, there is probably no need for a computer program to handle the payroll. If, however, that company expands to 400 people, whatever method is used to process the payroll for the smaller group would probably be a seven-day-a-week job when performed for the larger group.

Another example of a problem that would make a small company need a computer: what if that company with four people on the payroll handles sales to 200 companies with an inventory that runs into hundreds of thousands of dollars? Unless all four people are doing nothing but inventory control seven days a week, nothing could be shipped! Now, this example might be a little exaggerated, but it illustrates the point at which an automated method of handling the business could become necessary. Then, once the computer was installed and set up for inventory control, the payroll could be computerized if time and resources permit.

DEFINING THE PROBLEM

Whatever the business need, the correct first step in finding a solution to it is defining just what has to be done, when it has to be done, how much is to be done, etc. This overall statement of objective is necessary to keep the process of finding the solution on course, without troublesome wrong turns and side issues.

A problem definition should state why action is necessary and just what is expected from any solution. A problem definition should also avoid placing restrictions on how a solution is to be achieved, because doing so could preclude a solution. In other words, you should not include any mention of what tools are to be used to construct the final solution, whether computer-based or not.

It is also important to include a description of the expected results in the problem definition. The description should not be vague and should be as complete as possible. This description will help you determine just what information is needed to produce the desired results. If a computer solution is to be implemented, extensive data entry work might be necessary to make the required information available to the computer system. Data entry time must also be taken into account when you are creating cost estimates of the new system.

A well-written problem definition will reduce the time spent on speculation, making the solution available faster.

DEFINING THE OUTPUT

The next step, after completing the problem's definition, is to define the exact content of what the solution is to produce; in short, defining the output. Output is any product that is essential to solving the business problem. The output in a payroll system is the checks, reports to management about the hours worked, vacation and sick time reports, reports to the IRS, and pay stubs. These are varied in form, and some at least from an employee's point of view, seem irrelevant. However, each output form helps to solve a part of the total business problem.

There might also be files to be kept for year-end reporting. These are also output.

A complete output definition would include a description of each data item to appear in the output. A proper description should include the data type (character or numeric), a name for each variable to be used, the length of the item, and its source, whether from an already existing file or through calculation. The necessity of this step should be apparent: without knowing the exact output specifications, it would be impossible to determine what input is needed. It is unlikely that all the input a new computer system must use would be available in usable form. Problems of data entry must, therefore, also be considered. If existing files are to be used, are they available for use, and in what format are they? Consideration of these key points at this time can save time and sweat later.

DOCUMENTATION AND DESIGN

After there is a complete, clearly-written definition of the problem, coupled with a complete, clearly-written set of specifications for the output, these two documents will be used as the basis for the rest of the problem solution. Any such important documents should be finished prior to coding any computer programs, the textbook writers will tell you. So why do most companies spend less time at these activities than at program coding?

The time spent up-front in designing a program is inversely proportional to the time that will be spent coding. In simpler terms, when the design of a program is complete and well-documented, the programs almost code themselves! When the necessary designing is skipped over in the name of productivity, coding takes many times longer because mistakes that should have been eliminated in the design phase did not surface until the program coding phase.

DEFINING THE INPUT

The next step in the design phase is defining the input necessary to produce the output that was just defined. Since, in the output definition, care was taken to note the source of all items, the input definition should be the process describing these data items and in what form they are available. They might need to be entered by hand, in which case this is probably a good time to find out who will do the work.

In new systems, probably all the input data items needed will be entered by hand. Fortunately, with R:base 5000, this is a task that is performed more easily than with most other languages. With R:base 5000, when you define what your data files/data-bases will look like, R:base will allow you to start entering data immediately. R:base 5000 generates input screens that allow easy entry of the items to be stored. This may be an answer to management's productivity obsession, because the data entry can start while the next step of the design process is going on. If management wants to see production, you can show them the data entry effort and give yourself some additional design time.

DEFINING THE PROCESS

Now the problem has been defined, the output specifications have been written, and the input has been determined. With these documents firmly in hand, you are ready to define the actual process of turning the input data items into the output information.

The overall functions of the system, as set out in the problem's definition, must each be divided into their component functions. This step is when the actual process of programming takes place. The problem, output, and input definitions were the beginning of this process, but only at this step is the actual process defined. You can use many different methods to define the process.

Chapter 3

Mapping the Process

The methods used by professional programmers to define processes most often are flowcharting and pseudocoding. These are representative of the two categories of process mapping. *Charting* a process involves drawing a pictorial representation of the flow of control using symbols that depict the functions. *Pseudocoding* means to define the process in terms of its functions using a structured style that mirrors the workings of computer programs.

Breaking down a process into its component functions makes the program coding phase go faster. This is because it is easier to master each piece of the solution than the entire solution all at once. By dividing the functions during the design state, coding becomes faster and more controlled.

FLOWCHARTING

Flowcharting has been used since the inception of computers in the business environment. There are some advantages and disadvantages you should be aware of before choosing the use of flowcharts as the standard for your business.

First, the pictorial representation of the logic of a program is very readable; that is, it can be understood easily and by anyone. Unfortunately, they are hard to draw. They are difficult to envision and cumbersome to change, and as a result, they are usually not finished before coding starts. A system design should be living and envolving as new, efficient paths are discovered. Flowcharts must be redrawn each time a change is made.

By using the flowchart symbols shown in Fig. 3-1, a programmer or process

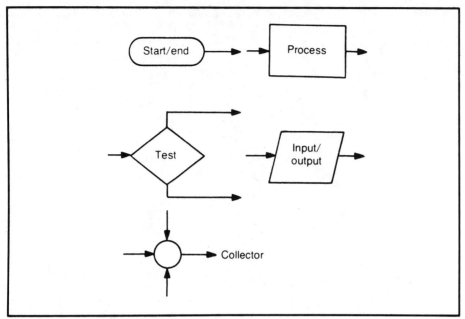

Fig. 3-1. The flowcharting symbols.

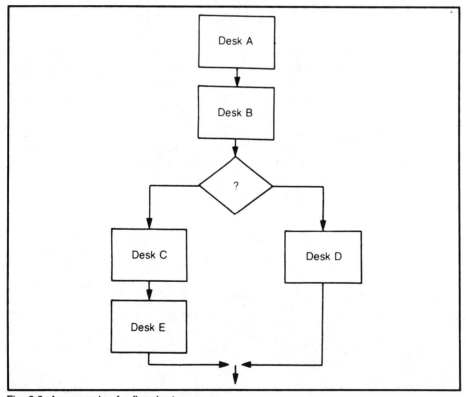

Fig. 3-2. An example of a flowchart.

designer can show the flow of paperwork through a department. Think of the rectangles as desks. The paperwork moves from desk to desk along the lines of control (Fig. 3-2). If there is a decision, a choice between desks, the decision point is denoted by a diamond.

Any process, whether a computer process or not, can be depicted with a flow-chart. For example, Fig.3-3 shows a flowchart of boiling water for tea.

In many programming classes, this type of flowchart is used to drill future programmers in breaking a process down into its simplest components. If you want to practice flowcharting, try making flowcharts of answering the phone, or choos-

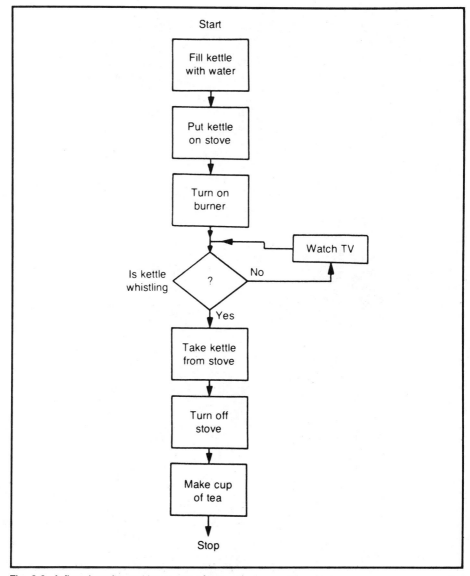

Fig. 3-3. A flowchart for making a cup of tea.

ing a television show. As you find simpler and simpler steps to break the process into, you will find yourself drawing and redrawing your flowchart.

Note that the following examples use *logical constructs*, which demonstrate how both flowcharts and pseudocódes are developed. These constructs are explained in detail in Chapter 5 and are used here only to help clarify the initial mapping process.

Let's look at another example of a flowchart. In this process, a company is looking through its employee records and choosing records that meet certain criteria. The employees that meet the qualifications are going to be asked if they would like to transfer to a foreign branch office. The process could be defined (flowcharted) as shown in Fig. 3-4.

The flowchart in Fig. 3-4 actually works; that is to say, it will perform the requested process. However, it is not very consistent or readable. Notice that all of the diamond blocks have "No" legs on the left, except the last one, which has a "Yes." This flowchart falls short on readability and consistency.

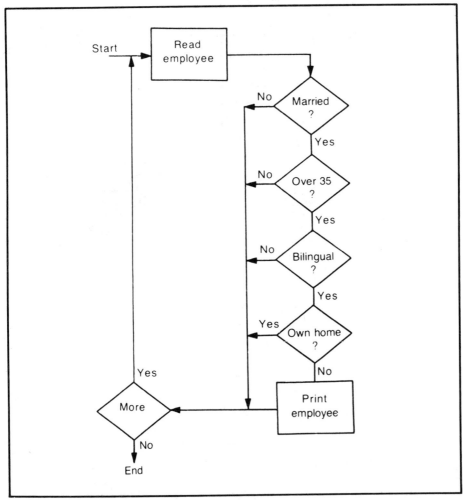

Fig. 3-4. A flowchart for an employee search.

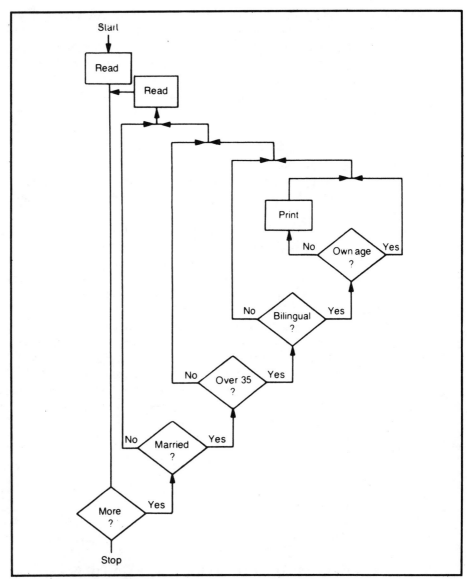

Fig. 3-5. A logical construct flowchart.

A better way of depicting the process can be accomplished by using the logical construct flowchart shown in Fig. 3-5. Notice that every diamond block has the Yes leg out to the right side. The entire process is contained in a *Read loop*, in which the records are read. After each read operation, a question is asked: "are there any more records to read?" This question determines whether or not the last record has been processed.

Another thing you might notice is that the flowchart could define the logical structure of a program or show the flow of paperwork in the office! If the records were sheets of paper in a file cabinet and all the questions were answered by human examination of the document, this flowchart would still be valid. A process definition does not have to be computer-based.

On first sight, the second flowchart seems to be larger and more complicated than the first. However, each logical construct is apparent, and the resulting chart is much more readable.

You can see the problems with trying to modify flowcharts. Usually the whole chart must be redrawn; in a growing, evolving system design this can be a drawback.

PSEUDOCODING

In recent years, pseudocoding has become the backbone of the programmer's tool chest. It reduces programming into the coding of the simplest relationships. Pseudocoding uses logical constructs, which appear in some form in most computer languages.

With logical constructs, processes may be mapped out in very general terms and slowly be made more detailed, until the final solution has evolved. Each subfunction may be concentrated on until it is solved and eventually becomes a part of the system. This divide and conquer method of problem solving is the answer to the problem of complexity. Functions are reduced to subfunctions of less complexity until a detailed, accurate map of the process has been obtained. Coding is now just a matter of translating the pseudocode into a real computer language. Coding takes less time, and testing can be started at the same time coding commences.

Pseudocode is a representation of a logic flow, but unlike the pictorial flowchart, pseudocode is written in plain language. This fact makes pseudocode easier to change or rewrite than a flowchart. Figure 3-2 showed the flow of paperwork from desk to desk in an office. That same process, shown as pseudocode, would look like this:

```
DESK A
DESK B
IF   X
   THEN
      DESK C
      DESK E
   ELSE
      DESK D
ENDIF
...
```

The diamond block, with its Yes and No legs, becomes an IF-THEN-ELSE logical construct. The THEN part is done if condition X is true; the ELSE part if condition X is false.

The "waiting for the teakettle" process shown in Fig. 3-3 would look like this in pseudocode:

```
PLACE KETTLE ON BURNER
TURN ON BURNER KETTLE IS ON
DOWHILE KETTLE NOT WHISTLING
   WATCH TV
ENDDO
REMOVE KETTLE FROM HEAT
TURN OFF BURNER
MAKE TEA!
```

16

The DOWHILE construct is a loop that is performed repeatedly while the condition "kettle not whistling" is true.

For a final example of pseudocode, let's look at the process flowchart in Fig. 3-5.

```
READ EMPLOYEE
DOWHILE MORE RECORDS
    IF MARRIED
      THEN
        IF OVER 35
          THEN
            IF BILINGUAL
              THEN
                IF OWNS HOME
                  THEN NOTHING
                  ELSE PRINT EMPLOYEE
                ENDIF
            ENDIF
        ENDIF
    ENDIF
    READ NEXT EMPLOYEE
ENDDO
```

First, notice the IF Owns Home construct. The THEN leg of the flow has no process associated with it. That construct could be changed to a negative comparison by the addition of NOT:

```
. . .
IF DOES NOT OWN HOME
  THEN PRINT EMPLOYEE
ENDIF
. . .
```

Also notice that there is a series of IF-THEN-IF-THEN . . .. These constructs could be replaced by a single IF if you make the condition complex by connecting the conditions with AND. The final version of the pseudocode would look like this:

```
READ EMPLOYEE
DO WHILE MORE EMPLOYEES
    IF MARRIED AND OVER 35 AND BILINGUAL
      THEN
        IF DOES NOT OWN HOME
          THEN
              PRINT EMPLOYEE
        ENDIF
    ENDIF
    READ MORE RECORDS
ENDDO
```

The pseudocode has become simpler than the flowchart by use of a complex condition. It is much easier to combine expressions in pseudocode than to type all those conditions in a little diamond block! Since pseudocode is so easily changed, it is much more desirable than a flowchart for a design tool. Flowcharts are excellent documentation tools; they should be drawn after the design is complete.

SUMMARY

In the first pages of this book, you have seen the initial stages of the development of a computer software system. This is the design phase, when the whole shape of the system is determined. After the design is completed, the actual process must be constructed. In the cases that are addressed by this book, that means that it is time to code the programs in a computer language: R:base 5000. The steps taken so far have been:

☐ Define the problem.
☐ Define the output.
☐ Define the input.
☐ Define the process.

Chapter 4

Designing Processes

The design phase of a project should be completed before you begin program coding. To make use of the design techniques advocated by this book, the completion of the design should be a hard-and-fast rule: be alert to and suspicious of any other course of action. An incomplete design will guarantee a late and unproductive solution.

Another obstacle that faces the programmer is alteration of the design during the coding phase. By changing the system requirements during coding, more time must be spent adding bells and whistles, and not enough time can be given to the construction of the required solution.

The new business computer programmer and those who find programming tedious, time consuming, and frustrating should consider these rules:

☐ Always complete the design phase prior to program coding.
☐ Freeze the design until coding and testing are complete.

Once coding and testing are done in a structured manner, enhancing the system or program is merely a problem of adding or changing already existing functions. A *plug-in* sort of structure can be changed with very little trouble.

DESIGNING THE PROCESS

Up to this point, you have been introduced to the system (or program) development process. The next step is to design the process. This step depends on understanding the three fundamental concepts involved in a good program (or system). They are: generality, modularity, and hierarchy. Also, it is important to keep in mind the *EZ2s* of development: easy to write, easy to read, easy to test.

Function Charting

The first step in system/program development is to chart the major functions of the system. These should be listed in the program definition that was developed earlier. Each of the major functions should be written in a box on a blank sheet of paper, one function to a sheet. These sheets of paper will become the function hierarchy charts for the system. Figure 4-1 shows a sample function hierarchy chart.

Fundamentals of a Good Program

The first fundamental of a good program, generality, means that the system will work for all input received by the system. In effect, this means that a program should check each input variable for validity and show error messages for any invalid data. The program accomplishes this task by making sure that numeric fields have numeric data in them, and by checking numeric data items for a proper range of values. Character data might have to be checked for specific values or formats. When one of the criteria is not met, an error message must be displayed somehow.

Modularity describes the result of breaking individual functions into separate programming problems. This approach means easier programming because only one function must be addressed at one time. With large systems, this approach is particularly necessary because, quite often, one person could not conceive and design the entire system.

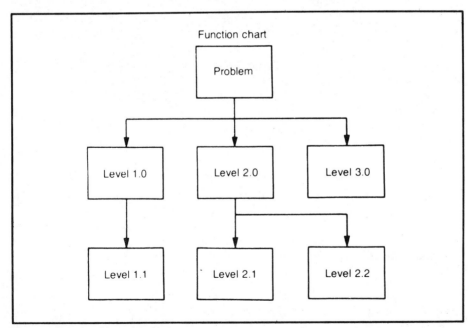

Fig. 4-1. Function hierarchy chart.

This method of system design also results in a hierarchy of functions. The top-level boxes that you have drawn on the otherwise blank sheets of paper become the top of the functional hierarchy of the system. Then, as each major function is divided into still smaller functions, you can add interconnecting boxes that describe the hierarchical relationship between the functions. In programming terms, each function becomes a module, or *subroutine*, each of which calls still other modules until the lowest level of function is reached. By using this top-down hierarchical approach, the lowest-level functions that are not unique can be seen readily. They can then be shared between modules as needed, without repeating the work.

The EZ2s of Programming

If you follow this type of approach to program design, the EZ2s take care of themselves. Once the functional hierarchy is determined, the first step is designing the logic for the top-level functions/modules. When the design of the major functions is complete, they can be coded and, using a programming trick called *program stubs*, can be tested for logical correctness. Since the major functions will become the most-used code in the program, they can also be the most-tested. As each lower-level function is designed and coded, it can be inserted into its stub and tested. When the lowest-level functions have been tested and the output approved, the system will be ready for implementation, with the program logic completely tested out.

Keep the fundamentals of a good program in mind as you step into the world of process design. They are, once again: generality, modularity, and hierarchy.

STYLES OF PROGRAMMING

There are two major styles of programming: interactive and passive. *Passive programs* are processes that can run from start to finish with no interruption by the operator. Sometimes misnamed *batch* programs by professional programmers, passive programs make up most of the work cycle at large installations. Huge number of transactions are accumulated during normal business hours and then processed during the second and third shifts. The series of passive programs processes these transactions, update files, create reports, print bills, and so forth. All this processing is done with little or no direct input from the computer operators; the operations staff has enough to do! They place the media containing transactions records, cards, tapes, or disks into the proper units, put paper in the printers, align the bill forms, and determine the order in which the programs are to be run.

Interactive programming, on the other hand, requires extensive communication with the operator. This type of program would not be welcome in a batch environment, since in big shops there are large numbers of programs running at any given time. The operations staff cannot (and will not!) devote a lot of attention to an individual program. Microcomputers, however, are ideal for interactive programming. They are usually run as *dedicated systems*, which means that only one program can be running at a time.

Interactive programs usually handle just one transaction at a time. The operator requests a function and enters the data, and a file is updated. He then requests another function, and a report is produced. The interactive quality of the program lets the operator control which functions are performed and in what order. Interactive programming also helps alleviate operator boredom by showing the operator that the system is working and by allowing him to have control over the outcome.

Selection Menus

One method of creating an interactive program is to design the use of a selection menu, as shown in Fig. 4-2. The program displays a list of the functions available on the computer monitor. The operator then chooses an option and enters data, and the file is updated. He can choose another function, and a report is produced. In this manner, the operator can choose the functions and the order in which the functions are to be performed.

Usually, the function selections are displayed with an option number for the operator to select. In some limited instances, the operator might have to type the first letter of the function name or the entire function name. Since the design and creation of the menus is up to you (the programmer), you may design your menus in a manner comfortable to you or your operator (probably you, also). There are, however, two guidelines you should observe:

☐ Don't make the operator enter too many characters because it is easy to make typing errors.
☐ Make the option choice easy to read and understand.

When you are considering interactive programming, remember that people make mistakes, and people will be interacting with your programs. Just as it is important for you to design the screens and menus for human understanding, it is important for the program to double-check input typed by a human. People make mistakes because of fatigue or misunderstanding, a trait that computers (fortunately) lack. Even a simple mistake, such as typing with the <Shift Lock> key engaged, can cause endless havoc with your data.

The computer program must judge the input data for itself. Each piece of input,

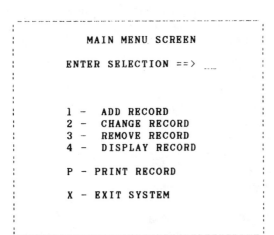

Fig. 4-2. An example of a menu screen.

```
 ------------------------------------------------
|               DATA ENTRY SCREEN                |
|                                                |
|     Name:      :                  :            |
|     Address:  :                  :             |
|     City:      :                  :            |
|     State:     :   :   Zip:  :      :          |
|                                                |
|     Date of Birth: :  /  /  :                  |
|                                                |
|     Credit Limit:  :            :              |
|                                                |
 ------------------------------------------------
```

Fig. 4-3. An example of a data entry screen.

including a menu selection, must be examined for validity before a function can be performed. If there is a list of functions and selection codes on the menu screen, the program must match the input from the operator against a list of the valid selections. If the code is typed wrong, an error message should be displayed. An error message of this type should be readable and list the valid choices for the operator.

Data Entry Screens

Interactive programs can use screens for the entry of data. A sample screen in shown in Fig. 4-3. These screens are forms for the data, just like any paper form that you fill out with a pencil. The data entry screen is filled out by using the keyboard to enter information into each area on the screen. This information is then stored into variables by the program. The program can then examine each entry for validity.

Data entry screens should be designed for ease of use. The operator must be able to read the screen and understand the placement of data on the form. Sometimes, when a shop is first automating, the input screens are designed directly from the paper form being replaced. This choice helps to add a sense of continuity to the system, but a better practice is to ask the people who fill out or read those forms for their suggestions. They can tell you what they would like to see changed and how to best design the screens for ease of data entry. Designing for ease of data entry is most important in companies where large number of transactions are entered daily, but it can help to cut down needless work and increase productivity even in small shops.

EDITING DATA

Once the operator has entered the data on the screen, the program must examine it for validity. In other words, the input data must meet certain predetermined rules.

First, the data must conform to the required data type. If the input data is numeric—that is, to be used in calculations—the program must be sure that the input contains only numbers. This type of edit is called a *class edit*. Database managers like R:base 5000 do not allow characters in a field defined as numeric data. The keyboard locks up or an audible alarm is sounded when the attempt is made. Most character data items are not checked since any character is valid. In some cases, however, you might want to check for improper data, such as numbers in a name field.

Second, if the input is numeric, the contents of the field might have to fall within a certain range of values. If, for instance, a field called Month is created, the value probably has to be between 1 and 12 inclusive. This type of edit is called a *range edit*.

Third, the data should conform to data already in the file; this is called a *correctness edit*. For example, in a payroll system, a transaction can be entered to pay an employee for overtime hours worked. If the employee is not eligible to receive overtime pay, the transaction is in error (or someone is trying to put one over on you).

Programs should check data for all possible violations. Any input presented to the program, even if *you* plan to be doing the data entry, should be edited for class, range, and correctness. Remember that anyone can make mistakes, and you want your data to be as error-free as humanly possible.

ERROR MESSAGES

When errors are detected in input data, it is necessary to notify the operator. In passive programming, this usually means producing an error report for the data entry staff to use the next day in correcting the input transactions. In interactive programming, it means telling the operator immediately that there is something wrong.

One means of informing the operator of an error is through the use of an audible alarm signal. Most microcomputers have a beep or bell character that sounds an alarm. Usually, the sound is used in conjunction with a message describing the error. When the alarm is used alone, the operator might not easily see the problem.

Error messages are displayed on the monitor screen. When use with the audible alarm, they alert the operator to the fact that a problem has occurred. The message should explain the problem and offer suggestions for correction. These are messages to be read by people; they should be easily understandable.

An example of a good error message from a menu selection screen is:

```
*** INVALID SELECTION ***
VALID OPTIONS ARE 1,2,3,4 AND X
     RE-ENTER SELECTION
```

The error is described in the first line; the correct choices are listed in the second line; and the next course of action is indicated in the third line. These are the three elements of a good error message. This is not to say that you must use three lines; there are also good one liners, and there are other enhancements to make the message stand out more. Error messages should always appear on the same part of the screen, preferably near the top, so that the operator will know where to focus his attention. When the alarm sounds, the operator will be trained to look at that place for the error message. Displaying the message in color or in high-intensity characters will also draw attention to it. You should not use blinking text, however, because it can be quite annoying. Another method is called *flowerboxing*. Using this technique, the message is surrounded by asterisks to make it very apparent:

```
*************************************
*          INVALID SELECTION        *
*  VALID OPTIONS ARE 1,2,3,4 AND X  *
*         RE-ENTER SELECTION        *
*************************************
```

SOME TYPICAL PROCESSES

One type of typical process has been discussed in detail: the edit, or *data validation*, process. This unit will show you some other frequently used data processes you will need in your programs.

The first process that will be discussed is the data search. Usually, a file of records is searched for individual records that meet certain conditions, called the *search criteria*. In the simplest cases, the searching involves comparing a field in each record to a value and listing the records in which the field contains the value. For example, you might be searching an employee file for a particular social security number. When the record with that number is found, you might want to perform some process using it; you might change or delete the record or just display its contents. This kind of search is called a *unique search*, because only one record will be retrieved.

A search could be used as a correctness edit for input data. If you are adding a new employee to the payroll file, you could first search the file for the social security number of the new employee. If a match is found, it may mean that:

☐ Something strange is going on
☐ You entered the wrong social security number (possibly)
  or
☐ The employee has already been added to the file (most likely)

In any case, if unique data is found in the file when it should not be there, something is wrong. The transaction should fail, and the program should give an appropriate error message. Pseudocode for a unique search could look like this:

```
DISPLAY "SSN TO BE SEARCHED FOR"
GET ANSWER
READ A RECORD
DO WHILE MORE RECORDS AND SSN NOT FOUND
   READ NEXT RECORD
ENDDO
DISPLAY RECORD IF FOUND
```

A *generic search* occurs when more than one record meets the search criteria. For example, you might want to list all employees with the last name of Smith. This search could result in several records being listed or processed in some other way.

One way of using a generic search is to display fields for use in another process. In the payroll system example, you might need the social security number to change an employee record. However, if all you know is the employee's name, you could use a generic search to display all the employees with that particular last name, along with their social security numbers. You could then choose the proper social security number to use for the change transaction. Pseudocode for a generic search could look like this:

```
DISPLAY "NAME TO BE SEARCHED FOR"
GET ANSWER
READ A RECORD
DO WHILE MORE RECORDS
  IF NAME FOUND
    THEN PRINT NAME AND SSN
  ENDIF
  READ NEXT RECORD
ENDDO
```

Another frequently used process is *totaling*. When you are billing a customer, the total of the bill is printed somewhere on the form that is sent to the customer. Administrative reports have totals of dollar amounts, employees, quantities, etc.

Totals are said to be *accumulated* in computer programs. That is, each required total is defined as a field in the program. Each time a record is read or an amount is calculated, that amount is added to the accumulated total. Using the payroll system example, an employee record might include regular hours worked and overtime hours worked. An administrative report generated by this system would include a total for regular hours, a total for overtime hours, and a total for the total of all hours worked. Each time a record is read, the Regular Hours and Overtime Hours are added to their respective totals. Then, after calculating the total hours worked for that employee (regular + overtime), that sum is added to the Total Hours total field. When the report is examined, the Total Hours should match the sum of the total Regular Hours plus the total Overtime Hours. This is called *cross footing* in the business vernacular and is another method of checking the correctness of the process.

SUMMARY

This chapter has discussed the basis for designing computer processes. Keep in mind the fundamentals of a good program: generality, modularity, and hierarchy. These three fundamentals should be used in conjunction with the EZ2s of programming: easy to read, easy to write, and easy to change.

This chapter also discussed the styles of interactive and passive programming, including the use of screens and menus as tools for data entry and process control. You also saw some typical processes found in computer programs: checking input data, searching files, and totaling amounts. These are not all of the possible processes—just a sample of those most frequently used.

In later chapters, you will see how the logical constructs work and how to examine your design for errors. You will also see some systems designed from start to finish.

Chapter 5

The Workings of Language

The design of a process is hierarchical in nature, proceeding from the major functions at the top of the function chart through the lowest functions at the bottom. The problem most new or non-programmers have is how low to go. To answer this question, it is important to understand how a computer language is put together.

TYPES OF STATEMENTS

The concept of statements in computer programs was discussed earlier. Each statement accomplishes some purpose within the program. The general types of statements are:

- ☐ Assignment statements.
- ☐ Decision statements.
- ☐ Input/output statements.
- ☐ Control statements (loops and branches).

Assignment Statements

The assignment statement is used to assign a value to a variable. It is the most common program statement at the lowest levels of the function hierarchy, but it becomes scarcer as you rise through the chart. However, you will be traversing the chart top-down. The first modules to be designed will be the major functions and will have few, if any, assignment statements.

Table 5-1 shows some examples of assignment statements in various languages.

Table 5-1. Defining Variables in Various Programming Languages.

Language	Statement
R:base 5000	Set Variable A to 3 + 4
BASIC	LET A = 3 + 4
dBASE II	STORE 3 + 4 TO A
dBASE III	STORE 3 + 4 TO A or A = 3 + 4
COBOL	MOVE 3 + 4 TO A
PL/I	A = 3 + 4;
Pascal	COMPUTE A = 3 + 4

Each statement assigns the value of 3 + 4 to the variable A.

In pseudocode, you can make up your own version of the assignment. Be sure that it can be easily understood by others. Most programmers tend to use the syntax (computer grammar) of the language with which they are familiar.

Calling Subroutines

The second most common statement, and the most common at the top level, is the *subroutine call*. It is a control statement that causes a subroutine or subfunction to be performed. When the function is complete, control returns to the statement following the call. Subroutine calls are used to establish the hierarchy of functions. Each major function module calls the functions listed in the second level in the function chart, and they in turn call the next level. A chart illustrating the flow of control that occurs when subroutines are used is shown in Fig. 5-1.

The program stubs mentioned earlier are empty lower-level modules that have not been coded yet. Because the function chart will tell you what subfunctions there will be, it is possible to set up stubs for them. As each subfunction is coded, it can be placed in the stub and lower-level stubs added. This way, the most-used program logic will be the most tested.

USING LOGICAL CONSTRUCTS IN PROCESS DESIGN

Keeping this idea of modularity in mind, let's discuss the actual form of the process design. As described before, process logic can be depicted in two ways: charting and pseudocoding. Both methods can be accomplished using a few logical constructs, which will be discussed next. Charting methods are good ways of documenting a complete design because they are pictorial in nature. However, they are difficult to change as the process evolves; so the recommended procedure is to design with pseudocode and document afterwards with a chart.

As you remember, pseudocode is a language-based way of designing processes. You can design your system by using the simple logical constructs combined with plainly written human-language statements that describe the logic the process will follow.

The logical constructs are:

☐ SEQUENCE
☐ IF-THEN-ELSE
☐ DOWHILE
☐ CASE

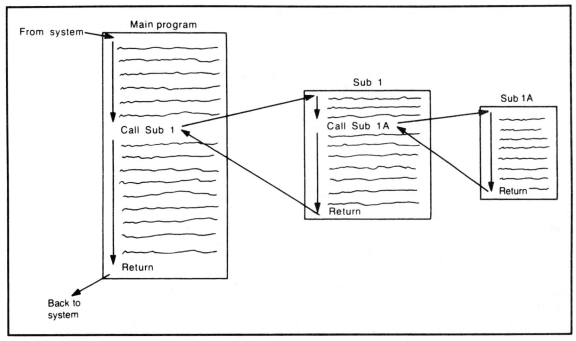

Fig. 5-1. The flow of control when calling subroutines.

The SEQUENCE logical construct is just that—one statement following another. This is the simplest form of construct, and simply depicts one action following another. A SEQUENCE flowchart and an example of SEQUENCE pseudocode are shown in Fig. 5-2.

Fig. 5-2. A sequence flowchart and pseudocode.

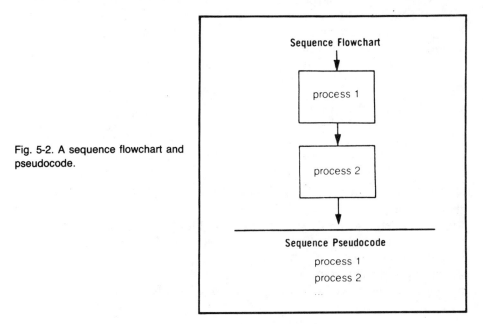

The others, IF-THEN-ELSE, DOWHILE, and CASE are decision statements, and most languages have them in one form or another. It might be necessary in some languages to use the statements available to create the construct. In R:base 5000 they exist in these forms.

Notice that there are no input/output type statements used in pseudocode. The reason is that the design process should not be tied down to the exact form to be used. This type of design allows flexibility, so that a change of computers or software does not affect the design. The only necessary references to input and output might be statements such as GET A RECORD, GET NEXT RECORD, and WRITE A LINE.

IF-THEN-ELSE

The IF-THEN-ELSE logical construct is the simplest form of decision statement. It asks a question in the form of a comparison; for example, **IF payroll code is 2**. There are two possible results from a comparison of this type: true or false. If the comparison in the IF is true, then whatever processing is invoked in the THEN part of the statement is performed, and when completed, the next statement following the IF construct is performed. If the result is FALSE, the ELSE section is performed.

Some IF statements have only a THEN following them. If the comparison is false, the THEN unit is not performed, and control falls to the next statement. A flowchart and pseudocode for an IF-THEN-ELSE construct is shown in Fig. 5-3.

IF-THEN-ELSE statements, and for that matter all the logical constructs, can be considered individual statements. Therefore, the THEN unit of an IF-THEN-ELSE construct can also have an IF statement in it. This occurrence is called *nesting* by programmers and is quite valid. Care should be taken, however, that IFs and THENs match up with the proper ELSEs. This task can be accomplished through the use of indentation to indicate which statements are on the same nesting level. It is not wise to nest too deeply because the statement can become unwieldy and unreadable. If necessary, another function should be created.

In R:base 5000, the IF statement looks like this:

```
IF conditional expression THEN
   statements to be performed if TRUE
  ELSE
   statements to be performed if FALSE
ENDIF
```

Notice that the word THEN is on the same line as the IF. R:base 5000 takes the statements after the THEN part of the construct as true. If the expression is FALSE, R:base 5000 looks for an ELSE in the code, and if ELSE is present, performs the statements following it. If there is no ELSE, the ENDIF is reached, and the next statement is executed.

Indentation is important in IF-THEN-ELSE constructs to make the code easier to read and understand. In R:base 5000, the end of an IF statement is marked by an ENDIF.

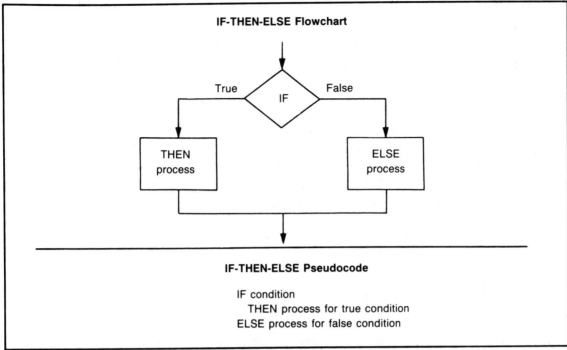

IF-THEN-ELSE Flowchart

True   IF   False

THEN process

ELSE process

IF-THEN-ELSE Pseudocode

IF condition
    THEN process for true condition
ELSE process for false condition

Fig. 5-3. An IF-THEN-ELSE flowchart and pseudocode.

Let's look at some examples of conditions in the IF-THEN-ELSE construct format. For example, if the program needs to perform some special processing when a date is in November, the pseudocode would look like this:

```
IF MONTH = 11 THEN
     perform "November processing"
  ELSE
     perform "normal processing"
ENDIF
```

In this example, the conditional expression is **month = 11** on the line starting with IF. The expression asks a question to which there can be only two possible answers: "Is month equal to 11? Yes or no?" When the system sees an expression like this, it examines the value of the variable Month and compares it to the literal value 11. If they are equal, the system signals a true, or yes, answer for the question, and the process contained in the THEN unit of the construct is performed. If the value of Month is not equal to 11, the ELSE unit gets control, and that processing is performed.

Here are other examples:

```
IF STATE = "CT"
  THEN ...

IF ZIP = 06040
  THEN ...
```

```
IF DATE = EXPIRE
   THEN ...
```

In the third example, the contents of the variable Date are compared against the contents of the variable Expire. Again there are only two possibilities: the contents are either equal or not equal; so the expression is either true or false. There is no other answer to a conditional expression.

Comparisons

The comparisons that can be made in a decision statement such as IF-THEN-ELSE can be simple or complex. The simplest form involves testing one variable against another or against a literal value.

The comparisons that can be made are:

☐ Equals (=)
☐ Not Equals (< >)
☐ Greater Than (>)
☐ Less Than (<)
☐ Greater Than Or Equal To (> =)
☐ Less Than Or Equal To (< =)

Some languages have two more, Not Greater Than and Not Less Than. These should be used with caution and replaced with Greater Than Or Equal To and Less Than Or Equal To when possible.

Complex Comparisons

Simple comparison expressions have two possible results: true or false. Comparison expressions can be combined to form complex expressions when they are connected with the *Boolean* operators AND and OR. A complex expression is evaluated by the AND and OR rules.

For an AND expression to be true, both sides of the expression must be true. If one of the expressions is false, the AND expression is false.

For an OR expression to be true, only one side of the expression must be true. If both sides are false, the OR expression is false.

ANDs and ORs can be used within complex expressions; for instance, two OR expressions could be connected by an AND, or the expression could be even more complex. The best rule to follow is the KISS rule: Keep It Simple, Stupid! Use complex expressions only where necessary.

Let's look at some examples of complex conditional expressions. In complex expressions, each conditional expression is evaluated separately, and then the results of the ANDs and ORs are evaluated according to the AND and OR rules. For example:

```
IF STATE = "CT" AND ZIP = 06040
   THEN ....
```

In this example, the value of the variable State is compared against the literal

CT. Likewise, the value of the variable Zip is compared to 06040. Only if both of these conditions are true is the entire expression true. If either is false, the entire condition is false.

In the following example, the two simple conditions are made into a complex expression by joining them with an OR:

```
IF STATE = "CT" OR STATE = "MA"
   THEN ...
```

It is obvious that at least one of these conditions must be false; State cannot have two different values! However, the OR rule states that only one of the joined expressions need be true for the entire condition to be true. In this case, if the value of State is CT, the condition is true. The condition is also true if the value is MA. If anything other than these two values is in State, the condition is false.

In more complicated conditional expressions, two expressions connected with an AND can be connected to still other expressions:

```
IF (STATE="CT" OR STATE="MA") AND NAME="SMITH"
   THEN ...
```

In this example, the condition inside the parentheses is evaluated first and then ANDed with the evaluation of the third expression. If the variable State contains either CT or MA, the condition in the parentheses is evaluated as true using the OR rule. Then the value of the variable Name is compared with the literal value Smith. Therefore, this complex condition is true if Name is equal to Smith, and if the State is either CT or MA.

When evaluating complex conditional expressions, it is important to evaluate the expressions inside parentheses first and to remember the AND and OR rules. Also, don't make conditions too complex, for readability's sake; the KISS (Keep It Simple, Stupid) method is the best compromise.

USING THE DOWHILE STATEMENT

DOWHILE is another type of conditional statement. A DOWHILE is a series of statements that is performed repeatedly WHILE the condition remains true. Each time the loop of statements is performed, the condition is reevaluated, and if it is still true, the process in the loop is performed again. A flowchart and pseudocode for a DOWHILE process is shown in Fig. 5-4.

Programmers use DOWHILE loops to perform a series of statements as long as some condition is true. This condition can be internal to the program, for example:

```
SET COUNTER TO 1
DOWHILE COUNTER <= 15
   ...
   statements
   ...
   add 1 to counter
ENDDO
```

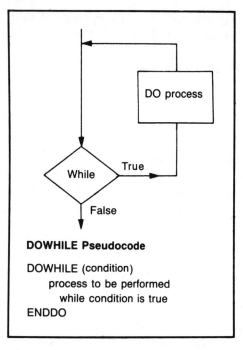

DOWHILE Pseudocode

DOWHILE (condition)
    process to be performed
      while condition is true
ENDDO

Fig. 5-4. A DOWHILE flowchart and pseudocode.

The DOWHILE loop will be performed 15 times; each time through the loop, the counter is incremented by one. The condition in the DOWHILE statement (Counter $< = 15$) is tested immediately after each time the counter is incremented. When the value of Counter exceeds 15, the loop is ended and control passes to the statement following the ENDDO.

Another way that DOWHILE is used is to test for a condition external to the program. One such condition is end-of-file, which answers the question "Are there any more records to read?" A DOWHILE loop will be performed once for each record in the file, regardless of the number of records. Most major function routines are based on this type of loop.

```
read a record
DOWHILE more records
   ...
   statements
   ...
   read next record
ENDDO
```

The condition is external to the program; the loop will be performed once for each record in the file. If records are added to the file in the future, the program will still work because the condition determines when the end-of-file is reached, regardless of the number of records in the file.

Notice also that the condition is tested after both READ statements. The condition is tested at the start of the loop, as well as after each subsequent READ. While the condition remains true, the loop is executed. When the condition becomes false, the statement after the ENDDO is executed, and the program continues from there.

The DOWHILE logical construct takes the following form in R:base 5000:

```
WHILE conditional expression THEN
  statements to be performed
  as long as the condition is TRUE
ENDWHILE
```

The loop continues to be executed as long as the conditional expression tests TRUE. It is tested each time the ENDWHILE is encountered. The end of the WHILE is marked by an ENDWHILE in R:base 5000.

THE CASE FIGURE

The last logical construct you need to learn is the CASE figure. A CASE is a decision point that allows more than two processes to be performed for various values of a variable. For instance, the variable Sex appears to have only two possible values. However, there are three: male, female, and invalid (not valid). Here the CASE condition has three possible processes to perform; one for MALE, one for FEMALE, and one for invalid data. The CASE figure would look like this:

```
CASE SEX
  WHEN MALE
    male processing
  WHEN FEMALE
    female processing
  OTHERWISE invalid sex code processing
ENDCASE
```

Figure 5-5 shows a flowchart and pseudocode for a case chart.

The CASE figure in R:base 5000 can be implemented by creating a table. You will see this construct in detail in the third section of this book.

CHECKING OUT YOUR PSEUDOCODE

When you have finished your pseudocode for a function, it is necessary to test it out; that is, to examine it for logical correctness and to make sure it does what you want it to do.

To check out your pseudocode, read each statement one at a time. This is the way the computer will execute your statements when you translate your pseudocode into R:base 5000 code. Point a pencil to each line as you read it. When you execute conditional statements, examine the flow of control for both true and false conditions.

Tracing the Flow in IF-THEN-ELSE Constructs

In an IF-THEN-ELSE logical construct, when the IF condition is true the statements in the THEN unit are executed, and control passes to the statement following the ENDIF. For example:

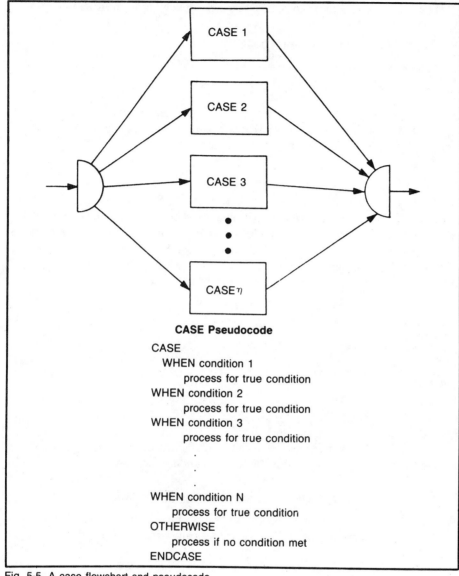

CASE Pseudocode

CASE
   WHEN condition 1
      process for true condition
   WHEN condition 2
      process for true condition
   WHEN condition 3
      process for true condition
        .
        .
        .
   WHEN condition N
      process for true condition
   OTHERWISE
      process if no condition met
   ENDCASE

Fig. 5-5. A case flowchart and pseudocode.

1. IF Month = 2
2.   Then Month name is "February"
3. ENDIF
4. . . .

If Month does equal 2, the flow of control, in terms of the line numbers, would be 1,2,3,4. On the other hand, if Month was anything other than 2, the flow would be 1,3,4. With no ELSE unit for a false condition, control passes out of the IF-THEN construct to the next statement (line 4).

If the IF construct includes an ELSE unit, slightly different processing occurs:

1. IF State = "CT"
2.   THEN perform in-state process
3.   ELSE perform out-of-state process
4.   ENDIF
5. . . .

A true condition in this example (State equal to CT) would result in the execution of statements 1,2,4,5. The ELSE unit is skipped over when the condition is true. A false condition in the example would result in the execution of statements 1,3,4,5; the THEN unit is skipped over.

Tracing the Flow in CASE Constructs

In a CASE construct, control is passed to the statements in the WHEN unit when the condition tests true and then jumps to the statement following the ENDCASE. If no WHEN condition tests true, control jumps to the OTHERWISE unit, if it exists. For example:

1. CASE
2.   When State = "CT"
3.   perform "in Connecticut"
4.   When State = "MA"
5.   perform "in Massachusetts"
6.   When State = "NY"
7.   perform "in New York"
8.   OTHERWISE
9.   perform "other state"
10. ENDCASE
11. . . .

When this construct is executed, and the value of state is CT, the statements will be performed 1,2,3,10,11. If State is MA, the flow of processing would be 1,4,5,10,11; for the state of NY, the flow would be 1,6,7,10,11. If the State was anything other than CT, MA, or NY, the flow would be 1,8,9,10,11.

Tracing the Flow in DOWHILE Constructs

In a DOWHILE construct, a loop of statements is performed as long as a condition is true. In the following example, a counter is incremented and then tested by the DOWHILE statement.

1. set Counter to 1
2. DOWHILE Counter < = 3
3.   add Counter to total
4.   add 1 to Counter

5. ENDDO

6. . . .

First, the variable Counter is set to one. The DOWHILE then tests the variable Counter against a literal (3). While Counter remains at three or below, this loop is executed. The flow of processing would be 1,2,3,4 (Counter now 2),5,2,3,4 (Counter now 3), 5,2,3,4 (Counter now 4), 5,2 (condition now false), 5,6.

The variable Total would now contain 6 (1 + 2 + 3), while Counter would be set to 4. Notice that the loop was performed three times; while Counter was 1, 2, and finally 3. The incrementation to 4 made the condition false, and the statements inside the loop were not performed after counter became 4.

Tracing the Values of Variables

Another aid in testing your pseudocode is to write any variable names down on a separate sheet of paper and write in the values you wish to test. As the values change, cross out the old values and write in the new ones. This procedure will show the exact values of the variables at each statement in the code.

This type of careful examination of the process design is called a *walk-thru* and is invaluable as a testing tool. By getting the design right before the actual computer program is written, you can save yourself a lot of aggravation caused by having missed problems in your design. Your program may even work the first time if you take the time to design it properly and test the design.

Chapter 6

Coding,
Testing, and Debugging

Now for the second phase of the project, the coding phase. In the design phase you defined the problem, the output, the input, and the process. Now it is time to code and test the new system.

DOCUMENTATION

The reference materials you will need during your coding phase are the manuals for whatever software you are using, the problem definition, the output definition, the input definition, and the process definition. These materials, aside from the reference manual, are the documentation for your system. Along with the program code, the design definition will become a package that is necessary to use for future changes.

When a system is to be changed or enhanced, the programmer will refer to the documentation package for a clearer understanding of the system. And to find the easiest way to make the enhancement. A poorly assembled documentation package can make changes difficult, if not impossible, to implement.

Some companies keep outdated computer equipment, some dating back to the early 1960s. Why? Because the programs were written then, and the documentation has become scattered, scrambled, and lost during the interim. In some cases, the source language for the program itself has been lost, rendering all change impossible. The executives' attitude is "The programs still work well, and we don't have the time to rewrite and redocument the system." Usually, the cost of keeping the old equipment is much greater than the cost of developing a new, rewritten and documented system.

The point is that the documentation package is important to you and to your business. Write it well, and keep two copies of everything!

READABILITY

Since the source code of the program is to become part of the documentation package, it is important to write it in a readable manner. Even the pseudocode or flow-chart should be painstakingly written, so that when you come back to it later, you can understand how the process works. Many professional programmers find themselves working on systems they designed and wrote years in the past and scratch their heads in wonder at how they could have forgotten what they did. With readable, understandable documentation, reworking is a much easier task.

One way of making programs (and pseudocode) more readable is to indent subordinate code. Any code that is inside a loop should be indented to differentiate it from the main code. This one act alone makes the program much easier to read.

Another method of making a program easier to read is to start each function at the top of a new page. In some languages, it is necessary to put comments in the code, showing the break between the end of one subfunction and the start of the next.

Finally, comment statements are available in virtually all computer languages. Use them to your advantage. By commenting effectively and changing those comments when necessary, you can put some documentation directly into the code. Comments are especially helpful when a complicated process is present; you can explain the process in plain language to programmers who might change the program in the future. Remember, it could be you!

MAKING SURE THE PROGRAM WILL WORK

There are two types of errors associated with program coding: *syntax errors* and *logic errors*. The logic errors should be obvious in the process design. Process designs (pseudocode) should be carefully examined, not only by the creator, but by other, even disinterested, parties. The examination can be done in an informal or formal walk-thru of the pseudocode. Each decision point can be evaluated, and errors can be worked out before coding begins.

Syntax errors are usually discovered when the program is run on the computer. They can also be avoided or minimized by careful examination of the coded program. It is also good to have the language manual handy (and open) while you are coding a program.

Testing During Coding

When the coding of a major function is complete, testing can begin, and from then on, testing can progress simultaneously with coding. Higher-level functions can be tested with stubs at the lower levels. When the high-level function works, the stubs may be filled in. Every decision path in the function should be tested before the next module is included for testing. Testing in this fashion means that any errors which appear are usually the fault of the last subroutine added, making error detection and correction much easier.

Using Test Data

At this point, some form of test input data is necessary. This data should be, whenever possible, actual live data, gleaned from already existing files. In the case of a new system, all of the test data might have to be generated by the tester. For each item of test input, there should be a written document stating the expected results when the program is presented with that item. Test data should include erroneous and invalid information.

The test data can also become part of the documentation package. The test data can be listed, along with the expected results. If, when you are testing a program, unexpected results occur, either the expected results are incorrect or there is a problem in the program (most likely). Unexpected results should not be blamed on the weather, cosmic rays striking the computer, or the computer itself. The problem lies with the program in most cases, and sometimes with the interpretation of the expected results.

Most of the time, the responsibility for creating test data falls to the programmer, which might not be a good idea. Usually, the programmer is the person most closely involved with the system, and therefore he could, either consciously or unconsciously, test the program with slanted data that will produce the desired results while not testing every possible program path. One company had a system that worked well for 6 years. One day, a transaction was entered and the system failed. Why? That particular type of transaction was never tested, not once, during the testing phase of the project; in fact, it was never entered until that fateful day when the system came crashing down at 2:00 A.M. Poor testing practices can let errors slip in when you least expect them as the poor on-call programmer found out that morning.

One solution to this problem is to have some other party create the test data. This choice may not be possible in small shops, where one person is responsible for everything. Once the test data is created, the programmer can evaluate the transactions and write expected results for them. This procedure will help maintain integrity in the system, while possibly testing for conditions not envisioned by the programmer.

Testing It Again

When coding is complete for the entire major function, test it again. Any final errors encountered should be small and easy to fix. The expected results should be compared to the actual results and then compared against the results required by the problem definition. When these comparisons have been done, the system is ready for use and can be implemented as new office procedure.

DESIGNING DATA

Just as important as developing the process is designing the database. Because systems are restricted by the data they have access to, deciding what data is necessary is an important step in development. This is why the output specifications are written before the input is defined. When a new system is being developed, care must be taken to include all information necessary for the system, as well as for any foreseen future uses.

Identifying Records

The first data items in a record should be those that provide a unique identification for the record. In a personnel system, the name of the employee is not a good primary identification item, but could be used as a secondary identification item. A better primary identification item would be a social security number, because it is unique to each employee. In a payroll or personnel system, the social security number would probably be the first data item in the record and would be the major *key* that identifies the record.

Arranging Data

An important guideline in deciding on the arrangement of data items in a record is that you should keep related fields together. The name information would be immediately followed by the address information if these are commonly used together in the output.

A third guideline is that you should describe the data in terms of entities. An *entity* is composed of all fields necessary to producing the output. This concept is most useful when more than one file is involved. In a personnel system, the major entity would be described as Employee, even if name and address information was in one file, the rate of pay in another, and hours worked in still another. Entities are used often in systems that use data which were intended for other purposes and would be costly to reenter. By using the entity approach, the system can be designed as if all data resided in the same place.

Letting the Computer Do the Work

One final guideline: do not include fields in the record that can be calculated from other fields already available. The computer should do any calculations; that is its purpose. Data entry people should not have to do any calculations, and their decisions should be kept to a minimum. The computer can do these things faster and more accurately, and the data entry process can be shortened accordingly.

SUMMARY

In Chapter 5 and 6 you have seen the seven-step method of program design:

☐ Define the problem.
☐ Define the output.
☐ Define the input.
☐ Define the process.
☐ Code.
☐ Test.
☐ Evaluate.

Also discussed were the three fundamentals of a good program:

- ☐ Generality.
- ☐ Modularity.
- ☐ Hierarchy.

You also learned the basic types of statements found in a computer language:

- ☐ Assignment statements.
- ☐ Input/Output statemetns.
- ☐ Decision statements.
- ☐ Loop control statements.

You also saw the workings of decision statements, and you were introduced to the last phase in program development, the coding phase. Finally, this chapter discussed documentating and testing the program and designing and arranging data fields. In the last two sections of this book, using data with R:base 5000 will be discussed in more detail.

Chapter 7

Business Considerations

This book so far has tried to generally describe some suggestions that apply to all sizes of business—from megabuck corporations to mom-and-pop operations. However, the method by which individual steps are accomplished changes with the size of the business.

LARGE VERSUS SMALL

Large corporations have large staffs of programming specialists and data entry personnel. Projects that these staffs perform can take years to complete and can cost the company a lot of person-power. The cost of the project is carefully measured against the benefits and savings that the company will realize.

On the other end of the business spectrum, even a small retail outlet can benefit from the use of a computer. The projects that would be undertaken would be shorter in duration, however, and all data entry and programming probably would be performed by the same person. Possibly the owners would have to do everything by themselves. If so programming might be done during off hours and weekends, and even be forgotten for long periods of time as the problems of running the business intervene.

In large businesses, a given department can go to the programming staff with a business problem, and the staff is expected to develop the answer. Small businesses do not have this advantage. Small business managers must decide the uses of automation themselves. They should ask themselves some questions such as "What takes the most time away from customer services? What part of my job is boring, repetitious? What information must be saved for long periods of time, and would take a lot of space to store?" Once these questions have been answered, the small business manager should have some idea of what aspects of the business to automate.

ADMINISTRATIVE AUTOMATION

By using the guidelines presented in this book, even the business manager who must program on weekends can be involved in the development of an automated system. Commonly, the first type of system that a small business would create is a payroll/personnel system. This area is often the most significant function of a company that is not directly related to increasing sales or profits. By automating administrative functions, the small business releases resources to concentrate on the profit-making areas of the business, which usually include customer relations. Automation can help you with your business, not run your business for you; data processing is notoriously a service function.

As the small business programmer becomes familiar with the equipment and language of automation, more and more uses will occur to him. It is important to adhere to the system development method described in this book while you are working on the second and third automation projects. In this way, you will prevent something that professional programmers know as *second-system syndrome*; that is, adding too many functions to a simple system. A system that has too many bells and whistles hanging off it will be unwieldly to use and manage effectively. Remembering the KISS maxim (Keep It Simple, Stupid) will make development more manageable.

INTERACTIVE PROGRAMMING

As mentioned earlier, the advent of terminals and microcomputers has made possible the use of a programming style known as interactive programming. In the past, programs were written to run without interruption from the operator. The process used files, and sometimes parameter cards, to communicate changing information such as report date (usually different from the real date), start/cutoff dates, and the like. This type of information is specific to the time and date the program is to be run and would have to be entered at run time. This idea of batch processing meant that once the program had started, the user had to wait while the program ran all its coded instructions without interruption.

Interactive programming is just that—having a conversation with the program. The program prints certain questions on the screen, and the user must answer them to allow the program to continue running. In the cases just mentioned, the program might print **ENTER REPORT DATE:**, and the user would enter the data that should appear at the top of the report.

The problem with interactive programming in the past was that terminals were not widely used to perform program execution. They were used to enter and modify programs. The computer operations staff—the trained professionals that actually run the computer in large installations—were too busy doing their job to answer questions from the program. Now terminal operators, who may or may not be programmers, are running their own jobs at the terminal. Because each one is the operator for his little piece of the system and would probably just sit and watch the program run anyway, he has time to respond to questions from the program. Interactive pro-

gramming not only gets needed data to the program, but also eliminates some boredom on the part of the operator. It is a way of letting him know that the program
is working for him.

Microcomputing

Microcomputers have brought the idea of interactive programming to its peak
usage. Game programs are the most obvious and notorious type of interactive program. They translate the input of the game controller (joystick) into motions of
graphic characters on the display screen and dole out rewards and punishments (for
the improper use of the controller). Interactive business programs do much the same
thing—if the data is entered incorrectly, the program will send an error message
to the user, who will immediately reenter the data.

The microcomputer has another advantage: the system is not being used by anyone other than the operator. This means that all resources available to the system
are available to you with no waiting. Because you are the operator, the questions
and answers that you use to interact with your program can be individualized to
you. Individualization can make the programming process more fun and the dry data
entry jobs less boring and more accurate.

Menus

One way of interacting with programs is with full-screen menus. *Menus* are lists
of functions that you may want to perform using the system and that you have programmed previously. For instance, let's say that you have created some R:base 5000
programs that you can use to do all your home budgeting functions. You might have
a checkbook balancing program, a loan calculation program, a bill register, and a
check-writing program. To produce a menu system from this, you would add the
top level of the hierarchy, a new module called Budget perhaps. This module would
display the choices available and ask you to enter an opinion number that is listed
beside the name of the option. As an option is selected, Budget would then call the
program that performs the chosen function. As the number of uses for the microcomputer grow, they can be added to the menu, or a new, higher-level menu could be
implemented. Now when you choose Budget from that higher menu, the menu that
was just discussed would appear on the screen. You could then choose a function
from that menu.

Another hierarchy has developed: a hierarchy of menus that should mirror the
hierarchy of functions discussed earlier. Note that in the example just discussed,
functions were added from lower to higher. This is a minor deviation from the top-
down approach, and would not have happened at all if the future uses for the computer had been foreseen. If you are using the machine to do budget work and sud-
denly decide to put a name and address list on the computer as well, you now have
two functions that are unrelated. By adding a higher level to the hierarchy, you can
bring the functions together in a bigger package, possibly called Home Management. Nothing detrimental, such as developing something "bottom-up," was done,
but functions were merged into a new hierarchy whole. This change will make use
of the system easier because the list of functions is clear to any operator. The
programmer has not undermined his control of the system.

Chapter 8

Screen, Report, and Application Generators

One day, some programmer, somewhere, had the revelation that computer programs can be used to generate other computer programs. This idea surely came about when the programmer in question realized that, with each application system he would write, some of the same functions were recreated over and over. Each new database needs a function to add new records, another to change existing records, still another to delete unwanted records, and, possibly still another to list the stored records.

The actual program code and structure that is used in each of these common functions is basically the same, allowing for differences in the number of fields, the particular edits performed, etc. The programmer probably noticed the number of times he had "cloned" these same functions for different databases.

One of the key phrases to for when you are deciding to perform a particular task using a computer is ". . . the same . . . over and over." One of the advantages of a computer is that it is very good at doing similar tasks or tasks with minor differences repeatedly without becoming tired or bored. So, this hypothetical programmer decided to let a program write the code for simple and common tasks, while freeing himself for other, more interesting tasks. Thus, the application generator was born.

HOW APPLICATION GENERATORS WORK

Simply put, an *application generator* is a program that creates another program, based on some form of input. The input can be in the form of a second, simplified lan-

47

```
┌─────────────────────────────────────────────────────────────────────┐
│                                                                       │
│  Before using the R:base Application Express choice                   │
│      "Define a new application"                                       │
│                                                                       │
│  1. Create your database using R:base 5000 Application Express menu   │
│        choice "Define a new database"                                 │
│                                                                       │
│  2. Create any custom data entry forms using the FORMS command from   │
│        the R:base command mode                                        │
│                                                                       │
│  3. Create any custom output report forms using the REPORTS command   │
│        from the R:base command mode                                   │
│                                                                       │
│  Next, choose the Application Express choice                          │
│      "Define a new application"                                       │
│                                                                       │
│  4. Choose the database to use in the application                     │
│                                                                       │
│  5. Define your menu structure using the menu generator               │
│                                                                       │
│  6. Define help screen for the menus                                  │
│                                                                       │
│  7. Choose the function of each menu                                  │
│        (Add, Change, Delete, Display, Print, Custom)                  │
│                                                                       │
│  8. Depending on function chosen select:                              │
│        Sort fields                                                    │
│        Selection Criteria                                             │
│        Data entry form name                                           │
│        Output report name                                             │
│        Custom program name                                            │
│                                                                       │
│  9. Create custom startup                                             │
│                                                                       │
│ 10. Run your application                                              │
│                                                                       │
└─────────────────────────────────────────────────────────────────────┘
```

Fig. 8-1. The steps to creating an application with EXPRESS.

guage; the program code can also be generated based on selections made interactively via a menu, as in the case of R:base 5000's Application EXPRESS.

Application EXPRESS is a combination of report writer, screen format, and code generator. It also performs the function of defining databases and tables. The programmer interacts with EXPRESS via a system of menus and screens. Through a step-by-step process, the developer is lead through the definition of the application from the top level down to the detailed functions. As each choice is made, the EXPRESS program is evaluating the choice and creating the program to perform the chosen options.

The application generator program merges an already-written function with input provided by the programmer to form simple, common routines. The size of the function library included in an application generator dictates how much power that generator will have. More sophisticated program generators might include a dozen functions or more; the Application EXPRESS provides seven of the simplest.

The reason that application generators like the Application EXPRESS work is because the programs that perform common database functions are similar in structure. In fact, the only difference between, for example, the Add functions for two different databases, is the name of the program, the name of the database accessed, and the names/definitions of the individual fields. These are supplied to the application generator by the programmer, and the changes are made to the stock ADD function from the generator's library of functions.

The Application EXPRESS creates a basic menu structure for each application. The action to be performed for each choice may be defined as one of the stock functions, or can include custom programs (those created outside of the EXPRESS). The creation of such a menu is also a stock function, because there are fewer differences between menu programs than between Add functions—all that changes are the options on the menu.

Using an application generator is relatively easy. The programmer just fills in the blanks, and the code is generated automatically by the program. The application can be quickly entered, and the programs be available for testing in a very short time, usually minutes, after the creation of the database.

Saving development time is especially important when you are starting an application that will require a large data entry effort at the outset. If, for example, a company wanted to computerize their customer list, someone must actually enter all of the information on their existing customer list into the computer. Simple data entry functions (add, change, delete, and browse) can be quickly provided using an application generator, allowing data entry to proceed while the application is still being developed. These functions can then be replaced by customized programs, or revised to fit the needs of the system.

GENERATING SCREENS

The simplest form of application generator is the screen *format generator*. This is usually a program that generates a screen format for data-entry purposes, giving a "picture" of how the screen is to look physically.

Most code to display text or fields on a screen looks pretty much the same. At the same time, it is hard to get an idea of what the screen will actually look like when it is displayed because the code bears no resemblance to the final product at all.

A programmer will *manually* produce a screen by writing the screen format down on paper, then counting or estimating the position of each item by row and column coordinates. He then writes the statements to display the information or retrieve the field from the screen. These statements all have the same format, differing only by the row/column position where the object is to be displayed, and the field name or text to be displayed at that position.

By providing a picture of the screen format to the screen generator, the row/column locations can be calculated automatically. The text to be displayed is placed at the position on the format screen that it is to occupy when the final screen is displayed. The program counts the position in row/column coordinates, and places these at their proper place in the program statement being generated. The text is then placed in the statement, and the generated statement is complete.

The screen generator must also be able to differentiate between text to be displayed and field names for fields whose contents are to be displayed (output fields) and those whose values are to be entered by the operator (input fields). You can differentiate by using special characters of the keyboard to indicate the start of a field name. Other special characters could provide the type of data (numeric or character) for editing purposes. Some sophisticated screen generators also provide range-checking and data-formatting features.

Application EXPRESS provides a very flexible screen format that can be altered completely. The screen is presented so that any section can be changed by moving the cursor to the proper area and typing in the new text or field name. Screens may be titled for easy identification. Fields are identified by name; the programmer is then asked a series of questions about the field for editing purposes. Most information about fields is already available from the database, which contains the size, data type, and location of each of the fields it contains.

The EXPRESS screen generator is described in detail in Chapter 13.

REPORT WRITERS

Another form of program generator is the *report writer*. Report writers produce program code to print lists of records or custom forms for use as reports, statements, bills, etc.

Report writers are similar to screen generators in that they take a formatted page and produce the program statements necessary to print that page. Printing and report commands look even less like the final product than screen display statements. Control breaks, loops, and other interspersed statements can make developing a report program a trial-and-error process, in spite of the fact that most report programs have the same structure.

There are two basic kinds of reports: the *line report*, where each line represents one database record, and *custom form report*, where each page may represent one database record. The lines or forms can be oriented to an entity, pulling the data to be printed from several tables or databases.

Manually creating a custom form report requires many of the same steps used to produce a screen format: the format is written on paper, the row/column coordinates are plotted, and so forth. Program code can be generated in the same way that screen format code can be generated once the position, data type, and output format of each individual field is known. Line reports are even easier to generate because even the column spacing can be calculated based on the sum of the field lengths and the size of the line.

The purpose of a report writer is to automate this process. The programmer provides a picture of what the report is to look like and how the output data is to be formatted. He determines the text for report and column headings and identifies which columns are to be totaled. The report writer builds the program code necessary to print the report in the correct format.

For some reports, it might be necessary to create a *control break*, a change in processing that occurs based on the contents of a data field. For example, a database of sales personnel might be sorted into sequence by a department number; the users of that report might want to see subtotals or some other information each time the department number changes.

This kind of processing requires several steps. First, the data must be sorted into sequence—either ascending or descending—by the control field, in this case Department Number. If the file is not in sequence by the control field, each time the contents of the control field changed the break routine would be performed, possibly at each record.

After each record is read from the database, and before the information is printed, the contents of the control field must be interrogated to determine if the value is different from that of the previous record. This procedure requires that you make a temporary field to hold the contents of the last record's control field. The holding area must be replaced with the contents of the current record's control field after you make the interrogation.

Finally, the break routine must be written. The routine prints any subtotals for the control break, in this case by department. The routine could also advance the paper to the next page and print new headings for the next department. The break routine must be executed after the last record in the file has been printed and prior to any grand totals.

The process of including a control break in a report may seem complicated, but it really is not. There is a holding field, a comparison, and a routine to perform if the comparison is unequal. The differences between control breaks are limited to the columns that are to be subtotaled on the report and the field that is the control field. This information can be quickly given to an interactive report generator like Application EXPRESS, which then uses the proper routine from its library.

The EXPRESS report generator is described in detail in Chapter 15.

CREATING APPLICATION SYSTEMS

Application generators are more sophisticated, allowing multiple menus, screens, reports, and functions to be coded rapidly. Programs thus created can be used immediately (after proper testing, of course).

An entire application system could be generated with the correct code generator, but usually an application system has several custom components or functions that could not be anticipated by the designers of the code generator. These must be programmed in the usual manner; the code generator, however, can offer several shortcuts.

Data entry functions that are needed prior to the completion of the system can be delivered immediately, allowing the initial data entry work to start even though the system is not ready. This feature can be a real time-saver, especially where an initial conversion to computer hardware is concerned.

Another use for generated code is as a base program that may later be modified by adding custom code to the generated code. This hybrid programming approach is useful when security routines are added to an application, or to log each function performed for possible later recovery.

THE DRAWBACKS OF CODE GENERATORS

The drawbacks that a system developer might encounter in using an application generator will sometimes cause him to choose another solution. The abilities of the code generator are limited to what its designers included in the library of functions. This fault cannot be corrected; anyone who can think of a complicated routine can always think of one still more complicated.

Although the application generator is useful for short and uncomplicated routines, the more complex processing required in an accounts receivable system, for example, would be beyond its abilities.

Another problem with the use of a code generator is that the program code produced lacks style and flexibility. The routine can be produced in one format only, with no extra routines for security or logging purposes. Sometimes the code generated is completely protected from change by special formatting or by using commands that are not available in custom programs.

There is also a Murphy's law of Application Generators: any application generated by an application generator will contain more bugs than the application generator. The application generator is a program, too, and like all programs can contain logic errors. An even greater problem exists when logic errors appear in the generated program, making the generated code useless.

The use of an application generator in creating a computer application system can help to accelerate the development process. That same development speed could be offset, however, by producing an application that is stale, stagnant, and not easily modified for future needs. As with any programming techniques, the trade-offs must be evaluated before you commit yourself to an unchangeable course of action.

Chapter 9

Fred's
Friendly Fish Market

Now that you have seen some of the activities involved in creating and using an automated system, let's develop a system that could be used for either business or personal purposes. For the purpose of this example, let's introduce a small business-person named Fred. Fred's business is small, that is, not him!

Fred owns a wholesale fish market. Fred is growing larger each month. Not Fred, his business! He sells all types of fish and seafood to area restaurants, supermarkets, and other smaller fish markets. Fred has decided that, in order to grow larger, he must be able to operate his business more efficiently. He is spending too much time running the business and not enough time with the lobsters and crabs. Fred's fish are ready to enter the computer age!

Fred sends circulars to his regular customers every month. This means that Fred himself needs to address every circular by hand each month, and this is excruciatingly boring work to Fred. He'd much rather be spending time with his family or improving the business, not typing out a hundred envelopes or so every month. So, after careful research, Fred has decided to purchase a personal computer that can use R:base 5000 software. Fred made this decision because he knows that, although this is the first use he has thought of for automating his business, there will be more uses in the future.

Before Fred purchased that personal computer, he defined his business problem in general terms: "I want to print labels, store an address/phone list, and produce a directory of these people."

Fred's purchase decision was based on his immediate needs (a computer, a disk drive for storage, and a printer). Looking ahead to the future, Fred decided that buying a good, all-purpose machine with a reliable service contract and useful, generalized software now and expanding his uses later was his best bet in automating his business.

DEFINING THE PROBLEM

Now that he has decided on his resources, even if he hasn't made the purchase yet, he can start designing the program he will use. As shown in Fig. 9-1, the definition of the problem is the basis upon which the whole system is built. Fred now adds

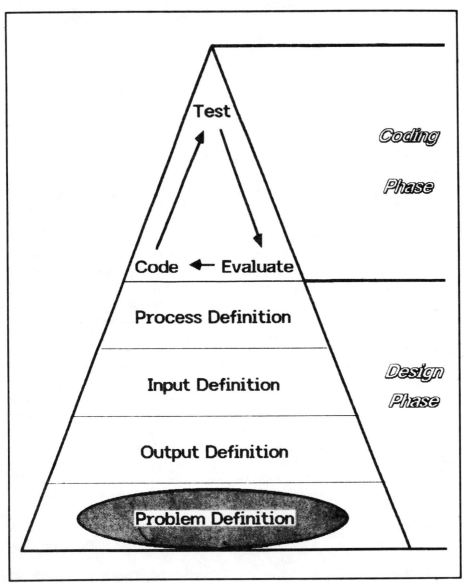

Fig. 9-1. The problem definition.

more detail to his problem definition:

- [ ] I need to enter and store information to be printed on mailing labels and on plain paper for a directory for use in mailing those darn circulars.
- [ ] R:base 5000 software that I have chosen can automatically handle data entry, storage, and editing when I supply disks to store the information on.
- [ ] Also, I will need backup copies of these disks, as well as backup copies of the software.
- [ ] On the mailing labels I need to have customer name, street address, city, state, and zip code.
- [ ] On the directory I also need to have the telephone number.

Now that Fred has written the definition in this form, breaking functions onto separate lines, he can see that the program will not be too difficult to write, and there is no calculation to be performed on the data. R:base 5000 will supply an entry and update facility for the information; so the thing to do now is to design the data.

DEFINING THE OUTPUT DATA

Since Fred decided to computerize his customer list, he must define precisely what he will need on that list. Fred knows that the customer directory and mailing labels are of utmost importance. Fred starts by thinking about what fields are needed in order to prepare those darn mailing labels and produce a customer directory.

The first field is name. Fred decides that, because he wants all output to be in alphabetical order by last name, he will put last name first in his database. He could put all names in one field called Name, in last-first order. However, Fred is still thinking of the future; someday, he might want to send personalized letters to his customers, and he would need to print the name in first-last order. Fred defines his first piece of output data as two fields: FName and LName. They are character data items, and each will be 20 characters long.

The next data item is address. Fred creates Address as a character field, up to 25 characters long. This field will hold the street address.

The city name field, Fred decided, would be 15 characters long, with the name City. Fred is being very careful not to use meaningless names in identifying his data items so that future enhancements will be easier. Good old Fred, always thinking about the future.

The state field is easy, says Fred, "Just two characters identify every state in the USA, and I only have customers in three!" So the field becomes State, with character data, two positions long.

Now comes a toughy, Fred thought. Zip code used to be five digits long, but isn't it supposed to be changed to nine digits in the near future? Fred decides to make zip code nine digits long to be sure; although, he could have easily changed this at a later time with R:base 5000. A zip code is an excellent example of a number that is not used in calculations. It could be defined as a character field. However, Fred wants R:base 5000 to edit the input data for him, and if he defines it as character data, the system would allow any character in the field. By defining it as a numeric field, it will accept only numbers nine positions long.

The last step is taking care of the phone number, so Fred uses the same reasoning as for Zipcode and comes up with Phone, which will be ten digits long and numeric.

Fred's output description looks like Table 9-1. The output definition is part of the evolving system design. Since it is still a design, the definition can be changed to reflect new requirements and developments. This definition is not "cast in stone!"

Format of the Output

Part of the output definition is also defining exactly what the output reports will look like. In a name/address file this step is usually easy because there are few fields to contend with, and because the format of mailing labels is defined by the post office and is rarely changed. (Look how long it will take American businesses to implement the nine-digit zip code—7 years!)

Format of the Mailing Labels

Fred has decided to buy blank labels that are three across a page, or *3-up*, as they are called. That means that three labels must be printed at one time, or the labels on the right side of the page will go to waste. The format that would be used if there are eight names on the mailing list is shown in Fig. 9-2.

The layout of the labels does not provide enough details to be useful as an output definition. The field names are really not enough. The length of each field should be part of the label definition to ensure the proper fit and alignment. Producing this type of format for the label will show the smallest possible size the label should be. The following shows a single label. Note that the space from one X to the next is the field length as defined previously.

```
X------FNAME-------X X------LNAME-------X
X--------ADDRESS--------X
X----CITY-----X, ST
X--ZIP--X
```

These field definitions reflect the largest possible variable that each field can hold.

Format of the Directory

The only real document Fred has to design is the directory he wants printed.

Table 9-1. Fred's Output Description for the Customer List.

Field	Data Type	Length
FNAME	character	20
LNAME	character	20
ADDRESS	character	25
CITY	character	15
STATE	character	2
ZIP	numeric	9
PHONE	numeric	10

```
 ---------------------    ----------------------    ----------------------
:                     :  :                      :  :                      :
:  FNAME1 LNAME1      :  :  FNAME2 LNAME2       :  :  FNAME3 LNAME3       :
:  ADDRESS1           :  :  ADDRESS2            :  :  ADDRESS3            :
:  CITY1, ST1         :  :  CITY2, ST2          :  :  CITY3, ST3          :
:  ZIP1               :  :  ZIP2                :  :  ZIP3                :
:                     :  :                      :  :                      :
 ---------------------    ----------------------    ----------------------
:                     :  :                      :  :                      :
:  FNAME1 LNAME1      :  :  FNAME2 LNAME2       :  :  FNAME3 LNAME3       :
:  ADDRESS1           :  :  ADDRESS2            :  :  ADDRESS3            :
:  CITY1, ST1         :  :  CITY2, ST2          :  :  CITY3, ST3          :
:  ZIP1               :  :  ZIP2                :  :  ZIP3                :
:                     :  :                      :  :                      :
 ---------------------    ----------------------    ----------------------
:                     :  :                      :  :                      :
:  FNAME1 LNAME1      :  :  FNAME2 LNAME2       :  :                      :
:  ADDRESS1           :  :  ADDRESS2            :  :         WASTE        :
:  CITY1, ST1         :  :  CITY2, ST2          :  :                      :
:  ZIP1               :  :  ZIP2                :  :                      :
:                     :  :                      :  :                      :
 ---------------------    ----------------------    ----------------------
```

Fig. 9-2. Mailing labels.

This should lead to more questioning on Fred's part. Does he want a hand-held, book size directory, or does he want it printed on 3 × 5 cards? Some printers can only handle forms with sprocket-feed holes on the sides; some work with regular typing paper. Fred must take these details into consideration, as well.

So Fred, for the time being, has decided on 8 1/2- × -11 inch paper because he has pin-feed paper for his new printer. If at a later time he wishes to convert to ROLI-DEX, he can do so without too many problems. And, if he ever runs out of the special forms, he can always convert to plain paper.

Fred decided to make his directory one column wide, with as many names as fit on each page. This is the most efficient form that he can think of, and it will probably not be used that often anyway. He just needs it to look up a name or phone number when he is not near the computer.

Fred now defines the format for an entry in the directory:

```
X------LNAME-------X,  X------FNAME--------X
                       X------ADDRESS----------X
                       X----CITY-----X  ST  X--ZIP--X

Phone:  X-PHONE--X
```

The format shows the maximum length of each field because the maximum length of the fields must be allowed for on the output forms. Otherwise, the fields may get chopped off, or *truncated*, if other fields on the form compete for the same space. Also the fields could print past the edge of a narrow form, which wastes ink and time, and doesn't do your printer much good either.

Now Fred can figure out how many of these entries will fit on a page. He already decided that he would use regular paper with a length of 11 inches for this listing. Fred's printer prints 6 lines per inch, so this means that there will be 66 lines available per page. Each individual entry takes 5 lines, and Fred wants 2 lines between entries; thus each entry will require 7 lines in all. Also, Fred decided that he didn't want the first and last entries on each page to print too near the top or bottom. He decides to leave 5 blank lines at the top and bottom of each page, or a total of 10 blank lines. With a little math, Fred figures:

66 total lines − 10 margin lines = 56 effective lines
56 lines/7 lines per entry = 8 entries per page.

Fred decides that he will print eight entries per page. Each entry will be formatted as shown previously.

TWO THINGS AT ONCE

Fred has defined his output pretty well. His next discovery is that he has also defined the input. This is because it's Fred's first stab at automation: he has no existing files, and all data that is needed will have to be present in the input or calculated from the input. Because there is no calculation involved in the solution to Fred's business problem, he has done the remarkable feat of defining his input and output in one step. Up-front planning has already paid off in this admittedly simple system.

Fred's input description looks just like his output description because there are no calculations. It is shown in Table 9-2.

REEXAMINING THE DESIGN

Now the problem has been defined and the output specified, and Fred is ready to tear into his process definition. As he looks carefully at the documents he has created, he notices that there is not much processing to do at all. The information has only to be retrieved from wherever it is now and placed on the output form. Fred takes the sensible approach and decides to look over his requirements one more time.

On closer inspection, he notices two things. First, the nine-digit zip code is broken into two parts: the five-digit zip code and the new four-digit part are separated by a hyphen. He decides not to create a Zip1 and Zip2 field for the two parts.

Second, the telephone number, when entered as a single number, is awkward to look at and needs to be divided into three parts: area code, exchange, and number. Instead of breaking up the telephone number into its component parts, Fred decides that he will make the field a character field and enter all punctuation manu-

Table 9-2. Fred's Input/Output Description for the Customer Directory.

Field	Data Type	Length
FNAME	character	20
LNAME	character	20
ADDRESS	character	25
CITY	character	15
STATE	character	2
ZIP	numeric	9
PHONE	numeric	10

ally. Now the numeric edit will not work; so Fred will have to edit the contents of the telephone number field by himself. He is prepared to do that to save processing time. So, both the zip code and the telephone number fields will be character fields. The zip code will be 10 characters long and have the form NNNNN-NNNN. The telephone number will have the form (AAA)NNN-NNNN and will be 13 characters long.

FRED DIVIDES TO CONQUER

Now that Fred has defined his output and input, he is ready to chart the hierarchy of the functions in the system. He first draws a square on the empty sheet of paper and labels it Customer System. This is the overall name of the major function. He then draws six more boxes in a line an inch or two under the first box. He labels these boxes, from left to right, Add Customer, Change Customer, Remove Customer, Print Mailing Labels, Print Mailing List. These are the overall kinds of actions that Fred will need his system to perform. He then connects the boxes with lines, denoting the hierarchy of the functions. The result is shown in Fig. 9-3.

Fred now adds a third level of boxes about an inch under the second row. He puts two boxes underneath the Print Mailing Labels box. He connects them to the box using the hierarchy lines and labels them as in Fig. 9-4. Because the function Print Mailing Labels will automatically print the labels each time a row of three labels are formatted, it is shown as a part of the second hierarchy rather than as a separate third level.

Fred feels that his hierarchy is now complete, and he is ready to start his screen design.

DESIGNING SCREENS

At this point in the design, Fred (or you) can take a look at how the data is to be entered. When a new customer is to be added to the file, all of the input fields must be entered; the record concerning the customer does not exist in computer-usable

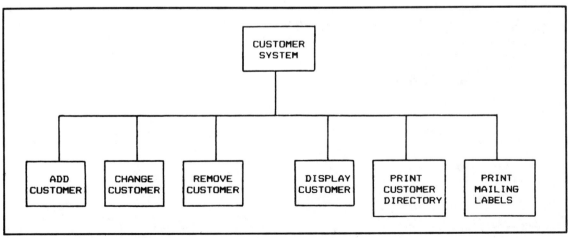

Fig. 9-3. The main function hierarchy chart.

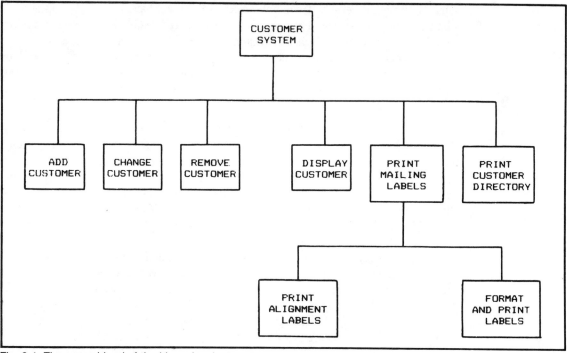

Fig. 9-4. The second level of the hierarchy chart.

form. So, in order to "capture" this information, Fred designs the data input screen for customer additions to look like the screen shown in Fig. 9-5.

With this screen, Fred can enter all the information needed for each customer. Notice that he allowed for the full length of each field; he also included a heading for the screen and a label for each field. You may notice a large space between the heading and the first field. Later you will learn how error messages and informational messages can also be programmed to appear in this space.

For the Change Customer function, Fred needs approximately the same screen as was defined for the Add Customer function, except that when it appears, it should

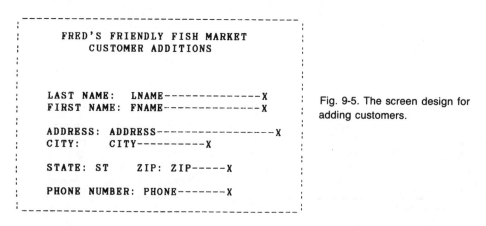

Fig. 9-5. The screen design for adding customers.

```
--------------------------------------------------
:                                                :
:          FRED'S FRIENDLY FISH MARKET           :
:               CUSTOMER CHANGES                 :
:                                                :
:     *** ENTER CUSTOMER TO BE CHANGED ***       :
:                                                :
:     LAST NAME:   LNAME---------------X         :
:     FIRST NAME:  FNAME---------------X         :
:                                                :
:                                                :
:                                                :
:                                                :
:                                                :
:                                                :
--------------------------------------------------
```

Fig. 9-6. The screen design for customer search.

have all the information already displayed. Then it can be changed and the record updated. With this type of process, however, Fred will have to tell his program which customer to change. He will need the screen shown in Fig. 9-6.

The name information will give the program a clue that indicates which record is to be retrieved for changes. If the record is not found, the computer can be programmed to display an error message, as shown in Fig. 9-7. The user will be requested to reenter the name. When the record is retrieved, it will be displayed on the screen (Fig. 9-8), with all the information filled in. Fred then has the ability to change any field on the screen. After changes have been made, he can tell the system to put the record with the changes back into its place in the file.

The screens for Display Customer, shown in Figs. 9-9 and 9-10, will look almost the same as those for Change Customer, except that no data can be changed.

For the Delete Customer function, Fred will need a screen to enter the name of the customer to be deleted, and some way of confirming the delete. If, by chance, the name was entered incorrectly or the wrong name was entered, he wants the ability to abort the deletion. The program should ask if the retrieve record is the correct one to remove from the file. Notice how Fred is using informational messages in the message area of the confirmation screen shown in Fig. 9-11.

After creating the screens for the customer data entry and the maintenance functions (called *file maintenance* in programmer talk), Fred turns to the actual application screen. The add, change, delete, and display functions are also applications,

```
-------------------------------------------
:                                         :
:      FRED'S FRIENDLY FISH MARKET        :
:           CUSTOMER CHANGES              :
:                                         :
:   *** NAME NOT FOUND - TRY AGAIN ***    :
:                                         :
:     LAST NAME:   LNAME---------------X  :
:     FIRST NAME:  FNAME---------------X  :
:                                         :
:                                         :
:                                         :
:                                         :
:                                         :
-------------------------------------------
```

Fig. 9-7. An example of a screen error message.

```
----------------------------------------
:                                        :
:     FRED'S FRIENDLY FISH MARKET        :
:          CUSTOMER CHANGES              :
:                                        :
:                                        :
:   LAST NAME:   LNAME--------------X    :
:   FIRST NAME: FNAME--------------X     :
:                                        :
:   ADDRESS: ADDRESS-----------------X   :
:   CITY:     CITY---------X              :
:                                        :
:   STATE: ST    ZIP: ZIP-----X          :
:                                        :
:   PHONE NUMBER: PHONE------X            :
:                                        :
----------------------------------------
```

Fig. 9-8. The Customer Changes data screen.

but they are support functions; that is, they exist only to facilitate the operation of the functions Print Mailing Labels and Print Directory. These last two are the output generators—the functions for which the system was written in the first place.

Fig. 9-9. The screen for a customer search.

```
----------------------------------------
:                                        :
:     FRED'S FRIENDLY FISH MARKET        :
:          CUSTOMER DISPLAY              :
:                                        :
: *** ENTER NAME TO BE DISPLAYED ***     :
:                                        :
:   LAST NAME:   LNAME--------------X    :
:   FIRST NAME: FNAME--------------X     :
:                                        :
:                                        :
:                                        :
:                                        :
:                                        :
----------------------------------------
```

The input screen for the Print Mailing Labels function is designed as shown in Fig. 9-12. This screen asks if alignment labels are to be printed. When a Y is entered, the test labels will be printed. The alignment routine will print a series of

```
----------------------------------------
:                                        :
:     FRED'S FRIENDLY FISH MARKET        :
:          CUSTOMER DISPLAY              :
:                                        :
:                                        :
:   LAST NAME:   LNAME-------------X     :
:   FIRST NAME: FNAME--------------X     :
:                                        :
:   ADDRESS: ADDRESS-----------------X   :
:   CITY:     CITY---------X              :
:                                        :
:   STATE: ST    ZIP: ZIP-----X          :
:                                        :
:   PHONE NUMBER: PHONE-------X           :
:                                        :
----------------------------------------
```

Fig. 9-10. The Customer Display screen.

```
-------------------------------------------------------
:              FRED'S FRIENDLY FISH MARKET             :
:                   CUSTOMER DELETION                  :
:                                                      :
:  ENTER "D" TO CONFIRM DELETE ===>  __                :
:                                                      :
:     LAST NAME:   LNAME--------------X                :
:     FIRST NAME:  FNAME--------------X                :
:                                                      :
:     ADDRESS:  ADDRESS----------------X               :
:     CITY:     CITY----------X                        :
:                                                      :
:     STATE: ST    ZIP: ZIP-----X                      :
:                                                      :
:     PHONE NUMBER: PHONE----X                         :
:                                                      :
:                                                      :
-------------------------------------------------------
```

Fig. 9-11. The deletion confirmation message.

Xs across the labels so the operator can properly adjust the printer. The <cr> symbol stands for carriage return and means that the operator should press the enter or return key. After the alignment labels are printed, this screen is displayed again. When Fred has aligned the printer to his satisfaction, he presses the enter key, and the customer labels are printed.

The Print Directory function really does not need a screen because the plain paper forms can be aligned without using the method described for the Print Mailing Labels function. Fred decides to display a screen anyway to confirm that the Print Directory function is the one that the operator wanted. So he designs the screen shown in Fig. 9-13.

When this screen is displayed, Fred will have to tell the program to start printing the directory. If he chose the option by mistake, he could abort it.

On closer examination of his screens, Fred describes that this screen could also be used in the Print Mailing Labels function in the same way. This project is still in the design phase; and writing another piece of paper is an easy task. This sort of change should be noted in the design, rather than changed when the full system is implemented. Fred now changes the Mailing Label screen to look like the one shown in Fig. 9-14.

```
---------------------------------------------
:                                            :
:      FRED'S FRIENDLY FISH MARKET           :
:         MAILING LABEL PRINT                :
:                                            :
:                                            :
:                                            :
:      ENTER "Y" FOR ALIGNMENT PRINT         :
:        OR <cr> TO BEGIN PRINT              :
:                                            :
:            ====>  ___                      :
:                                            :
:                                            :
:                                            :
:                                            :
---------------------------------------------
```

Fig. 9-12. The Mailing Label Print screen.

```
FRED'S FRIENDLY FISH MARKET
CUSTOMER DIRECTORY PRINT



ENTER <cr> TO BEGIN PRINT
  OR "N" TO ABORT PRINT

     ====>  ___
```

Fig. 9-13. Customer directory and screen.

Fred has one more screen to design: the menu screen for the entire customer system. This screen (and program) is the top level on the hierarchy chart, and will allow Fred to initiate any of his functions by entering a number or letter. Fred's menu screen is shown in Fig. 9-15.

The **ENTER SELECTION** line is where the selection is entered. This is called a *prompt* because you are prompted for the right answer. If you enter anything besides 1-6 or X, the system will prompt you for a correct answer by printing **INVALID SELECTION—TRY AGAIN** on the message area of the screen.

Now, Fred is ready to tackle the design of the processes his system will perform.

A MENU SYSTEM

Fred envisions the top level of the hierarchy as a menu that will invoke the next-lower level of functions. This means that when he runs the program, a list of choices will appear on the screen with an option number beside each one. The operator (probably Fred) will enter the number of his choice, and the function will be performed. It's just like ordering food in a restaurant, thought Fred. No wonder they are called menus.

```
FRED'S FRIENDLY FISH MARKET
    MAILING LABEL PRINT



ENTER "Y" FOR ALIGNMENT PRINT,
      "A" TO ABORT PRINT,
   OR <cr> TO BEGIN PRINT

        ====>  ___
```

Fig. 9-14. The revised Mailing Label Print screen.

```
┌─────────────────────────────────────────────┐
│          FRED'S FRIENDLY FISH MARKET         │
│             CUSTOMER SYSTEM MENU             │
│                                              │
│                                              │
│        ENTER SELECTION ===>  __              │
│                                              │
│            1 - ADD CUSTOMER                  │
│            2 - CHANGE CUSTOMER               │
│            3 - REMOVE CUSTOMER               │
│            4 - DISPLAY CUSTOMER              │
│                                              │
│            5 - PRINT MAILING LABELS          │
│            6 - PRINT DIRECTORY               │
│                                              │
│            X - EXIT SYSTEM                   │
└─────────────────────────────────────────────┘
```

Fig. 9-15. The main Customer system menu.

Fred then writes the pseudocode shown in Fig. 9-16 for his menu program. Inside the DOWHILE loop, Fred places a CASE construct to test for the options he listed on his menu screen. He includes an OTHERWISE unit in case the number entered was not one listed on the screen. Fred then ends the DOWHILE loop with an ENDDO and notes that this will be the end of the program because it has fulfilled all the functions.

Fred uses a switch, which is called Exit, to determine if the operator has chosen the exit option. The first statement sets the switch for exiting the system to no exit. As long as this code is N, the menu is to be displayed so that another option can be chosen. Fred wrote the statement Display Menu Screen and then used a DOWHILE to see if the exit option (he called it option X) had been chosen.

Fred now walks-thru his pseudocode to determine if it is correct and if it performs the processes he wants when he wants. He writes Exit on a separate sheet

```
                    MENU PROGRAM

      SET EXIT TO "N"
      DISPLAY MENU SCREEN
      READ OPTION
      DOWHILE EXIT = "N"
        CASE
          WHEN OPTION = 1 PERFORM "ADD CUSTOMER"
          WHEN OPTION = 2 PERFORM "CHANGE CUSTOMER"
          WHEN OPTION = 3 PERFORM "REMOVE CUSTOMER"
          WHEN OPTION = 4 PERFORM "DISPLAY CUSTOMER"
          WHEN OPTION = 5 PERFORM "PRINT MAILING LABELS"
          WHEN OPTION = 6 PERFORM "PRINT MAILING LIST"
          WHEN OPTION = X SET EXIT TO "Y"
          OTHERWISE WRITE "INVALID OPTION"
          DISPLAY MENU SCREEN
          READ OPTION
        ENDCASE
      ENDDO
```

Fig. 9-16. Pseudocode for a menu selection.

of paper and writes below it. After Exit he adds Option and writes an X below it, showing that he has chosen the Exit System option on his (as yet) imaginary menu. Fred has decided to test this option first (a very good idea).

Exit   Option

N   X

The next statement to be performed is the DOWHILE. The condition asks if Exit is equal to N. Looking at his sheet of paper, Fred sees that Exit is equal to N, because N was assigned to it in the first statement; Exit has not been changed by another assignment. "This isn't right," thought Fred. The program should not get into the loop if the X option was chosen. On close examination of the code, Fred sees that the condition would be met on the next time through the loop, but only after the menu is displayed another time.

So, Fred makes a modification to the pseudocode as shown in Fig. 9-17. Now when he chooses option X, the WHEN unit for the condition Option-X is performed, and the value of Exit is changed to Y. Control jumps out of the CASE figure to the ENDDO, and the condition is tested. Since Exit now equals Y, the condition is no longer true, so control then passes out of the DOWHILE to the statement following the ENDDO.

THE FUNCTIONS

Now Fred begins to code the functions on the second level of the hierarchy chart. As he looks at the functions, Fred realizes that the add, change, remove, and display functions are probably performed easily in a powerful database manager like R:base 5000.

Because the major purpose of a database management program is to add, change, delete, and display records in a database file, he can probably use very few R:base 5000 commands to perform these functions. His pseudocodes for these functions look like this:

```
SET EXIT TO "N"
DOWHILE EXIT = "N"
   CASE
      DISPLAY MENU SCREEN
      READ OPTION
      WHEN OPTION = 1 PERFORM "ADD CUSTOMER"
      WHEN OPTION = 2 PERFORM "CHANGE CUSTOMER"
      WHEN OPTION = 3 PERFORM "REMOVE CUSTOMER"
      WHEN OPTION = 4 PERFORM "DISPLAY CUSTOMER"
      WHEN OPTION = 5 PERFORM "PRINT MAILING LABELS"
      WHEN OPTION = 6 PERFORM "PRINT MAILING LIST"
      WHEN OPTION = X SET EXIT TO "Y"
      OTHERWISE WRITE "INVALID OPTION"
   ENDCASE
ENDDO
```

Fig. 9-17. Redesigning the pseudocode.

```
ADD A CUSTOMER

  ACCESS CUSTOMER FILE
  ADD CUSTOMER DATA IN LAST NAME ORDER
  CLOSE FILE

CHANGE A CUSTOMER

  ACCESS CUSTOMER FILE
  ENTER CUSTOMER NAME
  VERIFY AND RETRIEVE RECORD
  CHANGE CUSTOMER DATA
  CLOSE FILE

REMOVE CUSTOMER

  ACCESS CUSTOMER FILE
  ENTER CUSTOMER NAME
  VERIFY AND DELETE RECORD
  CLOSE FILE

DISPLAY CUSTOMER

  ACCESS CUSTOMER FILE
  ENTER CUSTOMER NAME
  VERIFY AND DISPLAY CUSTOMER
  CLOSE FILE
```

Fred has now pseudocoded all but the last two functions the system is to perform. These functions are a little more involved:

```
PRINT MAILING LABELS

    PERFORM "ALIGNMENT PRINT"
    ACCESS CUSTOMER FILE
    READ A CUSTOMER RECORD
    DOWHILE MORE RECORDS
    PERFORM "FORMAT FOR LABELS"
      IF LABEL COUNTER = 3
        THEN
           PRINT A ROW OF LABELS
           RESET LABEL COUNTER
      ENDIF
      READ NEXT RECORD
    ENDDO
    CLOSE FILE
```

In this program, notice that Fred has put off defining the two subfunctions in the PERFORM statements. No matter how simple they may be, they are still on the next level of the hierarchy, and the second level is not finished yet.

```
PRINT MAILING LIST

    ACCESS CUSTOMER FILE
    READ CUSTOMER RECORD
    DOWHILE MORE RECORDS
      PRINT DIRECTORY ENTRY
```

```
   READ NEXT RECORD
ENDDO
CLOSE FILE
```

Again, Fred has postponed the definition of the third-level modules until later. Notice that these programs will still be valid, no matter what format the final labels or directory take. This means that if Fred starts out using sheets that contain 3 labels across the page (3-up labels) and later switches to 2-up labels, the only modules that need to be changed are the Print Alignment and Format For Labels modules. This is an advantage of modular programming—changes to the lower-level functions do not require the recoding of any higher modules.

THE SUBFUNCTIONS

Now Fred turns to his third and final level:

```
PRINT ALIGNMENT LABELS

   ASK IF ALIGNMENT NEEDED
   DO WHILE ALIGNMENT NEEDED
      PRINT LABEL WITH X'S FILLING EVERY FIELD
      ADVANCE TO NEXT LABEL
      ASK IF ALIGNMENT IS NEEDED
   ENDDO


   FORMAT FOR LABELS

      ADD 1 TO LABEL COUNTER
      MOVE CUSTOMER FIELDS TO LABEL 1, 2 OR 3,
         DEPENDING ON LABEL COUNTER
```

These two functions could probably be coded in the Print Mailing Labels pseudocode. Do not be tempted to join short modules, however. Always break the process down into functional components, as Fred has done. Always traverse the module hierarchy from top to bottom; beware of shortcuts.

Fred now codes the final function:

```
PRINT DIRECTORY ENTRIES

   PRINT THE DIRECTORY ENTRIES
   BLANK OUT THE DIRECTORY FIELDS
   ADVANCE PAPER
   IF TOO CLOSE TO BOTTOM OF PAGE FOR MORE ENTRIES
      THEN ADVANCE TO TOP OF PAGE
   ENDIF
```

Notice that Fred did not say exactly how he is going to know when the printer is nearing the bottom of the page. This step will have to be done in R:base 5000 code, and Fred hasn't learned it yet. Therefore, he leaves the pseudocode statements deliberately vague; he will not be tied down to a particular method.

An important advantage of top-down coding is that the basic system can be made available quickly, before all the modules are coded in R:base 5000. In the customer system example, the Add Customer function could be the first one done. Then, while Fred is coding the other modules, someone else can be entering the customer data (Fred's wife Elsa, for instance). Then, when the PRINT functions are ready to be placed on-line, the data will be available to test them, and the system will be ready to go.

Chapter 10

Fred Gets Ambitious

Fred has finished the design for his customer information system. He is feeling very proud of himself, but he still doesn't feel perfect; it seems too easy! Fred wants to automate as much as he can. He thinks of other sections that he can automate most easily.

"Gee whiz, I should automate orders next. There are so many each day that we work many hours after the docks close just to do the paperwork. Also, we could do the daily inventories so we know what to order each day. My brother Frank always orders too much mackerel and not enough lobster. He says, 'Don't worry, what we sell, we sell.' But I do worry; we need to track our inventories so we don't run out. Murphy's Restaurant came to us for crab last month, and we were out; they haven't ordered from us since. So, I want to automate our customer orders and our inventories. That way I will know what my customers are ordering and what I need to have in our warehouse. Finally, I want to automate the payroll here. We are always paying too much to the dockhands or the checks are late or something. I will do all these things."

Fred has gone off the deep end! Because of one success, he is ready to tackle the world (and all he has done is the design). The next logical step is to chart the whole system. This will become the new top level of the hierarchy chart, and everything else will move down one level. The customer system becomes part of a bigger system and will be represented as such. The resulting hierarchy chart is shown in Fig. 10-1, and the Main Menu screen is shown in Fig. 10-2.

After charting and designing his Main Menu screen, Fred thinks he is now ready to tackle the rest of the system. He remembers that a beginner should design a little

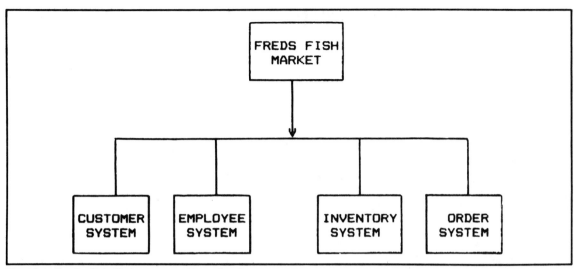

Fig. 10-1. Fred's Fish Market system hierarchy chart.

at a time. One module can be finished before the others are started.

Fred is now ready to automate the next part of his system, the ordering system. When customers place orders with Fred, the smallest part of the process that he goes through is actually sending out the order. The rest of the process is filling out the order form, keeping track of the inventory, and keeping orders on the file for long periods of time. Fred has just about outgrown his four-drawer file cabinet. In the fish business there are no backorders. If you don't have it, the customer will go somewhere else to get it. There are many standing orders. One of Fred's customers, The Fish Depot in Somersville, has a lobster special twice a week. They expect 62 one-pound lobsters every Tuesday and Saturday. They don't even call in the order; the lobsters are expected to be there (and it's a long walk). They do call in other items each day, though. Fred and Frank (his brother) spend a lot of time remembering who gets what, and when.

So with one design already under his belt, Fred starts the design for the Customer Order System.

Fig. 10-2. Fred's Fish Market main screen design.

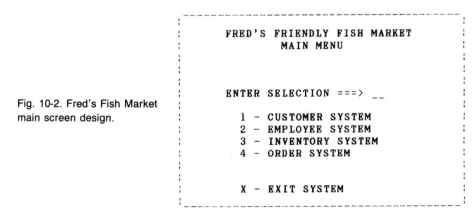

```
FRED'S FRIENDLY FISH MARKET
         MAIN MENU


ENTER SELECTION ===>  __

   1 - CUSTOMER SYSTEM
   2 - EMPLOYEE SYSTEM
   3 - INVENTORY SYSTEM
   4 - ORDER SYSTEM


   X - EXIT SYSTEM
```

THE PROBLEM DEFINITION

Fred needs certain information to create this system. In processing orders now, he has

- ☐ Customer information
- ☐ An order number to uniquely identify orders
- ☐ The date of the order
- ☐ The quantity, description, and price of each item ordered

As Fred examined his current way of processing orders, he saw that there were two forms of output: the order form that goes to Fred's shipping department to indicate what is to be packed and shipped, and the shipping form (bill of lading), which is also the invoice. (Fred's Fish is C.O.D. only—not codfish, cash on delivery—he doesn't give credit.)

Fred defined his problem like this:

```
"I need to record and store
order information
to be used to produce
order forms and shipping labels.
The order forms should have:
    the order number and customer name
    each item and quantity number.
The shipping form should have:
    the order number and all customer information
    each item and quantity
    along with prices and a total."
```

Fred immediately noticed that the shipping form has some information on it that can be retrieved from the customer system he has finished designing! That means that he will not have to reenter the information; he will just have to retrieve it when he wants it.

THE OUTPUT DEFINITION

Now Fred defines the fields he will need for his output, as shown in Table 10-1. Six out of the 11 items of output that Fred defined are fields from his previous system! Because that information will be available in computer usable form, Fred doesn't have to worry about entering it again. Fred wonders how to retrieve it from the customer file, but he realizes that problem should be figured out as a part of the input design.

The length of the Price field is 5.2. This means it will contain a total of five digits, with two representing pennies. The largest price you could have would be 999.99.

Fred defines the shipping form so that it will look just like the ones he wrote by hand (Fig. 10-3). The order form would be the same, but would not have prices or the customer's address.

THE INPUT DEFINITION

The total price fields including the Total Owed would not be input fields. They can

Table 10-1. Order Form Output Definition.

Field	Type	Length
FNAME	Character	20
LNAME	Character	20
ADDRESS	Character	25
CITY	Character	15
ST	Character	2
ZIP	Character	10
ORDER NUMBER	Numeric	5
DATE ORDERED	Character	8
QUANTITY	Numeric	3
ITEM	Character	25
PRICE	Numeric	5.2

be calculated by multiplying QTY times Price as the items are printed on the form.

Fred now can define his input. The fields from the customer system can be retrieved; only fields that need to be input for the order system are given in Table 10-2.

Now Fred can address a question that has been bothering him. "How can I use my customer file with my new order file? Each order must be related to a unique customer, and if at some point, I have two customers named Bill Smith, how could the program tell them apart using the information I have given it?"

A good question—as things are designed now, there is no unique identification for a customer, apart from the customer's last and first names. When Fred was envisioning his customer system, it wasn't important. If he somehow asked to delete the wrong customer, he could always abort the delete and find the next record that had the name he entered. Now, however, when he will be accessing that file from a program, Fred cannot rely on his own judgment because a computer cannot make judgments of this type. Another way must be found.

Fred decides that he must change his customer system to include a field called

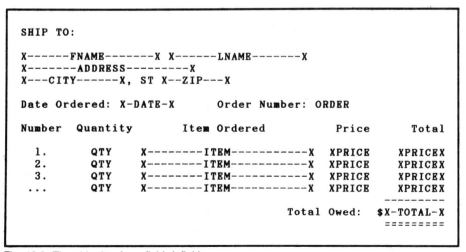

```
SHIP TO:

X------FNAME-------X X------LNAME-------X
X-------ADDRESS---------X
X---CITY------X, ST X--ZIP---X

Date Ordered: X-DATE-X      Order Number: ORDER

Number   Quantity      Item Ordered        Price       Total

  1.       QTY     X--------ITEM----------X  XPRICE     XPRICEX
  2.       QTY     X--------ITEM----------X  XPRICE     XPRICEX
  3.       QTY     X--------ITEM----------X  XPRICE     XPRICEX
 ...       QTY     X--------ITEM----------X  XPRICE     XPRICEX
                                                      ---------
                                        Total Owed:  $X-TOTAL-X
                                                      =========
```

Fig. 10-3. The shipping form field definition.

Table 10-2. Order Form Input Definition.

ORDER NUMBER	Numeric	5
DATE ORDERED	Character	8
QUANTITY	Numeric	3
ITEM	Character	25
PRICE	Numeric	5.2

Customer Number. This will be a unique identifier. It will be first on the record and will be assigned by Fred when the customer data is initially added to the file.

Fred has also decided to add something he always wanted and never even did in the manual system—the customer's business name. When Fred started, he sold mainly to other distributors. He always dealt with the owner and would ship the items with the owner's name on the label. As Fred has gotten larger (the business, not Fred: he only weighs 130 lbs), he has not been able to meet all of his customers. The business name is more important than the owner's or seafood buyer's name in a large supermarket chain.

Fred's new input description for the customer system looks like Table 10-3. Fred makes this change to his customer system design, and looks for more changes. He knows that his customer information screens will change; for example, the Add Customer screen now will have to include customer number and company, as shown in Fig. 10-4.

Also, the screens for Change Customer, Delete Customer, and Display Customer can be changed to retrieve the customer record by the customer number, rather than by the more unreliable customer name. For example, the Change Customer screens would look like the one shown in Fig. 10-5.

Fred had to make these changes to the Customer Name screens for Delete Customer and Display Customer, as well. He also had to make the change to his directory format, as shown in Fig. 10-6.

With these changes made, Fred feels that he can now produce an input definition for the order system. (See Table 10-4.)

A TWO-FILE SYSTEM

Now that Fred has decided on the input fields, he looks at the design of the data.

Table 10-3. Input Definition for the Customer System.

Field	Data Type	Length
CUSTNO	Numeric	5
COMPANY	Character	20
FNAME	Character	20
LNAME	Character	20
ADDRESS	Character	25
CITY	Character	15
STATE	Character	2
ZIP	Character	10
PHONE	Character	13

```
            FRED'S FRIENDLY FISH MARKET
                CUSTOMER ADDITIONS


    CUSTOMER NUMBER: CUSTN

        COMPANY:      COMPANY------------X
        LAST NAME:    LNAME-------------X
        FIRST NAME:   FNAME-------------X

        ADDRESS: ADDRESS-----------------X
        CITY:      CITY----------X

        STATE: ST     ZIP: ZIP-----X

        PHONE NUMBER: PHONE-------X
```

Fig. 10-4. A new Customer Additions screen.

One order record, as just defined, has one item associated with it. "This is no good." Fred thought. "Most of the orders I process are for more than one item." He could put Item1, Item2, etc., directly on the order record, but doing so would make the record very large and difficult to use. It would also limit the number of items that could be assigned to one order number. Fred is about to experience the realities of relational database design, and he doesn't even know what that means—yet.

In the Database section of this book, you will learn in detail how to analyze and design databases. For now, only a brief mention of the *two-file* system is necessary.

The solution is for Fred to create two files: one for order number, customer number, and date; and another for the quantities, items, and prices. The "bridge" between the files is the order number, which will appear in both. In the Order file, one record will appear for each order. In the Order Items file, one record will appear for each different item ordered. The order number will be placed in the Order Items file, and all item records with the same order number will be the corresponding order on the Order file.

The Order file itself will be a bridge between the Customer file and the Order

```
        FRED'S FRIENDLY FISH MARKET
              CUSTOMER CHANGES


    CUSTOMER NUMBER: CUSTN

    LAST NAME:    LNAME--------------X
    FIRST NAME:   FNAME--------------X

    ADDRESS: ADDRESS-----------------X
    CITY:      CITY----------X

    STATE: ST     ZIP: ZIP-----X

    PHONE NUMBER: PHONE-------X
```

Fig. 10-5. A revised Customer Changes screen.

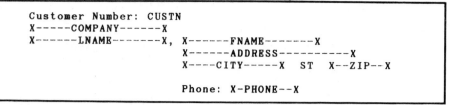

```
    Customer Number: CUSTN
    X-----COMPANY------X
    X------LNAME-------X,  X------FNAME-------X
                          X------ADDRESS----------X
                          X----CITY-----X  ST  X--ZIP--X

                          Phone: X-PHONE--X
```

Fig. 10-6. A revised directory format.

Items file because of the inclusion of the customer number. The definitions that Fred has arrived at are given in Table 10-5.

By using the two-file approach, Fred has made his system easier to use. Also, he can have any number of items on a single order, which makes the system more flexible.

THE FUNCTION HIERARCHY

Fred's major function is called the *order system*. What would an order system consist of? Well, Fred has a good example of an order system right now—the one he uses currently. So, he examines what exactly it is that he does now with orders. Figure 10-7 presents a comparison between a manual order system and an automated order system.

One thing he does now is write new orders as they come in. Therefore, the system will need a function for Enter Orders.

Table 10-4. Input Definition for the Order Form.

Field	Type	Length
ORDER NUMBER	Numeric	5
CUST NUMBER	Numeric	5
DATE ORDERED	Character	8
QUANTITY	Numeric	3
ITEM	Character	25
PRICE	Numeric	5.2

Table 10-5. Two-File System Definitions.

ORDER FILE		
Field	Type	Length
ORDER NUMBER	Numeric	5
CUST NUMBER	Numeric	5
DATE ORDERED	Character	8
ORDERITM FILE		
Field	Type	Length
ORDER NUMBER	Numeric	5
QUANTITY	Numeric	3
ITEM	Character	25
PRICE	Numeric	5.2

Fig. 10-7. A comparison between a manual order system and an automated order system.

Now when a customer calls to change an order, Fred makes the correction using a pencil, crossing off and adding items in the list. Also, if a customer calls and says "Forget it," he just throws that order form away (after a few choice words). So, his system will need to perform the functions Change Orders and Delete Orders.

Another thing that Fred does is look up an order in that old four-drawer file cabinet when there is a question about it. A Display Order function is also necessary. Fred also needs to have standing orders on the system. These are orders that are basically the same each week. Fred decides to input those once and use the order number over and over, changing the date.

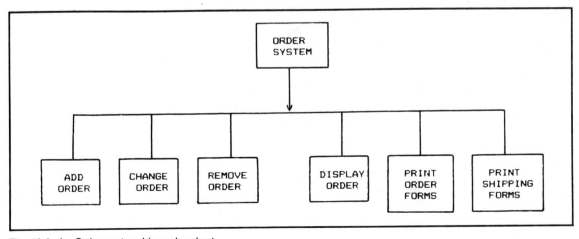

Fig. 10-8. An Order system hierarchy chart.

Finally, the system will need a function to print the order forms that are to be sent to the shipping department and the shipping forms with the prices that Fred has already defined in his output definition. The shipping department will enter the prices and make any changes for any out-of-stock items after the order has been packed. Remember, there are no backorders in the fresh fish business—only lost sales—and Fred doesn't want to see any get away! The function hierarchy chart, showing the main functions, is presented in Fig. 10-8. Now, Fred can design his main menu for the order system, as shown in Fig. 10-9.

All system functions are available from this menu—or will be when Fred gets the system coded and tested! Fred's pseudocode for the menu program looks like this:

```
SET EXIT TO "N"
DISPLAY MENU SCREEN
DOWHILE EXIT = "N"
  READ OPTION
  CASE
    WHEN OPTION = 1 PERFORM "ADD ORDERS"
    WHEN OPTION = 2 PERFORM "CHANGE ORDER"
    WHEN OPTION = 3 PERFORM "REMOVE ORDER"
    WHEN OPTION = 4 PERFORM "DISPLAY ORDER"
    WHEN OPTION = 5 PERFORM "PRINT ORDER FORMS"
    WHEN OPTION = 6 PERFORM "PRINT SHIPPING FORMS"
    WHEN OPTION = X SET EXIT TO "Y"
    OTHERWISE WRITE "INVALID OPTION"
  ENDCASE
ENDDO
```

With the menu out of the way, Fred moves to the next level of his hierarchy chart. The establishment of an Add Order function is the first and most important step in creating an order system, so Fred tackles this function first.

THE ADD ORDER FUNCTION

Something about this system has been bothering Fred. Each time an order is entered, one or more items are going to be entered. How can the items be entered at the same time as the order is created?

```
------------------------------------------
:   FRED'S FRIENDLY FISH MARKET          :
:        ORDER SYSTEM MENU               :
:                                        :
:                                        :
:   ENTER SELECTION ===>  __             :
:                                        :
:     1 - ADD ORDERS                     :
:     2 - CHANGE ORDERS                  :
:     3 - REMOVE ORDER                   :
:     4 - DISPLAY ORDER                  :
:                                        :
:     5 - PRINT ORDER FORMS              :
:     6 - PRINT SHIPPING FORMS           :
:                                        :
:     X - EXIT SYSTEM                    :
:                                        :
------------------------------------------
```

Fig. 10-9. The Order system main menu.

```
    ---------------------------------------------------
    :              FRED'S FRIENDLY FISH MARKET           :
    :                   ORDER ADDITIONS                  :
    :                                                    :
    :         ORDER NUMBER:        ORDRN                 :
    :                                                    :
    :         CUSTOMER NUMBER:  CUSTN                     :
    :                                                    :
    ---------------------------------------------------
```

Fig. 10-10. The Order Additions preliminary screen.

Fred can land this fish by accessing both files in his program. The first screen will ask for information that is specific to that order; in other words, the customer number and order date. When this information is entered, the program will display a second screen for adding items.

The second screen will have room for the operator to enter ten items. If there are more than ten items, the screen will be redisplayed with enough space for the next ten items. Each screen will allow ten items to be entered under that order number; by redisplaying the screens, the operator can add any number of items.

What if the order number that is entered already exists on the order file? This would be an invalid condition, since according to Fred's design, the order number is supposed to be unique. It would be irritating to enter the customer number and date, just to find out that the order number already exists and the information must be reentered.

One way of eliminating this problem is to use an entry screen. An *entry screen* is a preliminary screen that would ask for the order number and customer number. Then, if an order with that number already exists, an error could be displayed. Otherwise, the order would be new (and valid), and the customer number could be used to pull the necessary customer fields from the customer file. The customer number would be checked to make sure that it did exist on the customer file, since the system can't retrieve information that is not there. By adding this entry screen, Fred makes his system more reliable because duplicate orders would not be possible. Fred's first input screen, the Entry screen, is shown in Fig. 10-10.

He can then create the next screen in the sequence, the Order Additions screen shown in Fig. 10-11. In this figure, you can see the customer information that was

```
----------------------------------------------
:      FRED'S FRIENDLY FISH MARKET            :
:            ORDER ADDITIONS                  :
:                                             :
:                                             :
:   ORDER NUMBER:        ORDRN                :
:                                             :
:   CUSTOMER NUMBER:  CUSTN                   :
:                                             :
:   COMPANY:       COMPANY------------X       :
:   LAST  NAME:  LNAME---------------X        :
:   FIRST NAME:  FNAME--------------X         :
:                                             :
:                                             :
:   DATE ORDERED:  MM/DD/YY                   :
----------------------------------------------
```

Fig. 10-11. The Order Additions screen.

drawn from the customer file. This information is displayed on the Add Order screen so that the operator can judge whether or not the correct customer number was chosen. If the customer did not exist on the customer file, an error message would be displayed, but there is no way that Fred can guard against an incorrect customer number entry. The computer can't read minds! Therefore Fred displays the customer information immediately so the operator will be able to double-check that the customer's name matches what he believes is the customer number.

Finally, Fred creates the Add Items screen, as shown in Fig. 10-12. Notice that the company and name information is displayed on this screen, also. This is another double-check; if the operator gets confused about which order is being entered, the name information will help figure it out.

The quantity and item number for 10 items can be entered on this screen. If there are less than 10 items, the operator enters the orders and enters blanks on the next line (actually just presses the enter key again), and the order is filed. If there are more than 10 items, the operator fills up the 10 items on the first screen, presses enter, and receives a fresh screen, presses enter, and receives a fresh screen with room to add ten more items. The # field changes to show records 11 to 20. When a blank line is entered on the screen, the programs will know that the operator is finished adding items.

Fred is almost ready to begin pseudocoding the Add Order function, but first, he notices that he needs to make a small change to the hierarchy chart. The Add Items function would go under the Add Order function in the hierarchy chart.

Fred has broken this function into its smallest parts. He can now design the process of adding items. The pseudocode Fred created for add order is shown in Fig. 10-13.

In this program, Fred decides that the entering of a blank order number will signal the end of the process. As long as the operator continues to enter order numbers and customer numbers on the screen, the program will continue to add orders to the file. This is done with the DOWHILE loop in conjunction with the IF statement; each time the screen is displayed, the IF statement checks for an order number. If it is blank, control shuttles around the processing to the end of the loop. The

```
------------------------------------------------
:        FRED'S  FRIENDLY  FISH  MARKET          :
:              ORDER  ITEM  ADDITIONS            :
:                                                :
:                                                :
:    ORDER  NUMBER:       ORDRN                  :
:                                                :
:    COMPANY:         COMPANY------------X       :
:    LAST   NAME:     LNAME--------------X       :
:    FIRST  NAME:     FNAME--------------X       :
:                                                :
:       #   QUANTITY   ITEM  NUMBER              :
:                                                :
:       1      QTY        ITEMN                  :
:       2      QTY        ITEMN                  :
:       3      QTY        ITEMN                  :
:      ...     QTY        ITEMN                  :
:      10      QTY        ITEMN                  :
:                                                :
------------------------------------------------
```

Fig. 10-12. The Order Item Additions screen.

```
ADD AN ORDER

      ACCESS ORDER FILE
      SET ORDER NUMBER TO NOT BLANK
      DO WHILE ORDER NUMBER NOT BLANK
         DISPLAY SCREEN
         ENTER ORDER NUMBER AND CUSTOMER NUMBER
         IF ORDER NUMBER NOT BLANK
            VERIFY ORDER NUMBER
            IF NEW NUMBER
               THEN
                  ACCESS CUSTOMER FILE
                  VERIFY CUSTOMER NUMBER
                  IF FOUND
                     THEN
                        DISPLAY CUSTOMER DATA
                        ENTER DATE FIELD
                        ADD TO ORDER FILE
                        PERFORM "ADD ITEMS"
                     ELSE
                        WRITE "CUSTOMER NUMBER NOT FOUND"
                  ENDIF
               ELSE
                  WRITE "ORDER NUMBER ALREADY ON FILE"
            ENDIF
         ENDIF
      ENDDO
```

Fig. 10-13. The Add Order pseudocode.

DOWHILE condition then becomes false, and control passes out of the loop to the end of the program.

Within the first IF statement, Verify Order Number means to check the order file for an identical order number.

The IF New Number statement following the Verify Order Number statement sees if a duplicate order number is found. If a duplicate is found, control passes to the ELSE unit, which causes an error message to be displayed. Within the THEN unit of the IF New Number statement, the customer number is treated in much the same way.

Once the order number and the customer number are verified, the display screen for Add Order is presented. The operator can see the customer information that was retrieved from the customer file and can enter the order date. When this screen is entered correctly, control passes to the Add Items function for the addition of items to the order.

Satisfied with this pseudocode, Fred moves on to define the Add Items process, as shown in Fig. 10-14. In this program, the Add Items screen has ten lines for item numbers and quantities. Each time a line is entered, the program verifies that the item number exists on the item file, and if it does, it retrieves the price. It then places the newly ordered item into the Order Items file. If the item number is not on the file, an appropriate error message is displayed.

As long as the item number entered is not blank, the system will continue to add records to the file. Each time the operator has entered ten records, an IF statement will clear the display and update the item number counter.

```
ADD ITEMS

    ACCESS ORDER FILE
    ACCESS ORDER ITEM FILE
    SET ITEMCOUNT TO 1
    SET QUANTITY TO NOT BLANK
    DO WHILE QUANTITY NOT BLANK
       DISPLAY SCREEN AND EXISTING ITEM NUMBERS
       ENTER QUANTITY AND ITEM NUMBER
       IF QUANTITY NOT BLANK
         VERIFY ITEM NUMBER
         IF FOUND
           THEN
               RETRIEVE PRICE
               WRITE RECORD TO ORDER ITEM FILE
               INCREMENT ITEMCOUNT BY 1
           ELSE
               WRITE "ITEM NUMBER NOT ON FILE"
         ENDIF
       ENDIF
       IF ITEMCOUNT IS A MULTIPLE OF 10
         THEN REDISPLAY ITEM SCREEN
       ENDIF
    ENDDO
```

Fig. 10-14. The Add Items pseudocode.

THE CHANGE ORDER FUNCTION

Fred is now ready for the next leg on the hierarchy—the Change Order function. In this function, Fred envisions that the only changes that should be necessary will be changes to the items. The customer number should never be incorrect because it is double-checked at entry time. Fred has learned that some controls are necessary, but too many controls or redundant controls only slow down processing and make the system overly complicated.

Other functions that come under the Change Order heading are: add items, change the quantity of an item, change an item number, and remove an item. On the advice of a friend, Fred has decided to combine them into one function. Fred's new hierarchy chart for the Change Order items function is shown in Fig. 10-15.

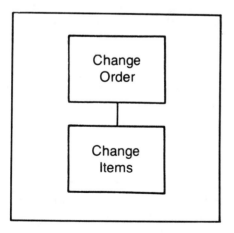

Fig. 10-15. The updated Order Changes hierarchy.

```
 ------------------------------------------------
|                                                |
|            FRED'S FRIENDLY FISH MARKET          |
|                 ORDER CHANGES                   |
|                                                |
|        ORDER NUMBER:        ORDRN               |
|                                                |
|                                                |
 ------------------------------------------------
```

Fig. 10-16. The Order Changes preliminary screen.

Now Fred can create the screens that the program will use. He again uses the Entry screen method, but with a minor difference, as shown in Fig. 10-16.

On this entry screen, Fred does not ask for the customer number. Why not? Because it already exists on the order file, there is no need to enter it again! The customer number had to be entered on the Add Order Entry screen because the order did not exist yet and the customer number was needed to retrieve the customer information. Now the the order record already exists on the file and can provide the customer number.

The next screen to develop is the Order Changes screen. This screen is merely a *pass-through* to the Change Order Items function. A *pass-through* screen is one that is displayed but allows no input to the system. The screen in Fig. 10-17 allows Fred to make sure that he has the right order before moving on to the Change Items function.

When this screen is displayed, the program asks the operator if there are changes to be made to the items in the order. If there are and the operator answers affirmatively, Fred will have the program display the Change Items screen.

Because the Change Items function seems a little tricky to Fred, he decides to first pseudocode the Change Order pass-through screen. The pseudocode is shown in Fig. 10-18.

Fred first verifies that the order exists, and if it does, he has the program display the Order Changes screen. The customer's number, company name, and contact's name are displayed to make sure that the right order has been retrieved. Then the operator can enter a carriage return to continue (<cr>), or an X to abort the change operation for that particular order number. When the operator enters a blank

```
 ----------------------------------------------------
|                                                    |
|       FRED'S FRIENDLY FISH MARKET                  |
|            ORDER CHANGES                           |
|                                                    |
|       CHANGE ITEMS? ===>  __                       |
|     ENTER <cr> TO CONTINUE, X TO ABORT             |
|                                                    |
|     ORDER NUMBER:        ORDRN                      |
|                                                    |
|     CUSTOMER NUMBER:   CUSTN                        |
|                                                    |
|     COMPANY:      COMPANY------------X              |
|     LAST   NAME: LNAME--------------X              |
|     FIRST  NAME: FNAME--------------X              |
|                                                    |
|     DATE ORDERED: MM/DD/YY                          |
|                                                    |
 ----------------------------------------------------
```

Fig. 10-17. The Order Changes screen.

```
CHANGE AN ORDER

    ACCESS ORDER FILE
    SET ORDER NUMBER TO NOT BLANK
    DO WHILE ORDER NUMBER NOT BLANK
      DISPLAY SCREEN
      ENTER ORDER NUMBER
      IF ORDER NUMBER NOT BLANK
        VERIFY ORDER NUMBER
        IF FOUND
          THEN
            ACCESS CUSTOMER FILE
            RETRIEVE CUSTOMER INFORMATION
            DISPLAY "CHANGE ITEMS" MESSAGE
            READ CHOICE
            IF CHOICE NOT X
              THEN PERFORM "CHANGE ITEMS MENU"
            ENDIF
          ELSE WRITE "ORDER NUMBER NOT FOUND"
        ENDIF
      ENDIF
    ENDDO
```

Fig. 10-18. The pseudocode for the Order Changes screen.

order number, the system will return to the main Order menu. After a carriage return is entered, the Order Items Change screen is displayed.

Originally, Fred was going to have functions that would add, change, and remove items. After thinking about it for several days, in between his arguments with Frank, the only design he could envision was a simple design that would show one item at a time and allow it to be changed. Fred knows he can improve on this design. He doesn't want to watch each and every item appear before him just to change the 22nd item. He wants a system that allows him to enter the quantity and item number he wants to change or delete. He will worry about adding items later.

Fred finished his design just as a friend of his named Myron strolled into the retail area of Fred's Friendly Fish. He showed his design to Myron who promptly talked him into trading three lobsters and a pound of scallops for a more difficult-to-implement but easier-to-use design. (Myron already computerized his business, a local personnel agency that does some computer work, too.)

Fred had explained to Myron that it was important that the operator be able to see all the items at once and be able to add, change, or remove items from the same screen. Myron told Fred that because of the screen size limitations the addition of only ten items could be displayed at a time. Through a *scroll* function more items could be displayed after the first ten. The resulting screen is shown in Fig. 10-19.

Myron also explained that there is a difference between adding items to a new order and adding items to an existing order. The Change Items menu displays ten items at a time, like the Add Items menu. However, only the items that already exist for that order will be placed on the Change Items menu for review and selection. Fred wondered how an item could be added. The answer struck him like a ton of mackerel. "If there are less than ten items on the screen, there will be some blank lines on the menu." If the operator (probably Fred or Elsa) asks to change

```
------------------------------------------------------
:            FRED'S FRIENDLY FISH MARKET              :
:                ORDER ITEM CHANGES                   :
:                                                     :
:            ENTER SELECTION ===>  __                 :
:            C/CHANGE,S/SCROLL,X/EXIT                 :
:                                                     :
:          ORDER NUMBER:        ORDRN                 :
:                                                     :
:          COMPANY:       COMPANY-------------X       :
:          LAST   NAME:   LNAME---------------X       :
:          FIRST  NAME:   FNAME---------------X       :
:                                                     :
:            #   QUANTITY   ITEM NUMBER               :
:                                                     :
:            1     QTY         ITEMN                  :
:            2     QTY         ITEMN                  :
:            3     QTY         ITEMN                  :
:          ...     QTY         ITEMN                  :
:           10     QTY         ITEMN                  :
:                                                     :
------------------------------------------------------
```

Fig. 10-19. The Order Item Changes screen.

a blank line, the item number and quantity that are typed for that line will be added to the file.

The best way to handle the change or removal of items was to think of each function as a variety of the change function. The easiest way to do that was to make changes or deletions one part of an IF statement and the additions another part. Myron impatiently explained to Fred: "If you retrieve an item that exists on the file, you can do two things to it: change the quantity, item number, or both; or remove the item by changing the quantity to zero."

Fred understands; Myron leaves. He can use the record numbers shown on the screen to retrieve the data. If there is no data for that record number, the record will be added. If there is data, the item is changed if the quantity is set to anything other than zero. The item is deleted if the quantity is set to zero. The first option

```
-----------------------------------------------
:        FRED'S FRIENDLY FISH MARKET          :
:            ORDER ITEM CHANGES               :
:                                             :
:        RECORD NUMBER ==>  __                :
:      ENTER RECORD NUMBER TO BE CHANGED      :
:                                             :
:      ORDER NUMBER:        ORDRN             :
:                                             :
:      COMPANY:       COMPANY-------------X   :
:      LAST   NAME:   LNAME---------------X   :
:      FIRST  NAME:   FNAME---------------X   :
:                                             :
:        #   QUANTITY   ITEM NUMBER           :
:                                             :
:        1     QTY         ITEMN              :
:        2     QTY         ITEMN              :
:        3     QTY         ITEMN              :
:      ...     QTY         ITEMN              :
:       10     QTY         ITEMN              :
:                                             :
-----------------------------------------------
```

Fig. 10-20. The Order Item Changes screen.

```
-------------------------------------------------
:                                               :
:        FRED'S FRIENDLY FISH MARKET            :
:             ORDER ITEM CHANGES                :
:                                               :
:   QUANTITY: QTY   ITEM NUMBER: ITEMN          :
:             ENTER CHANGES                     :
:                                               :
:    ORDER NUMBER:       ORDRN                  :
:                                               :
:    COMPANY:       COMPANY------------X        :
:    LAST   NAME: LNAME--------------X          :
:    FIRST NAME: FNAME--------------X           :
:                                               :
:      #    QUANTITY    ITEM NUMBER             :
:                                               :
:      1     QTY        ITEMN                    :
:      2     QTY        ITEMN                    :
:      3     QTY        ITEMN                    :
:     ...    QTY        ITEMN                    :
:     10     QTY        ITEMN                    :
:                                               :
-------------------------------------------------
```

Fig. 10-21. The Order Item Changes screen.

listed on the menu is C for change, which means Add, Change, or Delete items. The S will allow Fred to page forward through the displayed items ten at a time. The X function will allow Fred to exit this function and return to the main Order Change screen to change other orders.

The next logical step is to design the screen to be displayed when the C option, Change An Item, is requested. (This screen is shown in Fig. 10-20.) This screen allows the operator to specify the record number of the items he wishes to change. The record number is the first field on the item list. The user must choose one of the record numbers displayed, or an error message will be displayed. Once the record number is entered and the record found, the next screen, shown in Fig. 10-21, will display the item to be changed.

Fred can now enter any changes he wishes. He can also not enter changes, which

```
-------------------------------------------------
:                                               :
:        FRED'S FRIENDLY FISH MARKET            :
:             ORDER ITEM CHANGES                :
:                                               :
:      RECORD NUMBER ==>  _ _                   :
:   ENTER RECORD NUMBER TO BE CHANGED           :
:                                               :
:    ORDER NUMBER:       ORDRN                  :
:                                               :
:    COMPANY:       COMPANY------------X        :
:    LAST   NAME: LNAME--------------X          :
:    FIRST NAME: FNAME--------------X           :
:                                               :
:      #    QUANTITY    ITEM NUMBER             :
:                                               :
:     11     QTY        ITEMN                    :
:     12     QTY        ITEMN                    :
:     13     QTY        ITEMN                    :
:                                               :
:                                               :
:                                               :
:                                               :
-------------------------------------------------
```

Fig. 10-22. The Order Items scroll screen.

will leave the item as is. Fred decides that there is no need for a delete confirmation. If the operator changes the quantity to 0, that is a very conscious decision. Fred is beginning to understand the use of controls.

These are all the screens needed for the Change Items function. Figure 10-22 shows a sample of the screen that would be displayed if the S command were entered. It shows a screen with items 11, 12, and 13. The operator would have to enter a number greater than 13 to add an item to the file.

Prior to pseudocoding the Change Items subfunction, Fred comes up with the final hierarchy chart for the order system, as shown in Fig. 10-23.

Fred starts the pseudocoding with the main part of the menu for changing items. He builds the menu just like other menus he has built before, using the CASE statement:

```
CHANGE ITEMS

    SET EXIT TO 'N'
    DISPLAY MENU SCREEN
    DOWHILE EXIT = 'N'
      DISPLAY ITEMS
      DISPLAY SELECTION
      READ SELECTION
      CASE
        WHEN SELECTION = 'X'
          SET EXIT TO 'Y'
        WHEN SELECTION = 'C'
          CHANGE RECORDS
        WHEN SELECTION = 'S'
          ADD 10 TO SCROLL COUNTER
      ENDCASE
    ENDDO
```

Here Fred has the program look for C, S, or X. Option C causes the section used to change the items to be accessed. Option S will add ten to the counter that keeps

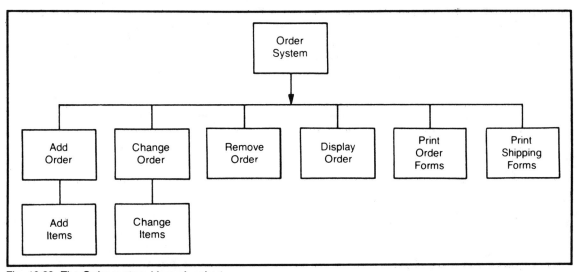

Fig. 10-23. The Order system hierarchy chart.

track of the record numbers displayed and cause the next ten to be displayed the next time the screen is shown. The X option is chosen when the operator wants to leave the menu and return to the Change Order function.

Now that Fred is finished with screen design for the Change Order Items function, he feels he understands the process better. With a little help from his friend, he will turn his hand to pseudocoding; Myron gets more lobsters. The resulting code is shown in Fig. 10-24.

Fred performs all three functions (Add, Change, and Delete) in this one piece of pseudocode. This may or may not be a good idea from the standpoint of modularity because the fewer functions a module is to perform, the easier it is to code later. However, Fred does (wisely) separate the functions within the pseudocode with some extra comments.

The first step in the pseudocode is to display the screen that requests the record number. All functions require the record number, and it is immediately checked to determine if that record number is currently displayed on the screen. If that record is not displayed, an error message is sent to the operator and another record number can be entered.

If the record is currently displayed on the screen, the Change Item panel is displayed, allowing the operator to change the quantity and item number shown on the screen. The program determines whether or not the line for that record number was blank by checking to see if the old fields were blank. If they are, this item is to be added, and after verifying the item number, the record is added to the item file.

If the quantity of the chosen item is changed to zero, Fred has the program recognize this as a Delete function, and the record is removed from the Order Items file.

If the item number is changed, Fred's program decides that this is a change to the item, checks to make sure that the new item number is on the item file, and retrieves the price. Finally the changed record is updated in the Order Items file.

Now, Fred adds pseudocode for the scroll function to the bottom of the pseudocode, and he is done. In this small program, Fred creates a *scroll counter* to keep track of the top item on the menu screen. The scroll counter is set to one in the Change Order program. The first item and the following 9 items are then displayed on the menu. When the S option is chosen, this program adds ten to the scroll counter, and the eleventh through twentieth items are displayed. No matter how many items are in the file for this order, the scroll program will display ten at a time, scrolling forward only.

```
CHANGE ITEMS

   SET EXIT TO 'N'
   DISPLAY MENU SCREEN
   DOWHILE EXIT = 'N'
     DISPLAY ITEMS
     DISPLAY SELECTION
     READ SELECTION
     CASE
       WHEN SELECTION = 'X'
         SET EXIT TO 'Y'
       WHEN SELECTION = 'C'
```

Fig. 10-24. The Order Item Changes pseudocode.

```
                ACCESS ORDER ITEM FILE
                SET RECORD NUMBER TO NOT BLANK
                SET SCROLL COUNTER TO 10
                DO WHILE RECORD NUMBER NOT BLANK
                   DISPLAY SCREEN
                   ENTER RECORD NUMBER
                   IF RECORD NUMBER NOT BLANK
                      THEN
                         VERIFY RECORD NUMBER IN THE 10 DISPLAYED
                         IF IN THE 10
                            THEN
                               RETRIEVE RECORD
                               DISPLAY QTY AND ITEMN
                               IF BLANK
                                  THEN
                                     DISPLAY ADD MESSAGE
                               ENDIF
                               ENTER CHANGES
                               IF QTY AND ITEMN NOT BLANK
                                  THEN                      /* ADD RECORD */
                                     IF OLD QUANTITY BLANK
                                        THEN
                                           VERIFY ITEM NUMBER
                                           IF FOUND
                                              THEN
                                                 RETRIEVE PRICE
                                                 WRITE RECORD TO ORDER ITEM FILE
                                              ELSE
                                                 WRITE "ITEM NUMBER NOT ON FILE"
                                           ENDIF
                                     ENDIF
                                        IF QTY OR ITEM NUMBER DIFFERENT THEN ORIGINAL
                                           THEN                      /* DELETE RECORD */
                                              IF QTY = 0
                                                 THEN
                                                    REMOVE RECORD FROM ORDER ITEM FILE
                                                 ELSE                 /* CHANGE RECORD */
                                                    VERIFY ITEM NUMBER
                                                    IF FOUND
                                                       THEN
                                                          RETRIEVE PRICE
                                                          WRITE RECORD TO ORDER ITEM FILE
                                                       ELSE
                                                          WRITE "ITEM NUMBER NOT ON FILE"
                                                    ENDIF
                                              ENDIF
                                        ENDIF
                                     ENDIF
                            ELSE
                               WRITE "RECORD NUMBER NOT ON DISPLAY"
                         ENDIF
                   ENDIF
                ENDDO
             WHEN SELECTION = 'S'
                ADD 10 TO SCROLL COUNTER
          ENDCASE
       ENDDO
```

Fig. 10-24. The Order Item Changes pseudocode. (Continued from page 88.)

```
FRED'S FRIENDLY FISH MARKET
      ORDER REMOVAL


ORDER NUMBER:       ORDRN
```

Fig. 10-25. The preliminary
Order Removal screen.

Fred has completed the toughest design he has had to tackle so far in his short data processing career, and he is now free to move on to the next function in the system.

THE REMOVE ORDER FUNCTION

For the Remove Order function, Fred again decided to use an entry screen to confirm that the order exists before any processing is performed. In the case of a Delete operation, this step is particularly important. It is easier to go through an extra confirmation step than it is to reenter an entire order that was deleted by mistake. The entry screen looks like the Change Order entry screen and is shown in Fig. 10-25.

Figure 10-26 shows the next screen that Fred designs—the confirmation screen for the delete. This screen looks like the other item screens; however, only the first ten items are displayed. Fred has decided not to give the Delete function a scrolling capability. "Anyone can tell if the order is the correct one from the first ten items," said Fred. "Why bother with unnecessary processing?" So Fred pseudocodes the Delete Order function as shown in Fig. 10-27.

After the order number is entered from the entry screen, the order is looked up in the order file. If it does not exist, an error message is displayed. If it does

Fig. 10-26. The Order Removal screen.

```
FRED'S FRIENDLY FISH MARKET
          ORDER REMOVAL

ENTER D TO CONFIRM DELETE ==>  __


ORDER NUMBER:       ORDRN

COMPANY:       COMPANY------------X
LAST   NAME:  LNAME--------------X
FIRST NAME:   FNAME--------------X

DATE ORDERED:  MM/DD/YY

  #   QUANTITY   ITEM NUMBER

   1     QTY        ITEMN
   2     QTY        ITEMN
   3     QTY        ITEMN
 ...     QTY        ITEMN
  10     QTY        ITEMN
```

```
REMOVE ORDERS

        ACCESS ORDER FILE
        SET ORDER NUMBER TO NOT BLANK
        DO WHILE ORDER NUMBER NOT BLANK
          DISPLAY SCREEN
          ENTER ORDER NUMBER
          IF ORDER NUMBER NOT BLANK
            VERIFY ORDER NUMBER
            IF FOUND
              THEN
                RETRIEVE ORDER
                ACCESS CUSTOMER FILE
                RETRIEVE CUSTOMER INFORMATION
                DISPLAY ORDER
                ACCESS ORDER ITEMS FILE
                DISPLAY 1ST 10 ITEMS
                ENTER DELETE CONFITMATION
                IF CONFIRM = D
                  THEN
                      DELETE MAIN ORDER RECORD
                      DELETE ALL ITEM RECORDS
                ENDIF
              ELSE
                WRITE "ORDER NOT ON FILE"
            ENDIF
          ENDIF
        ENDDO
```

Fig. 10-27. The Order Delete pseudocode.

exist, the order, customer, and ordered items information is retrieved from their respective files, and the Delete Order confirmation screen is displayed. If a D is entered from this screen, the order will be removed from the order file, and all items with that order number will be removed from the ordered items file.

Fred is satisfied with the documentation of his system so far. He is ready to dive into the next function.

THE DISPLAY ORDER FUNCTION

Fred can now design the Display Order function, and he designs it almost like the Remove Order function. If you look closely at the screens and pseudocode, you can see many similarities. Instead of deleting orders, Fred just has the program display the information on the screen. He also allows scrolling forward through the items by pressing the enter key. The screens are shown in Figs. 10-28 and 10-29. The pseudocode is shown in Fig. 10-30.

Fig. 10-28. The preliminary Order Display screen.

```
        FRED'S FRIENDLY FISH MARKET
              ORDER DISPLAY


        ORDER NUMBER:      ORDRN
```

```
----------------------------------------
:                                        :
:      FRED'S FRIENDLY FISH MARKET        :
:            ORDER DISPLAY                :
:                                        :
:      ENTER <cr> TO CONTINUE             :
:                                        :
:                                        :
:  ORDER NUMBER:       ORDRN              :
:                                        :
:  CUSTOMER NUMBER:  CUSTN                :
:                                        :
:  COMPANY:      COMPANY------------X     :
:  LAST   NAME: LNAME--------------X      :
:  FIRST  NAME: FNAME-------------X       :
:                                        :
:  DATE ORDERED: MM/DD/YY                 :
:                                        :
:                                        :
:     #  QUANTITY   ITEM NUMBER           :
:                                        :
:     1    QTY        ITEMN               :
:     2    QTY        ITEMN               :
:     3    QTY        ITEMN               :
:    ...   QTY        ITEMN               :
:    10    QTY        ITEMN               :
:                                        :
----------------------------------------
```

Fig. 10-29. The Order Display screen.

First, the order number is entered and checked against the Order file. If the order exists, the order and customer information are displayed, along with the first ten item records for that order. By placing the item displays within a DOWHILE loop, Fred has taken care of the scrolling facility. When the enter key is pressed,

```
DISPLAY ORDERS

      ACCESS ORDER FILE
      SET ORDER NUMBER TO NOT BLANK
      DO WHILE ORDER NUMBER NOT BLANK
        DISPLAY SCREEN
        ENTER ORDER NUMBER
        IF ORDER NUMBER NOT BLANK
          VERIFY ORDER NUMBER
          IF FOUND
            THEN
              RETRIEVE ORDER
              ACCESS CUSTOMER FILE
              RETRIEVE CUSTOMER INFORMATION
              DISPLAY ORDER
              ACCESS ITEM FILE
              DO WHILE MORE RECORDS
                DISPLAY 10 ITEMS
                ENTER CONTINUE CONFIRMATION
              ENDIF
            ELSE
              WRITE "ORDER NOT ON FILE"
          ENDIF
        ENDIF
      ENDDO
```

Fig. 10-30. The pseudocode for the Order Display function.

```
      Fig. 10-31. The Print Order
      Forms screen.
```

```
      FRED'S FRIENDLY FISH MARKET
            ORDER FORMS PRINT


      ORDER NUMBER:        ORDRN
```

more items are looked for in the Order Items file, and if found, they are displayed. When there are no more item records for that order, the process is complete and the entry screen is displayed again.

Now Fred has all the administrative functions out of the way. The Add, Change, Delete, and Display functions all exist for only one purpose: to add and manipulate the information necessary to produce the output—the order form and the shipping form.

THE PRINT ORDER FORM FUNCTION

To print the order form, Fred uses the entry screen concept to find the order in the file. If the order is not present, an error message is displayed. The entry screen, shown in Fig. 10-31, looks almost like the other order number entry screens.

Another design consideration is the way the printed order form will appear on paper. Fred will use the form he uses now; so he defines his output to ensure that he remembers all the fields and can easily code the line and column numbers in his final program. The layout of the form is shown in Fig. 10-32.

Because this function does not require a "confirm" screen, like Remove Order, Fred can jump right into his process definition, as shown in Fig. 10-33. In this program, the entry screen is displayed and the order number is entered by the operator. The program searches the Order file for that order number and when it is found,

```
          Order Number: ORDRN

          X-----COMPANY------X
          X------FNAME-------X  X------LNAME-------X

          Order Date: MM/DD/YY

  ITEM #      QUANTITY       ITEM NUMBER          DESCRIPTION
     1          QTN            ITEMN        X----------DESC---------X
     2          QTN            ITEMN        X----------DESC---------X
     3          QTN            ITEMN        X----------DESC---------X
     4          QTN            ITEMN        X----------DESC---------X
     5          QTN            ITEMN        X----------DESC---------X
     6          QTN            ITEMN        X----------DESC---------X
     7          QTN            ITEMN        X----------DESC---------X
     8          QTN            ITEMN        X----------DESC---------X
```

Fig. 10-32. The Print Order Form layout.

```
PRINT ORDER FORM

    STORE BLANK TO ORDER NUMBER
    DO WHILE ORDER NUMBER NOT BLANK
       DISPLAY SCREEN
       ENTER ORDER NUMBER
       IF ORDER NUMBER NOT BLANK
          ACCESS ORDER FILE
          VERIFY ORDER NUMBER
          IF FOUND
             THEN
                PRINT HEADER OF ORDER
                ACCESS CUSTOMER FILE
                RETRIEVE CUSTOMER INFORMATION
                DISPLAY ORDER INFORMATION
                ACCESS ORDER ITEM FILE
                DO WHILE MORE RECORDS
                   RETRIEVE QUANTITY AND ITEM NUMBER
                   ACCESS ITEM FILE
                   RETRIEVE DESCRIPTION
                   PRINT RECORD
                ENDDO
             ELSE
                WRITE "ORDER NUMBER NOT ON FILE"
          ENDIF
       ENDIF
    ENDDO
```

Fig. 10-33. The pseudocode for the Print Order Form.

the program retrieves the customer information. The order and customer information are printed, and then the Order Item file is searched for all items belonging to that order. As each item record is retrieved, the Item file is searched for that item number so that the item description can be printed on the order form. The program then loops back, using the inner DOWHILE loop, to search for more items.

THE PRINT SHIPPING LABEL FUNCTION

The last function of Fred's order system is to print the shipping label for an order from the stored order information. Again, the entry screen concept is used, as it was in the Print Order Form function. The screen is shown in Fig. 10-34.

The final design consideration is the way the printed shipping form will appear on paper. Fred will use the form he uses now so he defines his output to ensure that he remembers all the fields and can easily code the line and column numbers

```
----------------------------------------
:                                        :
:     FRED'S FRIENDLY FISH MARKET        :
:        SHIPPING FORMS PRINT            :
:                                        :
:                                        :
:                                        :
:   ORDER NUMBER:      ORDRN             :
:                                        :
:                                        :
----------------------------------------
```

Fig. 10-34. The Print Shipping Forms screen.

in his final program, as he did for the order form. The format of the output is shown in Fig. 10-35. The pseudocode is shown in Fig. 10-36.

In this process, the order number is searched for on the Order file, and if it is not present, an error message is displayed. If an order is on file, however, the order and customer fields are retrieved and printed on the shipping form. Then, Fred has the program search for the items that belong to the order. As each item is found, the item description and its price are retrieved from the Item file. The program calculates the price to the customer for each item by multiplying quantity times the item price. The total is accumulated so that the bottom line, the total cost, can be printed on the form. The program then loops to get any further items for the order.

If Fred has decided that a particular customer gets a discount, the discount percentage is retrieved from the customer file; the amount of the discount is then calculated and subtracted from the total price of all items on the order. Finally, the total cost is printed at the bottom of the form.

THE INVENTORY SYSTEM

Fred's friend Myron made some other suggestions for Fred to try. One of these is to incorporate an inventory system. This is a logical extension of the Item file that Fred would like to build. Fred hasn't realized yet, but he has to find a way to add,

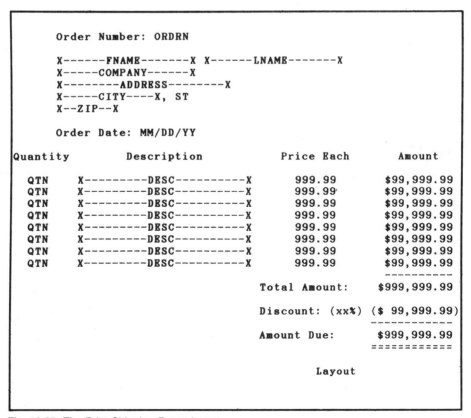

Fig. 10-35. The Print Shipping Forms layout.

```
PRINT SHIPPING FORM

    STORE BLANK TO ORDER NUMBER
    DO WHILE ORDER NUMBER NOT BLANK
      DISPLAY SCREEN
      ENTER ORDER NUMBER
      IF ORDER NUMBER NOT BLANK
        ACCESS ORDER FILE
        VERIFY ORDER NUMBER
        IF FOUND
          THEN
            PRINT HEADER OF ORDER
            ACCESS CUSTOMER FILE
            RETRIEVE CUSTOMER INFORMATION
            PRINT ORDER INFORMATION
            ACCESS ORDER ITEM FILE
            SET TOTAL TO 0
            DO WHILE MORE RECORDS
              RETRIEVE QUANTITY AND ITEM NUMBER
              ACCESS ITEM FILE
              RETRIEVE DESCRIPTION AND PRICE
              AMOUNT = QUANTITY X PRICE
              ADD AMOUNT TO TOTAL
              PRINT RECORD
            ENDDO
            WRITE TOTAL
            DISCOUNT AMOUNT = DISCOUNT/100 X TOTAL
            WRITE DISCOUNT
            SUBTRACT DISCOUNT FROM TOTAL
            WRITE AMOUNT DUE
          ELSE
            WRITE "ORDER NUMBER NOT ON FILE"
        ENDIF
      ENDIF
    ENDDO
```

Fig. 10-36. The Print Shipping Forms pseudocode.

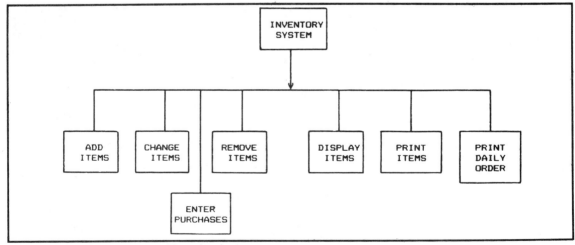

Fig. 10-37. The Inventory system hierarchy chart.

change, or delete items in the Item file. Fred has produced the design shown in Fig. 10-37 and will tackle it in the future. For now, Fred will simply establish the Item file using the R:base 5000 user functions.

SUMMARY

In the last two chapters, you have followed Fred as he designed systems for his business. You saw the logical constructs at work in his pseudocode; you saw him develop his systems from scratch; and you saw his documentation package slowly grow as he aimed to automate his entire business.

Fred had to change his original design for the customer system as other systems started to need access to that data. His design was growing and evolving, bending to his needs as he defined his business problems.

You will be seeing more of Fred in the next two sections of this book, as he learns R:base 5000 and sees how to turn his designs into working reality.

Section II

DATABASE FUNDAMENTALS

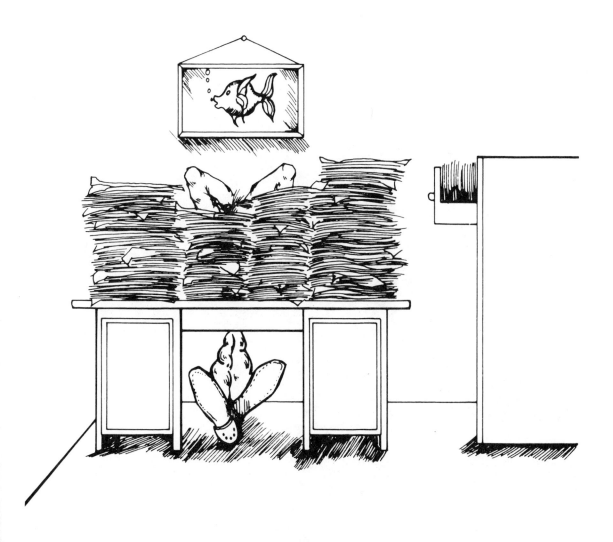

Chapter 11

What is a Database?

Database is a term given to the physical area and logical means of storing your data in a computer system. A database is simply data that has been transformed into meaningful information by logically grouping and storing it.

There are endless numbers of databases in the world. One of the more common databases in any business is the file of customers. This file in the simplest form would contain the customer's name, address, and telephone number. The database might contain many other files, such as customer accounts, lists of items the customers have purchased, etc. In a retail business there would be other files, such as inventory files, price files, stock number, and description files. Together, all these files make up the database for the business. The terms *database, tables,* and *files* are used interchangeably in this book. In R:base 5000 you could think of all related files, which R:base 5000 calls tables, as comprising a database.

Another example of a database is a dictionary system. The files, or tables, that make up the database would include the dictionary file and the thesaurus file. For each word, the dictionary file would include a single entry that contains three fields: the word, the type (noun, verb, etc.) and the definition. The thesaurus file contains many entries for each word. Each entry has the word from the dictionary file, along with other words that mean the same thing.

A database is an organized collection of records. Such things as newspapers and magazines are not a database. An index of magazine articles that tells the subject, magazine name, and date is a database. Information must be in some order and must be retrievable by some means in order. That is the difference between information and chaos.

USES FOR A DATABASE

Why would you need a database? This is a commonly asked question. A database will enable you to ask questions and quickly receive answers about your data. "How many customers bought $200 worth of product this month? Which of my customers live in Connecticut? How many customers in New England pay their bills on time?" These are all typical questions that you might ask if you had a database.

What can a database management system like R:base 5000 do for you? Besides enabling you to easily enter, change, and delete data, it enables you to change the description of your records at any time. For example: For ten years you have had two stores in Connecticut. Now you are adding stores in Massachusetts, Rhode Island, and New York. Your database has a place for store name and city, but not state. If you have many records already on a computer, would you have to change them all? The answer is yes. With most languages this would be a difficult process. With a database manager like R:base 5000, it is simple and easy.

A database manager can also let you ask questions in many forms. "How many fish did we sell this month? The last 3 months? How about all year? How many customers live out of CT?" Questions such as these are simple to ask. It's almost as simple as English! R:base 5000 also lets you produce reports with just one command. The true beauty of R:base 5000, however, is that apart from being a database manager, it is also a programming language.

In the first section of this book, you learned how to program. That section discussed proper design of a program and all the logical constructs. In this chapter you will learn more about how to plan your database and use R:base 5000 programming commands to manipulate the database. First, let's learn a little bit more about databases.

RELATIONAL DATABASES

R:base 5000 is a *relational* database management system. This means that each record is stored just as you might have entered it. Each record is the same size and has the same fields, each the same size. The records are collections of fields. Each file, or table, is a collection of records; one or several tables can constitute a database.

Keys

Usually, when you are using several files in a database system, you need to have some way to use them together. This is where the concept of a common key comes in. In the customer example, a key might be the customer name. If you had one file with the customer names, addresses, and telephone numbers, while another file had the customer names and account balances, you could use the name as a key to retrieve information from both files.

These keys allow you to tie many files together. For example, a parts file from a typical business might look like the one shown in Table 11-1. This file can be accessed and information retrieved about the part number and its corresponding description, but in this example there are two other pieces of information needed: the price of a part and how many are in stock. This company has several tables in their database; the other files are shown in Fig. 11-1.

Table 11-1. Parts File for a Typical Business.

Description File		
Part__No	**Weight**	**Description**
6HD	6 oz.	Heavy Duty Nails
8LT	8 oz.	Light Weight Nails
8LTS	8 oz.	Light Weight Screws
6BT	6 oz.	Light Weight Bolts
10WA	10 oz.	Heavy Duty Washers
6RN	6 oz.	Roofing Nails
ES-28	28 in.	Electric Saw

To produce a report that will include the part number, description, price per item, and quantity in stock, you would have to check three different tables. In Fig. 11-1, you see that both tables contain the same part numbers, but have no other common information. This is one way to organize your information. The part number is called the key; all other information is related to it.

The part number need not be the only key in the database. For example, in the inventory file, location may be another key to a file called Hours. This file might have the building location, the hours the building is open, and what state it is in. So, the concept of keys is an important one to use in organizing your data and retrieving it again later.

Files

In R:base 5000, a table is synonymous with a file. An R:base 5000 database can be made up of many tables. Figure 11-2 is an example of a table. This one is aptly

```
                            PRICE  TABLE

        PART  NO      UNIT        PRICE  EA   PRICE  10   PRICE  100
          6HD         1000           22.34      182.30     1595.00
          8LT         1000           22.34      162.70     1256.00
          8LTS         100            3.56       33.50      295.00
          6BT          100            4.35       41.30      386.00
          10WA        1000           18.45      174.50     1663.00
          6RN         1000           22.34      162.70     1200.00
          ES-28          1           89.50      695.00     5950.00

                        INVENTORY  TABLE

        PART  NO    QTY  INSTK   ORDER  QTY   ORDER  LVL   LOCATION
          6HD         63000        50000       10000      WHSE1
          8LT         56000        50000       15000      WHSE2
          8LTS         3000         5000        4000      BIN37
          6BT          5000         5000        4000      WHSE4
          10WA         6000        20000       10000      WHSE2
          6RN         12000        10000        5000      WHSE3
          ES-28          78           50          25      STORE
```

Fig. 11-1. Sample Price and Inventory tables.

```
                    CUSTOMER TABLE

   NAME          STREET        CITY    ST   ZIP      PHONE
Joe Smith   23 Daring Lane   Enfield   CT   06268   5552345
Bill  Jones  156 East St     Windsor   CT   06234   5551645
Mark Ames   10 South Rd      Branford  CT   05455   5553774
```

Fig. 11-2. An example of a table.

named Customer File. All the information in the table makes up the file or, as some people refer to it, the database. As just described, there really is no key associated with this file. A likely key would be Name; however, if you are interested in Location, State, or Zip Codes, any of these might be keys instead.

Records

A database file (table) is made up of records. Each *record* would be a line in the table. In the customer record example, each record consists of a name, several address fields, and a telephone number. There are three records in the file: one each for Joe Smith, Bill Jones, and Mark Ames.

Fields

Each *field* is a column in the table and has its own title. The customer file has the following fields:

Name, Street, City, ST, Zip, and Phone.

These fields are defined when the database is created. Whenever you wish to use this data you must call each field by its name. Later, if you want to print the information, you could change the name of the column header from Name to Person's Name or anything else you want. The field names exist only to help you use the data in the program.

R:base 5000 refers to fields as columns. You can have many columns in a database. When you have more than one table in a database, you might want to use some of the same columns in different tables. This is a totally acceptable procedure as long as you keep the column definition the same between tables. In fact, R:base 5000 will force you to keep the column definition the same if it is used in more than one table.

If you have more than one database, they will be totally unrelated except for the fact that they might occupy space on the same diskette. R:base can only deal with one database at a time, but it understands everything about a single database and all of its tables.

DATABASE STRUCTURES

Your database structure is the dictionary to your data. You will sometimes hear the database structure referred to as the *data dictionary*. The database structure is made up of several elements, including the database name, the name of each table in the database, the name of each field in each table, the maximum size of each field, and the field type.

Database Names

The database name should be something meaningful. Actually all names you use in a computer system should be meaningful. Remember, some day someone else might have to use this program. Even though you have two lovely children named Sue and Bobby, these names are inappropriate in your computer system. Choose names that will indicate what the database contains. In R:base 5000 there are several rules for creating the database name:

☐ A maximum of seven characters.
☐ The first character must be a letter.
☐ The other six characters may be letters, numbers, or most special characters except the colon.
☐ No "blanks" are allowed in the name.

Good database names include Sales for a sales file, Invntry for an inventory file, and Sale__10 for an October sales file. Examples of illegal names are 1957Dat (it must start with a letter), Customer (name is too long), and Car Jan (no blanks are allowed).

By properly naming your files, you will be able to easily recognize and use your databases—and so will everybody else!

Table Names

Table names are very similar to database names, except they have a slightly different set of rules.

☐ A maximum of eight characters.
☐ The first character must be a letter.
☐ The other seven characters may be letters, numbers, or special characters.
☐ No "blanks" are allowed in the name.

Good database names include Customer for a customer file, Invntory for an inventory file, and Sale__Oct for an October sales file. Examples of illegal names are 1957Sale (it must start with a letter), Customers (name is too long), and Car Part (no blanks are allowed).

Table names do not appear on your diskette when you do a directory. They are stored as part of your database name in the database files on your disk and can only be read by R:base 5000.

Column Names

Records do not have names. They can be identified by their record number; each record is assigned a number by R:base 5000. Usually this number is the sequence number of creation. The first record entered is record 1; the next is record 2, etc. When the records are sorted, they will have different numbers, but more about that later.

Each column has a column name. It is this name that you use to search, sort, report, change, or do anything to the database. Each column name in a file must be unique; that is, no two may be the same. You may use the same name in different files; when two files share a common key, the same column name should be used.

As with database names, each column name should be meaningful. Use Name to represent a person's name, and Zip_Code for the zip code. Remember, these names will be used extensively in your program; so they should be easily recognizable, and if possible, short. This way when the column name is used in calculations or expressions, they won't go on forever. Column names have rules just like table names:

☐ A maximum of eight characters.
☐ The first character must be a letter.
☐ The other seven characters may be letters, numbers, or underscores.
☐ No "blanks" are allowed in the name.

COLUMNS

Column names allow us to identify a column of data such as Name, or Zip_Code, but what is actually in those columns? Why the data, of course. Each data item is called a column, or *variable*, because the Name in record 3 may be changed at any time. Its value can vary. However, the program will never change the value unless you tell it to do so.

You will find that there are many ways to change a column. You can directly input data into the column; you can edit a value already there; you can use an assignment statement that changes it. No matter what, you always have control over the contents of a column.

Column Types

There are six types of columns:

☐ Text.
☐ Date.
☐ Time.
☐ Dollar.
☐ Integer.
☐ Real Number.

Text columns are columns that will not be used in mathematical expressions. Text columns may contain any value; letters, numbers, special characters, anything! Don't forget that values of all numbers, such as zip codes and social security numbers, should also be character columns because they will never be used in calculations.

Date columns are special columns used for date calculations. They are in the form of *mm/dd/yy* (month,day,year). Date columns are always eight characters long, including the separating slashes.

Time columns are special columns used for time calculations. They are in the form of *hh:mm:ss* (hours, minutes, seconds). Time columns are always eight characters long, which includes the separating colons.

Dollar columns are those numbers with two decimal places that contain dollar amounts such as sales figures or prices.

Integer columns are whole numbers with no decimal places. They are used to represent quantities or whole number amounts.

Real-number columns also contain numbers. Like the dollar amounts, they may contain decimal points. All numeric columns may contain a negative sign on the left side. The real-number columns are used for precision, especially in calculations. They may have many decimals and are stored as binary numbers.

Column Rules

As with column names, the columns themselves have a few rules to follow:

- ☐ Text—maximum length 1500 characters.
- ☐ Date—always 8 characters in the form *mm/dd/yy*.
- ☐ Time—always 8 characters in the form *hh:mm:ss*.
- ☐ Dollar—range of +/– $99,999,999,999,999.99.
- ☐ Integer—range of +/– 999,999,999.
- ☐ Real Number—range of +/– 9 × 10 +/– 37 with six-digit accuracy in scientific or decimal notation.

SUMMARY

In the next chapter, you will learn how R:base 5000 allows you to create your data dictionary. However, there are a few things to remember first.

- ☐ Every database has a name of seven or less characters.
- ☐ Every table has a name of eight or less characters.
- ☐ There can be 40 tables per database.
- ☐ Columns are the columns of your database.
- ☐ Each column has a name of 8 characters or less.
- ☐ Each column has a type and a length.
- ☐ There can be a maximum of 400 columns in a database.
- ☐ Together, the columns make up the rows, which are the records.
- ☐ In one table, the length of all columns together cannot exceed 1530 characters.
- ☐ Make your names mean something!

Chapter 12

Creating and Using the Database Structure

The first thing you will do after your program design is completed is to begin the database design. Your database should have all the columns needed for your program. Output columns are of no concern at this point; you already have used the output columns to determine the input columns. These input columns are the only columns that belong on your database. Any columns that can be calculated should not be on the database; they can be calculated at any time.

DESIGNING THE DATABASE

When you are creating a database, keep these limits in mind:

☐ Databases can have a maximum of 400 columns and 40 tables.
☐ Total length of a record cannot exceed 1530 characters.
☐ Databases can have an unlimited number of records up to the physical size of the floppy disk or hard disk.

Let's take our small businessman, Fred. The first task that Fred has decided to computerize is his customer file. So far you know that Fred has decided to include the customer's name, address, and telephone number. Should our database look like Table 12-1?

No, of course not! If you had defined your database this way, it would be very difficult to ask questions of it and group common types of customers. Rather, let's divide the database into a format that is easier to query; that is, to get answers from.

Table 12-1. Incorrect Database Format.

Columnname	Type	Length
NAME	CHAR	20
ADDRESS	CHAR	29
PHONE	CHAR	10
		- - - -
Total		59

The correct format is shown in Table 12-2.

You can see that the size of the total database has not changed, but it is now easier to use if you wish to see all customers in Connecticut or Massachusetts. This method of breaking each column into the smallest part is important in database design. Note that there is a column called Street. You could have divided it into Street#, Strtname, and Strttype, but this would not have made any sense. You would never care how many people lived on lanes as opposed to streets and roads. You would never ask to see customers who lived at addresses whose number was 32. However, you might ask to see all customers who live on Main Street. You can do so regardless of the street number, and you will see how later in this chapter.

RUNNING R:base 5000

There are several ways to run R:base 5000. If you have 320K or more you can use the R:base menu system. This system, shown in Fig. 12-1, lets you automatically choose from several different R:base programs, including:

☐ EXPRESS—Automatic application and database generator.
☐ GATEWAY—A file conversion program between R:base and other software.
☐ RBASE—R:base command mode.
☐ RBEDIT—The R:base editor.
☐ RCOMPILE—The R:base compiler.
☐ CLOUT2—Natural language query for R:base data files.

Table 12-2. Acceptable Database Format.

Columnname	Type	Length
LASTNAME	CHAR	10
FSTNAME	CHAR	10
STREET	CHAR	12
CITY	CHAR	10
STATE	CHAR	2
ZIPCODE	CHAR	5
PHONE	CHAR	10
		- - - -
Total		59

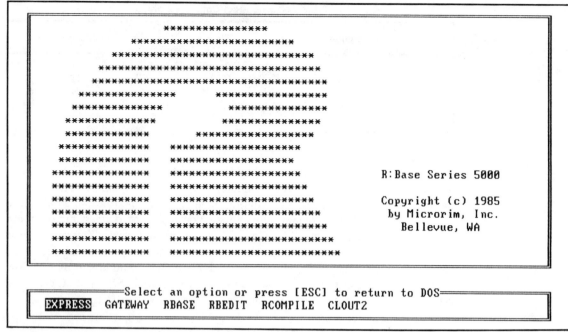

```
                    ****************
                 **************************
              *******************************
            ********************************
          *********************************
        ***************        ****************
       **************          ****************
      **************           ****************
     **************          ******************
    **************         ********************
   **************         ********************
  **************         *********************
 ***************        **********************           R:Base Series 5000
 **************         ********************
 **************         *********************            Copyright (c) 1985
 **************         **********************              by Microrim, Inc.
 **************         **********************              Bellevue, WA
 **************         ***********************
 **************         ***********************
```

```
═══════════Select an option or press [ESC] to return to DOS═══════════
 EXPRESS  GATEWAY  RBASE  RBEDIT  RCOMPILE  CLOUT2
```

Fig. 12-1. The R:base menu system.

You can customize this menu by using any editor or word processor, including the R:base editor, to edit the file RB5000.dat, which contains the menu items.

If you don't have 320K, you can access any of these programs individually by inserting the proper diskette and typing any of the command names just given.

The menu is simply a way to access all the various programs that make up R:base 5000 without having to remember the various commands. Whether you type a command or use the menu system to run a command, the results are the same.

When you use the R:base command mode, you will see the following symbol:

R>

This symbol means that R:base is waiting for you to enter an R:base command. In order to create a database definition, you can issue the proper string of commands or use the EXPRESS system to define the database.

It is easier to use EXPRESS to create the database. Later you will see the string of commands needed in R:base to create the database.

CREATING THE DATABASE STRUCTURE

Once you have entered the R:base 5000 Application EXPRESS from your operating system, you are given six choices, as shown in Fig. 12-2.

Application EXPRESS is used for several tasks:

☐ Defining or changing a database definition.

110

☐ Defining or changing an entire application.

☐ Displaying a file directory.

☐ Exiting back to the operating system or R:base menu.

You would choose the first option, *Define a new database*, to create your database structure. R:base 5000 will ask you for the database name. You must provide a name for R:base 5000 to use to store the database on your diskette. The R:base 5000 prompt looks like this:

```
Enter your database name (1-7 characters)
```

After you create an R:base 5000 database, you will see three files on your disk that begin with the characters that you used to name the database. The last character will be a one, two, and three, respectively, followed by the DOS file extension rbs. For example, if you create a database called Mydata, you would find on your disk:

```
MYDATA1.RBS
MYDATA2.RBS
MYDATA3.RBS
```

R:base has added the numbers and file extensions to the name that you gave the database. This is the reason that database names can only be seven characters long. With the addition of the extra character, you reach the DOS file name maximum of eight characters. The rbs extension identifies the file as an R:base database to R:base 5000.

R:base creates three different files on your disk in order to better manage your data. The file with the 1 in it contains the database structure definition (the data dictionary) and the location of the data. The file with the 2 in it contains the data itself, and the file with the 3 in it contains the "index" for the key columns. You will learn more about keys later.

After you name the database, you can begin to name your table and its columns. EXPRESS gives you a screen that lets you move around freely, entering your columns. First you must enter your table name. Figure 12-3 shows the table name

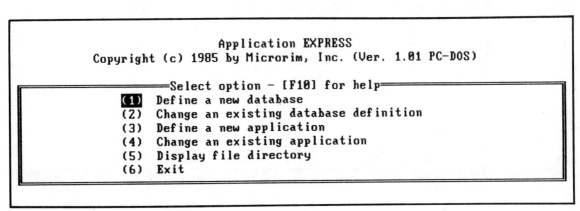

```
                     Application EXPRESS
         Copyright (c) 1985 by Microrim, Inc. (Ver. 1.01 PC-DOS)

                 ═Select option - [F10] for help═
            (1)  Define a new database
            (2)  Change an existing database definition
            (3)  Define a new application
            (4)  Change an existing application
            (5)  Display file directory
            (6)  Exit
```

Fig. 12-2. The Application EXPRESS menu.

```
     Enter your database name (1-7 characters) BOOK
```

Fig. 12-3. The EXPRESS Define Table screen.

already entered as Customer. When the screen first appeared it was blank. The message:

```
Enter the name for this table
```

was displayed at the top of the screen. The cursor highlight was in the table name area. After the table name is entered, the screen changes, as shown in Fig. 12-3. Once you begin entering the column definitions, you can always change the table name by pressing <PgUp>. This key will move the cursor to the Table Name block and let you change the name.

R:base 5000 is now ready for you to describe the table. You will be asked to enter three items for each column. Each column must have a Name, Type, and Width.

You are now ready to enter your columns. First you would enter a column name. Figure 12-4 shows the first column name entered. The first column has been named Lastname.

As soon as the column name is entered, the middle of the screen changes. A

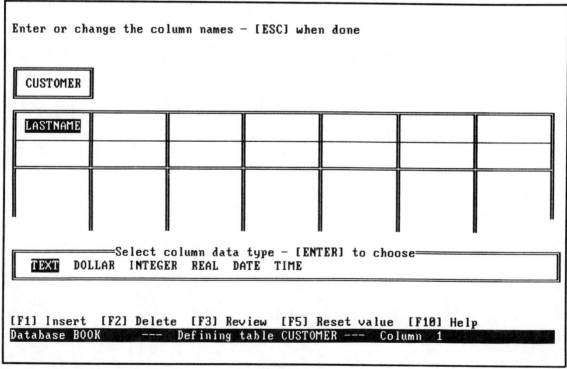

Fig. 12-4. The EXPRESS Define Table screen choosing data types.

112

menu is displayed to let you choose the proper data type for the column. One of the six choices must be chosen.

If you choose *TEXT* as your data type, you will also be asked to enter the length. You would type a number from 1 to 1500. This would be the maximum length of the text field. The other data types do not need to have their lengths specified.

Figure 12-5 shows the first field completely entered. The field's name is Last-name. It is a text field with a length of 10. The cursor automatically moves to the next column to let you begin entering its definition.

After you enter each column's name, type, and for text fields the width, you can change columns you have already defined by using the cursor keys to move between the field names. By pressing <Return> when you are on a column name, you can change the column type if you want.

Figure 12-6 shows the completed database. There are seven columns defined. As you can see, the total length is 59 characters.

If your database contains more than seven columns, you will have to use your cursor keys to see them all. You can only see seven columns at a time. Pressing the <Home> and <End> keys will take you between the first and last columns you have defined. This is a fast way to move between your fields.

You can also see the entire database in list form by pressing <F3>. Figure 12-7 shows this database in list form. <F3> is known as the Review key and can be used in many different functions of R:base 5000.

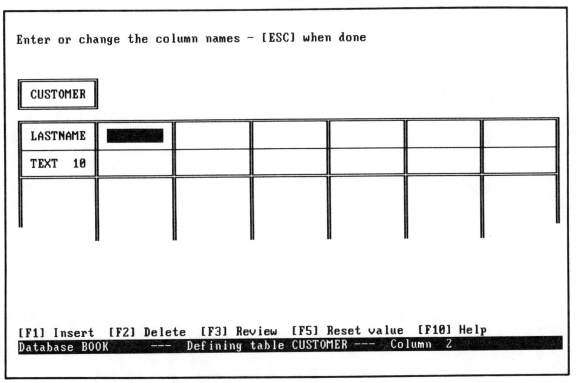

Fig. 12-5. One field defined with EXPRESS.

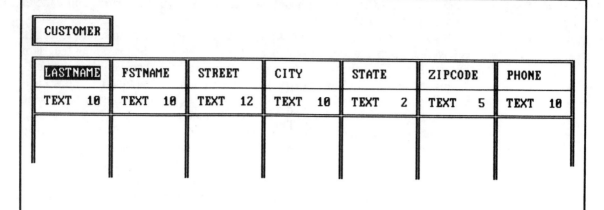

Fig. 12-6. The complete database.

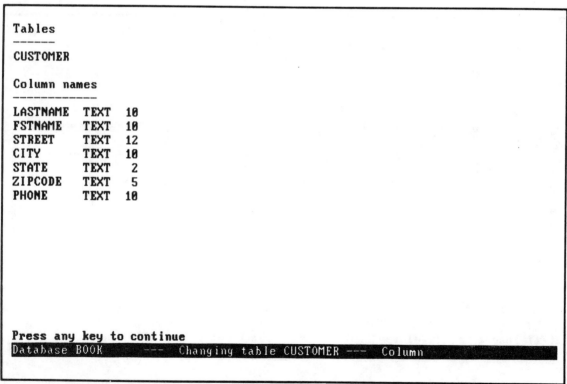

Fig. 12-7. Reviewing the database.

Once you are done creating the table, you would press the <ESC> key. Before doing so make sure you have created your table to fit your needs. Even if you need to make a change after you have saved the table definition, R:base 5000 lets you quickly and easily change the table definition.

CHANGING A TABLE DEFINITION

Once you have created and saved a table, the Application EXPRESS program can help you change the definition. The second option in the EXPRESS menu, shown in Fig. 12-2, lets you change an existing database definition. Choosing that option displays another menu that lets you add, change, or remove tables from a database.

This menu is shown in Fig. 12-8. As long as you have already created a database name, you can add new tables to the database, change existing table names and columns, and remove a table from the database.

Once you choose the appropriate action, R:base will list all the tables in your database and ask you to choose which one you want to change or remove. If you are adding a table, it will ask you for a new name.

Once you choose the table you want to work with, you can display the table in exactly the same form as when you saved it last by pressing <ESC>.

There is no difference between the way you move within a table or change a table once you get to it than when you first created it.

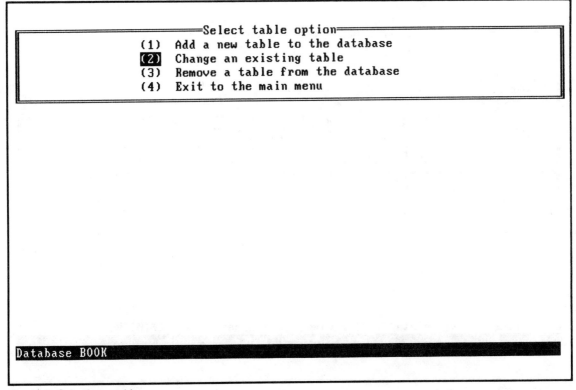

Fig. 12-8. Selecting a table.

There are several function keys that make it easy for you to change the table. You can use the cursor keys to move between the field names. Once you are on a column name you can rename it by simply typing in a new name. By pressing <Return> when you are on a column name, you can change the column type and length if you want.

The <F1> function key lets you insert a new field between two existing fields. When you move the cursor to an existing field and press <F1>, the columns to the right will all move over one column to the right, allowing a new column to be defined.

Figure 12-9 demonstrates the effect of pressing <F1> in the Customer database. Once the column is inserted, you can type a column name and then define the column type.

To delete a column, you must move the cursor to a column name and press <F2>. The column you are in disappears, and all remaining columns to the right move over to close up the space.

Once you are done changing your database, you must press <ESC> to save the table to disk.

Once you have placed data in a table, you cannot use the Application EXPRESS to change a column definition. Instead, you must use commands from the R:base command mode.

```
Enter or change the column names - [ESC] when done


  CUSTOMER


 LASTNAME   FSTNAME    STREET                  CITY       STATE      ZIPCODE

 TEXT  10   TEXT  10   TEXT  12                TEXT  10   TEXT   2   TEXT   5








 [F1] Insert  [F2] Delete  [F3] Review  [F5] Reset value  [F10] Help
 Database BOOK        --- Changing table CUSTOMER ---  Column  4
```

Fig. 12-9. Inserting a column.

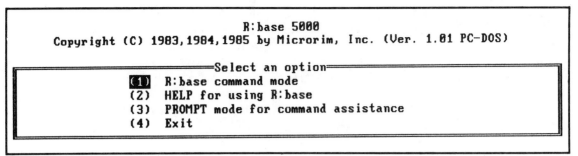

Fig. 12-10. R:base 5000 command mode menu

R:base 5000 COMMAND MODE

R:base command mode is the normal way to use most functions of R:base 5000. Although many commands use menus to let you choose the many options of R:base, there are many commands that can be run much more quickly through simple commands. R:base also features a Prompt mode to assist you in learning these commands.

You can enter R:base command mode by typing **RBASE** from the system disk or, as shown in Fig.12-1, choosing RBASE from the menu. After entering R:base command mode, you will see the menu shown in Fig. 12-10.

This menu has several choices. Choosing the first item will place you directly into the R:base command line. You will always see the R> prompt when you are in the R:base command mode.

When you see this prompt, you know that R:base is asking you to give it a command. You can enter any valid R:base command. Of course, you have to know what the valid R:base commands are and which one you need to use.

The other items in the menu allow you to get assistance on a particular R:base command and to use the R:base prompting mode.

When you enter an R:base command, there will be a short delay while R:base processes your command. Some commands will not display anything to let you know they were successfully completed. You will simply see a new line with the R> prompt.

Using the Database and Tables

Once you have created the database, you can begin to use it. The first command you need is the command to Open the database. *Opening the database* means choosing the database you wish to use. When you have many databases, this will become even more important than when you only have one. To use the database, you must enter the R:base 5000 command mode. Then choose the command **OPEN** to open the database. Following is an example of this command:

```
R> OPEN BOOK
```

R:base 5000 knows to go to the default disk drive and open the files called Book1.rbs, Book2.rbs, and Book3.rbs. In opening the database, R:base 5000 checks to make sure the database exists.

117

The extension of rbs is used only by DOS. R:base 5000 knows that to use a file it must be a database file. Later, you will learn of other file extensions that R:base 5000 uses. When you are done with the database you should close it so R:base will free memory and allow you to access other databases. In R:base 5000 you don't have to close your database, but it is a good idea. R:base 5000 performs some of its updating only at the time the file is closed. If an error occurs while a file is open there can be problems. To close a database, simply type **CLOSE** by itself. R:base 5000 remembers the database in the original CLOSE and closes it for you, for example:

```
R> CLOSE
```

Once you open a database, you can retrieve any information about the database you want. This includes displaying:

☐ The tables that make up the database.
☐ The columns in each table.
☐ The data in the tables.

Figure 12-11 shows the screen after the R:base command mode is selected and the Book database is opened. When you open a database, the message **Database exists** tells you that the database was opened.

Viewing the Table Structure

The LIST command is used to display different information about your database. Options for LIST can include databases, tables, and columns.

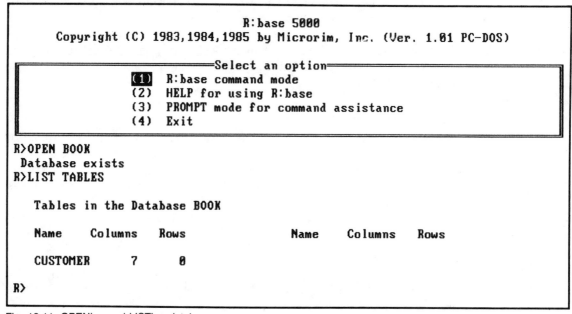

Fig. 12-11. OPENing and LISTing databases.

```
R>LIST CUSTOMER

    Table: CUSTOMER
    Read Password: NO
    Modify Password: NO

    Column definitions
    # Name       Type      Length        Key
    1 LASTNAME   TEXT      10 characters
    2 FSTNAME    TEXT      10 characters
    3 STREET     TEXT      12 characters
    4 CITY       TEXT      10 characters
    5 STATE      TEXT       2 characters
    6 ZIPCODE    TEXT       5 characters
    7 PHONE      TEXT      10 characters

    Current number of rows:        0

R>
```

Fig. 12-12. The LIST command.

LIST Databases will read your disk directory and display a list of all databases on your disk. **LIST Tables** can only be used after you have opened a database, as shown in Fig. 12-11. It will display all the tables in your database, the number of columns in each table, and the number of rows (records).

The **LIST Columns** command will list all the different columns, their type, and their width for all the tables in your database. It also tells you in what tables each column is used. Because you can use a column in more than one table, the LIST COLUMNS command is invaluable for keeping track of your columns.

So far, you have defined only one table. Figure 12-11 only shows the one table, Customer, defined in the database Book. The Customer table has seven columns. Because you have not added any data, there are no rows.

You can also list all the columns in a single table. Many times you will deal with one table at a time, or even a single table in a database. The LIST command can be coupled with a table name. Figure 12-12 shows the LIST Customer command. Its column names, type, and length are listed.

Creating a Database with R:base Commands

You can also create the database and table structures without using EXPRESS. There are times when you might find it easier to not use EXPRESS. In particular, when you are creating tables that use many of the same columns, you will define your tables in a different way than if you were defining separate tables with unique columns.

In R:base 5000 command mode, you would typically set up a database as follows:

☐ Define the name of the database.

- [ ] Define all the columns in all of the tables.
- [ ] Assign columns to each table.
- [ ] Repeat the third step for each table defined.

This procedure is a little different than when you are using EXPRESS. With EXPRESS you:

- [ ] Define the name of the database.
- [ ] Define the name of the table.
- [ ] Define each column in the table.
- [ ] Repeat the second and third steps until all tables are defined.

When you are using EXPRESS, once you define a table and its columns they are known to the database. When you define a column in one table and then use it in another table, R:base automatically knows its type and width. In order to set up each table, you must create a new table name and fill in the columns. If they are columns you haven't used before, you will also need to define the column type.

The commands to define the Book database and the Customer table are shown in Fig. 12-13. First the DEFINE command is used to define the name of the database and then to enter Define mode. If you are changing a database definition, you would still use the DEFINE command to enter DEFINE mode.

After you have created or specified the database and entered DEFINE mode, you are ready to define or change columns or tables.

```
R>DEFINE BOOK
 Begin R:base Database Definition
D>
D>COLUMNS
D>
D>LASTNAME TEXT 10
D>FSTNAME   TEXT 10
D>STREET    TEXT 12
D>CITY      TEXT 10
D>STATE     TEXT 2
D>ZIPCODE   TEXT 5
D>PHONE     TEXT 10
D>
D>TABLES
D>
D>CUSTOMER WITH LASTNAME FSTNAME STREET CITY STATE +
D>ZIPCODE PHONE
D>
D>END
 End R:base Database Definition
R>
```

Fig. 12-13. Defining a database in command mode.

Defining columns is accomplished through the COLUMNS command. Once you enter the keyword COLUMNS, you can define as many columns, column types, and widths as you want. You would define all your columns for all your tables. Figure 12-13 shows the definition of the same seven columns that were defined with EX-PRESS earlier in this chapter.

Once you have defined all of your columns, you would assign them to your tables. In the DEFINE mode, the TABLES keyword tells R:base that you will be defining your tables and assigning the columns to them.

One table is defined in this example. The Customer table is defined by using all of the seven columns. When you are through defining your database, the END command returns you to the R:base command mode.

PASSWORDS

R:base 5000 lets you set and use passwords at two different levels: the database level and the table level.

Database Passwords

Passwords at the database level prohibit anyone without the password from changing the database structure. The command to set a password for the database is the OWNER command.

```
D> OWNER mypswd
```

This command sets the database password to **mypswd**. Once you have set the password, you must enter it each time you restart R:base.

If you wanted to change the database structure, you would have to enter the password. There are two ways to enter the password. From the R:base command mode you can type:

```
R> USER mypswd
```

The other way to enter the password is the same way you created it:

```
D> OWNER mypswd
```

Once you have created the database password, you might want to change it. The password can be changed by typing:

```
R> RENAME OWNER mypswd to newpswd
```

This command changes the existing password **mypswd** to **newpswd**.

You can also remove the password entirely by typing:

```
R> RENAME OWNER mypswd to none
```

None is a keyword to tell R:base to remove the password.

Table Passwords

There are also passwords that can be set for each table. They safeguard the data in the table from being read, changed, or both.

When you prevent someone from changing the data, it is called *write protection*. Usually write protection does not stop someone from looking at the data. When you prevent someone from looking at the data, it is called *read protection*. Usually if there is read protection, there is automatically write protection. If you can't look at the data, you shouldn't be able to change it either.

R:base 5000 does not work this way. You set the different types of protection independently of each other. To get the most protection, you must set both.

To define table passwords, you must get into DEFINE mode and type:

```
D> PASSWORDS
```

You can then set the passwords. R:base refers to read passwords as RPW (read password) and write passwords as MPW (modify passwords). To set a read password to **pwl** and the write password to **nono**, you would enter:

```
D> RPW for CUSTOMER is pwl
D> MPW for CUSTOMER is nono
```

Remember that you must have entered PASSWORDS first in the Define mode before you entered the RPW and MPW commands.

If you have set an RPW, the user can only read the data after he enters the password. If you set an MPW, the user can read and modify the data after he enters the password.

If you have table passwords, you must also have a database password.

To change a password, you would just reenter the RPW and MPW commands with new passwords or use the RENAME command. Of course, you would first have to enter them as they presently exist. To remove table passwords, you would use **none** as the password.

SETTING RULES

In the next section you will see how to enter data into your database. When you enter data, you are performing one of the most critical phases of using a database. Your output can only be as good as your input. The old saying garbage in, garbage out is very applicable here.

R:base 5000 features a unique way of helping you enter your data correctly without any programming. You can specify a set of rules to check your data entry. There are several things you can check:

☐ Ranges—Is the data within a specified range?
☐ Lists—Does the entry exist in a predetermined list?
☐ Duplicates—Has the data already been entered?

When you enter a rule, you enter a message that will be displayed if the entry

```
D>RULES
D>
D>"Salary amount too large" SAL IN PAYROLL LT 1000
D>
D>"Illegal Quantity" AMOUNT IN INVNTRY GE 0 AND +
D>AMOUNT IN INVNTRY LT 1000
D>
D>"Duplicate customer number" CUSTNO IN CUSTOMER NEA +
D>CUSTNO IN CUSTOMER
D>
D>"Item not in inventory list" ITEMNO IN SALES EQA +
D>ITEMNO IN INVNTRY
D>
D>END
 End R:base Database Definition
R>
```

Fig. 12-14. Using RULES to enter verification rules.

fails the rule test. You can enter up to 20 rules for each table.

These rules are called *verification rules* because you are verifying the data for each entry. To enter rules you must be in the DEFINE mode of a database. The RULES keyword lets you start to enter rules. Some examples of these are found in Fig. 12-14.

The first DEFINE tells R:base that we are going to enter some rules. The first rule checks the column called Sal in the table called Payroll. The value of Sal must be less than 1000, or the message is displayed and the data for that column must be reentered.

The second rule checks for a range instead of a single amount. The data in the column called Amount in the Invntry table must be larger than 0 and less than 1000 or the message **Illegal Quantity** is displayed.

The third rule checks for duplicates in the Customer table by checking to see that the value entered into the CustNo column of the same table doesn't already exist.

```
R>LIST RULES
    RULE checking = ON
RULE   1    SAL IN PAYROLL LT 1000
    Message:Salary amount too large
RULE   2    AMOUNT IN INVNTRY GE 0
        AND AMOUNT IN INVNTRY LT 1000
    Message:Illegal Quantity
RULE   3    CUSTNO IN CUSTOMER NEA CUSTNO IN CUSTOMER
    Message:Duplicate customer number
RULE   4    ITEMNO IN SALES EQA ITEMNO IN INVNTRY
    Message:Item not in inventory list
R>
```

Fig. 12-15. LIST RULES.

The final rule checks for a list comparison. If you have a list of items in inventory, you can't sell an item that is not in the inventory. This rule checks the value of the ItemNo entered into the Sales table against all the other item numbers in the Invntry table. If it doesn't find a match, then the item is not in the inventory list and cannot be sold. You could also check to make sure that if the item is in the inventory list, its quantity is not 0.

If you want to see all the rules you have defined, use the LIST RULES command in R:base command mode. Figure 12-15 displays the "LIST RULES" command.

When you create rules for a database, R:base actually creates a table called Rules. Later if you want to delete rules you have created, you can use the DELETE ROWS command from the Rules table. For example, to delete the fourth rule, you would enter the command as follows:

```
R>DELETE ROWS FROM RULES WHERE NUMRULE EQ 4
```

Rows and Numrule are keywords in this expression.

CHANGING A TABLE STRUCTURE

Up to this point you have seen how to create a database and open it for use. You have not yet learned how to put data into it or how to use this data. First, a very important subject is how to change the database once it is defined.

You may always change a database using EXPRESS as long as it is empty. Once it contains data, however, you must use some special commands to change the database.

If you wanted to simply change an existing column, you would use the CHANGE COLUMN command. This command allows you to change an existing column definition and convert the data in it to the new definition. Obviously, changing a text column that contains letters would convert the values to zero.

As an example, using the Customer table, you could change the definition of Street to make it wider and change the name to StrtAddr by entering the command:

```
R>CHANGE COLUMN STREET IN CUSTOMER TO STRTADDR TEXT 20
```

You can change just the data type and length or just the name by only entering that much of the command. There are also other commands to let you add or delete columns.

First let's take the customer database. Assume you have already entered some data. Now, you want to keep several columns from the Customer database and create a new table with some new columns.

The PROJECT command lets you copy columns and their data to create a new table. Figure 12-16 shows the PROJECT command creating a new table from the Customer table. Remember that it is shown after some data has been entered.

Now that you have created a new table with several fields, you want to create some new fields. In this way, you can build a new table but retain the existing customer list.

```
R>OPEN BOOK
 Database exists
R>PROJECT CUSTCRDT FROM CUSTOMER USING LASTNAME FSTNAME STATE
 Successful project operation      14 rows generated
R>SELECT ALL FROM CUSTCRDT
 LASTNAME     FSTNAME      STATE
 ----------   ----------   --------

 SMITH        JOHN         MA
 JONES        BILL         CT
 SMITH        ROBERT       NJ
 ROBERTS      PHIL         CT
 CHARLES      LARRY        CT
 CLARK        SEYMOUR      CT
 SMITH        KIRK         MA
 YOUNG        SUE          MA
 JOHNSON      GEORGE       MI
 MITCHELL     HENRY        CT
 YORK         JOHN         CT
 BATES        MARK         MA
 JAMES        GEORGE       CT
 SHERRI       JOE          CT
 R>
```

Fig. 12-16. PROJECTing a new table.

The EXPAND command lets you enter new columns in a table with data. Figure 12-17 shows the EXPAND commands to add three new columns.

The new columns are Since, an integer field which contains the year that the customer first bought from Fred's Fish Market. Buy85 is a one-character text field that is Y if the customer has bought anything in 1985 and N if they haven't been seen. This field helps to purge the file of customers who are no longer customers or to help Fred send out mailings to his old customers reminding them to come back.

```
R>EXPAND CUSTCRDT WITH SINCE INTEGER

EXPAND    command complete
R>
R>EXPAND CUSTCRDT WITH BUY85 TEXT 1

EXPAND    command complete
R>
R>EXPAND CUSTCRDT WITH AMOUNT DOLLAR

EXPAND    command complete
R>
```

Fig. 12-17. EXPANDing the table.

```
R>SELECT ALL FROM CUSTCRDT
  LASTNAME    FSTNAME    STATE    SINCE      BUY85     AMOUNT
  ----------  ---------  -------  ---------  --------  --------
  SMITH       JOHN       MA       -0-        -0-       -0-
  JONES       BILL       CT       -0-        -0-       -0-
  SMITH       ROBERT     NJ       -0-        -0-       -0-
  ROBERTS     PHIL       CT       -0-        -0-       -0-
  CHARLES     LARRY      CT       -0-        -0-       -0-
  CLARK       SEYMOUR    CT       -0-        -0-       -0-
  SMITH       KIRK       MA       -0-        -0-       -0-
  YOUNG       SUE        MA       -0-        -0-       -0-
  JOHNSON     GEORGE     MI       -0-        -0-       -0-
  MITCHELL    HENRY      CT       -0-        -0-       -0-
  YORK        JOHN       CT       -0-        -0-       -0-
  BATES       MARK       MA       -0-        -0-       -0-
  JAMES       GEORGE     CT       -0-        -0-       -0-
  SHERRI      JOE        CT       -0-        -0-       -0-
R>
```

Fig. 12-18. The new table.

The last column is called Amount and is a dollar field that will contain the amount that is owed to Fred.

You can also remove unwanted columns with the REMOVE command. It is similar to the EXPAND command except that you only have to enter the column name.

Figure 12-18 shows the new table that was created with the EXPAND commands. The new column's values are all set to -0- until data is entered.

Chapter 13

Database Records

Once the database structure has been created, you can begin to input records. You can input records with the LOAD command.

ADDING RECORDS

R:base 5000 automatically generates a sort of entry form for you. The form appears one line at a time and displays each column in the table. You then can fill in each line in the form just like you would fill in any other form. Figure 13-1 shows the screen after opening the database and running the data entry command LOAD.

The WITH PROMPTS keyword tells R:base to tell the name and data type of each column as it asks for the data entry. Without this keyword, you would have to know exactly what the data looks like. R:base would let you know you are in that data entry mode by changing the prompt to a L> instead of the now familiar R>.

The first column in the customer database is displayed. The cursor appears after the colon (:). You can then enter the data for the first record. After you enter the Lastname and press <Enter>, the screen displays the next column, Fstname.

As you press the <Enter> key, the cursor will skip to the next column. After you enter the last field (Phone) and hit <Enter>, a message is displayed allowing you to end the data entry or to continue entering records. Figure 13-2 shows the screen after the first two records are entered.

To quit entering records, you would simply press the <ESC> key at any time. If you have not finished the record you are entering, it will not be saved. Only completed records are saved. After you press <ESC>, R:base 5000 will return you to

```
R>OPEN BOOK
 Database exists
R>LOAD CUSTOMER WITH PROMPTS
 Begin R:base Data Loading

 Press [ESC] to end, [ENTER] to continue
LASTNAME (TEXT   ):
```

Fig. 13-1. Using the LOAD command.

the R> prompt. You can enter as many records as you wish until you hit <ESC>.

Entering text data is the easiest. Whatever you place in a column will be its value. Numeric fields work a little differently. As you enter the value, the number is checked to make sure it is the correct type. If you have created a column, such as Dollar, Real, or Integer, you must enter a value in that form. For example, an integer cannot have any decimals.

If you make a mistake, like entering a letter in a Dollar field, R:base will beep and display a message telling you that the entry is not valid. You can then correct the entry.

```
R>OPEN BOOK
 Database exists
R>LOAD CUSTOMER WITH PROMPTS
 Begin R:base Data Loading

 Press [ESC] to end, [ENTER] to continue
LASTNAME (TEXT   ):SMITH
FSTNAME  (TEXT   ):JOHN
STREET   (TEXT   ):PILGRIM WAY
CITY     (TEXT   ):PLYMOUTH
STATE    (TEXT   ):MA
ZIPCODE  (TEXT   ):05634
PHONE    (TEXT   ):6173442654

 Press [ESC] to end, [ENTER] to continue
LASTNAME (TEXT   ):JONES
FSTNAME  (TEXT   ):BILL
STREET   (TEXT   ):15 SAMOAN DR
CITY     (TEXT   ):WESTVILLE
STATE    (TEXT   ):CT
ZIPCODE  (TEXT   ):04663
PHONE    (TEXT   ):2034662837

 Press [ESC] to end, [ENTER] to continue
```

Fig. 13-2. Entering several records.

If you have created a set of rules for your table and you violate one of the rules, you will also get a message and have to reenter the value.

Entering data is the same whether you enter it when there is no data in the table or when there is a lot of data in the table. If there are already records in the database, R:base 5000 will position the record pointer to the last record on the file, and the new records will be placed after the existing ones. R:base 5000 takes care of adding the records regardless of the number of records in the database.

CREATING DATA ENTRY FORMS

Using the LOAD command is easy, but it gives you little control over entering your data. You cannot enter the data in the order you want. You cannot change an entry once you move to another column without leaving the LOAD command. You cannot display messages on the screen or display a different prompt than the column name and data type.

The FORMS command allows you to do all of these things. It provides an easy way for you to create your own form and then to use it over and over. To start the forms definition, you would type the command FORMS along with a name to store it with. For example:

```
R> FORMS CUSTFORM

Begin R:base forms definition

Enter table name (for variables form press [ENTER]): CUSTOMER
```

After telling R:base to create or use a form called Custform, R:base asks the name of the table to use. This is necessary so R:base can access the table description when you place your columns in the form.

A *variables form* is a form that provides much more customizable control. It will be described in the Programming section as it is used when you are programming R:base 5000.

After you enter the form name and table name, the screen changes to a menu:

```
----Edit------Locate-----Quit--------------------
```

These three items let you create and edit the text that appears on the entry form and then locate where the data will be entered into the columns.

Once you choose *Edit*, you are placed in a blank screen except for the message at the top right side of the screen:

```
< 2, 1>  [F3] to list, [ESC] to exit
```

The <2, 1> tells you that the cursor is on location line 2, column 1 of the screen. As you move the cursor, the cursor locator will move to tell you its location. You may move the cursor anywhere on the screen. Because FORMS let you move about the screen, there are some keys you should understand. Table 13-1 shows the keys that let you move around the screen more quickly.

Creating an entry form is done in two parts. First, all the text you want on the screen must be entered. This text will be titles, instructions, column labels, or anything else you want.

Table 13-1. Keys Used to Create or Edit Forms.

KEY	EFFECT
↑	Moves the cursor up one line
↓	Moves the cursor down one line
→	Moves the cursor right one space
←	Moves the cursor left one space
Ctrl →	Moves the cursor to end of line
Ctrl ←	Moves the cursor to beginning of line
Tab	Moves the cursor ten spaces to the right
Shift-Tab	Moves the cursor ten spaces to the left
Del	Deletes the character over the cursor
Ins	Inserts a space at the cursor position
F1	Inserts a blank line at the cursor position
F2	Deletes the line at the cursor position
F3	Lists columns in the table
F4	Turns Repeat mode on and off

The second part is to locate each column's entry area on the entry form. The entry areas may be placed anywhere. Even if you label a line Name, you can place the entry area for City on that line. Hopefully you wouldn't want to, though.

Figure 13-3 shows the form after the text has been entered. The cursor locator is on < 15, 31> after the last text, Phone Number:, has been entered.

The next step is to press <ESC> and return to the menu:

```
----Edit------Locate-----Quit--------------------
```

This time the LOCATE command should be used to position the column entry areas on the form. The data entry form you have so far defined will remain on the screen when the menu is displayed and while you locate the entry positions.

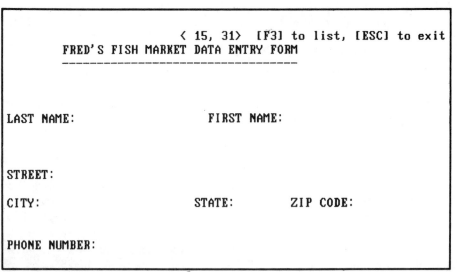

Fig. 13-3. Entering text on an entry form.

130

R:base 5000 will prompt you to move the cursor on the entry form to the area where you want to enter the data. You are asked to put an S for start at the beginning of the entry area and an E at the end of the area. You must mark the beginning and end of each column in your data entry screen.

When you first choose LOCATE, the following message appears at the top of the screen:

```
Enter column name:                    [F3] to list, [ESC] to exit
```

R:base wants to know what column you are going to define first. The <F3> function key will display a list of the columns in your table. Pressing <F3> will display Fig. 13-4. Once you have seen your columns, press <ESC> to return to the data entry form.

The first column to define is the Lastname column. The message would look like this after you enter **LASTNAME**:

```
Enter column name: LASTNAME
```

The message then changes to:

```
Move cursor to start location for LASTNAME and press [S]
```

You would move the cursor to the space to the right of Lastname: and enter an **S**. (See Fig. 13-5.)

Notice that the message has changed to:

```
Move cursor to end location for LASTNAME and press [E]
```

You can enter the **E** any number of positions to the right of the S as long as it is

```
[ESC] to return to Form Editing
Form: CUSTFORM    Table: CUSTOMER


Columns:

    # Name      Type     Length

    1 LASTNAME  TEXT     10 characters
    2 FSTNAME   TEXT     10 characters
    3 STREET    TEXT     12 characters
    4 CITY      TEXT     10 characters
    5 STATE     TEXT      2 characters
    6 ZIPCODE   TEXT      5 characters
    7 PHONE     TEXT     10 characters
```

Fig. 13-4. Columns list in a data entry form.

```
Move cursor to end location for  LASTNAME and press [E]              < 6, 37>
                         FRED'S FISH MARKET DATA ENTRY FORM
                        ------------------------------------


           LAST NAME: S                    FIRST NAME:



           STREET:

           CITY:                     STATE:          ZIP CODE:


           PHONE NUMBER:
```

Fig. 13-5. Positioning the first column.

not longer than the column length entered when you created the table. A text field
that has a length of 15 can have a distance between the S and the E of anywhere
from 1 to 15 characters.

You will repeat this procedure for all of the columns in the table you want on
the data entry form. Usually you want all of them on the form. When you are finished, press <ESC> to return the Edit/Locate menu.

Figure 13-6 shows the final data entry form created from the Customer table.
You can edit the text on the form or the locations simply by repeating the processes
used to create the form. You may add, change, or delete text, and you may change
the locations of the S and E areas of the screen.

```
——Edit—Locate—Quit——————————————————————————————————————
                         FRED'S FISH MARKET DATA ENTRY FORM
                        ------------------------------------


           LAST NAME: S          E      FIRST NAME: S         E



           STREET: S          E

           CITY: S         E          STATE: SE     ZIP CODE: S    E


           PHONE NUMBER: S        E
```

Fig. 13-6. The final data entry form.

```
Storing FORM
End R:base FORMS definition
R>LIST FORMS

   Form        Table
   _____    _____

   CUSTFORM    CUSTOMER

R>
```

Fig. 13-7. Storing and LISTing entry forms.

When you are through, choose *Quit* from the menu. Figure 13-7 shows the message as the form is stored. You can see all the forms you have defined at any time with the LIST FORMS command. Like RULES, FORMS becomes a table in your database.

ENTERING DATA WITH DATA ENTRY FORMS

Once you create the data entry form, you can begin to use it. The ENTER command enables you to use a data entry form to enter data. To use the data entry form you have just seen created, you would type:

```
R> ENTER CUSTFORM
```

The blank data entry form would be displayed as shown in Fig. 13-8 with the entry bar in the first area.

Once you are in the data entry area, you can move from area to area with the <Enter> or <Tab> keys. You can change data in areas you have already entered. Use the <Enter> or <Tab> key to move to the area you want to change and change it. When the screen looks as you want it to, press the <ESC> key. A menu will be displayed at the top of the screen, as shown in Fig. 13-9.

```
Press [ESC] when done with this data
              FRED'S FISH MARKET DATA ENTRY FORM
              ------------------------------------


       LAST NAME: ████████████      FIRST NAME:



       STREET:

       CITY:                    STATE:       ZIP CODE:


       PHONE NUMBER:
```

Fig. 13-8. The Data Entry screen.

```
┌─────────────────────────────────────────────────────────────────────┐
│ ─Add─Reuse─Edit─Quit──────────────────────────────────────────────── │
│                     FRED'S FISH MARKET DATA ENTRY FORM                │
│                     ------------------------------------              │
│                                                                       │
│                                                                       │
│          LAST NAME: DEBRIS              FIRST NAME: DAVEY             │
│                                                                       │
│                                                                       │
│          STREET: 212 LOVE RD                                          │
│                                                                       │
│          CITY: SMALLTOWN          STATE: OH     ZIP CODE: 56474      │
│                                                                       │
│                                                                       │
│          PHONE NUMBER: 5462334658                                     │
│                                                                       │
└─────────────────────────────────────────────────────────────────────┘
```

Fig. 13-9. The data entry menu.

R:base automatically creates a programmed routine to let you choose one of four options:

☐ Add—Add the record, clear the areas, and continue.
☐ Reuse—Add the record, keep the data, and continue.
☐ Edit—Don't add the record yet, reedit the areas.
☐ Quit—Don't add the record, leave the menu.

Both the *Add* and *Reuse* options will add the record to the database and then let you enter another record. The *Add* option clears out all the entry areas so you start with an empty screen, but the *Reuse* option keeps the existing data on the screen. If you are only changing one column, why reenter all the columns?

The *Edit* option simply puts you back into the screen area and lets you change the record on the screen. The Quit option returns you to the R:base command mode. Normally to quit you first Add the record then press <ESC> from the empty screen and choose *Quit*. If you choose *Quit* without adding the last record, it will be lost.

Entry screens can be used by many commands. Later in this chapter you will see other uses for the entry screen, including when you are displaying or changing existing records.

The routine that displays the *Add, Reuse, Edit,* and *Quit* options is part of the Forms Manager. When you program your own application and use an entry form, you will probably not want that routine. The variables form described in the Programming section of this book gives you more control over data entry.

If you had created rules for your table, you could not add the record until all the rules were satisfied.

Assume that 15 records are now in the database. These records will be used to demonstrate some of the capabilities of the R:base 5000 database manager.

DISPLAYING RECORDS

There are many ways to display records. The easiest is to ask R:base 5000 to list all records. The SELECT command tells R:base 5000 to list all the records in the database. If you have a lot of records, R:base will stop at the bottom of the screen and prompt you to see more records. R:base displays one screen full of data at a time. Between each screen, you have the option of stopping by pressing <ESC> or continuing by pressing any key.

Let's use the SELECT command to display all the records in the table. The correct syntax or computer grammar to see all the records in a table is **SELECT all from Customer**. Customer is the table name that contains the data you want to display. Figure 13-10 shows the result of using the SELECT command.

As you can see, all of the records have been displayed as they were entered, records 1 to 15. The SELECT command also puts the column names at the top of the screen. Later you will see how to resort these records by any of the fields. Now you will see some of the power of the SELECT command. You can use the SELECT command to selectively display certain records and, at the same time, only display certain columns.

Let's look at the table again. Using other options of the SELECT command, you can change the looks of the display.

First, let's only look for customers with addresses in the state of CT. Figure 13-11 shows these customers.

The WHERE clause is used to subset the table and only display rows that meet the condition in the WHERE phrase. The WHERE phrase has a number of different possible operators.

The phrase **WHERE State = CT** means to choose records that contain CT

```
R>SELECT ALL FROM CUSTOMER
 LASTNAME    FSTNAME    STREET        CITY        STATE   ZIPCODE   PHONE
 --------    -------    ------        ----        -----   -------   -----
 SMITH       JOHN       PILGRIM WAY   PLYMOUTH    MA      05634     6173442654
 JONES       BILL       15 SAMOAN DR  WESTVILLE   CT      04663     2034662837
 WILLIAMS    DANNY      17 ALOHA DR   HONOLULU    HA      67355     8081257688
 SMITH       ROBERT     15 APPIAN DR  TRENTON     NJ      16645     2075663343
 ROBERTS     PHIL       GEORGIA LANE  HARTFORD    CT      06105     2034662777
 CHARLES     LARRY      45 DOG LANE   HARTFORD    CT      06105     2032663885
 CLARK       SEYMOUR    26 WHITE LN   E HARTFORD  CT      06034     2037546663
 SMITH       KIRK       27 INN AVE    SPRINGS     MA      16646     4132774883
 YOUNG       SUE        27 VISTA DR   WESTVIEW    MA      16646     4133664828
 JOHNSON     GEORGE     3445 OHIO LA  DETROIT     MI      35535     5742553773
 MITCHELL    HENRY      23 DENNIS DR  W HARTFORD  CT      06117     2037333232
 YORK        JOHN       34 CAPE DR    HARTFORD    CT      06334     2033664773
 BATES       MARK       CHARLES RD    BOSTON      MA      46638     6173552626
 JAMES       GEORGE     24 PIE LANE   S WINDOW    CT      47744     2033665737
 SHERRI      JOE        14 CUP ROAD   BUCKSVILLE  CT      46627     2032663737
R>
```

Fig. 13-10. Displaying records.

```
R>SELECT ALL FROM CUSTOMER WHERE STATE = CT
LASTNAME     FSTNAME     STREET        CITY        STATE    ZIPCODE   PHONE
----------   ----------  ------------  ----------  -------  --------  ----------
JONES        BILL        15 SAMOAN DR  WESTVILLE   CT       04663     2034662837
ROBERTS      PHIL        GEORGIA LANE  HARTFORD    CT       06105     2034662777
CHARLES      LARRY       45 DOG LANE   HARTFORD    CT       06105     2032663885
CLARK        SEYMOUR     26 WHITE LN   E HARTFORD  CT       06034     2037546663
MITCHELL     HENRY       23 DENNIS DR  W HARTFORD  CT       06117     2037333232
YORK         JOHN        34 CAPE DR    HARTFORD    CT       06334     2033664773
JAMES        GEORGE      24 PIE LANE   S WINDOW    CT       47744     2033665737
SHERRI       JOE         14 CUP ROAD   BUCKSVILLE  CT       46627     2032663737
```

Fig. 13-11. The Connecticut records only.

in the State field. Notice that there is nothing special about the way that the value CT is entered. This is because it is a literal value. CT is the value of State in the records to be displayed. If you wished to compare the column State to a column named CT, the WHERE clause would have looked like the following:

WHERE STATE =A CT

When you are referring to a pair of columns, an A must follow the operator. With column comparisons, the A is the only way to tell the difference between a variable or column and a value.

R:base 5000 uses a very standard set of operators in comparisons. These include equal, not equal, greater than, less than, and, for value operators, contains. Tables 13-2 and 13-3 display the operators for values and columns.

You can use the operator itself or the symbol shown in Tables 13-2 and 13-3. It makes no difference which way you use the symbols.

EQ is the same as = . *LEA* is the same as < =A. As long as you make sure to use the right type of combination when you are comparing values or columns, you will have the correct results.

In addition to the comparison operators, there are several operators that locate specific information (Table 13-4). The EXISTS clause tests a column to see if there

Table 13-2. Value Operators.

Operator	Symbol	Definition
EQ	=	Equal
NE	< >	Not equal
GT	>	Greater than
GE	> =	Greater than or equal to
LT	<	Less than
LE	< =	Less than or equal to
CONTAINS		Embedded in the Text column

Table 13-3. Column Operators.

Operator	Symbol	Definition
EQA	= A	Equal
NEA	< > A	Not equal
GTA	> A	Greater than
GEA	> = A	Greater than or equal to
LTA	< A	Less than
LEA	< = A	Less than or equal to

is some data in the column. If it is blank, EXISTS would not be true. FAILS is the exact opposite:

R> SELECT ALL FROM CUSTOMER WHERE LASTNAME FAILS

This statement would only display the rows whose Lastname column was blank.

The **COUNT** = **n** clause lets you display the *n*th row in the table by number. The following statement displays the tenth record in the table:

R> SELECT ALL FROM CUSTOMER WHERE COUNT= 10

COUNT = **LAST** finds the last row in the table, while **LIMIT** = **n** only displays *n* number of rows.

There will be many times that you want to display your data in other ways. When you have many columns, you might want to only see some of the columns and in a different order than the data actually exists. Figure 13-12 shows a display of only the name and telephone number of all the records.

Notice that you are able to show only three of the columns by listing the names of the columns you want. Simply type the column names to suppress the listing of all the columns. You will also notice that they are listed in the order you have specified.

Figure 13-13 shows how you can also combine the two SELECT commands to only list those records that are from the state of CT. Notice that you are able to display the Connecticut records without showing the state in the display.

Let's learn one more way of selecting records using the SELECT command, with the use of the Contains operator. This is a special operator to R:base 5000.

Table 13-4. Specific Information Operators.

Operator	Definition
EXISTS	Column contains some data
FAILS	Column contains no data
COUNT = *n*	A specific row number
COUNT = LAST	The last row in a table
LIMIT = *n*	Only *n* number of rows are displayed

```
R>SELECT FSTNAME LASTNAME PHONE FROM CUSTOMER
 FSTNAME      LASTNAME    PHONE
 -----------  ----------  ----------
 JOHN         SMITH       6173442654
 BILL         JONES       2034662837
 DANNY        WILLIAMS    8081257688
 ROBERT       SMITH       2075663343
 PHIL         ROBERTS     2034662777
 LARRY        CHARLES     2032663885
 SEYMOUR      CLARK       2037546663
 KIRK         SMITH       4132774883
 SUE          YOUNG       4133664828
 GEORGE       JOHNSON     5742553773
 HENRY        MITCHELL    2037333232
 JOHN         YORK        2033664773
 MARK         BATES       6173552626
 GEORGE       JAMES       2033665737
 JOE          SHERRI      2032663737
 R>
```

Fig. 13-12. Limiting the scope of the display.

It is used to search for partial matches. Let's assume that Fred wants to see his customers who live in any city that contains the word Hartford. Fred would type the command like this:

`SELECT ALL FROM CUSTOMER WHERE CITY CONTAINS HARTFORD`

The resulting display is shown in Fig. 13-14. This form of the SELECT command allowed Fred to display the records in the table whose city field contains the word Hartford.

```
R>SELECT FSTNAME LASTNAME PHONE FROM CUSTOMER WHERE STATE = CT
 FSTNAME      LASTNAME    PHONE
 -----------  ----------  ----------
 BILL         JONES       2034662837
 PHIL         ROBERTS     2034662777
 LARRY        CHARLES     2032663885
 SEYMOUR      CLARK       2037546663
 HENRY        MITCHELL    2037333232
 JOHN         YORK        2033664773
 GEORGE       JAMES       2033665737
 JOE          SHERRI      2032663737
 R>
```

Fig. 13-13. Limiting the search and scope of the display.

```
R>SELECT ALL FROM CUSTOMER WHERE CITY CONTAINS HARTFORD
LASTNAME     FSTNAME      STREET        CITY         STATE      ZIPCODE    PHONE
----------   ----------   -----------   -----------  --------   --------   --------

ROBERTS      PHIL         GEORGIA LANE  HARTFORD     CT         06105      2034662777
CHARLES      LARRY        45 DOG LANE   HARTFORD     CT         06105      2032663885
CLARK        SEYMOUR      26 WHITE LN   E HARTFORD   CT         06034      2037546663
MITCHELL     HENRY        23 DENNIS DR  W HARTFORD   CT         06117      2037333232
YORK         JOHN         34 CAPE DR    HARTFORD     CT         06334      2033664773
R>
```

Fig. 13-14. Searching for a containing phrase in a field.

The SELECT command is extremely important for ad-hoc reports. In later chapters you will learn how to create more complex reports with the REPORTS command and how to add titles, column headers, totals, and subtotals (for your numeric fields). You will also learn some other commands for quick reporting and how to use all these commands with compound phrases. A *compound phrase* provides ways of asking compound questions; for example, if you want to see people from Connecticut, but only if they live in Hartford. Compound phrases can produce very specific extractions from the database. This topic will be discussed later in this chapter.

HANDLING ERRORS IN R:base 5000 COMMANDS

When you enter an R:base command, there will be a short delay while R:base processes your command. Some commands will not display anything to let you know they were successfully completed. You will simply see a new line with the R> prompt. When you make an error, however, R:base will show you the correct *syntax*, or computer grammar, needed to properly execute the command.

Figure 13-15 shows an example of an R:base error that occurred when the SELECT command was used. After the error message is displayed, R:base shows you the syntax diagram to let you try to enter it correctly the next time. As for all computer systems, you have to be very precise about how you use a command.

The command:

```
R> SELECT ALL WHERE STATE EQ CT
```

was typed at the R:base prompt. This command is supposed to display all the Connecticut records. However, an error was made. The SELECT command requires that you tell R:base the name of the table that the data is in. The correct command is:

```
R> SELECT ALL FROM CUSTOMER WHERE STATE EQ CT
```

Once you have some familiarity with R:base commands, you will learn how to use the syntax charts to enter corrected commands.

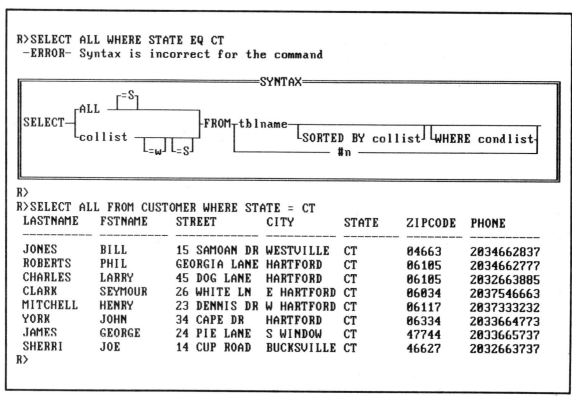

```
R>SELECT ALL WHERE STATE EQ CT
 -ERROR- Syntax is incorrect for the command

┌──────────────────────────────SYNTAX──────────────────────────────┐
│         ┌ALL┐  ┌=S┐                                               │
│ SELECT─┤    ├─────────┬─FROM─tblname─┐                            │
│         └collist┘ ┌=W┐┌=S┐           └SORTED BY collist┘└WHERE condlist─│
│                   └──┘└──┘              #n                        │
└──────────────────────────────────────────────────────────────────┘

R>
R>SELECT ALL FROM CUSTOMER WHERE STATE = CT
  LASTNAME    FSTNAME     STREET        CITY        STATE   ZIPCODE  PHONE
  ----------  ----------  ------------  ----------  -----   -------  ----------

  JONES       BILL        15 SAMOAN DR  WESTVILLE   CT      04663    2034662837
  ROBERTS     PHIL        GEORGIA LANE  HARTFORD    CT      06105    2034662777
  CHARLES     LARRY       45 DOG LANE   HARTFORD    CT      06105    2032663885
  CLARK       SEYMOUR     26 WHITE LN   E HARTFORD  CT      06034    2037546663
  MITCHELL    HENRY       23 DENNIS DR  W HARTFORD  CT      06117    2037333232
  YORK        JOHN        34 CAPE DR    HARTFORD    CT      06334    2033664773
  JAMES       GEORGE      24 PIE LANE   S WINDOW    CT      47744    2033665737
  SHERRI      JOE         14 CUP ROAD   BUCKSVILLE  CT      46627    2032663737
R>
```

Fig. 13-15. R:base 5000 error message.

USING THE R:base PROMPT MODE

When you are first using R:base 5000, you might need some help in using some of the more complex commands. R:base 5000 features a PROMPT mode to help you get started. The PROMPT mode is used by selecting RBASE from the RB5000 menu or by entering the command RBASE from DOS. When you start R:base, the main menu is displayed as shown in Fig. 12-10. The third choice, *PROMPT mode for command assistance*, lets you use the R:base PROMPT mode.

Figure 13-16 displays the main PROMPT mode menu. As you can see, prompts are available for nearly every R:base command. Since you are now familiar with the SELECT command, it will be used as an example.

The PROMPT screen shown in Fig. 13-17 contains a menu at the top of the screen. The *Go Execute* choice lets you enter the PROMPT mode and make a selection. Once you enter the PROMPT mode, the familiar R> prompt is replaced by a P> prompt to let you know you are in PROMPT mode.

By entering the command you want to be prompted through, R:base will display a new screen that you can fill in. R:base then automatically will execute the command. After entering SELECT in the prompt line, the screen changes to the SELECT prompt screen (Fig. 13-17).

The top half of Fig. 13-17 in the box is all that was originally displayed. In this example you can fill in the table name, a list of the columns to display, the sort or-

140

der, and search conditions. The SELECT prompt screen also tells you a little about the command and displays some new information that you haven't learned yet.

The table used in this figure is a table you will see again later. It contains the same data as the Customer table and also contains a column called Since, which is the year the customer first became a customer. There is also a column called Amount, which lists the amount that the customer owes.

R:base can automatically sum a column. By listing the column name followed by =S, the column will be automatically summed. This works in normal R:base command mode, too.

After the information in the box is filled in, the <ESC> key is pressed, automatically executing the command and displaying the results. As you can see in the bottom half of Fig. 13-17, the SELECT command is run using the information entered at the prompts. The data is displayed, and the amount column is totaled.

Although you still would have to know some of the R:base syntax even to use this simple prompting scheme, it makes entering commands easier when you first use R:base 5000.

CHANGING RECORDS

After adding records, you might discover a mistake has been made. This is a situation where changing records is necessary. You can work with the entire table in a full screen mode, viewing all the records and columns (or at least as many as you can see on the screen at once) and moving freely among them changing any values you want. To do so you would use the EDIT command. You can also change a table by entering conditions in which to change the entire table. This action requires the use of the CHANGE and ASSIGN commands.

The CHANGE command enables you to change one or more rows with a single

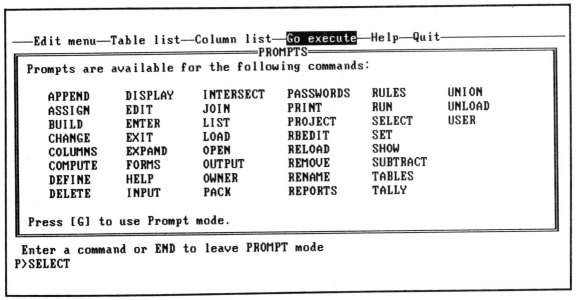

Fig. 13-16. R:base 5000 PROMPT screen.

```
 Press [ESC] when done with this data
╔═════════════════════════════════════PROMPTS═══════════════════════════╗
║ SELECT                                                                 ║
║ ──────                                                                 ║
║ Use the SELECT command to retrieve data from a table. Specify          ║
║ the table and the columns. To display all columns, enter ALL.          ║
║ To sum a column, add =S to the column name.  To set a display          ║
║ width for a column, add =w to the column name, where w is a            ║
║ number from 1 to 256.                                                  ║
║                                                                        ║
║ Name of table to display : ▌CUSTCRDT▐                                  ║
║ Name(s) of columns to display (or ALL) :                               ║
║ FSTNAME LASTNAME STATE AMOUNT=S                                        ║
║ Sort order (optional list of column names) :                          ║
║ AMOUNT=D                                                               ║
║ Condition that selects rows to display (optional) :                    ║
║ SINCE >= 1978                                                          ║
╚════════════════════════════════════════════════════════════════════════╝



SELECT FSTNAME LASTNAME STATE AMOUNT=S FROM CUSTCRDT SORTED BY AMOUNT=D WHERE +
SINCE >= 1978
 FSTNAME      LASTNAME     STATE     AMOUNT
 ──────────   ──────────   ────────  ─────────────────

 JOHN         YORK         CT           $54,324.00
 BILL         JONES        CT           $21,533.00
 KIRK         SMITH        MA           $12,456.34
 JOHN         SMITH        MA            $2,356.00
 GEORGE       JAMES        CT            $1,798.98
 JOE          SHERRI       CT               $23.00
 ROBERT       SMITH        NJ                $0.00
 SEYMOUR      CLARK        CT                $0.00
 ──────────   ──────────   ────────  ─────────────────
                                        $92,491.32
 Enter a command or END to leave PROMPT mode
 P>
```

Fig. 13-17. R:base 5000 PROMPT SELECT screen.

command. It is used to set the value of all rows meeting a specific condition. For example, if Mary Edwards gets married and changes her name to Smith:

R> CHANGE LASTNAME TO SMITH WHERE LASTNAME = EDWARDS

You could also change the value of many rows:

R> CHANGE DEPT TO DATA PROCESSING WHERE DEPT = COMPUTERS

Many rows might be changed if the name of the Computer department changes to Data Processing department.

You can also change rows based on the comparisons of columns:

```
R> CHANGE CREDIT TO N WHERE AMT_OWED GTA CRED_LMT
```

This command will change the Credit column to N if a customer has purchased more than his credit limit.

In order to change the value of all columns using a numeric expression, you must use the ASSIGN command.

```
R> ASSIGN SALARY TO SALARY * 1.05 WHERE SALARY EXISTS
```

This command increases all the salaries by 5 percent, as long as the salary column wasn't blank for each record.

Numeric expressions in R:base 5000 include the four standard expressions:

☐ Addition +
☐ Subtraction −
☐ Multiplication ×
☐ Division /

There is also a symbol to calculate the first item as the percentage value of the second item:

☐ Percentage %

The last two symbols are *concatenation* symbols. This is a fancy word meaning putting two text strings together.

☐ Concatenation with space &
☐ Concatenation without space +

50% PAYROLL would take the value of the column Payroll and multiply by 50 percent. If Payroll was 200:

```
ASSIGN PAYROLL TO 50% PAYROLL
```

would make the value of Payroll 100.

FSTNAME + LASTNAME would put two strings together without any spaces in between. Fstname&Lastname would put two strings together with a space between.

If Fstname was John and Lstname was Smith, the values of the following two expressions would be the following:

```
ASSIGN NAME TO   FSTNAME+LASTNAME
```

yields **JOHNSMITH.**

```
ASSIGN NAME TO  FSTNAME&LASTNAME
```

yields **JOHN SMITH.**

EDITING A TABLE

You can also edit the entire table with the EDIT command. Figure 13-18 shows the screen after the following command has been typed.

```
R> EDIT ALL FROM CUSTOMER
```

The entire Customer file is displayed. You may move freely throughout the screen changing any of the values you want. You may even delete individual rows by pressing the <F2> key and then confirming the delete by pressing <Enter>.

If there were more columns or rows, you would have to scroll up and down or left and right to see and edit them. Table 13-5 shows the list of cursor movements for the EDIT screen.

When you are through editing all the values you want, you can leave the edit screen by pressing <ESC>. All of your changes are automatically saved.

When you use the EDIT command, you don't have to see all of your table at once. You can use the WHERE clause to only see as much of the file as you want. For example:

```
R> EDIT CITY FSTNAME LASTNAME FROM CUSTOMER WHERE STATE=CT
```

```
            Press [ESC] to quit, [F2] to delete, [F5] to reset
  LASTNAME    FSTNAME    STREET        CITY        STATE    ZIPCODE    PHONE
  ---------   --------   -----------   ---------   -----    -------    ----------
  SMITH       JOHN       PILGRIM WAY   PLYMOUTH    MA       05634      6173442654
  JONES       BILL       15 SAMOAN DR  WESTVILLE   CT       04663      2034662837
  WILLIAMS    DANNY      17 ALOHA DR   HONOLULU    HA       67355      8081257688
  SMITH       ROBERT     15 APPIAN DR  TRENTON     NJ       16645      2075663343
  ROBERTS     PHIL       GEORGIA LANE  HARTFORD    CT       06105      2034662777
  CHARLES     LARRY      45 DOG LANE   HARTFORD    CT       06105      2032663885
  CLARK       SEYMOUR    26 WHITE LN   E HARTFORD  CT       06034      2037546663
  SMITH       KIRK       27 INN AVE    SPRINGS     MA       16646      4132774883
  YOUNG       SUE        27 VISTA DR   WESTVIEW    MA       16646      4133664828
  JOHNSON     GEORGE     3445 OHIO LA  DETROIT     MI       35535      5742553773
  MITCHELL    HENRY      23 DENNIS DR  W HARTFORD  CT       06117      2037333232
  YORK        JOHN       34 CAPE DR    HARTFORD    CT       06334      2033664773
  BATES       MARK       CHARLES RD    BOSTON      MA       46638      6173552626
  JAMES       GEORGE     24 PIE LANE   S WINDOW    CT       47744      2033665737
  SHERRI      JOE        14 CUP ROAD   BUCKSVILLE  CT       46627      2032663737
```

Fig. 13-18. The Edit screen.

144

Table 13-5. Cursor Movements in the Edit Screen.

Key	Function
↑	Moves highlighting up one row
↓	Moves highlighting down one row
Tab	Moves highlighting one column to the right
Shift-Tab	Moves highlighting one column to the left
→	Moves the cursor one character to the right
←	Moves the cursor one character to the left
Ctrl →	Moves highlighting to the last column in the row
Ctrl ←	Moves highlighting to the first column in the row
Home	Moves highlighting to the top of the screen
End	Moves highlighting to the bottom of the screen
PgUp	Shows the previous screenful of data
PgDn	Shows the next screenful of data
Del	Deletes the character over the cursor
Ins	Inserts a space at the cursor position
F2	Deletes the currently highlighted row
F5	Resets the contents of the currently highlighted item

would put you in the EDIT mode but only looking at the columns City, Fstname, and Lastname. Only the customers in the state of Connecticut would be displayed. The rest of the records in the table are still there, but you can only edit the ones you specify.

If you have created a data entry form, you can use it to edit your data one record at a time. The command EDIT USING will use your form to serve as an edit mask for each row.

R> EDIT USING CUSTFORM

will display the screen as shown in Fig. 13-19. The form is displayed with a menu at the top. This menu has seven choices that let you perform all the necessary functions.

☐ Skip—Skips to the next record and displays it on the form.
☐ Edit—Moves the cursor into the form to make changes.
☐ Change—Makes the change to the record. Change is only used after Edit.
☐ Add—Adds a new record from the contents of the screen.
☐ Reset—If changes were made with Edit, they are reversed.
☐ Delete—Deletes the current row.
☐ Quit—Exits from the EDIT USING function.

After you have used the *Edit* option to move the cursor into the record and make any changes, the record is not actually changed. You must then press one of the active commands.

Change will update the existing record with any changes you made while you were in the entry form. If you made no changes, the Change command does nothing but rewrite the record to itself.

```
┌─────────────────────────────────────────────────────────────────┐
│ ──Skip──Edit──Change──Add──Reset──Delete──Quit──────────────────  │
│                    FRED'S FISH MARKET DATA ENTRY FORM             │
│                    ------------------------------------           │
│                                                                   │
│                                                                   │
│         LAST NAME: SMITH              FIRST NAME: JOHN            │
│                                                                   │
│                                                                   │
│         STREET: PILGRIM WAY                                       │
│                                                                   │
│         CITY: PLYMOUTH          STATE: MA     ZIP CODE: 05634     │
│                                                                   │
│                                                                   │
│         PHONE NUMBER: 6173442654                                 │
│                                                                   │
└─────────────────────────────────────────────────────────────────┘
```

Fig. 13-19. Edit using a form.

Add will actually create a new record. This command can create duplicate records if you are not careful. This choice can be used to edit existing records and create variations of them.

As you want to move from one record to the next, the *Skip* command will display each record in succession. When you find a record you want to change, the *Edit* command will move you into the record.

The entry form is an integral part of R:base 5000. It can be used to enter your records or to change and delete them later.

DELETING RECORDS

In most computer systems, deleting records is a slow and arduous process because, as records are deleted, the file must somehow regain the recovered space. In R:base 5000, deleting records is a two-step process. First, you will use the DELETE command. This command is very similar to the SELECT command; if you give the command DELETE, it will delete the records the WHERE clause specifies. Using the command:

`R> DELETE ROWS FROM CUSTOMER WHERE STATE = HA`

will delete all the records with the state of HA. The command

`R> DELETE DUPLICATES FROM CUSTOMER`

will delete duplicate records from the table.

Records deleted by the DELETE command are not really gone. You can't see them or get to them, but they still occupy space on the table. Again, deleting is a two-step process. The records won't physically disappear until the PACK command is issued. This command copies the file over without the deleted records. It takes a fair amount of time and should be done only after deleting is completed. Do all your deletions first, then use PACK once, as follows:

```
R> PACK
```

Now, all of the undeleted records are copied. This procedure is how R:base 5000 takes care of freeing up the space that was used by the now deleted records in the file. PACKing actually copies the undeleted records, and then renames the new file while deleting the old file.

Chapter 14

Sorting the Table

Most of the time you will want your table in a certain order. Possibly, you want to see your customers in alphabetical order by last name; maybe you will want a list by the state in which they live. There are even times you might want a list of your customers in the order of the customer who owes the most money to the one who owes the least money. No matter what order you wish to see the table, some type of rearrangement will be necessary.

The most common way to rearrange data in a file is to sort the data. This method, however, means physically moving the records. Each time you want to change the way you see the data, you must move the records.

There is another way to sort your data that might be faster in some searches. Building Keys is a method where a separate list of pointers is kept. This list contains the order of the records in the table based upon the sort criteria you have specified. A table can be keyed far quicker than it can be sorted because keying a table assigns values to a list of pointers, while sorting means physically rearranging the data. Updating keys is also very quick because no physical rearrangement of the data is necessary.

To illustrate the concept of sorting and pointers, let's assume the data in Table 14-1. You can see that there is no special order to this sample file. There are two ways to sort a table: ascending or descending order. If a table is sorted by an ascending key, then the record with the lowest value in the key field is the first record, and the record with the highest value of the key field is the last record. In a descending sort, the highest values come first. Character values are sorted from Z to A, and

Name	Test Score
WILLIAM	85
SAMUEL	57
FRED	63
GEORGE	98
ADAM	91
JOHN	89
ZACHARY	76
CORY	34

Table 14-1. Data for Sorting by Pointers.

numbers from the largest positive value to the largest negative value. The opposite is true for an ascending sort.

Let's look at the data as if it had been sorted by name. The data would be physically rearranged and would now look like Table 14-2. Sorting by descending score yields Table 14-3.

Notice that in these two examples the data itself was physically rearranged. Figure 14-1 shows a conceptual model of the same two sorts done with keys. As you can see, with keys there is a separate column (actually the file labeled filename3.RBS contains the keys) that contains the order of each record for the sort desired. In this case there are two separate index files.

For a final analogy of index pointers, imagine what you would do when you want to see a product that you know is in a software catalog, but you cannot remember the product name. The product you are searching for is indexed in several ways in the back of the catalog. Usually these indexes are in order by the product type, manufacturer, and the product name itself. There are three separate indexes, all pointing to the same page in the catalog.

SORTING A TABLE

R:base 5000 does not keep the data sorted at any time. The SORTED BY phrase in commands such as SELECT and EDIT will let you see your data in a sorted order.

To display all the records in the Customer file in a sorted order sorted by state, you would type the following statement:

R> SELECT ALL FROM CUSTOMER SORTED BY STATE

Name	Test Score
ADAM	91
CORY	34
FRED	63
GEORGE	98
JOHN	89
SAMUEL	57
WILLIAM	85
ZACHARY	76

Table 14-2. Data Sorted by Name in Ascending Order.

Sorting it by DESCENDING score yields:	
Name	**Test Score**
GEORGE	98
ADAM	91
JOHN	89
WILLIAM	85
ZACHARY	76
FRED	63
SAMUEL	57
CORY	34

Table 14-3. Data Sorted by Score in Descending Order.

Figure 14-2 shows the sorted table.

The records are now sorted by state. The State column does not have to appear first in the table. Only if you use the SELECT command to display it that way will it be shown first.

You can also sort the table in descending order. To display all the records in the Customer file in a descending sorted order sorted by state, you would type the following statement:

R> SELECT ALL FROM CUSTOMER SORTED BY STATE=D

Figure 14-3 shows the sorted table. Notice that the order of State is now in descending order. The New Jersey record is first and the Connecticut records are last.

The problem of multiple keys has not yet been addressed. Using the Customer file, for example, how would you sort the file if you later wanted to report by state, and within the report for each state you wished to see the people sorted by name? This sort would allow you to group the people from Connecticut, then Massachusetts, etc. in alphabetical order in each state.

The data is sorted first by state, and the people within each state are sorted by name. This type of sort would be created by simply having the two sort columns in the SORTED BY clause. Figure 14-4 shows a multiple sort.

In this example, the SELECT command specifies both the columns to appear

NAME	TEST SCORE	ASCENDING NAME INDEX	DESCENDING TEST SCORE INDEX
WILLIAM	85	7	4
SAMUEL	57	6	7
FRED	63	3	6
GEORGE	98	4	1
ADAM	91	1	2
JOHN	89	5	3
ZACHARY	76	8	5
CORY	34	2	8

Fig. 14-1. The table with key pointers.

150

```
R>SELECT ALL FROM CUSTOMER SORTED BY STATE
 LASTNAME     FSTNAME     STREET         CITY          STATE   ZIPCODE   PHONE
 ----------   ----------  ------------   ----------    -----   -------   ----------

 CHARLES      LARRY       45 DOG LANE    HARTFORD      CT      06105     2032663885
 JONES        BILL        15 SAMOAN DR   WESTVILLE     CT      04663     2034662837
 YORK         JOHN        34 CAPE DR     HARTFORD      CT      06334     2033664773
 ROBERTS      PHIL        GEORGIA LANE   HARTFORD      CT      06105     2034662777
 JAMES        GEORGE      24 PIE LANE    S WINDOW      CT      47744     2033665737
 CLARK        SEYMOUR     26 WHITE LN    E HARTFORD    CT      06034     2037546663
 MITCHELL     HENRY       23 DENNIS DR   W HARTFORD    CT      06117     2037333232
 SHERRI       JOE         14 CUP ROAD    BUCKSVILLE    CT      46627     2032663737
 SMITH        KIRK        27 INN AVE     SPRINGS       MA      16646     4132774883
 SMITH        JOHN        PILGRIM WAY    PLYMOUTH      MA      05634     6173442654
 YOUNG        SUE         27 VISTA DR    WESTVIEW      MA      16646     4133664828
 BATES        MARK        CHARLES RD     BOSTON        MA      46638     6173552626
 JOHNSON      GEORGE      3445 OHIO LA   DETROIT       MI      35535     5742553773
 SMITH        ROBERT      15 APPIAN DR   TRENTON       NJ      16645     2075663343
R>
```

Fig. 14-2. Displaying a sorted Customer table.

on the report and how the report should be sorted. Within the state of Connecticut records, the people are sorted by Lastname. Also within the Massachusetts records, the people are sorted by Lastname. You can specify up to 10 levels in any sort clause.

In these examples, the columns used in the SORTED BY clause also appeared in the display. You could sort by one column and not display it. R:base always uses all the columns, even if it doesn't display them all.

```
R>SELECT ALL FROM CUSTOMER SORTED BY STATE=D
 LASTNAME     FSTNAME     STREET         CITY          STATE   ZIPCODE   PHONE
 ----------   ----------  ------------   ----------    -----   -------   ----------

 SMITH        ROBERT      15 APPIAN DR   TRENTON       NJ      16645     2075663343
 JOHNSON      GEORGE      3445 OHIO LA   DETROIT       MI      35535     5742553773
 BATES        MARK        CHARLES RD     BOSTON        MA      46638     6173552626
 YOUNG        SUE         27 VISTA DR    WESTVIEW      MA      16646     4133664828
 SMITH        JOHN        PILGRIM WAY    PLYMOUTH      MA      05634     6173442654
 SMITH        KIRK        27 INN AVE     SPRINGS       MA      16646     4132774883
 JONES        BILL        15 SAMOAN DR   WESTVILLE     CT      04663     2034662837
 CLARK        SEYMOUR     26 WHITE LN    E HARTFORD    CT      06034     2037546663
 CHARLES      LARRY       45 DOG LANE    HARTFORD      CT      06105     2032663885
 MITCHELL     HENRY       23 DENNIS DR   W HARTFORD    CT      06117     2037333232
 YORK         JOHN        34 CAPE DR     HARTFORD      CT      06334     2033664773
 ROBERTS      PHIL        GEORGIA LANE   HARTFORD      CT      06105     2034662777
 JAMES        GEORGE      24 PIE LANE    S WINDOW      CT      47744     2033665737
 SHERRI       JOE         14 CUP ROAD    BUCKSVILLE    CT      46627     2032663737
R>
```

Fig. 14-3. Displaying a sorted Customer table in descending order.

```
R>SELECT STATE FSTNAME LASTNAME FROM CUSTOMER SORTED BY STATE LASTNAME
STATE       FSTNAME       LASTNAME
─────────   ───────────   ───────────
CT          LARRY         CHARLES
CT          SEYMOUR       CLARK
CT          GEORGE        JAMES
CT          BILL          JONES
CT          HENRY         MITCHELL
CT          PHIL          ROBERTS
CT          JOE           SHERRI
CT          JOHN          YORK
MA          MARK          BATES
MA          KIRK          SMITH
MA          JOHN          SMITH
MA          SUE           YOUNG
MI          GEORGE        JOHNSON
NJ          ROBERT        SMITH
R>
```

Fig. 14-4. Displaying a sorted Customer table with multiple columns.

The SORTED BY clause is available almost everywhere the WHERE clause is. This includes the SELECT and EDIT commands, and commands you will see later, such as PRINT.

In the Programming section, you will see how important the SORTED BY clause can be. When you process the data in a sorted order using the SET POINTER command, you can completely control the processing of data.

BUILDING KEYS

Building keys into a table is a very simple operation. The command:

R> BUILD KEY FOR LASTNAME IN CUSTOMER

will set up a key for the column Lastname in the Customer table. When you are using commands that select records and the WHERE phrase meets all of the following conditions, keys will save you time.

☐ The last condition in the WHERE clause uses the key.
☐ The last operator in the WHERE clause is an EQ.
☐ The last connector is an AND.

The following SELECT command meets those conditions:

R> SELECT ALL FROM CUSTOMER WHERE STATE EQ CT AND LASTNAME EQ SMITH

There is a more important reason to use keys, however. In the next chapter you will see some *relational concepts*; that is, where two or more tables are related to each other. Relational operators automatically take advantage of keyed columns. It is, therefore, important to build keys for the columns in your tables that will be commonly used to relate one table to another.

When you use a nonkeyed file to search for records, R:base 5000 will check every record sequentially until it finds a match or reaches the end of the file. If there are thousands of records to search, this process may take a long while. R:base 5000 will read the whole file just to find a single or a few records. When a table has been sorted, the situation will still not be improved. Sorting the table only rearranges the data; it does nothing to help R:base 5000 locate records faster. Keying, on the other hand, helps R:base 5000 locate records quickly.

Chapter 15

Searching the Database—A Second Look

In this chapter, you will see some advanced ways to search a database and begin to see the difference in using R:base 5000 as a database manager and using the R:base 5000 programming statements.

COMPOUND EXPRESSIONS

Compound expressions involve the use of connectors, such as AND, OR, and NOT. These connectors allow you to ask far more specific questions than just querying the state in which someone resides. With compound expressions you can ask questions such as: "Show me all my customers that live in apartments which are not in Connecticut or Massachusetts. How many customers do I have that have not had an order in 2 years but whose last order was over $20.00? Which of my largest ten customers owe the most money for more than 60 days?"

Obviously, these pieces of data would have to be on the database in order to ask these types of questions. Without the compound expression, however, they could not be asked then.

Let's discuss the first two connectors, AND and OR. *AND* is a connector that allows you to evaluate several comparisons and make a positive decision only if all the comparisons are true. (If you are asked to compare the variable *Amt__Spent* to *less than 500*, if the value of Amt__Spent is less than 500, the expression is true. If Amt__Spent is equal to or greater than 500, the expression is false.) Using AND you may ask a question such as the following:

```
SELECT ALL FROM CUSTCRDT WHERE AMT_SPENT < 500 AND STATE=CT
```

This pseudocode representation illustrates the use of AND. Only if the customer has spent less than 500, as well as residing in Connecticut will he be printed out. Just living in Connecticut is not enough; he must also have spent less than 500.

The connector *OR* allows you to evaluate several expressions and make a decision if any of the comparisons are true.

```
SELECT ALL FROM CUSTCRDT WHERE AMT_SPENT < 500 OR STATE=CT
```

This pseudocode representation shows the use of OR. If the customer has spent less than 500, the expression is true regardless of the state in which he lives. Likewise, if he lives in Connecticut, the expression is true regardless of the amount spent. Only if both pieces of the expression are false is the expression false. To be false in this example, the person must not live in Connecticut and must have spent at least 500.

The final connector, NE, is always used in conjunction with the expression itself, rather than allowing two expressions to be combined. For example:

```
SELECT ALL FROM CUSTCRDT WHERE STATE NE CT
```

DISPLAYING SELECTED RECORDS

Assume the database shown in Fig. 15-1. Let's look at several examples and results of the SELECT command using compound expressions. For example:

```
R> SELECT ALL FROM CUSTCRDT WHERE STATE = CT AND BUY85 = Y
```

```
R>SELECT ALL FROM CUSTCRDT
  LASTNAME    FSTNAME    STATE    SINCE      BUY85    AMOUNT
  ----------  ---------  -------  ---------  -------  ----------------
  SMITH       JOHN       MA       1981 Y              $2,356.00
  JONES       BILL       CT       1979 Y              $21,533.00
  SMITH       ROBERT     NJ       1980 N              $0.00
  ROBERTS     PHIL       CT       1975 Y              $423.12
  CHARLES     LARRY      CT       1973 Y              $18,435.00
  CLARK       SEYMOUR    CT       1983 Y              $0.00
  SMITH       KIRK       MA       1983 Y              $12,456.34
  YOUNG       SUE        MA       1971 Y              $123.40
  JOHNSON     GEORGE     MI       1976 N              $7,685.00
  MITCHELL    HENRY      CT       1976 Y              $34,567.00
  YORK        JOHN       CT       1984 N              $54,324.00
  BATES       MARK       MA       1973 Y              $2,345.00
  JAMES       GEORGE     CT       1980 Y              $1,798.98
  SHERRI      JOE        CT       1978 Y              $23.00
  R>
```

Fig. 15-1. A sample database.

```
R>SELECT ALL FROM CUSTCRDT WHERE STATE = CT AND BUY85 = Y
LASTNAME    FSTNAME    STATE    SINCE      BUY85    AMOUNT
----------  ---------  -------  ---------  -------  ----------------
JONES       BILL       CT        1979 Y             $21,533.00
ROBERTS     PHIL       CT        1975 Y                 $423.12
CHARLES     LARRY      CT        1973 Y             $18,435.00
CLARK       SEYMOUR    CT        1983 Y                   $0.00
MITCHELL    HENRY      CT        1976 Y             $34,567.00
JAMES       GEORGE     CT        1980 Y              $1,798.98
SHERRI      JOE        CT        1978 Y                  $23.00
R>
```

Fig. 15-2. Using the AND connector.

Using the AND connector, you have asked for R:base 5000 to display all records
for customers in Connecticut who have bought from you this year. As you can see,
the records that were selected and displayed have been shown in Fig. 15-2.

Changing the AND connector to OR yields the following:

R> SELECT ALL FROM CUSTCRDT WHERE STATE = CT OR BUY85 = Y

Now you have changed what you are asking for. You want to see a customer if he
lives in Connecticut or if he has bought from you this year. It doesn't matter which
of those conditions he met; even if he meets both you want to see him.

```
R>SELECT ALL FROM CUSTCRDT WHERE STATE = CT OR BUY85 = Y
LASTNAME    FSTNAME    STATE    SINCE      BUY85    AMOUNT
----------  ---------  -------  ---------  -------  ----------------
SMITH       JOHN       MA        1981 Y              $2,356.00
JONES       BILL       CT        1979 Y             $21,533.00
ROBERTS     PHIL       CT        1975 Y                 $423.12
CHARLES     LARRY      CT        1973 Y             $18,435.00
CLARK       SEYMOUR    CT        1983 Y                   $0.00
SMITH       KIRK       MA        1983 Y             $12,456.34
YOUNG       SUE        MA        1971 Y                 $123.40
MITCHELL    HENRY      CT        1976 Y             $34,567.00
YORK        JOHN       CT        1984 N             $54,324.00
BATES       MARK       MA        1973 Y              $2,345.00
JAMES       GEORGE     CT        1980 Y              $1,798.98
SHERRI      JOE        CT        1978 Y                  $23.00
R>
```

Fig. 15-3. Using the OR connector.

```
R>SELECT ALL FROM CUSTCRDT WHERE STATE NE CT OR AMOUNT < 10000
 LASTNAME      FSTNAME      STATE     SINCE       BUY85     AMOUNT
 ----------    ----------   --------  ----------  --------  ----------------
 SMITH         JOHN         MA        1981 Y                      $2,356.00
 SMITH         ROBERT       NJ        1980 N                          $0.00
 ROBERTS       PHIL         CT        1975 Y                        $423.12
 CLARK         SEYMOUR      CT        1983 Y                          $0.00
 SMITH         KIRK         MA        1983 Y                     $12,456.34
 YOUNG         SUE          MA        1971 Y                        $123.40
 JOHNSON       GEORGE       MI        1976 N                      $7,685.00
 BATES         MARK         MA        1973 Y                      $2,345.00
 JAMES         GEORGE       CT        1980 Y                      $1,798.98
 SHERRI        JOE          CT        1978 Y                         $23.00
 R>
```

Fig. 15-4. Using the NOT connector with OR.

Using the NOT expression with an OR connector, you will be able to see a customer if he has spent less than 10,000. Whether he has spent less than this amount or not, you want to see him if he is not from Connecticut. Note that you want to see the names of those not residing in Connecticut no matter how much they have spent.

```
R> DISPLAY ALL OFF FOR STATE .NOT. = 'CT' OR AMOUNT < 10000
```

The resulting display is shown in Fig. 15-4. Figure 15-5 shows the same NE clause with AND instead of OR.

Using the NOT expression with an AND connector, you will be able to see a customer if he has spent less than 10,000 and he lives outside of Connecticut.

A double compound expression is shown in the next example:

```
R> SELECT ALL FROM CUSTCRDT WHERE STATE EQ CT AND   +
R> (SINCE <= 1980 OR AMOUNT > 10000)
```

```
R>SELECT ALL FROM CUSTCRDT WHERE STATE NE CT AND AMOUNT < 10000
 LASTNAME      FSTNAME      STATE     SINCE       BUY85     AMOUNT
 ----------    ----------   --------  ----------  --------  ----------------
 SMITH         JOHN         MA        1981 Y                      $2,356.00
 SMITH         ROBERT       NJ        1980 N                          $0.00
 YOUNG         SUE          MA        1971 Y                        $123.40
 JOHNSON       GEORGE       MI        1976 N                      $7,685.00
 BATES         MARK         MA        1973 Y                      $2,345.00
 R>
```

Fig. 15-5. Using the NOT connector with AND.

In this example, there are three conditions: State = CT, Since < = 1980, and Amount > 10,000, but because of the parentheses, the expression is reduced to two conditions. The first condition is simply that the customer must live in Connecticut (State = CT); the second is a complex expression itself and must be evaluated before being joined for evaluation to the first condition.

The second expression is true if the customer has been a customer since 1980. The second expression is also true if the customer has spent 10,000. Only if the customer meets neither condition is the second expression false.

After evaluating the simple first expression and the compound second expression, you can evaluate the expression as a whole. Since there is an AND clause between them, both sides must be true for the expression to be true. Remember that the plus sign indicates that the statement couldn't fit on one line and had to be split on two lines.

After careful examination, only people in Connecticut who have been customers since 1980 or have spent 10,000 should be listed. Figure 15-6 shows the resulting display.

The SELECT command with compound expressions can use all of the other features of the SELECT command. These include the SORTED BY clause and also column selection. The EDIT command can also use compound expressions.

Figure 15-7 is an example of a SELECT command using all the possible clauses. The command uses only four columns in the report: Fstname, Lastname, Amount, and State. The Amount column will be totaled with the = S option, while State will be displayed with a width of 5 characters, as shown by the = 5 option.

The data is taken from the Custcrdt table and is sorted by Amount in descending order; that is, the largest amount to the smallest amount. The only records that are selected are those whose value of Since is greater than or equal to 1978. Only records from customers who are relatively new, since 1978 will be displayed. The column Since will not be displayed in the report, but doesn't affect the selection process.

```
R>SELECT ALL FROM CUSTCRDT WHERE STATE = CT AND +
R>  SINCE <= 1980 OR AMOUNT > 10000
   LASTNAME      FSTNAME     STATE     SINCE         BUY85     AMOUNT
   ----------    ---------   -------   -----------   -------   ------------

   JONES         BILL        CT        1979  Y                 $21,533.00
   ROBERTS       PHIL        CT        1975  Y                    $423.12
   CHARLES       LARRY       CT        1973  Y                 $18,435.00
   SMITH         KIRK        MA        1983  Y                 $12,456.34
   MITCHELL      HENRY       CT        1976  Y                 $34,567.00
   YORK          JOHN        CT        1984  N                 $54,324.00
   JAMES         GEORGE      CT        1980  Y                  $1,798.98
   SHERRI        JOE         CT        1978  Y                     $23.00
R>
```

Fig. 15-6. A double compound expression.

```
R>SELECT FSTNAME LASTNAME AMOUNT=S STATE=5 FROM CUSTCRDT +
R>SORTED BY AMOUNT=D WHERE SINCE >= 1978
  FSTNAME      LASTNAME     AMOUNT             STATE
  -----------  -----------  -----------------  -----
  JOHN         YORK         $54,324.00 CT
  BILL         JONES        $21,533.00 CT
  KIRK         SMITH        $12,456.34 MA
  JOHN         SMITH         $2,356.00 MA
  GEORGE       JAMES         $1,798.98 CT
  JOE          SHERRI           $23.00 CT
  ROBERT       SMITH             $0.00 NJ
  SEYMOUR      CLARK             $0.00 CT
  -----------  -----------  -----------------  -----
                            $92,491.32
  R>
```

Fig. 15-7. All the possible options.

The SELECT command is the basis of ad-hoc reporting in R:base 5000. In the next chapter you will learn about the REPORTS command to create totally customizable reports. Although the SELECT command is rarely used in a programmed system, it is very important to the ad-hoc reporting that people who use your system will need. It also displays all of the concepts necessary to create your own reports.

CALCULATING AMOUNTS: COMPUTE AND TALLY

When you use the SELECT command, you can display the data in your table. You can total numeric columns, and choose the order and scope of the columns you display, and the sort order of the rows.

There may be times when you need some simple statistics. The COMPUTE command can give you some simple statistics about your data. You can get these statistics about your entire database or only a portion of your database. Table 15-1 shows the statistics available from the COMPUTE command.

The average, minimum, maximum, sum, count, and rows are displayed as requested when you are using the COMPUTE command.

Table 15-1. Statistics Available with the COMPUTE Command.

Statistic	Description
Ave	Computes the average of a numeric column
Count	Counts how many entries are in a column
Max	Selects the highest number, alphabetically highest Text string, or latest date from a column
Min	Selects smallest number, alphabetically lowest Text string, or earliest date from a column
Rows	Determines how many rows are in a table
Sum	Computes the sum of numeric data in a column
All	Computes all of the above

Figure 15-8 shows some sample uses of the COMPUTE command. The first example displays the SUM of the Amount column for all the records in the Custcrdt table. The sum is displayed along with the column name.

The second example shows the use of the WHERE clause to limit the scope of the COMPUTE command to only the Connecticut records. Notice that the total displayed in the second example is smaller, reflecting the exclusion of all the non-Connecticut records.

The last example shows the COMPUTE ALL command. All of the statistics are displayed as shown in Fig. 15-9. When you need some simple statistics, the COMPUTE command can be a ready asset.

Also important is the TALLY command. This command lists the number of occurrences for each different value in a column.

Figure 15-9 shows two examples of the TALLY command. The first example displays the various occurrences of the State column. As you can see, Connecticut is found eight times, Massachusetts four times, and Michigan and New Jersey once each. The second example shows the many values of the column Since and the number of occurrences for each of the values.

CREATING A REPORT FORM

You have already seen how to use the SELECT command to display your records. The SELECT command enables you to display some or all of your records and also allows you to display only certain fields. You can also calculate simple grand totals and sort your data into any order. The REPORTS command will enable you to do all that, but with a more formal display. The REPORTS command also enables you to save the format; so you can see the formatted report whenever you want without having to redefine the format.

Creating and using the report formats is a two-step process. The first step is to create the report, while the second step is to use the form to produce your report. Later you will see the OUTPUT command, which is used to run the report.

After you open your database and type **REPORTS**, R:base 5000 asks you for the name in which to store the report definition. This will be the name you will later

```
R>COMPUTE SUM AMOUNT FROM CUSTCRDT
AMOUNT    Sum =                    $156,069.84
R>
R>COMPUTE SUM AMOUNT FROM CUSTCRDT WHERE STATE = CT
AMOUNT    Sum =                    $131,104.10
R>
R>COMPUTE ALL AMOUNT FROM CUSTCRDT
AMOUNT    Count =           14              Minimum =                 $0.00
          Maximum =         $54,324.00 Sum =              $156,069.84
          Average =         $11,147.85 Rows =        14
R>
```

Fig. 15-8. The COMPUTE command.

```
R>TALLY STATE FROM CUSTCRDT

    STATE       Number of Occurrences
    ----------  -----------------------
    CT                 8
    MA                 4
    MI                 1
    NJ                 1
R>
R>TALLY SINCE FROM CUSTCRDT

    SINCE        Number of Occurrences
    ----------   -----------------------
            1971          1
            1973          2
            1975          1
            1976          2
            1978          1
            1979          1
            1980          2
            1981          1
            1983          2
            1984          1
R>
```

Fig. 15-9. The TALLY command.

use to print the report again and again. Figure 15-10 shows the initial creation of the report.

The name of the report form will Custrept. You can name your reports any-

```
R>OPEN BOOK
  Database exists
R>
R>REPORTS
Begin R:base REPORTS definition
Enter REPORT name:CUSTREPT
Enter table name:CUSTCRDT
```

Fig. 15-10. The REPORTS command.

thing you want, as long as you keep within the eight-character maximum and other rules of table names. When you create a report, you must associate the report with a table in the database. You may use columns from other tables in a database, but you must select one table to be associated with the report.

Once you begin the process, a menu is displayed, as shown in Fig. 15-11. These options let you create the report format.

There are seven choices represented by a menu at the top of the screen. You can also display the column names of your table and any variables you have defined by pressing the <F3> key.

In this section of the book, all of these options will be explained. The first thing you should do is lay out the report format on a piece of paper.

Fred decides that he will want a lot of the same information he could produce with the SELECT command. He wants the first and last name, how long the person has been a customer, and the amount the customer has spent this year. However, Fred also wants some things you can't get from a SELECT statement. He wants subtotals by state and the State column to appear at the top of each group. He also wants the subtotals and totals underlined. Fred draws a diagram (Fig. 15-12) of what he envisions will be his report.

Fred decides to create the report without the subtotal and totals first. As he is new at this process, he wants to take it one step at a time.

The Define Screen

Fred begins by defining any variable he might need. There are only two Fred really needs: the page number variable and the date variable. These are both internal variables to R:base 5000, but they must be set in the variables definition.

Fred chooses **D** from the REPORTS menu to *Define or change report variables*.

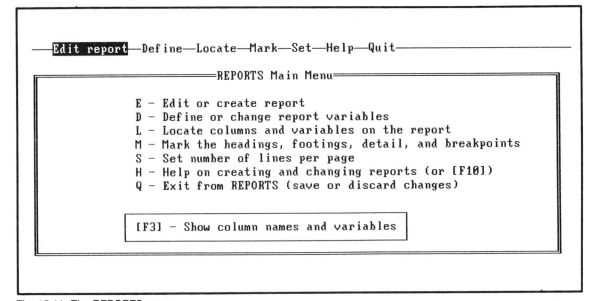

Fig. 15-11. The REPORTS menu.

Customer Credit by State

Page No: _____

<table>
<tr><td>First
Name</td><td>Last
Name</td><td>Customer
Name</td><td>Total
spent</td></tr>
</table>

Date } Page Header

State: _____ } Break Header

| John | Smith | 1978 | $63,061 | } Detail |

Subtotal } Break Footer

State: _____ } Break Header

} Detail

Subtotal } Break Footer

Total } Report Footer

Fig. 15-12. Fred sketches the report.

The screen changes to a screen very similar to the Forms screen. It is completely blank except for the prompt *[F3] to list, [ESC] to exit* at the top right part of the screen and the entry area labeled *Expression:* where each variable will be entered.

Fred decides to create three variables. Figure 15-13 shows the screen after the three variables were defined. Fred defined the first variable as follows in the Expression: entry area:

Expression: PAGE = #PAGE

The #PAGE is a special R:base 5000 function that stores the present page number. Fred sets a variable called Page to be equal to that special variable. Likewise Fred uses the special function #DATE and sets it to a variable Date. The last variable that Fred creates is one that he may not use. In case he changes his mind about the way he will display the first and last name and wants to display the names together, he creates a single variable called Name that will be equal to the first and last names together.

When each variable is defined, the type is automatically defined. You only have to define the expression, the name you want to use, and what it equals. For example, if the table contained two columns, Salary and Raise, you could calculate several new variables for the report, such as:

Newsal = Salary + Raise
Raisep = Raise/SalaryX100

to calculate the new salary and the raise percentage. Any proper mathematical expressions can be defined in the variable list.

The next step is to define the page header. A *page header* is a header that belongs on the top of every page. There are also *report headers* that only appear at the top of the first page. Fred does not need any report headers, so he will start by defining his page header. There really isn't any order you need to know when you are defining header text on the report form. Later, after all your text and output areas are defined (just like the data input form), you will tell R:base where the different types of headers are through a process known as *marking*.

After you leave the Define screen by pressing <ESC>, you will return to the REPORTS main menu. After you define the variables, the menu in the center of

```
                                              [F3] to list, [ESC] to exit
  Expression:

    1:INTEGER : PAGE     = #PAGE
    2:DATE    : DATE     = #DATE
    3:TEXT    : NAME     = FSTNAME  & LASTNAME
```

Fig. 15-13. Fred defines the variables.

Table 15-2. Cursor Movement Keys in the REPORT Command.

Key	Definition
→	Moves the cursor right one space.
←	Moves the cursor left one space.
↑	Moves the cursor up one line.
↓	Moves the cursor down one line.
Ctrl->	Moves the cursor to column 131 (the rightmost column).
Ctrl-<	Moves the cursor to column 1 (the leftmost column).
PgUp	Moves the cursor up 20 lines.
PgDn	Moves the cursor down 20 lines.
Tab	Moves the cursor right 10 spaces.
Shift Tab	Moves the cursor left 10 spaces.
Ins	Inserts a space at the cursor position.
Del	Deletes the character at the cursor position.
F1	Inserts a blank line at the cursor position.
F2	Deletes the line at the cursor position.
F3	Displays the column names and variables.
F10	Displays an online help screen.
Esc	Exists from editing.

the screen disappears, and only the top menu remains. You will then always see your report form unless you are defining variables or choosing from other menus.

The Edit Report Screen

You will choose *Edit report* to enter text into the form screen. After you choose *Edit report*, you are placed in a blank screen except for the messages at the top right side of the screen:

```
< 2, 1>  [F3] to list, [ESC] to exit
```

The <2, 1> tells you that the cursor is on the location line 2, column 1 of the screen. As you move the cursor, the cursor locator will move to tell you its location. You can move the cursor anywhere on the screen. Because Forms let you move about the screen, there are some keys you should understand. They are shown in Table 15-2.

Figure 15-14 shows the screen after Fred enters some header text. There is little difference between entering text in a report form and in a data entry form. The text that has been entered gives a blueprint to where the report data will go. This placement will be defined next with the *Locate* option.

The text **Page No.:** was entered at the top left to help display the page number on each page. Without this text, when the page number was displayed there would be a number in the middle of nowhere. The text is entered solely as a guide to the location of the output data. Notice there is no text for the Date variable. The date needs no explanation on the output report. Everyone will recognize the date for what it is.

The other header text consists of the title of the report and the column headers.

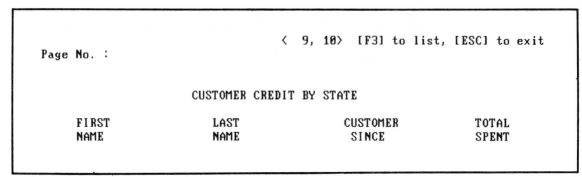

<   9, 10> [F3] to list, [ESC] to exit

Page No. :

CUSTOMER CREDIT BY STATE

FIRST   LAST   CUSTOMER   TOTAL
NAME   NAME   SINCE   SPENT

Fig. 15-14. Fred defines the page headers.

Notice how the headers can be totally customized and placed in a two-line format, giving you complete control over output. The word **FIRST** appears above **NAME**, taking up two lines. The SELECT command can only display the column name as a header.

You can move freely as you enter the text in the report form. You can even insert and delete lines by using the first two function keys. A complete list of the cursor movement keys appear in Table 15-2.

The Locate Screen

After the text is defined, the next step is to mark the location of the columns and variables. After pressing <ESC> to leave the *Edit report* screen, you would choose the *Locate* option.

The *Locate* option is used to position the column entry areas on the form. A menu appears at the top of the screen:

----Locate----Relocate----Help-----Quit--------------------

You will choose *Locate* to position the start and end areas of the output form for each variable or column. Once you have defined the location of these areas, you must choose *Relocate* to make changes.

R:base 5000 will prompt you to move the cursor on the entry form to the area to which you want to enter the data. You are asked to put an **S** for start at the beginning of the entry area and an **E** at the end of the area. You must mark the beginning and end of each column in your data entry screen.

When you first choose *Locate*, the following message appears at the top of the screen:

Enter column name or variable:

R:base wants to know what column or variable you are going to define first. The <F3> function key will display a list of the columns in your table. (See Fig. 15-5.) Once you have seen your columns, press <ESC> to return to the Report Form menu.

Pressing <F3> will display a list of all the columns in the Custcrdt table and the variables you have defined separately. This list will always tell you what you need to know to enter your column or variable names.

The first variable to locate is the Page variable. You will see the following message after you enter Page:

Enter column name: PAGE

The message then changes to:

Move cursor to start location and press [S]

Move the cursor to the space to the right of **Page No.:** and enter an S. The message then changes to:

Move cursor to end location and press [E]

You can enter the **E** any number of positions to the right of the **S** as long as it is not longer than the column length you entered when you created the table. A text field that has a length of 15 can have a distance between the **S** and the **E** of anywhere from 1 to 15 characters.

You will repeat this process for all of the columns and variables you want on the report form. Usually you want all of them on the report from. When you are finished, press <ESC> to return to the *Locate* menu.

Figure 15-16 shows all of the columns and areas defined in the report form. No-

```
                                        [ESC] to return to REPORT definition
Report: CUSTREPT    Table: CUSTCRDT

Variables:

 1:INTEGER : PAGE     = #PAGE
 2:DATE    : DATE     = #DATE
 3:TEXT    : NAME     = FSTNAME   & LASTNAME

Columns:

    # Name      Type      Length

    1 LASTNAME  TEXT      10 characters
    2 FSTNAME   TEXT      10 characters
    3 STATE     TEXT       2 characters
    4 SINCE     INTEGER    1 value(s)
    5 BUY85     TEXT       1 characters
    6 AMOUNT    DOLLAR     1 value(s)
```

Fig. 15-15. Columns and variables list in a report form.

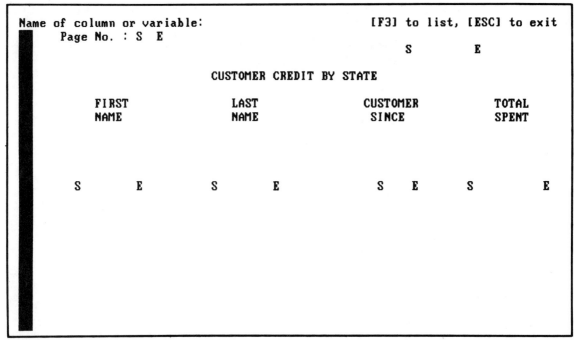

Fig. 15-16. Locating the columns and variables.

tice the **S** and the **E** for **Date** just below the prompt at the top right of the screen. There is no text associated with this location.

The Mark Screen

After returning to the Locate menu, you can choose *Quit* to return to the main menu. The last procedure involves marking the form. You might notice that there has been a vertical stripe on the left side of the form. This is there for a very important reason. When Fred created his sketch of the different parts of the form, he was actually marking the form. There are several different marks for the different areas. Table 15-3 shows a chart of the different marks that might be necessary in a report.

Table 15-3. The Types of Marks.

Mark	Type	Description
HR	Report heading:	Appears on the first page of the report only.
HP	Page heading:	Appears once at the top of each page in the report.
H1	Break heading:	Appears at the top of each subtotal break.
D	Detail:	Data printed once for each row within a subtotal section.
F1	Break footing:	Footing displayed at the bottom of each subtotal break.
FP	Page footing:	Footing printed once at the bottom of each page.
FR	Report footing:	Footing displayed once at the end of the entire report.

Headers go at the beginning of something, while footers go at the end of something. Report headers would appear only once, at the very top of the report. A report header could be an entire title page or even a single line heading at the beginning of the report. Report footers are traditionally grand totals. You could, however, have a credits or summary page after your detail records, which would be a report footer.

A *page heading* is the heading or lines that appear at the top of each and every page. These include the title, date, page number, and column headers. Most reports have many lines of page headers. Page footers are used much less frequently. They are used for page totals or notes that must appear on the bottom of each page. Page numbers can also appear at the bottom of each page rather than the top. In those cases, the page number would be a page footer.

Break headers and footers are actually part of the detail records. The detail records themselves determine when the break headers and footers are used. A *break* is the beginning or end of a logical grouping of data. If your data is sorted by state, you might want to see totals for each state. The total is called a *break footer*. The header that tells what state you are processing is the *break header*. In R:base 5000 you can have up to 10 break headers and footers, numbered H1 through H10 for the break headers and F1 through F10 for the break footers. Break footers are traditionally used for subtotals. If you are processing a lot of hierarchical (grouped) data such as Year, Company, Dept, Partno, and Qty, you might want individual breaks on quantity for the part numbers for the first three fields mentioned. The H1 and F1 would be Year, H2 and F2 for Company, and H3 and F3 for Dept.

To place marks on the form you must choose *Mark* from the main REPORTS menu. This choice will display the Mark menu (Fig. 15-17).

The Mark menu has seven choices that let you mark the headers and footers at the report, page, and break levels, mark the detail lines, list the various settings defined, get help, and quit back to the main REPORTS menu.

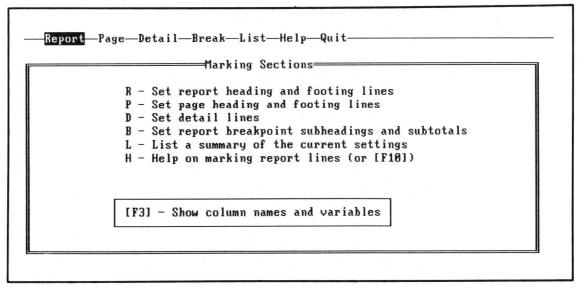

```
──Report──Page──Detail──Break──List──Help──Quit────────────────────

        ╞══════════════════Marking Sections══════════════════╡
        │                                                      │
        │    R - Set report heading and footing lines          │
        │    P - Set page heading and footing lines            │
        │    D - Set detail lines                              │
        │    B - Set report breakpoint subheadings and subtotals│
        │    L - List a summary of the current settings        │
        │    H - Help on marking report lines (or [F10])       │
        │                                                      │
        │    ┌──────────────────────────────────────────┐     │
        │    │ [F3] - Show column names and variables    │     │
        │    └──────────────────────────────────────────┘     │
        │                                                      │
```

Fig. 15-17. The Mark menu.

When you choose any of the header and footer choices, you are asked a series of questions. For example, if you choose *Report* to mark report headers and footers, you are asked the following questions:

```
Do you want to remove the initial carriage return[NO]?
Page eject before report[NO]?
Page eject after report heading[NO]?
Page eject before report footing[NO]?
Page eject after report footing[NO]?
```

These questions enable you to control the page ejects at various places. If you are creating a one-line report header for the very top of the first page, you don't want a page eject after the report heading. However, if your report heading is a separate title page, you would. The same is true for a report footing. If you are creating a one-line grand total, you want it at the end of the last page, not on a separate page. The default for all of these questions is *no*, and that is chosen by simply pressing <Enter>.

Choosing *Page* doesn't ask you about page breaks, but rather the resetting of variables. You might create a variable that continually adds up the amounts of whatever you are reporting. This variable might be set up to continually add the value of Amount to the variable. When you are calculating any type of totals you must set up this type of variable, called a *SUM OF* variable. This variable will be explained later in this section. If you are using this variable to display page totals, you would want to zero out the variable after each page footer displays the page total. A simple menu lets you add the name of each variable to the internal list of page break variables to reset.

When you choose *Break* to set any detail breaks you might have, you are also asked a series of questions:

```
Do you want to manually reset break variables[NO]?
Break number, 1- 2[2]?
Break column or variable:
Page eject before break heading[No]
--Add--Delete--Quit----------Variables to reset after break
```

Because you can create up to ten different breaks in a report, you can only work with one at a time. The questions let you control when to reset the breaks for totals, which break number to work with, the name of the variable or column to be used in the break, and whether or not there should be a page eject before each new break. For example, you would want a page eject if you want each State on a new page.

You can then define the name of any variables to reset after each break if you are not manually resetting the variables. As with page breaks, these are usually SUM OF variables.

If you choose *Detail*, there are no questions to answer. You simply mark the detail line(s).

Figure 15-18 shows the screen after the page headers and the detail line have been marked. Those two items are all Fred defines so far. He wants to test his re-

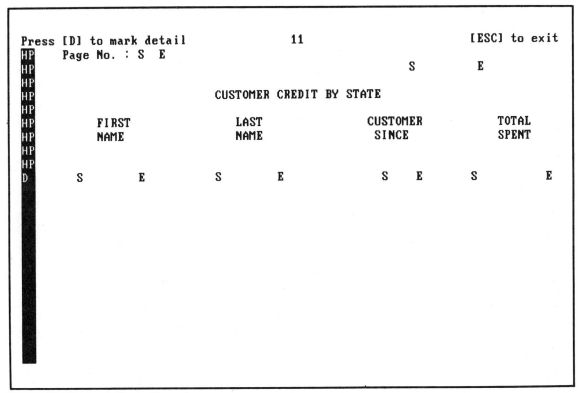

Fig. 15-18. The report form with marks.

port before he enters the total variables and detail breaks. The report he will produce will simply show the data with the titles and columns he has so far defined.

After answering the questions for whatever option you choose, you are placed in the Report Form in the vertical border and asked to mark the lines you want. A sample prompt for a page header would look like the following:

Press [H] to mark page heading

If you are marking report headers or footers, you are asked to place an **H** where you want any report headers. As you place an **H** in each row you want, the row mark automatically is displayed as **HR**. When you press <ESC> after you are through entering any report headers, you can then enter the report footers in the same way. As you place an **F** in each row you want, the row mark automatically is displayed as **FR** for the row footers.

The page headers work in exactly the same way, except as you press the **H** and **F**, they are displayed as **HP** and **FP**. The break headers and footers are slightly different. You will only enter one break at a time. As you enter the break headers and footers, they are displayed as **H** and **F**, followed by a number. The header and footer for the first set of breaks are displayed as **H1** and **F1** respectively. Detail lines are displayed and entered with a **D**.

Just because you have only created one detail line, don't think that only one line will print. The detail line tells every line to print in the table as selected by any WHERE clause in the PRINT command.

Summary

To create a report form requires four separate steps: creating any calculated variables, editing the text on the screen, locating the columns and variables, and marking the sections. Once you have created the form, it can be used in many ways.

USING THE REPORT FORM

The simplest way to use the report form is with the PRINT command. You may use this command after you return to the R:base command mode by using the <ESC> key and the *Quit* option from the main Report menu. The command PRINT Custrept will print the report shown in Fig. 15-19. The data is printed in the same order as it appears in the table.

The PRINT Command can also be used with the SORTED BY and the WHERE clause, as shown in Fig. 15-20. You do not have to specify a table with the PRINT command because the PRINT command uses the table specified when creating the

```
R>PRINT CUSTREPT
    Page No. :     1
                                                01/05/86

                    CUSTOMER CREDIT BY STATE

          FIRST              LAST            CUSTOMER            TOTAL
          NAME               NAME             SINCE              SPENT


        JOHN               SMITH              1981           $2,356.00
        BILL               JONES              1979          $21,533.00
        ROBERT             SMITH              1980               $0.00
        PHIL               ROBERTS            1975             $423.12
        LARRY              CHARLES            1973          $18,435.00
        SEYMOUR            CLARK              1983               $0.00
        KIRK               SMITH              1983          $12,456.34
        SUE                YOUNG              1971             $123.40
        GEORGE             JOHNSON            1976           $7,685.00
        HENRY              MITCHELL           1976          $34,567.00
        JOHN               YORK               1984          $54,324.00
        MARK               BATES              1973           $2,345.00
        GEORGE             JAMES              1980           $1,798.98
        JOE                SHERRI             1978              $23.00
    R>
```

Fig. 15-19. The PRINT command.

```
R>PRINT CUSTREPT SORTED BY AMOUNT WHERE STATE = CT
    Page No. :    1
                                              01/05/86

                  CUSTOMER CREDIT BY STATE

          FIRST           LAST          CUSTOMER        TOTAL
          NAME            NAME          SINCE           SPENT


          SEYMOUR         CLARK         1983              $0.00
          JOE             SHERRI        1978             $23.00
          PHIL            ROBERTS       1975            $423.12
          GEORGE          JAMES         1980          $1,798.98
          LARRY           CHARLES       1973         $18,435.00
          BILL            JONES         1979         $21,533.00
          HENRY           MITCHELL      1976         $34,567.00
          JOHN            YORK          1984         $54,324.00
    R>
```

Fig. 15-20. The PRINT command with SORTED BY and WHERE.

report form. In Fig. 15-20 only those records from Connecticut are printed on the report.

CREATING BREAKS AND TOTALS

This simple report doesn't do much more than the SELECT command. The greatest use of the REPORTS command is the ability to create breaks with subtotals and totals. The first step is, again, to define any variables needed for the report. Figure 15-21 shows the variables needed for the final report.

Two new variables have been added: SUBTOTAL and TOTAL. Like any variable, you can call them anything you want. Obviously, if you have more than one break, you will need to create some more unique names than these. Each of these

```
                                        [F3] to list, [ESC] to exit
  Expression:

  1:INTEGER : PAGE      = #PAGE
  2:DATE    : DATE      = #DATE
  3:TEXT    : NAME      = FSTNAME   & LASTNAME
  4:DOLLAR  : SUBTOTAL  = SUM       OF AMOUNT
  5:DOLLAR  : TOTAL     = SUM       OF AMOUNT
```

Fig. 15-21. Variables list for the CUSTREPT.

variables use the SUM OF notation to tell R:base 5000 to continue to sum the AMOUNT variable.

Notice that they both are summing the AMOUNT variable. The reason is that the SUBTOTAL variable will be *reset* after each break; that is, set back to 0. You don't want the report variable TOTAL reset; so it must be a different variable name. Any numeric variable may be used in the SUM OF. After you have created the variables you need, you must then go through the other three steps:

☐ Edit the text in the form for any changes.
☐ Locate the new columns and variables.
☐ Mark the types of lines.

Figure 15-22 shows the form after these steps have been performed. Text has been added to show the break and the report footer. The word **STATE:** appears above the detail line. The location is also marked and will be where the state will be placed. This will be the break header and will display the group header for each state. Notice that there are three H1 lines; this will allow a space to be skipped before and after the break header.

The break footer, labeled F1, takes two lines. An underline has been placed after the detail line to tell R:base to place an underline at the end of each group. The second break footer line is the subtotal. The text **SUBTOTAL** is entered. The vari-

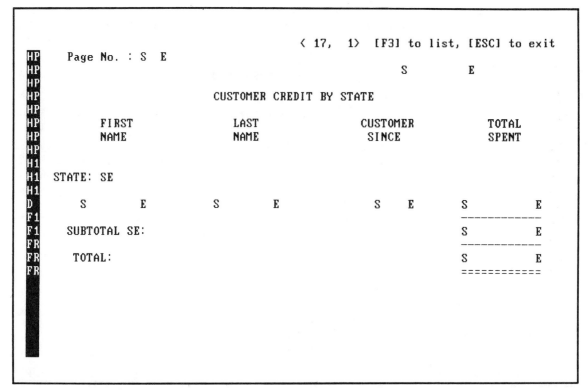

Fig. 15-22. The report screen in its final form.

```
                                                    Any key to continue

Report: Heading    [NOT] marked    [NO] eject before    [NO] eject after
        Footing    [   ] marked    [NO] eject before    [NO] eject after

Page:   Heading    [   ] marked       0 reset variables
        Footing    [NOT] marked

Detail:            [   ] marked


Break #  Column or   Heading   Footing   Eject   # of reset
         variable    marked    marked            variables
-------  ----------  -------   -------   -----   ----------
   1     STATE         yes       yes      no         1
```

Fig. 15-23. The Mark menu List screen.

able STATE was also located after the text to print out the name of the state in the footer as well as the header. There is no reason that you can't use the same variable or column more than once in the report.

The SUBTOTAL variable is located in the Total Spent column to print the subtotal of each group. The variable SUBTOTAL was also added to the list of variables to reset after each break.

Finally a report footer was entered at the bottom, signified by the code **FR**. An underline is placed after the break or subtotal. The variable TOTAL is located in the column, and text is added at the beginning of the line to let you know that the value displayed is the total. A double underline finishes the report.

The Mark menu has an option called *List* to list the options defined. Figure 15-23 displays this screen after the report form in Fig. 15-22 has been created.

This screen lists the options you have defined. It tells you that the report heading is not marked, but the report footing is, and there are no ejects before or after. There is a page heading with no reset variables because the heading is only used for text. There is a detail line and one break field. The break field is STATE, it has both a heading and footing and one variable (SUBTOTAL) to reset after each break. This screen can be very valuable as your reports get complicated.

OUTPUTTING TO A PRINTER OR FILE

Printing this report is the same as printing the last report. Because of the breaks, however, the report will not fit on one screen. Instead of viewing it on the screen, it may be better to see it on the printer.

The OUTPUT command lets you redirect output before printing it. The command:

R> OUTPUT PRINTER

sends output to the printer. There is also the command:

```
R> OUTPUT SCREEN
```

to send it to the screen. This command is the default for all output.

You can also use the OUTPUT command with a valid file name and optional drive and directory to send the output to a disk file. The command:

```
R> OUTPUT B:\1985\REPORTS\CUST.RPT
```

would send the report to the 1985 \ REPORTS directory on the B drive to the file Cust.rpt. The file name may be any legal DOS filename.

You can also send the output to more than one device at a time. Using the OUTPUT command, you specify a primary device and then secondary devices. The command:

```
R> OUTPUT PRINTER WITH SCREEN
```

or

```
R> OUTPUT SCREEN WITH PRINTER
```

will send the report to the printer and the screen.

You can send a report (or any output) to all three devices simultaneously with the command:

```
R> OUTPUT CUST.RPT WITH BOTH
```

The phrase *BOTH* means the screen and the printer.

You can also use the word *TERMINAL* in place of the word *SCREEN*. If you send output to the printer or a file, remember to reset the output to the screen alone to see your messages and prompts after you have printed your report. You can reset the device with the command:

```
R> OUTPUT SCREEN
```

Figure 15-24 shows the result of the following two commands.

```
R> OUTPUT PRINTER
R> PRINT CUSTREPT
```

CREATING FORM LETTERS FROM MULTIPLE TABLES

So far you have seen how to create a very simple report. A more complicated report would use columns from different tables. In this section you will see the creation and printing of a form letter, typically known as *mail merging*.

First the variables that will be needed in the report are created. These are shown

                                                02/09/86

                    CUSTOMER CREDIT BY STATE

         FIRST   LAST   CUSTOMER   TOTAL
         NAME   NAME   SINCE   SPENT

STATE: CT

     LARRY   CHARLES   1973 $18,435.00
     BILL   JONES   1979 $21,533.00
     JOHN   YORK   1984 $54,324.00
     PHIL   ROBERTS   1975 $423.12
     GEORGE   JAMES   1980 $1,798.98
     SEYMOUR   CLARK   1983 $0.00
     HENRY   MITCHELL   1976 $34,567.00
     JOE   SHERRI   1978 $23.00

     SUBTOTAL CT: $131,104.10

STATE: MA

     KIRK   SMITH   1983 $12,456.34
     JOHN   SMITH   1981 $2,356.00
     SUE   YOUNG   1971 $123.40
     MARK   BATES   1973 $2,345.00

     SUBTOTAL MA: $17,280.74

STATE: MI

     GEORGE   JOHNSON   1976 $7,685.00

     SUBTOTAL MI: $7,685.00

STATE: NJ

     ROBERT   SMITH   1980 $0.00

     SUBTOTAL NJ: $0.00

     TOTAL: $156,069.84
                                                        =============

Fig. 15-24. The printed report.

in Fig. 15-25. As you can see, this report form is called Credltr and uses the table Custcrdt. There are five variables defined. NAME is defined as the first name concatenated to the last name.

The fifth variable, CREDIT, is equal to 10 percent (Amount X .1) of the amount spent in the current period. These two variables are calculated from columns in the Custcrdt table.

```
                                      [ESC] to return to variable definition
  Report: CREDLTR     Table: CUSTCRDT

  Variables:

  1:TEXT      : NAME     = FSTNAME  & LASTNAME
  2:TEXT      : STREET   = STREET   IN CUSTOMER WHERE FSTNAME = FSTNAME AND
                            LASTNAME = LASTNAME
  3:TEXT      : CITY     = CITY     IN CUSTOMER WHERE FSTNAME = FSTNAME AND
                            LASTNAME = LASTNAME
  4:TEXT      : ZIPCODE  = ZIPCODE  IN CUSTOMER WHERE FSTNAME = FSTNAME AND
                            LASTNAME = LASTNAME
  5:DOLLAR    : CREDIT   = AMOUNT   X .1

  Columns:

      # Name       Type      Length

      1 LASTNAME  TEXT       10 characters
      2 FSTNAME   TEXT       10 characters
      3 STATE     TEXT        2 characters
      4 SINCE     INTEGER     1 value(s)
      5 BUY85     TEXT        1 characters
      6 AMOUNT    DOLLAR      1 value(s)
```

Fig. 15-25. Creating variables.

The other three variables—STREET, CITY, and ZIP—are taken from the Customer table because they do not exist on the Custcrdt file and are needed for the report.

The name of the variable created (which is also STREET) can be anything you want. The notation **Street in Customer** tells the report to get the value of the column Street from the Customer table. However, how does R:base know which row to get the values from? You must provide a unique combination using a WHERE condition for R:base to understand which row to use.

The clause:

WHERE FSTNAME = FSTNAME AND LASTNAME = LASTNAME

tells R:base to find the row in the Customer table where the first name and last name of the Custcrdt table are the same as the first name and last name in the Customer table. Assuming that there are no people with the same name, R:base will correctly identify the row.

You may use any columns in the main table and any other table to create the variables needed for the report.

The marked report form is shown in Fig. 15-26. The top half of the form is defined as being a large page header. The locations that have no text markings con-

178

```
Press [F] to mark page footing              1                    [ESC] to exit
HP  S                        E
HP  S                        E
HP  S                        E
HP  SE  S            E
HP
HP
HP  Dear  S                              E
HP
HP
FP      Thank you very much for shopping with us at ABC Corporation this
FP  year. We know that you have been a customer since S  E and we want
FP  to reward this patronage very much.
FP
FP      Based on the amount you have spent this year or still owe from last
FP  year we are giving you a merchandise credit of 10% of that amount. Our
FP  records indicate that you have spent S       E in our store. Your credit
FP  appears below.
FP
FP      Thanks again,
FP
FP      Albert B. Chisolm
FP      President, ABC Corporation
FP                                  Total Credit: S              E
```

Fig. 15-26. A mailing list report form.

```
JOHN SMITH
PILGRIM WAY
PLYMOUTH
MA    05634

Dear  JOHN SMITH


    Thank you very much for shopping with us at ABC Corporation this
year. We know that you have been a customer since 1981 and we want
to reward this patronage very much.

    Based on the amount you have spent this year or still owe from last
year we are giving you a merchandise credit of 10% of that amount. Our
records indicate that you have spent  2,356.00 in our store. Your credit
appears below.

    Thanks again,

    Albert B. Chisolm
    President, ABC Corporation
                              Total Credit:        $235.60
```

Fig. 15-27. A mailing list letter.

tain the variables NAME, STREET, and CITY, the column from the Custcrdt table, State; and then the variable ZIP. The text **Dear** precedes the variable NAME, which is used again.

The body of the letter and the salutation is a large page footer. Each page is a new letter, and that is the reason for the page headers being used.

In the body of the letter, which is primarily text, there are some located variables and columns. In the second line of the body of the letter is the column variable SINCE to be placed after the word *since*. The next to the last line in the body of the letter uses the column Amount to tell the customer how much has been spent. At the very bottom of the letter, the variable CREDIT is used to tell the amount of the merchandise credit.

When this report is printed, the located variables and columns are all filled in. The first page of the report (there will be as many pages as there are rows in the Custcrdt table) is shown in Fig. 15-27.

Chapter 16

Data Relations

So far you have learned about using one table at a time. You have examined a customer table used to store such things as name, address, and telephone number. You also examined a table that contained the customers' names and some history about their buying levels and longevity. These could easily be seen in a single table.

DATA REDUNDANCY

What about a file of customer purchases, though? A record could consist of the well-described items shown in Fig. 16-1. What is shown here is a symbolic record, which has a customer name and address information, along with shipping information. The record has 12 items on the order.

Can this be implemented with a relational database manager such as R:base 5000? Of course, but you would not do it in this way. Having this type of record would:

☐ Require every record to have 12 different Quantity, Item Number, List Price, Discount, Netprice, and Amount fields whether there were 12 items on the order or 1.
☐ Limit the record to 12 items. If the order had 20 items, you would have to split it up.
☐ How would you query a record of this type? Each quantity, item number, etc., would have different field names.

The way you can implement this type of data structure is with a record for each

```
CUST_NAME
BILL_STREET
BILL_CITY
BILL_STATE
BILL_ZIP
SHIP_STREET
SHIP_CITY
SHIP_STATE
SHIP_ZIP
PHONE
DATE

   QTY              QTY              QTY              QTY
   ITEM_NO          ITEM_NO          ITEM_NO          ITEM_NO
   LIST_PRICE       LIST_PRICE       LIST_PRICE       LIST_PRICE
   DISC             DISC             DISC             DISC
   NET_PRICE        NET_PRICE        NET_PRICE        NET_PRICE
   AMOUNT           AMOUNT           AMOUNT           AMOUNT

   QTY              QTY              QTY              QTY
   ITEM_NO          ITEM_NO          ITEM_NO          ITEM_NO
   LIST_PRICE       LIST_PRICE       LIST_PRICE       LIST_PRICE
   DISC             DISC             DISC             DISC
   NET_PRICE        NET_PRICE        NET_PRICE        NET_PRICE
   AMOUNT           AMOUNT           AMOUNT           AMOUNT

   QTY              QTY              QTY              QTY
   ITEM_NO          ITEM_NO          ITEM_NO          ITEM_NO
   LIST_PRICE       LIST_PRICE       LIST_PRICE       LIST_PRICE
   DISC             DISC             DISC             DISC
   NET_PRICE        NET_PRICE        NET_PRICE        NET_PRICE
   AMOUNT           AMOUNT           AMOUNT           AMOUNT
```

Fig. 16-1. A sample database.

quantity, item number, etc. The record might look like the following:

ORDER_NO
CUST_NAME
BILL_STREET
BILL_CITY
BILL_STATE
BILL_ZIP
SHIP_STREET
SHIP_CITY

```
SHIP_STATE
SHIP_ZIP
PHONE
DATE
QTY
ITEM_NO
LIST_PRICE
DISC
NET_PRICE
AMOUNT
```

There will be a separate record for each item ordered. Notice the new field at the top called Order_No. This is the key. Each record that belongs to the order will have the same order number (along with all the same customer information). With the database structured in this fashion, you can easily query the database to see the items for each order number. If you have only one item in the database, there will be only one record. You have the ability to have an endless (or almost endless) number of items. If there are 75 items, there will be 75 records. This occurrence, however, poses another problem: data redundancy.

Data redundancy occurs when normalization has not taken place. *Normalization* is a fancy term applied to database design and meaning that you have one data field in only one place unless it is the key. You do have a key in your database—Order_No. Each record for a specific order will have the same order number. Look at the beginning of each record: the name, billing and shipping address, telephone number, and date will be the same for each record with the same order number. Only the fields that contain the quantity, item number, discount, and prices will be different. This is data redundancy at its worst.

There is a solution. Through the use of multiple databases, you will see how to transform this record structure into several smaller ones, save much storage space, and eliminate data redundancy.

MULTIPLE DATABASES

Let's first define the present structure. (See Table 16-1.) Each record is 163 characters long. You also have to add 4 bytes because the minimum storage amount for text is four characters, and there are two text items that are only two characters wide. To find the length of a row, you also have to add 6 bytes for any pointers, making the storage value of this record 173 bytes.

If an order has 15 items, it will produce 15 records each 173 characters long. Each record will have the same customer information; only the actual quantity and item information will be different. Looking at these figures, you see that 15 records will create about 38,400 characters to be added to the table. When you realize that the customer information—which includes name, address, telephone number, and order date—need only be entered once, you will realize that, of the 38,400 characters added to the table, 23,040 are redundant (14 × the number of redundant bytes).

The solution is to break up this record into two tables. The first will contain the order number and customer information. The second will contain the order number and order information. (See Table 16-2.)

Now there are two tables. The Customer table will have only one record for

Table 16-1. Database Structure Defined.

ORDER__NO	TEXT	15
CUST__NAME	TEXT	15
BILL__STREET	TEXT	15
BILL__CITY	TEXT	15
BILL__STATE	TEXT	2
BILL__ZIP	TEXT	5
SHIP__STREET	TEXT	15
SHIP__CITY	TEXT	15
SHIP__STATE	TEXT	2
SHIP__ZIP	TEXT	5
PHONE	TEXT	13
DATE	DATE	8
QTY	INTEGER	4
ITEM__NO	TEXT	6
LIST__PRICE	DOLLAR	8
DISC	INTEGER	4
NET__PRICE	DOLLAR	8
AMOUNT	DOLLAR	8
TOTAL		163 bytes

each order, while the Order table will have one record for each item in the order. This solution is the way large applications are designed using relational tables. It allows you to program large applications very efficiently. The next step is to further eliminate redundancy. If there are many repeat customers who will have many

Table 16-2. A Record Broken into Two Tables.

CUSTOMER TABLE		
ORDER-NO	TEXT	15
CUST__NAME	TEXT	15
BILL__STREET	TEXT	15
BILL__CITY	TEXT	15
BILL__STATE	TEXT	2
BILL__ZIP	TEXT	5
SHIP__STREET	TEXT	15
SHIP__CITY	TEXT	15
SHIP__STATE	TEXT	2
SHIP__ZIP	TEXT	5
PHONE	TEXT	13
DATE	DATE	8
TOTAL		125 bytes
ORDER TABLE		
ORDER__NO	TEXT	15
QTY	INTEGER	4
ITEM__NO	TEXT	6
LIST__PRICE	DOLLAR	8
DISC	INTEGER	4
NET__PRICE	DOLLAR	8
AMOUNT	DOLLAR	8
TOTAL		53 bytes

different orders on the table, it would make a lot of sense to have a separate customer file. Also, if you have a lot of records with the customer's name, address, and telephone number and the customer moves, you want to be able to update only one record.

You can create a third table called Customer, while renaming the existing tables Order and Orderitm. This solution would produce Table 16-3.

Let's do some quick analysis. Assuming 15 orders per customer with each order having 15 items, it would take the following amount of space to store the records:

ONE TABLE	TWO TABLES	THREE TABLES
38,400 bytes	16,896 bytes	16,896 bytes

Later you will see how these numbers are precisely calculated.

Let's not stop here. If you analyze the Orderitm table, you can see some redundancies here. The overhead of adding an additional table did not overcome the reduc-

Table 16-3. A Record Broken into Three Tables.

CUSTOMER TABLE		
CUST_NO	TEXT	5
CUST_NAME	TEXT	15
BILL_STREET	TEXT	15
BILL_CITY	TEXT	15
BILL_STATE	TEXT	2
BILL_ZIP	TEXT	5
SHIP_STREET	TEXT	15
SHIP_CITY	TEXT	15
SHIP_STATE	TEXT	2
SHIP_ZIP	TEXT	5
PHONE	TEXT	13
TOTAL		107

ORDER TABLE		
ORDER_NO	TEXT	5
DATE	DATE	8
CUST_NO	TEXT	5
TOTAL		18

ORDERITM TABLE		
ORDER_NO	TEXT	5
QTY	INTEGER	4
ITEM_NO	TEXT	6
LIST_PRICE	DOLLAR	8
DISC	INTEGER	4
NET_PRICE	DOLLAR	8
AMOUNT	DOLLAR	8
TOTAL		43

tion in the number of redundant bytes. However, by going one step further you can eliminate even more bytes.

List_Price can be found on a file. This file could be keyed off of Item_No. Creation of this file will save additional resources.

Another possible reduction in storage space is Net_Price and Amount. These fields are calculated and have no business being on the table. Net_Price is really List_Price × Disc. Amount is really Qty × Net_Price.

Table 16-4. The Final Table Solution.

CUSTOMER TABLE		
CUST_NO	TEXT	5
CUST_NAME	TEXT	15
BILL_STREET	TEXT	15
BILL_CITY	TEXT	15
BILL_STATE	TEXT	2
BILL_ZIP	TEXT	5
SHIP_STREET	TEXT	15
SHIP_CITY	TEXT	15
SHIP_STATE	TEXT	2
SHIP_ZIP	TEXT	5
PHONE	TEXT	13
**TOTAL		107

PRICE TABLE		
ITEM_NO	TEXT	6
LIST_PRICE	DOLLAR	8
TOTAL		14

ORDER TABLE		
ORDER_NO	TEXT	5
DATE	DATE	8
CUST_NO	TEXT	5
TOTAL		18

ORDERITM TABLE		
ORDER_NO	TEXT	5
QTY	INTEGER	4
ITEM_NO	TEXT	6
DISC	INTEGER	4
TOTAL		19

Table 16-5. Number of Orders that Can Be Put on Disks.

# of Tables	360K Diskette	20Mb Hard Disk
ONE TABLE	10 orders	533 orders
TWO TABLES	22 orders	1212 orders
THREE TABLES	22 orders	1212 orders
FOUR TABLES	34 orders	1905 orders

Let's make these changes and see the final table solution. The tables would look like Table 16-4.

Let's do some more analysis. Assuming 15 orders per customer with each order having 15 items that are the same items each time, it would take the following amount of space to store the records:

ONE TABLE	TWO TABLES
38,400 bytes	16,896 bytes

THREE TABLES	FOUR TABLES
16,896 bytes	10,752 bytes

This solution would totally eliminate any redundancies. Notice that the amount of space necessary to store only 15 orders has been reduced from 38,400 characters to 10,752 characters. To put this solution in a better perspective, with a 360K diskette or a 20MB hard disk, you could have the number of orders on a disk shown in Table 16-5.

You can see that the saving from the original design to the final design represents an almost four-fold increase in space saving. The saving in diskettes alone would be worth the few minutes it might take to do a good table analysis.

Chapter 17

Fred and
the Database Design

So far in this section you have seen some examples of how the database commands work in R:base 5000. However, you have not seen any of the databases or tables that Fred must actually create for his application. In this chapter you will actually see Fred create his database and all its tables.

In the *Programming Fundamentals* section of this book, you learned about program design. Throughout Chapters 9 and 10, our small businessman, Fred, defined his problems. As you may remember, Fred wants to computerize his customer lists so he can have a directory at his fingertips. He wants to maintain a mailing list so he can print labels each month to send his monthly Fish Specials circular to his customers. He also wants a customer order system to keep track of his customer's orders to help his shipping department ship the orders and to help his billing department price and bill the orders.

Fred spent a lot of time defining the input data that he would need to produce his reports and forms. Without knowing it, Fred did most of his database design! However, Fred still needs to look at the big picture. Can he design even more flexibility into his programs with the database design? If there are some special ways Fred might want to look at his data with ad-hoc reports, Fred might want to add some fields to his database, even if the defined reports don't need them.

For example, Fred could put a field called Credit into his Customer file. This field would be maintained by Fred as a credit rating. Although Fred is cash on delivery only now, with a computer he could begin to extend credit to some customers. If they always pay their bills, he could put a **1** in the field. If they are always 30 days behind, perhaps a **2**. He could set up the rating system any way he wants. Later, he could look up people that have bad ratings to see how much they buy. A customer who pays only twice a year but buys hundreds of dollars' worth of fish might be worth having as a customer. The restaurant that only buys two lobsters every other month and then pays 6 months later might not be.

When you are designing a database, you should look at all aspects of the database. You should begin by listing all the input files you have so far defined and see if there are any more fields that are necessary. Then check if any fields can be eliminated because of redundancy or because they can be calculated. Check to see if any table can be split by a common key to create a new file or if any new files must be created (apart from keyed files). You should determine your keys for the file. Finally, you should calculate the amount of storage needed for your system before you purchase the hardware. R:base 5000 will run on almost any IBM-compatible system, but you may want to buy a specific system for your own reasons.

FRED DEFINES HIS CUSTOMER TABLE

There is little to do in this section. Fred has done a wonderful job of defining his customer database. In Chapter 9, he used his head and was able to define his customer table almost perfectly. The record structure looked like Table 17-1.

Fred could create his customer table now with R:base 5000, but remember, he must look at the big picture first.

In Chapter 10, Fred looked at the order system. When he decided on his input formats for his order system, he realized the need for a two-table system. He also realized the need for a key to the customer file, which meant rewriting the customer file to include the customer number. Fred discovered that without a customer number he could not tell the difference between John Smith of John's Seafood and John Smith of Smith's Dairy Bar.

Fred decided that it would also be nice to have the customer's business name on the file. As long as he only had to enter it once and could retrieve it at any time by the customer number, he decided that in his automated system he would add the business name.

Fred redefined his customer table to look like Table 17-2. He could enter this table into R:base 5000 now, but Fred knows that he still hasn't finished looking at the big picture. As Fred defines further, there may be more to change.

FRED DEFINES HIS ORDER TABLE

In Chapter 10, Fred defined his order tables. Fred began with the conceptual design in Table 17-3.

Table 17-1. Record Structure of the Customer Table.

Column name	Data type	Size
FNAME	TEXT	20
LNAME	TEXT	20
ADDRESS	TEXT	25
CITY	TEXT	15
STATE	TEXT	2
ZIP	TEXT	10
PHONE	TEXT	13

CUSTOMER TABLE		
Column name	Data type	Size
CUSTNO	TEXT	5
COMPANY	TEXT	20
FNAME	TEXT	20
LNAME	TEXT	20
ADDRESS	TEXT	25
CITY	TEXT	15
STATE	TEXT	2
ZIP	TEXT	10
PHONE	TEXT	13

Table 17-2. Redefined Customer Table.

Fred quickly realized that there were too many columns to enter each time; so he divided the fields into two tables. One of these is the Customer table he had already defined. "Wow," thought Fred. "I am automating already! I can use the Customer table for the orders. It takes me almost 2 hours each night just to write the names and addresses on the shipping forms and order forms. I can't wait until this is done. Elsa and Fred Jr. will be happy too."

Fred redefined his tables as shown in Table 17-4. Fred now has his Order file keyed to the Customer file by the Customer Number. All Fred has to do is enter the customer's number, and the customer information will be retrieved when it is time to print the orders.

The last analysis that Fred performed in Chapter 10 was to realize that he would have many order records in the file for each order number. Although each one must have a quantity, item description, and price, there is no need for each record to also have the customer number and date ordered. In more complex applications there would probably be other information that is only needed once, such as shipping address, customer purchase order number, and shipping method.

Fred realizes that he can save some space with the two-file system described in Chapter 10 of Section I. Fred therefore has divided his order file into two tables, the ORDER table and the Order Items table. (See Table 17-5.)

The Order Table contains only the data needed for each order, while the Order Items table contains only the data needed for each item of the order. Instead of each

Table 17-3. Conceptual Design for the Order Table.

ORDER TABLE		
Column name	Data type	Size
FNAME	TEXT	20
LNAME	TEXT	20
ADDRESS	TEXT	25
CITY	TEXT	15
STATE	TEXT	2
ZIP	TEXT	9
ORDNO	TEXT	5
ORDDATE	DATE	4
QTY	INTEGER	4
ITEM	TEXT	25
PRICE	DOLLAR	8

190

CUSTOMER TABLE		
Column name	Data type	Size
CUSTNO	TEXT	5
COMPANY	TEXT	20
FNAME	TEXT	20
LNAME	TEXT	20
ADDRESS	TEXT	25
CITY	TEXT	15
STATE	TEXT	2
ZIP	TEXT	9
PHONE	TEXT	10
ORDER TABLE		
ORDNO	TEXT	5
CUSTNO	TEXT	5
ORDDATE	DATE	4
QTY	INTEGER	4
ITEM	TEXT	25
PRICE	DOLLAR	8

Table 17-4. Customer and Order Tables Redefined.

record having the extra burden of the customer number and date ordered, there is one record in the Order file for each order, and as many records in the Order Items table as there are items ordered.

FRED REDESIGNS THE ORDER FILES

So far, Fred has done a good job. He has almost normalized his data fully. He is able to analyze what he has done and says: "When I create an order, I will add the main part of the order record to the Order table and each item to the Order Items table. The only table that will be accessed will be the Customer table, and that table is only accessed once for each record. In this way I can add items to the Order table

ORDER TABLE		
Column name	Data type	Size
ORDNO	TEXT	5
CUSTNO	TEXT	5
ORDDATE	DATE	4
ORDER ITEMS TABLE		
ORDNO	TEXT	5
QTY	INTEGER	4
ITEM	TEXT	25
PRICE	DOLLAR	8

Table 17-5. Two-File System for the Order File.

about as fast as I can type. All I have to add is the quantity, item number, and price for each item. I can get the order number for each record from the main Order table."

But wait! Fred is still thinking: "This still doesn't seem right. Why can't I make another table called *Item*? This table can contain all the item descriptions and prices. I wouldn't have to look up the prices each day, since some only change every week as the different boats bring different types of seafood to market. Why not set up a new table with the prices in it? That way we could change those prices that change in the morning, and as the orders come in, the new prices would be put on the orders. A lot of times we don't have the right prices and undercharge or overcharge our customers."

Fred designs the new table as shown in Table 17-6. It is time for Fred to get some help. Do you see what is wrong? Although Fred has made a new database, he didn't use his head. His key is a 25-character field that is actually the item description. Fields like that do not make good keys. They are too long and are often entered incorrectly; they must be reentered when the data entry screen tells the operator *ITEM NOT FOUND*. What about changing the order tables to look like Table 17-7?

Now Fred thinks he has the final Order table design. The Item table is now usable by the order system and can be updated separately. Look at the Order Items database. All that will be stored is the order number, item number, and quantity. What happens if Fred wishes to do some analysis in later weeks? The price that would be retrieved from the Item table would be the present price, instead of the price on the day the order was shipped. Fred realizes this problem and, after taking a nice break for a bowl of Elsa's clam chowder, has an idea. "I will retrieve the price from the Item table when the order is shipped, and then store the price on the Order Items database. That way I will have the price that is correct for that day, and I still won't have to enter it each time I ship an order."

Fred is learning. Sometimes in the ever-changing world of data, you must store

ORDER TABLE		
Column name	Data type	Size
ORDNO	TEXT	5
CUSTNO	TEXT	5
ORDDATE	DATE	4
ORDER ITEMS TABLE		
ORDNO	TEXT	5
QTY	INTEGER	4
ITEM	TEXT	25
ITEM TABLE		
ITEM	TEXT	25
PRICE	DOLLAR	8

Table 17-6. Order File Tables Keyed to Item Description.

ORDER TABLE		
Column name	Data type	Size
ORDNO	TEXT	5
CUSTNO	TEXT	5
ORDDATE	DATE	4
ORDER ITEMS TABLE		
ORDNO	TEXT	5
ITEMNO	TEXT	5
QTY	INTEGER	4
ITEM TABLE		
ITEMNO	TEXT	5
ITEM	TEXT	25
PRICE	DOLLAR	8

Table 17-7. Order File Tables Keyed to Item Number.

something even though it exists somewhere else. There is a difference between when you store data in a master table and in a transaction table. A field like Price changes all the time, and you have to know what you charged the customer that day. If a customer address changes, however, you don't want to send a bill to the old address just because they lived there when they bought your merchandise. If you want to get paid, you must send the bill to the new address. If a customer goes out of business, you might still keep the customer data for a while, or mark that customer by putting **out of business** in the Company Address field.

FRED GETS THE BIG PICTURE

Fred looks at his present database structures. He is trying to get the big picture. He has made two subtle changes. He has increased the size of Phone to 13 characters. He has decided to display and store the telephone number as *(AAA)NNN-NNNN* for easier readability. He has also changed Zip to 10 characters so he can store the 9-character zip codes as *ZZZZZ-ZZZZ*. (See Table 17-8.)

Fred is satisfied. He thinks he is ready to think about the rest of the system. As he thinks, he realizes that he can make one more enhancement to the database and some other new ideas.

Fred thinks aloud. "Ok, I have my Customer file that will be used by both the customer system and the order system, and I have the Item file that will be used by the item system. Am I missing anything? Oh, customer discounts! Each customer gets a discount on his order. Different customers get different discounts. That means that I can add Discount to the main Customer file. When I retrieve the information for an order, I can retrieve that, too. I will have to change my screen design again to input the discount, but at this time that's easy!"

Fred is performing good design analysis. You won't think of everything at once.

CUSTOMER TABLE		
Column name	Data type	Size
CUSTNO	TEXT	5
COMPANY	TEXT	20
FNAME	TEXT	20
LNAME	TEXT	20
ADDRESS	TEXT	25
CITY	TEXT	15
STATE	TEXT	2
ZIP	TEXT	10
PHONE	TEXT	13
ORDER TABLE		
ORDNO	TEXT	5
CUSTNO	TEXT	5
ORDDATE	DATE	4
ORDER ITEMS TABLE		
ORDNO	TEXT	5
ITEMNO	TEXT	5
QTY	INTEGER	4
PRICE	DOLLAR	8
ITEM TABLE		
ITEMNO	TEXT	5
ITEM	TEXT	25
PRICE	DOLLAR	8

Table 17-8. Tables with Two Fields Changed.

Even though this is the final design phase, you may still think of new things. As long as your original design is good, additions are no problem.

FRED REMEMBERS HIS INVENTORY SYSTEM

Fred also thought about two other systems: the inventory system and the employee system. Fred decides that the employee system is totally separate from the rest of his system and can wait until later. The inventory system, however, can use the Item file. Fred decides to design the database now and do the rest of it later.

The inventory system should have the quantity on hand of each item, and the amount Fred orders when the on-hand amount drops below a certain number. Fred thinks quickly and decides that his inventory file will just be a reworking of his Item file. Fred was wondering if he was going to have to design a whole system to keep track of the items, descriptions, and prices. The Customer file is a file used by the order system but is maintained by the customer system, which also uses it. By doing the inventory system now, Fred will catch two fish with one hook (Is that how it goes?). He can add, change, and delete the items in the inventory system along with the other inventory information. He designs it as shown in Table 17-9.

The item number is the key that the Order file uses to retrieve descriptions and prices. The On Hand amount tells the computer what the present inventory is. Fred will use this file to determine when an item is out of stock, rather than checking the warehouse for each order. The system can automatically subtract the amount of an order from the amount on hand, and add to the on-hand amount when new seafood is delivered. The Stock Level is the inventory amount that Fred wishes to maintain. This means that if the Stock Level is 500, then Fred wants to have at least 500 of that item at all times. Stock Level is sometimes called EOQ, or economic order quantity, when it is computed by a scientific method. In Fred's case, he just knows through years of experience. The Order Amount is the amount Fred wants to buy when the On Hand amount drops below the Stock Level. The Order Flag is a logical field to tell the inventory system that an order has been placed for the item.

Fred has designed the inventory system in his head! Each day he will run a program that will run through all the items on the file and place orders for those whose On Hand amount has fallen below the Stock Level. The Order Flag is then "turned on," or changed to **Y**, to indicate that an order has been placed with the fishermen. This step is done just in case the delivery takes a few days. Fred does not want to order the same thing twice!

FRED CALCULATES STORAGE SIZE

Fred's final database design for the system (after all those changes) is shown in Table 17-10. The last step is to determine the storage requirements for the system. Fred estimates the following:

☐ 200 customers in the Customer file.
☐ 300 items in the Item file.
☐ 500 orders per month in the Order file.
☐ 10 items per Order in the Order Items file.

R:base 5000 requires three files on your disk to keep a database.

☐ The first file always contains 9600 bytes and keeps the database description.
☐ The second file contains the data. This file can grow very large, depending on the amount of data you store in it. In order to calculate the storage size for the

Table 17-9. Inventory System File.

ITEM TABLE		
Column name	Data type	Size
ITEMNO	TEXT	5
ITEM	TEXT	25
PRICE	DOLLAR	8
ONHAND	INTEGER	4
STOCKLVL	INTEGER	4
ORDAMT	INTEGER	4
ORDFLAG	TEXT	1

database, you must calculate the size of each table. This is a five-step process for each table.

1. Calculate the total row length of a table. Add 6 bytes for pointers to each row. Text length is the length specified. Minimum length of a text field is 2 bytes. Date, integer, real, and time columns are 4 bytes. Dollar columns are 8 bytes. All column storage is in even 2-byte segments.

2. Divide 1536 by the row length to find #Rows/Block.

3. Estimate the number of rows per table.

4. Divide the number of rows by #Rows/Block to find #Blocks.

5. Multiply #Blocks by 1536.

6. Add the amounts together for all the tables.

CUSTOMER TABLE		
Column name	Data type	Size
CUSTNO	TEXT	5
COMPANY	TEXT	20
FNAME	TEXT	20
LNAME	TEXT	20
ADDRESS	TEXT	25
CITY	TEXT	15
STATE	TEXT	2
ZIP	TEXT	10
PHONE	TEXT	13
DISCOUNT	REAL	4
ORDER TABLE		
ORDNO	TEXT	5
CUSTNO	TEXT	5
ORDDATE	DATE	4
ORDER ITEMS TABLE		
ORDNO	TEXT	5
ITEMNO	TEXT	5
QTY	INTEGER	4
PRICE	DOLLAR	8
ITEM TABLE		
ITEMNO	TEXT	5
ITEM	TEXT	25
PRICE	DOLLAR	8
ONHAND	INTEGER	4
STOCKLVL	INTEGER	4
ORDAMT	INTEGER	4
ORDFLAG	TEXT	1

Table 17-10. Final Database Design.

Table 17-11. Calculations for Storage Requirements of Fredfsh Database.

File 1 - FREDFSH1.RBS			=	9,600
File 2 - FREDFSH2.RBS			=	525,312
Customer Table 200 Customers × 146 bytes/customer	=	29,184b		
Item Table 300 Items × 62 bytes/item	=	18,432b		
Order Table 500 Orders/month × 22 bytes/order × 3 months	=	33,792b		
Order Items Table 10 Items/order × 500 orders/month × 30 bytes/order item × 3 months	=	443,904b		
		525,312b		
File 3 - FREDFSH3.RBS 17000 rows at approximately 20 bytes/row			=	340,000
Total Storage Needed for 3 Months Data				874,912

☐ The last file keeps track of the keys. The average overhead per row because of keys is 10 to 37 bytes per row in this table.

Fred wants to keep the last three months' orders in the order files. Table 17-11's calculations determine storage requirements for the database he will call Fredfsh.

Fred has finished his database design. He calls the local computer stores and each assures him that they have storage medium that will hold 875,000 bytes. Fred's only problem is that they gave him 875,000 different prices and choices, too. Oh, well, if the fish don't byte, Fred will.

In the final section of this book, you will see Fred's entire design again, and you will see Fred program his design. Fred's Fish are moving closer to the computer age!!!

Section III

PROGRAMMING WITH R:base 5000

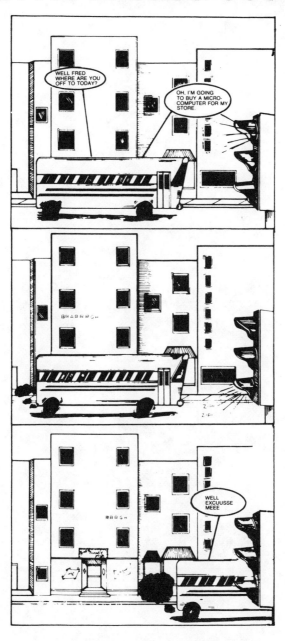

Chapter 18

Reexamining
Fred's Design

In the first two sections of this book, you saw how to go about producing a business design, database design, and programming design. The next step is to begin the actual coding using R:base 5000. A good place to start is to lay out the final design. In the first two sections, the design was scattered throughout several chapters. In Appendix A of this book you can find the design of Fred's Fish Market System in its entirety, as well as all the programs that make up Fred's system.

Many of the techniques shown in this section are abbreviated as they are shown in detail in Section II. Techniques such as creating a database or using the SELECT command are found in Section II. If you are a novice R:base user, read Section II before starting this section.

In this section you will see Fred, our small businessman, as he begins to code his system. Fred will start with the Customer system and the Order system. Fred will save the Inventory and Employee system for you to do.

In this section, you will first learn about the Application EXPRESS and how to create the entire Customer system with EXPRESS. EXPRESS can produce workable code, but unfortunately it cannot produce everything you may want to do. So, you will see how to create the same customized system without EXPRESS.

You will learn how to create several different types of menus, including one that controls other menus and one that controls processes. You will learn how to produce customized input screens, input screens that use several tables, and input screens that take more than one screen. You will learn how to write, add, change, delete, and display programs. You will learn how to use the REPORTS command to produce reports from multiple tables and even learn how to write R:base 5000 code to totally customize output when a report form doesn't do the job.

You may see some small changes in the final design presented in this section of the book and the appendices compared to the design shown in Sections I and II. These changes allow you to see more of the commands of R:base 5000 in the explanations of the program code.

Fred wants to test his programs just as quickly as he writes them. He knows that you cannot test the programs without the database. The first thing Fred wants to do is to create his database and tables. He can add data to them after he creates the program to add data to each module. You should create the database in native R:base 5000 commands or EXPRESS and not from a command procedure (program).

THE CUSTOMER SYSTEM

Fred begins with the Customer system. He knows that the Customer system is designed to print the mailing labels for his circulars and produce a customer directory so he can look up data such as telephone number or discount. The Customer database will also be one of the files needed by his Order system, which he will code after he finishes the Customer system. The Customer system seems the most logical place for Fred to start.

Actually, the real reason is Fred's brother, Frank. After Fred went out and bought a book on how to program and design databases using R:base 5000, Frank was very upset. Fred spent most of the day reading and writing these strange charts. Instead of cutting through the paperwork each day, Fred was creating this huge computer design. Now Fred wants to go and spend 6 months profit on a computer.

Frank says, "Fred, since you bought that book, Elsa and Fred Jr. haven't seen you, I haven't seen you, and the lobsters are beginning to wonder. If you can really save us 6 hours a day then go buy the machine. But if we don't save that time, you and that computer are going into the ocean." Fred has heard enough. He is already on his way to the bus stop.

Fred quickly sets his machine up and is ready to go. He has been practicing on his friend Myron's computer and is all set. Fred decides to start with the database. He knows that he can't test his programs until the data is set up. Fred begins

CUSTOMER TABLE		
Fieldname	Data Type	Length
CUSTNO	TEXT	5
COMPANY	TEXT	20
FSTNAME	TEXT	20
LSTNAME	TEXT	20
ADDRESS	TEXT	25
CITY	TEXT	15
STATE	TEXT	2
ZIP	TEXT	9
PHONE	TEXT	13
DISCOUNT	REAL	2

Table 18-1. Fred's Customer Table.

```
                        Application EXPRESS
        Copyright (c) 1985 by Microrim, Inc. (Ver. 1.01 PC-DOS)

        ═══════════Select option - [F10] for help═══════════
         (1)  Define a new database
         (2)  Change an existing database definition
         (3)  Define a new application
         (4)  Change an existing application
         (5)  Display file directory
         (6)  Exit
```

Fig. 18-1. The Application EXPRESS main menu.

by reviewing his Customer file design, starting R:base 5000, and creating his Customer table (see Table 18-1).

Creating the Database

Fred's Customer database is ready to be typed in. All the fields he has defined in his reports as well as those needed by other programs, such as the discount field used by the Order program, are there. Fred starts R:base 5000 and creates the Customer database.

There are two ways to create a database. The first is to use the Application EXPRESS, and the other is to enter commands such as DEFINE, TABLES, and COLUMNS that let you create a database.

If you like using menus, it is much easier to use EXPRESS. Also, you can make changes, such as inserting or deleting columns or changing their specification if you make a mistake. Figure 18-1 shows the EXPRESS main menu.

Application EXPRESS is used for several tasks:

☐ Defining or changing a database definition.
☐ Defining or changing an entire application.
☐ Displaying a file directory.
☐ Exiting back to the DOS or R:base menu.

You would choose the first option, *Define a new database*, to create your database structure. R:base 5000 will ask you for the database name. You must provide a name for R:base 5000 to use to store the database on your diskette.

Fred is very proud of his fish market. Although Frank would like to change the name to *Frank's Fish Market*, Fred owns 51 percent of the company and never will change the name. So, Fred decides to name his database Fredfsh. Remember, he could use only seven characters because R:base adds a character to the name for the DOS file names.

The R:base 5000 prompt looks like the following after Fred enters his name:

Enter your database name (1-7 characters) FREDFSH

After you create an R:base 5000 database, you will see three files on your disk that begin with the characters you used to name the database. The last character will be a one, two, and three, respectively, followed by the DOS file extension rbs. For example, if you create a database called Fredfsh, you would find on your disk:

```
FREDFSH1.RBS
FREDFSH2.RBS
FREDFSH3.RBS
```

R:base has added the numbers and file extensions to the name that you gave the database. This is the reason that database names can only be seven characters long. With the addition of the extra character, you reach the DOS file name maximum of eight characters. The rbs extension identifies the file as an R:base database to R:base 5000.

R:base creates three different files on your disk in order to better manage your data. The file with the **1** in it contains the database structure definition (the data dictionary) and the location of the data. The file with the **2** in it contains the data itself, and the file with the **3** in it contains the index for the key columns.

Naming a Table and Columns

After naming the database, you can begin to name your table and its columns. EXPRESS gives you a screen that enables you to move around freely entering your columns. First you must enter your table name. Figure 18-2 shows the table name already entered as Customer. When the screen first appeared, it was blank. The message:

```
Enter the name for this table
```

was displayed at the top of the screen. The cursor highlight was in the table name area.

After the table name is entered, you can begin entering the column definitions. You can always change the table name by pressing <PgUp>. This key will move the cursor to the table name block and let you change the name.

R:base 5000 is then ready for you to describe the table. You will be asked to enter three items for each column. Each column must have a name, type, and width.

Fred has already entered all his columns. First, he entered a column name. The first column has been named Custno.

As soon as the column name is entered, the middle of the screen changes. A menu is displayed to let you choose the proper data type for the column. One of the six choices must be chosen.

If you choose Text as your datatype, you will also be asked to enter the length. You should type a number from 1 to 1500, the maximum length of the text field. The other data types do not need to have their lengths specified.

After you enter each column's name, type, and for text fields the width, you can change columns you have already defined by using the cursor keys to move between the field names. By pressing <Return> when you are on a column name, you can change the column type if you want.

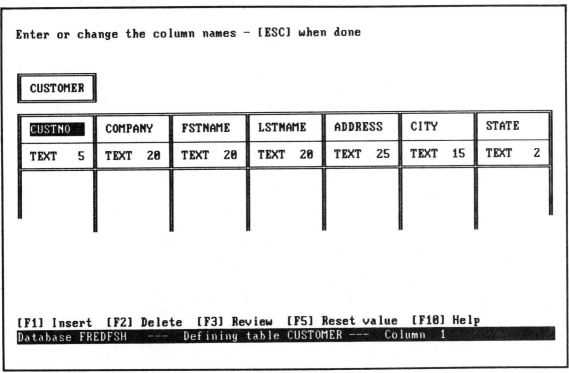

Enter or change the column names - [ESC] when done

CUSTOMER						
CUSTNO	COMPANY	FSTNAME	LSTNAME	ADDRESS	CITY	STATE
TEXT 5	TEXT 20	TEXT 20	TEXT 20	TEXT 25	TEXT 15	TEXT 2

[F1] Insert [F2] Delete [F3] Review [F5] Reset value [F10] Help

Database FREDFSH --- Defining table CUSTOMER --- Column 1

Fig. 18-2. The EXPRESS Define Table screen.

Figure 18-2 shows the complete database. There are ten columns defined. As you can see, only the first seven are shown. You must scroll to the left or right to see more columns.

If your table contains more than seven columns, you will need to use your cursor keys to see them all. You can only see seven columns at a time. Pressing the <Home> and <End> keys will take you quickly to the first or the last columns, respectively, that you have defined. This is a fast way to move between your fields.

The Order Tables

Fred now decides to define the rest of his tables. He will create the Order tables. He looks up his design for the order tables. (See Table 18-2.)

These are Fred's databases for the Order program. Just because the Order Items database will contain multiple records for each order number does not mean that anything in the creation of the databases is different.

Once you create a table with EXPRESS, you then have to select the option *Change an existing database definition* from the main EXPRESS menu. You are then presented with the *Select table Option* menu, as shown in Fig. 18-3. To add a new table you would select the first option, *Add a new table to the database*.

A new, blank table will appear on the screen, and you can begin entering your next table. The Order tables will be created exactly the same as the Customer database. Figure 18-4 shows the Order tables being created.

ORDER TABLE		
Column name	Data type	Size
ORDNO	TEXT	5
CUSTNO	TEXT	5
ORDDATE	DATE	4
ORDER ITEMS TABLE		
ORDNO	TEXT	5
ITEMNO	TEXT	25
QTY	INTEGER	4
PRICE	DOLLAR	8

Table 18-2. Order Table Design.

Fred has created the two order tables. He has called the main table Order and the order items table Orderitm. He decides to create just one more table at this time. The Item table is needed by the Order program. Even though he doesn't plan to write that program now, he will need it in order to test the Order program.

The design for the Item table that Fred designed in Chapter 17 looked like Table 18-3.

Building the Keys

The last thing to do for these tables is to set up the index keys. There will be at least one index in each table: Customer Number in the Customer and Order tables, Order Number in the Order and Order Items table, and Item Number in the Order and Item table.

That's all there is to it. Whenever a record is added to the tables, it will automatically be keyed by the key field. It doesn't matter that there are no records in the table yet; R:base 5000 only sets up the initial pointers.

To build the keys for the tables, you would use the following R:base 5000 commands from the native R:base 5000 command mode.

Building keys into a table is very simple operation. The command:

```
R> BUILD KEY FOR CUSTNO IN CUSTOMER
```

will set up a key for the column Custno in the Customer table. Keys will save you

```
================Select table option================
          (1)  Add a new table to the database
          (2)  Change an existing table
          (3)  Remove a table from the database
          (4)  Exit to the main menu
```

Fig. 18-3. Selecting a table.

```
Enter or change the column names - [ESC] when done


 ┌─────────┐
 │ ORDER   │
 └─────────┘

 ┌──────────┬──────────┬──────────┬──────────┬──────────┬──────────┬──────────┐
 │ ORDNO    │ CUSTNO   │ ORDDATE  │ ██████   │          │          │          │
 ├──────────┼──────────┼──────────┼──────────┼──────────┼──────────┼──────────┤
 │ TEXT   5 │ TEXT   5 │ DATE     │          │          │          │          │
 └──────────┴──────────┴──────────┴──────────┴──────────┴──────────┴──────────┘



 [F1] Insert  [F2] Delete  [F3] Review  [F5] Reset value  [F10] Help
 Database FREDFSH   ---   Defining table ORDER   ---   Column  4
```

Fig. 18-4. Creating the Order table.

time when you are using commands that select records and the WHERE phrase meets all of the following conditions:

☐ The last condition in the WHERE clause uses the key.
☐ The last operator in the WHERE clause is an EQ.
☐ The last connector is an AND.

The following SELECT command meets those conditions:

R> SELECT ALL FROM CUSTOMER WHERE STATE EQ CT AND CUSTNO EQ A-152

There is a more important reason to use keys, however. In the next chapters

Table 18-3. Item Table Design.

ITEM TABLE		
Column name	Data type	Size
ITEMNO	TEXT	5
ITEM	TEXT	25
PRICE	DOLLAR	8
ONHAND	INTEGER	4
STOCKLVL	INTEGER	4
ORDAMT	INTEGER	4
ORDFLAG	TEXT	1

```
Table: CUSTOMER
Read Password: NO
Modify Password: NO

Column definitions
 # Name        Type       Length        Key
 1 CUSTNO      TEXT           5 characters yes
 2 COMPANY     TEXT          20 characters
 3 FSTNAME     TEXT          20 characters
 4 LSTNAME     TEXT          20 characters
 5 ADDRESS     TEXT          25 characters
 6 CITY        TEXT          15 characters
 7 STATE       TEXT           2 characters
 8 ZIP         TEXT          10 characters
 9 PHONE       TEXT          13 characters
10 DISCOUNT    REAL           1 value(s)

Current number of rows:          0

Table: ORDER
Read Password: NO
Modify Password: NO

Column definitions
 # Name        Type       Length        Key
 1 ORDNO       TEXT           5 characters yes
 2 CUSTNO      TEXT           5 characters yes
 3 ORDDATE     DATE           1 value(s)

Current number of rows:          0

Table: ORDERITM
Read Password: NO
Modify Password: NO

Column definitions
 # Name        Type       Length        Key
 1 ORDNO       TEXT           5 characters yes
 2 ITEMNO      TEXT           5 characters yes
 3 QTY         INTEGER        1 value(s)
 4 PRICE       DOLLAR         1 value(s)
```

Fig. 18-5. The LIST ALL command.

```
Current number of rows:          0

Table: ITEM
Read Password: NO
Modify Password: NO

Column definitions
#  Name       Type      Length          Key
1  ITEMNO     TEXT        5  characters  yes
2  ITEM       TEXT       25  characters
3  PRICE      DOLLAR      1  value(s)
4  ONHAND     INTEGER     1  value(s)
5  STOCKLVL   INTEGER     1  value(s)
6  ORDAMT     INTEGER     1  value(s)
7  ORDFLAG    TEXT        1  characters

Current number of rows:          0
```

Fig. 18-5. The LIST ALL command. (Continued from page 208.)

you will see some relational concepts; that is, where two or more tables are related to each other. Relational operators automatically take advantage of keyed columns. It is therefore, important to build keys for the columns in your tables that will be commonly used to relate one table to another.

When you use a nonkeyed file to search for records, R:base 5000 will check every record sequentially until it finds a match or reaches the end of the file. If there are thousands of records to search, this process may take a long while. R:base 5000 will read the whole file just to find a single or a few records. When a table has been sorted, the situation still will not be improved. Sorting the table only rearranges the data; it does nothing to help R:base 5000 locate records faster. Keying, on the other hand, helps R:base 5000 locate records quickly.

To building the keys, Fred enters the following commands from R:base 5000 command mode:

```
R> BUILD KEY FOR CUSTNO IN CUSTOMER
R> BUILD KEY FOR ORDNOO IN ORDER
R> BUILD KEY FOR CUSTNO IN ORDER
R> BUILD KEY FOR ORDNO  IN ORDERITM
R> BUILD KEY FOR ITEMNO IN ORDERITM
R> BUILD KEY FOR ITEMNO IN ITEM
```

DISPLAYING THE DATABASE

After you have created your database and tables, you will want to see or print out a complete list of what you have defined. Figure 18-5 shows the results of the following command:

```
R> LIST ALL
```

This command will display all the tables in the open database and list their

```
Tables in the Database FREDFSH

Name      Columns   Rows              Name      Columns   Rows

CUSTOMER     10       0               ORDER        3        0
ORDERITM      4       0               ITEM         7        0




Column definitions
    Name       Type      Length          Table       Key
    ADDRESS    TEXT      25 characters   CUSTOMER
    CITY       TEXT      15 characters   CUSTOMER
    COMPANY    TEXT      20 characters   CUSTOMER
    CUSTNO     TEXT       5 characters   ORDER       yes
                                         CUSTOMER    yes
    DISCOUNT   REAL       1 value(s)     CUSTOMER
    FSTNAME    TEXT      20 characters   CUSTOMER
    ITEM       TEXT      25 characters   ITEM
    ITEMNO     TEXT       5 characters   ORDERITM    yes
                                         ITEM        yes
    LSTNAME    TEXT      20 characters   CUSTOMER
    ONHAND     INTEGER    1 value(s)     ITEM
    ORDAMT     INTEGER    1 value(s)     ITEM
    ORDDATE    DATE       1 value(s)     ORDER
    ORDFLAG    TEXT       1 characters   ITEM
    ORDNO      TEXT       5 characters   ORDERITM    yes
    PHONE      TEXT      13 characters   CUSTOMER
    PRICE      DOLLAR     1 value(s)     ITEM
                                         ORDERITM
    QTY        INTEGER    1 value(s)     ORDERITM
    STATE      TEXT       2 characters   CUSTOMER
    STOCKLVL   INTEGER    1 value(s)     ITEM
    ZIP        TEXT      10 characters   CUSTOMER
```

Fig. 18-6. LISTing the tables and columns in a database.

columns, type, length, keys, and passwords. It will also display the number of records in each table.

Because each table in the database is known to every other table, you might also want a cross-reference of your columns as they relate to each table. The command:

```
R> LIST COLUMNS
```

will display this cross-reference for you. In Fig. 18-6 the results of the following two commands are shown:

```
R> LIST TABLES
R> LIST COLUMNS
```

Chapter 19

Creating Applications with R:base 5000

Fred has finished creating the database structure. He is now ready to begin programming. Fred will review his design to remind himself what there is to program. This step is where his design techniques are put to the test. Depending on how good his screen designs and pseudocode are will depend on how long it will take to code and test the programs.

There are two ways to program your design with R:base 5000. The first is to use the Application EXPRESS program generator to create your program. An application generator, as described in Chapter 8, will automatically write programs for you. There are several standard functions that most application generators can create, including menus, add routines, change routines, delete routines, display routines, and printing routines.

R:base's generator also lets you use custom-defined forms and reports to enhance the data entry and output functions. It will also create a simple form and report for you if you haven't created any forms. You can also enter the file name of the R:base code you have already written that the generator can add to its program.

Although the Application EXPRESS program can create very sophisticated programs, it cannot do everything. When you need totally customized programs, you will have to use the R:base command language to transform your design into a workable program.

R:base 5000 even gives you the best of both worlds. You can use the Application EXPRESS to create the menus and then either choose the canned code that EXPRESS creates for the standard functions such as ADD, CHANGE, DELETE,

DISPLAY, and PRINT, or write your own and then attach them to the menus for custom applications.

In this chapter you will see how to use EXPRESS to create the Customer System with the design Fred created. First, however, a thorough discussion of the EXPRESS itself is necessary.

EXPRESS

EXPRESS is one of the best application generators available for any database management software. The fact that it works perfectly with R:base 5000 makes it even better.

There are a series of steps you must go through before you can actually generate the application. Even if you forget some of these steps while you are running EXPRESS, you can still go back and change any part of the EXPRESS-generated code and then run the application.

Databases and Tables

The first step in using the Application EXPRESS program is to create your database and its tables. Fred has already defined his tables in the Fredfsh database.

You must create a database and at least one table. EXPRESS cannot create an application without at least one table to use for each selection. Although you can use more than one table with each application, you can only use one table with each function.

If you are not quite sure what tables you need in your database, then don't turn on the computer yet. Complete at least an initial design on paper, which must include the output reports, the input data necessary to create those reports, and therefore the tables.

Rules

Because you are attempting to use EXPRESS so that you can do as little programming as possible, you should create any rules next. Rules allow you to give an automatic error message to the data entry person at the time data is entered if the data being entered does not conform to some predetermined rules.

The method for creating these rules is described in detail in Chapter 12. A rule might prevent the operator from entering a customer number that has already been entered. A rule might prevent a part number that doesn't exist on the Parts file from being added to the Order file. A rule might also check for ranges, such as a payroll amount having to be less than $10,000 for a single month.

The alternative to using rules is to design complex error-trapping routines, which can be very complicated for the average programmer. Rules let you avoid complex programming in many cases.

Forms

Once you have created your tables and entered your rules, you need to create your data entry forms. The form is used for adding your data. The FORMS command in R:base will help you create entry forms. This command is described in Chapter 13 in detail.

In the system that Fred has designed, he expected to use the form for displaying records and for confirming records before deleting them. He also expected to use the form for changing records.

R:base 5000 only uses the form for data entry when you are using the ADD and CHANGE functions of EXPRESS. You can modify the EXPRESS code after R:base produces it, or you can use custom macros to use the form for other functions. Later in this chapter, you will see what EXPRESS uses for each function.

You can have as many forms as you need for your system. If you don't have any forms created when you run EXPRESS, you can tell EXPRESS the name of the form you will use. It will create a very simple input form that you can later change as you want.

Reports

Just as R:base uses forms for data entry, it uses report forms for the Printing function. The R:base REPORTS command lets you create output reports. The report forms R:base can create are excellent forms that allow you to tie an unlimited number of tables and produce reports using these many tables.

If you haven't created a form yet when you choose the R:base Printing function from EXPRESS, it will create a very simple form for you. Later you can change that form and make it as complicated as you want.

The report forms can save you hundreds of programming statements. The REPORTS command is described in detail in Chapter 15.

Menus

Your menus are the backbone of your system. They control the flow from one area of the system to another. Menus simplify a system by giving the operator all the possible choices in a (hopefully) single, easy-to-read screen. Instead of having to remember the command to add a record, you can choose the *Add a record* choice from a menu.

Menus serve two different purposes: the first is to run a procedure such as add records, or print records; the second is to run other menus. Generally, every system starts with a main menu, and each choice on the main menu is a subsidiary menu such as *Customer System*, and *Inventory System*.

The choices on each subsidiary menu usually are functions such as *add, change*, or *print*. There is no reason, however, that you cannot have many levels of menus without reaching an actual function.

As you will see later in this chapter, R:base even offers two different types of menus: horizontal menus that appear across the top of the screen (like Lotus 1-2-3 has) and the old-fashioned vertical menus that take up the entire screen.

Menus are not created before you start the EXPRESS program, but they must be designed completely before you start. Because they are used to assign functions to each menu choice, they must be correct before you start.

Whether you use EXPRESS to create your menus or you create them yourself,

	Vertical	Horizontal
Table 19-1. Menu Code for Vertical and Horizontal Menus.	COLUMN Our Main Menu CUSTOMER SYSTEM EMPLOYEE SYSTEM ORDER SYSTEM INVENTORY SYSTEM EXIT SYSTEM	ROW Our Main Menu CUSTOMER EMPLOYEE ORDER INVENTORY EXIT

both types of menus work in the same way. Sample R:base 5000 menu code for the two types of menus appear in Table 19-1.

The vertical menus take up the entire screen. They appear as shown in Fig. 19-8. A number is placed in front of each selection for ease of selection. The horizontal menus are displayed on one line, much like Fig. 19-1. You may only have one-word selections on horizontal menus.

The code as shown in Table 19-1 can be placed in a file as shown and run with the CHOOSE command. Later you will see how the files can be combined into one file.

ENTIRE APPLICATIONS

Once you have performed the following steps, you are ready to create the entire system:

☐ Create the database and associated tables.
☐ Define data entry rules.
☐ Create the data input forms.
☐ Create the output report forms.
☐ Design the menu structure.

As you will see, EXPRESS is capable of creating very complex systems.

The Main Menu

EXPRESS will begin by asking you to create a main menu. This menu is used to run all the command files that make up each function of the system. It can perform the functions shown in Table 19-2 for any menu choice.

Table 19-2. EXPRESS Main Menu and Functions.

Function	EXPRESS Name	R:base 5000 Command
Add Records	Load	ENTER formname
Change Records	Edit	EDIT
Delete Records	Delete	DELETE ROWS
Display Records	Browse or Select	EDIT or SELECT
Print Records	Print	PRINT formname
Custom Functions	Custom or Macro	your program
Create a Menu	Menu	use EXPRESS

In Table 19-2, the column labeled *Function* is the task the function performs. The column labeled *EXPRESS Name* is the name that EXPRESS calls the function on the menu. Later you will see this list again in an R:base 5000 menu that lets you select the various functions. The last column is the R:base 5000 command that is used when R:base 5000 generates the command file for the particular menu function. An R:base command file that EXPRESS creates is nothing but a series of R:base commands put together in precisely the right way to produce the results that you want.

Remember that you create your system specification by answering a series of question, prompts, and menus, R:base is storing your answers. When you are through describing your system, R:base actually creates an R:base program that does everything you told it to do. Each function creates the code using the R:base commands in Table 19-2.

In the next section of this chapter, you will see Fred create the Customer System and the code that R:base produced. In the rest of the chapters of this book you will see Fred as he creates his entire program from scratch and his struggle to create a workable program in R:base 5000.

The R:base Files

After you have created your specifications for the EXPRESS application generator, R:base will take several minutes to produce the code. Four files are produced, each named from the name of the application that you choose.

Fred will be choosing the name Fishmkt as the name for his application. Later Fred will find three files on his disk in addition to the database files:

```
FISHMKT.API
FISHMKT.APP
FISHMKT.APX
```

The api file is an internal file that stores pointers needed for the execution of the program. The apx file is the compiled program that R:base creates. (More on compilers in the next section). The app file is a file that you can change if you want with any word processor or the built-in R:base word processor, RBEDIT.

When R:base creates the app file, it creates three different types of code: commands, menus, and screens. Each section is labeled with the words $COMMAND, $MENU, or $SCREEN, along with the name of the command, menu, or screen that precedes the code itself.

In this way, you can see where R:base has placed code for the command files along with the menu that it created and any help screens. When the code is in this form, it cannot be run directly. It must be first compiled when it is in this combined form. Later in this book you will see both a combined command file and a system that is broken up into almost 20 separate files.

Compiling

Compiling means translating normal program statements written in the application language (R:base) to a form readable by the computer. This means that R:base

216

can process the program faster because it doesn't have to translate the code from R:base code, which only R:base understands, to machine language, which the personal computer you are using understands.

This is a very simple process that only involves using the command:

R> RCOMPILE

As you will see later, you are presented with a menu that lets you select from the different options of the compiler. When you run the compiler with an R:base command file, your R:base program will run much more quickly because it saves the time it normally takes to translate each statement and perform the required actions.

Although you don't have to compile an R:base program, you will find it works much more quickly if you do.

CREATING THE CUSTOMER SYSTEM WITH EXPRESS

Before you start EXPRESS, you should have created your database and its tables. In Chapter 18, Fred created the customer database. You can see Fred's database again in Figs. 18-2 and 18-5. Fred used EXPRESS to create the database and its tables.

When you begin the EXPRESS, you see the main menu as shown in Fig. 18-1. When you are ready to begin creating the application, you would choose the third choice, *Define a new application*. Choosing this option will begin the application generation process. Figure 19-1 shows the first screen that you will see. First Fred chose the database that he would use. The name of Fred's database is Fredfsh. As you can see, Fred moved the menu bar to Fredfsh and pressed <Return>.

```
┌──────────────────Select database - [ENTER] to choose──────────────────┐
│ JOINS   COMPUCO   BOOK   FREDFSH                                        │
└────────────────────────────────────────────────────────────────────────┘




    Enter the name for this application  FISHMKT




    Enter the name of the main menu  MAIN
```

Fig. 19-1. Beginning the Application EXPRESS.

R:base 5000 then asked Fred for the name of the application. This would be the name of the DOS files that R:base would create with the app, apx, and api extensions. Fred chooses Fishmkt because he is proud of his store.

R:base then asks Fred for the name of the main menu. Everything is controlled from the main menu. Fred calls it Main. Before Fred continues to create his application, let's review the forms and rules Fred created.

Creating the Entry Forms and Rules

Fred created one entry form and called it Custform. The data entry form is shown in Fig. 19-2. Fred created it with the forms command and then will use it when he creates the ADD and CHANGE functions of the customer system.

The entry form is a simple one with just text and the corresponding entry fields. Fred will use this form for his data entry.

After the entry form is created, Fred wants to create the one rule that is needed for data entry. There can only be one record for each customer number in the file. No two customers can have the same number. Fred creates the rules as shown in Fig. 19-3.

Fred has set the rule and has told R:base to display the message **Duplicate customer number** whenever a customer number is entered that already exists on the file.

Figure 19-4 shows an example of that message after a duplicate customer has been entered. This figures also shows a data entry session in process for the form that Fred created.

```
                                   < 1,  1>  [F3] to list, [ESC] to exit
                       FRED'S FRIENDLY FISH MARKET
                          CUSTOMER ENTRY FORM



     CUSTOMER NUMBER:  S    E

     COMPANY:      S                    E
     LAST NAME:    S                    E
     FIRST NAME:   S                    E

     ADDRESS:   S                    E
     CITY:      S              E

     STATE:  SE          ZIP:  S        E

     PHONE NUMBER:  S          E

     DISCOUNT: S        E
```

Fig. 19-2. The Customer entry form.

```
R>LIST RULES
     RULE checking = ON
RULE   1    CUSTNO IN CUSTOMER NEA CUSTNO IN CUSTOMER
    Message:Duplicate customer number
R>
```

Fig. 19-3. Setting the rules.

Creating the Report Forms

Fred created one report format and let R:base created the other one. There are two reports in Fred's design of the Customer System. The first is the Customer Directory, which will be a book that Fred keeps at his desk when he calls his customers. The book must have all the information about Fred's customers that he will ever need. Figure 19-5 shows the form that Fred has created.

The second form that Fred needs is the Customer Mailing List. Fred decides that this list should be printed on sticky labels. Because Fred hasn't gotten his labels yet from the printer, he doesn't know what the spacing of the labels will be. Fred decides not to create the form yet. When he runs EXPRESS to create the application, he will tell R:base that he wants a Printing routine, and he will worry about the form later. Figure 19-6 shows the simple type of form that R:base will create if you do not give it a form name that you have already created.

```
-ERROR- Duplicate customer number              - Press [ESC] when corrected
                         FRED'S FRIENDLY FISH MARKET
                            CUSTOMER ENTRY FORM



          CUSTOMER NUMBER:  A-001

          COMPANY:     KAREN'S CHOWDER POT
          LAST NAME:   HAYDEN
          FIRST NAME:  KAREN

          ADDRESS:  25 KRAWSKI RD
          CITY:     N. WINDSOR

          STATE:  CT              ZIP:  06047

          PHONE NUMBER:  (203)555-2371

          DISCOUNT: 95
```

Fig. 19-4. Displaying the error message.

```
HR                          FRED'S FISH MARKET
HR                        CUSTOMER DIRECTORY PRINT
HR
HR
D
D
D    Customer Number:   S    E
D
D    S                        E
D    S                                                            E
D                             S                    E
D                             S                                        E
D
D                        Phone:  S            E
D
D                        Discount: S        E
```

Fig. 19-5. The Customer Directory form.

```
HP
HP
D
D  FSTNAME: S                    E
D  LSTNAME: S                    E
D  COMPANY: S                    E
D  ADDRESS: S                          E
D     CITY: S              E
D    STATE: SE
D      ZIP: S          E
```

Fig. 19-6. R:base's simple output form.

As you can see, the form is very simple. The column names are listed, along with a place for their output values. Notice that the columns Phone and Discount are missing. As you will see, when R:base creates a form for you in EXPRESS it lets you select the columns to be displayed, as well as any selection criteria and sorting orders.

CREATING THE MENUS

Once the forms are created, it is time to begin the application creation process. After you choose the name of the main menu, which Fred called Main (Fig. 19-1), you are ready to create your menus.

There are two types of menus in R:base 5000: horizontal and vertical. Horizontal menus are used often, by R:base 5000. Figure 19-7 shows a horizontal menu used by R:base 5000. Figure 19-7 shows a horizontal menu used by R:base 5000. It is the menu that lets you choose the type of menu you want. Horizontal menus are generally needed when you want to use the rest of the screen for something else, such as displaying data.

In horizontal menus you choose the selection by moving the highlighted menu bar from side to side with the cursor keys or by entering the first letter of the menu choice.

```
┌───────────────────────────────────────────────────────────────────────────┐
│                                                                             │
│                                                                             │
│      ┌═══════════════════════════Select menu type═══════════════════════┐  │
│      │ Vertical   Horizontal                                            │  │
│      └──────────────────────────────────────────────────────────────────┘  │
│                                                                             │
│                                                                             │
│                                                                             │
│                                                                             │
│                                                                             │
│                                                                             │
│                                                                             │
│                                                                             │
│                                                                             │
│                                                                             │
│                                                                             │
│                                                                             │
│                                                                             │
│                                                                             │
│  [F3] Review   [F5] Reset value   [F10] Help                                │
│  Database FREDFSH    - Defining Application FISHMKT   - Menu MAIN            │
│                                                                             │
└───────────────────────────────────────────────────────────────────────────┘
```

Fig. 19-7. Choosing the menu type.

```
┌────────────────────────────────────────────────────────────────┐
│  Enter or change the menu choices - [ESC] when done            │
│                   ════════FRED'S FISH MARKET MAIN MENU═══════    │
│  ┌──────────────────────────────────────────────────────────┐  │
│  │   (1)  CUSTOMER SYSTEM                                    │  │
│  │   (2)  EMPLOYEE SYSTEM                                    │  │
│  │   (3)  ORDER SYSTEM                                       │  │
│  │   (4)  INVENTORY SYSTEM                                   │  │
│  │   (5)  EXIT SYSTEM                                        │  │
│  │                                                          │  │
│  │                                                          │  │
│  │                                                          │  │
│  └──────────────────────────────────────────────────────────┘  │
│                                                                │
│                                                                │
│                                                                │
│                                                                │
│  [F1] Insert  [F2] Delete  [F3] Review  [F5] Reset value  [F10] Help │
│  Database FREDFSH   - Defining Application FISHMKT   - Menu MAIN   │
└────────────────────────────────────────────────────────────────┘
```

Fig. 19-8. Entering a menu.

Choosing the Menu Type

Fred decides to choose a vertical menu. He wants to use the entire screen to display his main menu. After he chooses *Vertical*, the screen changes to a large, empty box. Fred is prompted to enter the title for the menu and any selections. Fred enters his menu as shown in Fig. 19-8.

The title is automatically centered as you type it. Each menu selection is placed on the left side of the box as you enter it. You can use the function keys to insert or delete menu choices as you create the menu. Each menu selection will lead you through a series of steps to create further processing.

Fred has created five items in his menu. He envisions that each menu item will run a program which will handle the different systems he has designed. Fred has actually only designed the Customer and Order systems so far. In this way, he will be ready when he designs and codes these systems.

After creating the menu, Fred presses <ESC>. Next R:base 5000 displays the menu as it will look (Fig. 19-9) and asks Fred a series of questions about the menu.

The first question is:

Is ESC to be used to exit this menu?

Fred wants to handle exiting with a menu choice and enters **No**. The next question is:

Is HELP to be defined for this menu?

222

Fred enters **Yes** because he wants to create a help screen for the data entry operator. After Fred types **Yes**, the screen changes as shown in Fig. 19-9.

Fred decides to call the help screen for the main menu Helpmain. A help screen will assist the operator in understanding each function. Help menus are retrieved by pressing <F10>. Later you will see the code that EXPRESS generates to select a help screen.

After Fred enters the name of the help screen, R:base gives Fred a blank edit screen in which to enter his help screen. This screen is the same as any other edit screen. He can move around the screen freely with the cursor keys entering any text he desires. He also can insert lines with the <F1> key and delete lines with the <F2> key.

Fred creates the help screen, as shown in Fig. 19-10. This screen will be invaluable to the operator who hasn't seen Fred's system. You can create very complex help screens with R:base 5000 if you desire.

Fred has finished creating the main menu. His next task is to assign a function to each of the 5 selections.

Assigning Functions to Each Menu Item

R:base and EXPRESS make it very easy to assign functions to each of the selections. Figure 19-11 displays the main menu and a menu of choices to assign the function to menu selection 1. This figure is also a good example of the difference between the vertical menu at the top of the screen and the horizontal menu in the center of the screen.

There are nine functions that you can choose. You may assign one or more function to each menu choice. Table 19-2 shows the table of choices and the R:base command that each one uses.

Fred starts by choosing *Menu*. When the operator chooses *Customer System* from the main men, he will go to another menu that will let him pick the various database management choices, such as ADD, CHANGE, or DELETE.

When a function is chosen, such as Menu, a series of prompts and menus are entered or chosen to let R:base know the various selections that are to be made. The selection *Menu* will let you create a subsidiary menu to Main in exactly the same way as the main menu was constructed.

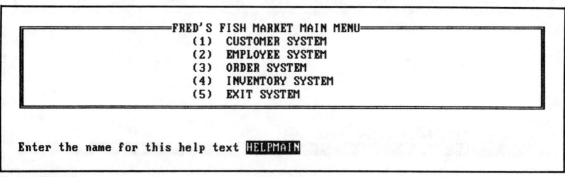

Fig. 19-9. Fred's main menu.

```
                        MAIN MENU HELP SCREEN
                        ---------------------


        CUSTOMER SYSTEM   - ADD/CHANGE/DELETE CUSTOMER RECORDS

        EMPLOYEE SYSTEM   - MANAGE EMPLOYEE LIST AND PRODUCE PAYROLL

        ORDER SYSTEM      - ADD/CHANGE/DELETE ORDERS FOR CUSTOMERS

        INVENTORY SYSTEM - MANAGE INVENTORY SYSTEM OF SEAFOOD PRODUCTS

        EXIT SYSTEM       - RETURN TO OPERATING SYSTEM




      * Note to Operator - If you have any serious problems call
                      Fred or Frank immediately
```

Fig. 19-10. The main menu help screen.

```
===============FRED'S FISH MARKET MAIN MENU===============
                (1)  CUSTOMER SYSTEM
                (2)  EMPLOYEE SYSTEM
                (3)  ORDER SYSTEM
                (4)  INVENTORY SYSTEM
                (5)  EXIT SYSTEM


The actions for menu selection  1 will be defined

================Select action for this menu selection================
  Load   Edit   Delete   Browse   Select   Print   Custom   Macro   Menu   Exit




[F3] Review  [F5] Reset value  [F10] Help
Database FREDFSH   - Defining Application FISHMKT   - Menu MAIN
```

Fig. 19-11. Assigning functions to a menu.

Figure 19-12 shows Fred's customer menu after it was entered. He named this menu Custmenu. Fred coded eight choices. He wants the ability to add, change, delete, and display his data. He also wants to print his mailing list and directory. Finally he wants to be able to exit to the main menu or to native R:base 5000.

After he enters this menu, R:base will then take Fred through the process of assigning of functions for all eight of the menu choices that Fred has added. The more levels of menus you have, the more questions you will answer and the more choices from menus you will choose. R:base will follow each menu branch to its conclusion before it returns to previous levels. In this case, R:base will ask Fred to assign all the functions to the Customer System before it returns to the main menu to assign choices to the Employee, Order, and Inventory systems.

Testing the Menus

R:base now displays the main again and asks Fred to choose the action to be

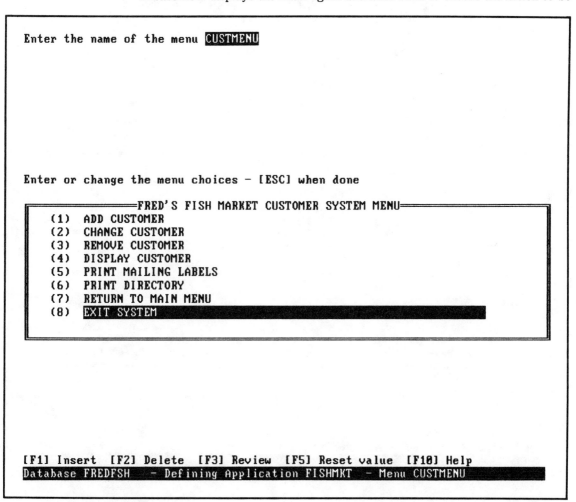

Fig. 19-12. Fred's Customer menu.

assigned to his first menu selection. Since the first function is *Add Customer*, Fred chooses *Load*, as shown in Fig. 9-13.

The screen immediately changes to that shown in Fig. 19-14. Fred is now asked to select the table he wants to load. Fred can only load one table at a time. Fred chooses the Customer table.

R:base then asks him to pick the form name from the list of forms in the database. Fred chose Custform, the form he created before using EXPRESS. If he hadn't created the form yet, R:base would create a very simple input form that Fred could modify later.

Because Fred has already created an entry screen, R:base 5000 knows the columns Fred will enter. If Fred had not already created an entry form, he would have been shown a menu with all the columns in the table and asked to choose the columns to be placed in the simple entry form. Fred would have chosen the keyword ALL because he wants the program generated to load all the columns in the table. Because Fred has created an input form, however, this step is skipped.

Before you move to the next selection, R:base displays the following question:

Do you want another action for the current menu pick:

This option lets you perform more than one task with a single menu item. In Fred's case, all he wants to do is enter a customer record. If Fred was using the Order

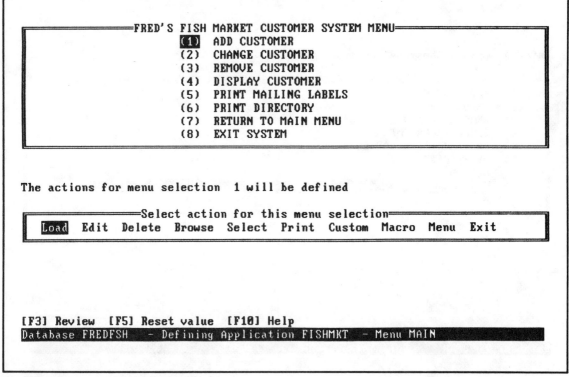

Fig. 19-13. Fred chooses the LOAD function.

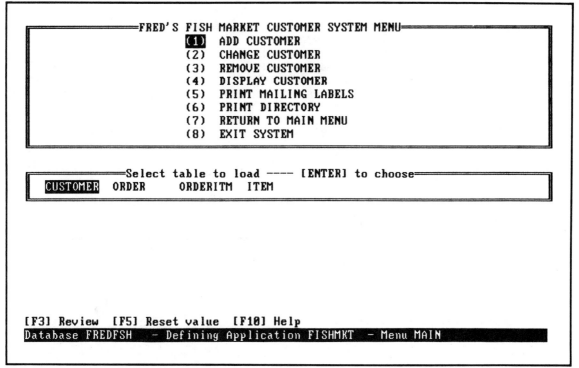

Fig. 19-14. Fred chooses the Customer table.

File, he might need several actions to add both the main order form and the form for multiple order items. Fred chooses **NO** and continues.

When EXPRESS creates the code for the first menu item, it will simply create the code:

```
ENTER CUSTFORM
```

Fred didn't specify any special options except to use the Custform form and the Customer table. You will see this code in the next section.

Fred chooses *Edit* for the *Change Customer* function and goes through the same steps as with ENTER. R:base will create the code:

```
EDIT CUSTFORM
```

for the second menu item. Fred thinks, "So far this has been easy. Answer a few questions and continue."

Fred now moves on to the third function, *Remove Customer*. R:base asks Fred a series of questions; the first is shown in Fig. 19-15. This question shows Fred that he must choose a column to be used for selecting the correct records to delete. Fred chooses his key, Custno.

Now Fred is asked what comparison operator should be used to compare the

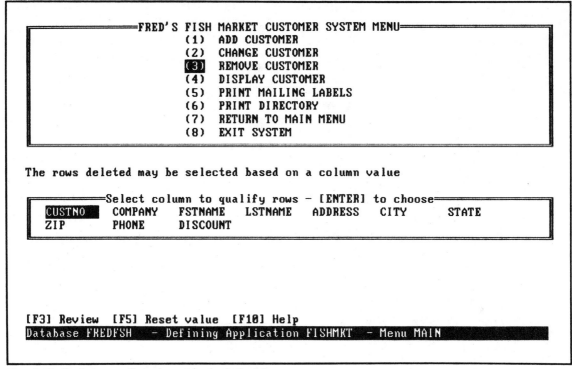

```
                   ═══FRED'S FISH MARKET CUSTOMER SYSTEM MENU═══
                       (1)  ADD CUSTOMER
                       (2)  CHANGE CUSTOMER
                      [(3)] REMOVE CUSTOMER
                       (4)  DISPLAY CUSTOMER
                       (5)  PRINT MAILING LABELS
                       (6)  PRINT DIRECTORY
                       (7)  RETURN TO MAIN MENU
                       (8)  EXIT SYSTEM


   The rows deleted may be selected based on a column value

         ═══Select column to qualify rows - [ENTER] to choose═══
       [CUSTNO]   COMPANY   FSTNAME   LSTNAME   ADDRESS   CITY      STATE
        ZIP       PHONE     DISCOUNT




   [F3] Review  [F5] Reset value  [F10] Help
   Database FREDFSH   - Defining Application FISHMKT  - Menu MAIN
```

Fig. 19-15. Fred chooses the column to selectively delete.

value that Fred will enter to the value of Custno. The choices include:

EQ NE GT GE LT LE CONTAINS EXISTS FAILS

Fred is also asked if he will enter the value to be compared at execution time. This means that Fred will be asked for a value to be used in the delete when the program is run.

The value that Fred will enter will be compared with one of those operators against the value of the column Custno in the Customer table. If Fred enters **EQ** for the operator and then **A-001** at execution time for the Custno, R:base will delete all records whose **Custno EQ A-001**.

Fred now moves on to the fourth selection, *Display Customer*. He chooses **Browse** from the menu choices. The Browse choice displays the table using the EDIT command, which allows you to make changes. Select uses the R:base command SELECT to display the table. Fred wants to be able to make changes with the *Display* function; so he chose Browse.

Fred now continues to the Printing functions. He starts with the *Print Mailing Labels* selection and chooses **Print** to create a PRINT function. Fred doesn't have any special form in mind since he doesn't know the spacing of the sticky labels he has ordered. R:base will create a form for him.

Fred is asked to choose the columns that will appear on the report. As you can see in Fig. 19-16, Fred has chosen seven of the ten columns in the table. Fred doesn't want to show his internal customer number, the customer's telephone number, or his discount on the mailing label.

Figure 19-6 shows the form that EXPRESS creates if you don't already have one. Later, Fred will modify this form to look the same way his label will look. *Print* also allows you to create a sorted order for your output. A menu lets you select from multiple sort columns and will add the SORTED BY clause to the PRINT statement.

Fred also chooses the *Print* function for the *Print Customer Directory*. Fred uses the report form Custdir, which he created. This form is shown in Fig. 19-5.

For the last two functions, which are exiting functions, Fred chooses *Exit*. These functions will simply return Fred to the main menu when the program is run.

Fred has now entered all the functions for the Customer menu. He is returned to the main menu to select choices for the other three systems—Employee, Order, and Inventory. Fred is anxious to see how the program runs; so he chooses *Exit* for the other three functions and gets ready to run the program.

UNDERSTANDING THE R:base CODE

Upon exiting the EXPRESS program, the files are created and the program compiled. Fred finds three new files on his disk:

```
FISHMKT.API
FISHMKT.APX
FISHMKT.APP
```

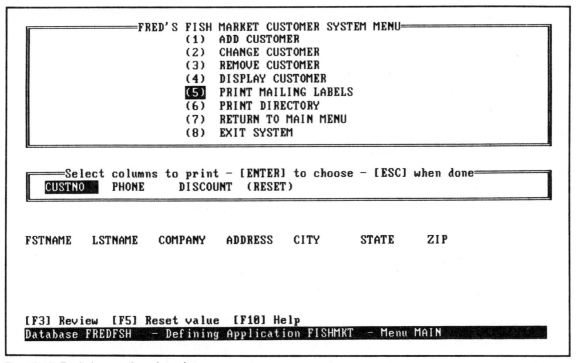

Fig. 19-16. Fred chooses the print columns.

Fred remembers that the api file contains some internal pointers. The apx file contains the compiled code that Fred will run. The final file, app, is an ASCII version of the program and its blocks. Fred decides to print out the code and look at it.

Fred views the printout shown in Figs. 19-17 and 19-18. Figure 19-17 shows the command file that EXPRESS created, while Fig. 19-18 shows the menu and screen files. R:base 5000 creates this as one long program.

Each section (command, menu, or screen) is known as a *block*. This program has five blocks: one command block named Fishmkt; three menu blocks named Prt$$$, Main, and Custmenu; and the screen, named Helpmain.

Figure 19-17 contains the code that runs the menus and its functions. It begins with $Command to let R:base know that it is a command block. The name of the block follows the header. You can have up to 40 blocks of any kind in a single file. Later you will see command files in detail. For now you will see the main parts of this file.

After some housekeeping statements, the first menu loop starts. The Choose Pick1 from Main statement displays the main menu and reads the selection. The

```
$COMMAND
FISHMKT
SET MESSAGE OFF
OPEN FREDFSH
SET ERROR MESSAGE OFF
SET VAR PICK1   INT
LABEL STARTAPP
   NEWPAGE
   CHOOSE PICK1   FROM MAIN
   IF PICK1   EQ -1 THEN
      NEWPAGE
      DISPLAY HELPMAIN
      WRITE "Press any key to continue "
      PAUSE
      GOTO STARTAPP
   ENDIF
   IF PICK1   EQ            1 THEN
      SET VAR PICK2   INT
      SET VAR LEVEL2 INT
      SET VAR LEVEL2 TO 0
      WHILE LEVEL2 EQ 0   THEN
         NEWPAGE
         CHOOSE PICK2   FROM CUSTMENU IN FISHMKT.APX
         IF PICK2   EQ          1 THEN
            ENTER CUSTFORM
         ENDIF
         IF PICK2   EQ          2 THEN
            EDIT USING CUSTFORM
         ENDIF
         IF PICK2   EQ          3 THEN
            FILLIN WHVAL USING "ENTER THE CUSTOMER NUMBER TO DELETE: "
            DELETE ROWS FROM CUSTOMER +
               WHERE CUSTNO   EQ      .WHVAL
               CLEAR WHVAL
         ENDIF
         IF PICK2   EQ          4 THEN
            EDIT   +
```

Fig. 19-17. The EXPRESS command code from the Fishmkt program.

230

```
                CUSTNO    +
                COMPANY   +
                FSTNAME   +
                LSTNAME   +
                ADDRESS   +
                CITY      +
                STATE     +
                ZIP       +
                PHONE     +
                DISCOUNT  +
                FROM CUSTOMER
            ENDIF
            IF PICK2  EQ              5 THEN
               CHOOSE PRNTOPT FROM PRT$$$ IN FISHMKT.APX
               IF PRNTOPT EQ "Both" THEN
                  OUTPUT PRINTER WITH SCREEN
               ELSE
                  OUTPUT .PRNTOPT
               ENDIF
               PRINT CUSTMAIL +
                  SORTED BY CUSTNO
               OUTPUT SCREEN
               IF PRNTOPT NE "PRINTER" THEN
                  WRITE "Press any key to continue "
                  PAUSE
               ENDIF
               CLEAR PRNTOPT
            ENDIF
              IF PICK2  EQ              6 THEN
                 OUTPUT PRINTER WITH SCREEN
                 PRINT CUSTDIR SORTED BY CUSTNO
              ENDIF
              IF PICK2  EQ              7 THEN
                 BREAK
              ENDIF
              IF PICK2  EQ              8 THEN
                 BREAK
              ENDIF
            ENDWHILE
            CLEAR LEVEL2
            CLEAR PICK2
            GOTO STARTAPP
          ENDIF
          IF PICK1  EQ            2 THEN
            GOTO STARTAPP
          ENDIF
          IF PICK1  EQ            3 THEN
            GOTO STARTAPP
          ENDIF
          IF PICK1  EQ            4 THEN
            GOTO STARTAPP
          ENDIF
          IF PICK1  EQ            5 THEN
            GOTO ENDAPP
          ENDIF
          GOTO STARTAPP
        LABEL ENDAPP
        CLEAR PICK1
        RETURN
```

Fig. 19-17. The EXPRESS command code from the Fishmkt program. (Continued from page 230.)

IF statements that check Pick1 are determining the menu paths for the main menu. If the <F10> key is chosen, Pick1 will be −1 and the screen Helpmain will be displayed as shown in Fig. 19-18.

The next section of the code checks Pick1 for being equal to 1. If it is, R:base will run the Customer menu. The statement displays the Customer menu and lets you choose one of the eight choices in the Customer menu. The variable Pick2 is used because Pick1 is used for the main menu.

This is where Fred defined his selections. The first selection, IF Pick2 = 1, corresponds to the first selection in the Customer menu. The code that is found there runs the command:

```
ENTER CUSTFORM
```

This command will display the Customer form and allow data entry. The second selection runs the command:

```
EDIT USING CUSTFORM
```

which uses the Custform while using the edit functions of R:base 5000.

The third function, which deletes records, uses code that is a little more complicated. It uses the FILLIN command, which you will learn in the next section, to ask the operator to enter a single value. That value is then compared to the CUSTNO column to determine which records to delete. After you enter the value, the statement:

```
DELETE ROWS FROM CUSTOMER WHERE CUSTNO EQ .WHVAL
```

deletes the correct rows in the Customer table. *.WHVAL* is the variable that the FILLIN command used.

The fourth selection uses the EDIT command to display the rows and columns. The command:

```
EDIT ALL FROM CUSTOMER
```

could have been used in place of the individual columns.

After the first four selections come the printing selections. Fred has made some changes to the code. In the fifth selection, *Print the customer mailing labels*, EXPRESS first displays a menu that lets the user select the destination of the printed output between a printer, file, screen, or any combination. This is a menu found in Fig. 19-18 called Prt$$$.

After choosing the print destination, the output is created with the command:

```
PRINT CUSTMAIL SORTED BY CUSTNO
```

Fred has changed the code in the second print selection. He has removed the print destination menu routine from the code. Fred always wants his Customer directory

```
$MENU
PRT$$$
ROW Select Print Routing
Printer
Screen
Both

$MENU
MAIN
COLUMN FRED'S FISH MARKET MAIN MENU
CUSTOMER SYSTEM
EMPLOYEE SYSTEM
ORDER SYSTEM
INVENTORY SYSTEM
EXIT SYSTEM

$MENU
CUSTMENU
COLUMN FRED'S FISH MARKET CUSTOMER SYSTEM MENU
ADD CUSTOMER
CHANGE CUSTOMER
REMOVE CUSTOMER
DISPLAY CUSTOMER
PRINT MAILING LABELS
PRINT DIRECTORY
RETURN TO MAIN MENU
EXIT SYSTEM

$SCREEN
HELPMAIN
```

                         MAIN MENU HELP SCREEN

          CUSTOMER SYSTEM - ADD/CHANGE/DELETE CUSTOMER RECORDS

          EMPLOYEE SYSTEM - MANAGE EMPLOYEE LIST AND PRODUCE PAYROLL

          ORDER SYSTEM   - ADD/CHANGE/DELETE ORDERS FOR CUSTOMERS

          INVENTORY SYSTEM - MANAGE INVENTORY SYSTEM OF SEAFOOD PRODUCTS

          EXIT SYSTEM   - RETURN TO OPERATING SYSTEM

     * Note to Operator - If you have any serious problems call
                          Fred or Frank immediately

Fig. 19-18. The menu and screen code from the Fishmkt program.

on the printer. He hardcodes the command:

`OUTPUT PRINTER`

in the program before running the PRINT command to print his Customer directory.

The last two options are exit options, and the BREAK command will exit from a loop.

The rest of the code are the menu stubs for later use that will someday run the other systems.

Figure 19-18 contains the rest of the EXPRESS program. This code is part of the code shown in Fig. 19-17. Normally it is one large set of statements with the blocknames between the blocks.

The $MENU statement signals the beginning of a menu block (and therefore the end of the previous block). After the menu statement is the name of the menu, followed by the type of menu and its name. The selection choices follow.

A $Screen file is displayed with the DISPLAY command. The DISPLAY command simply writes what it finds in the file to the screen. What you see is what you get.

RUNNING THE PROGRAM

Fred has now examined his code. He thinks to himself, "I'm not sure this is what I designed. I want a program that does what I want it to do. As I remember, R:base does a lot more than just display the screen."

Fred decides to run the program to see if it is what he wants. Fred starts by typing:

`RUN FISHMKT.APX`

That file is where the compiled version resides, and that is the only version that can be *run*. If you decide to modify the app file, you must recompile it before running it.

After a few seconds, the system displays the main menu screen, as shown in Fig. 19-19. Notice that the numbers have added to the screen from the menu file shown in Fig. 19-18.

Fred can move the highlight up and down among the numbers with the cursor keys. When he is ready to choose a selection, he presses <Return>.

```
════════════════════FRED'S FISH MARKET MAIN MENU════════════════════
                    (1)  CUSTOMER SYSTEM
                    (2)  EMPLOYEE SYSTEM
                    (3)  ORDER SYSTEM
                    (4)  INVENTORY SYSTEM
                    (5)  EXIT SYSTEM
```

Fig. 19-19. The main menu.

234

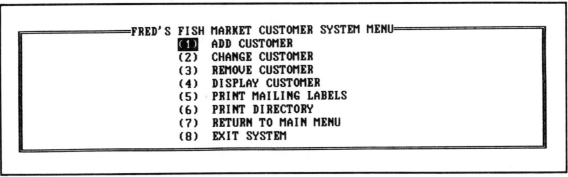

```
══FRED'S FISH MARKET CUSTOMER SYSTEM MENU══
        (1)  ADD CUSTOMER
        (2)  CHANGE CUSTOMER
        (3)  REMOVE CUSTOMER
        (4)  DISPLAY CUSTOMER
        (5)  PRINT MAILING LABELS
        (6)  PRINT DIRECTORY
        (7)  RETURN TO MAIN MENU
        (8)  EXIT SYSTEM
```

Fig. 19-20. The Customer menu.

The screen changes to the Customer main menu, as shown in Fig. 19-20. It works exactly the same as the main menu. You can move up and down with the cursor keys or move directly to the number you want to choose by entering that number. Fred is ready to start using his first selection; so he presses <Return> with the highlight on item number one.

Fred enters his first record into the empty form. The message:

`Press [ESC] when done with this data`

appears at the top of the screen. Fred finishes entering the record and presses <ESC>. The top of the screen displays the menu shown in Fig. 19-21.

Fred says, "What is this? I've entered my record." Then he remembers; R:base is actually using the ENTER Custform command. Fred has remembered that this

```
          FRED'S FRIENDLY FISH MARKET
             CUSTOMER ENTRY FORM



   CUSTOMER NUMBER:  A-001

   COMPANY:     LEE SIDE FISHERIES
   LAST NAME:   KAY
   FIRST NAME:  LEE JAY

   ADDRESS:   151 CLEMENS COUTHOUSE
   CITY:      ROCKVILLE

   STATE:  CT              ZIP:  06073

   PHONE NUMBER:   (203)555-6134

   DISCOUNT: 5
```

Fig. 19-21. The entry form in the Add function.

menu is standard when the ENTER command is used; it is automatic in R:base. Fred knows that he will have to choose *Add* to add the record and get a new blank screen. He can also choose *Reuse* to enter the record and keep the data on the screen. He can also choose *Edit* to change the data on the form before saving it, or he can choose *Quit* and not save the last record. Fred chooses *Add* and enters a few more records.

Fred quits back to the customer menu and presses **2** and then <Return> to *Change Customer*. The first record is displayed with a new menu at the top of the screen. Fred presses <Return> a few times and the fourth record is displayed.

The menu at the top gives Fred seven choices. He can skip to the next record, edit the record on the screen, or change the record to any new values he has entered on the screen with the EDIT function. Fred can also add the record he has edited as a new record, reset any columns he has changed, delete a record from the file, or quit back to the main menu. Fred looks at the screen in Fig. 19-22 and is not happy.

Fred thinks, "This is not at all what I designed. I want my CHANGE function to ask for the customer number and then display and let me change it. After I enter my 300 customers, I would have to spend hours finding the last one. So far, EX-PRESS is great, but it's not for me!"

Fred tries the DELETE function next. The system asks for the customer number that Fred wants to delete from the system. Fred is happy with that, but it doesn't show him to whom the customer number belongs. "I could delete my best customer by mistake," Fred says.

```
——Skip—Edit—Change—Add—Reset—Delete—Quit————————————————
                  FRED'S FRIENDLY FISH MARKET
                     CUSTOMER ENTRY FORM



        CUSTOMER NUMBER:  B-001

        COMPANY:    A PECK OF CHOWDER
        LAST NAME:  HAROLD
        FIRST NAME: DAVID

        ADDRESS:  23 NEWBORN RD
        CITY:     HARTFORD

        STATE:  CT          ZIP:  06115

        PHONE NUMBER:  (203)555-7463

        DISCOUNT: 35.0000
```

Fig. 19-22. The Customer Change function.

```
        Press [ESC] to quit, [F2] to delete, [F5] to reset    More→
CUSTNO   COMPANY              FSTNAME          LSTNAME           ADDRESS
-------- -------------------- ---------------  ---------------   --------
A-001    LEE SIDE FISHERIES   LEE JAY          KAY               151 CLEM
A-002    SAMS LOX HAVEN       SAMUEL           BURTON            18465 TR
A-003    SYLVIA'S SMOKE HOUSE EDITH            ZARSKY            1534 WET
B-001    A PECK OF CHOWDER    DAVID            HAROLD            23 NEWBO
```

Fig. 19-23. The Customer Display function.

Fred tries one more function, the DISPLAY function. Fred chooses the fourth selection from the Customer menu, and the screen in Fig. 19-23 appears. Fred says, "That's it. I want to display one record at a time so I can see all the columns. I don't want to be able to change or delete a record!" Fred throws his disk across the room into a lobster tank as Frank walks by.

Frank asks, "So Fred, your ideas about computerizing the business aren't working. Can I throw the darn thing into the ocean now!"

Fred responds, "Look Frank, you said I could have 3 weeks. So far I have spent 2 hours."

"You obviously haven't gotten anywhere," Frank says. "You're throwing things around the office and you almost hit Julie, our pet crab."

Fred apologizes, "Well, I'm just frustrated. Do you want to see what I have so far?"

Frank agrees. "If it will help you get back to the fish, OK."

Fred shows Frank the EXPRESS program. Frank goes wild! "Fred, you did this! This is great, and in only 2 hours. You're brilliant. I'm amazed! You can barely tell the difference between the lobsters and the crabs and yet you did this. Wow! Can I get a computer too?"

Fred is happier. Fred thinks to himself, "OK, EXPRESS is amazing, the system does do everything I want it to do. It just doesn't do it the way I want. I'm now ready to spend the time to learn how to program myself." Fred's fish are ready to be satisfied!

REUSING EXPRESS CODE FOR CUSTOM PROGRAMMING

Fred knows that EXPRESS can quickly create programs, but that the programs cannot do exactly what he wants. Fred realizes that he first should learn the programming commands that are necessary to write the programs.

So far you have seen EXPRESS create a simple program using the same database statements that you learned in Section II of this book. The rest of this book is dedicated to teaching you how to write code without EXPRESS and how to use and modify that code.

However, you and Fred must learn the programming commands that are unique to R:base 5000 before you start your coding. Of course, as you begin, remember that you can always use the R:base 5000 code produced by EXPRESS as a start. Fred starts by copying the Fishmkt.app file to a new file he calls Fishmkt.cmd. Later he will use that file as a base to start his coding. His menus are perfect; so why reinvent the transistor?

Chapter 20

R:base 5000 Programming Commands

You can create command files by using the R:base command RBEDIT. This command places you in the same simplistic editor that is used for input forms and output reports. The R:base editor is adequate for simple edits. It lets you scroll around the screen and see as many lines of code as you have by viewing sets of 24 lines. You can also insert a line or delete a line. You cannot, however, copy or move a line.

The editor makes it very laborious when you are creating large programs. You can, however, use almost any word processor, as long as you create an ASCII text file.

I personally use Personal Editor II from IBM's Personally Developed Library. You can use any word processing software, such as Microsoft Word, Framework II, WordStar, WordPerfect, or even MultiMate. You might find that text editors such as Personal Editor or KEDIT actually work better than full-fledged word processors.

COMMAND FILES

A *command file* is nothing more than a series of R:base commands strung together in just the right way. There is no real limit to the number of statements you may have in a single command file. You will find that good programming techniques dictate that you should break up your programs into small, workable modules of no more than 100 or 200 statements. Actually, code with about 60 statements in a module is excellent.

Splitting Long Command Lines

If you are writing code that sometimes needs more than 80 characters, you will have to split the line with a plus (+) character. For example:

```
FILLIN CHOICE USING "Enter your choice for the menu: "  +
   AT 3 25
```

The command could not fit on one line on the screen; so it was split with the plus character. Be careful not to split a line where R:base will get confused or add extra blanks.

Commenting Your Code

When you create command files, you will eventually want to document them. The reason for documenting files is not a selfish one. Chances are someday someone else may be looking at or changing your code. The neat coding trick you came up with today will be long forgotten in 6 months. In fact, you might be long forgotten in 6 months.

There is another reason for commenting your code. You might be looking at it in 6 months. There is nothing more embarrassing than not being able to remember what you did or why you did it way back when.

Comments are added to R:base 5000 code by starting the line with an asterisk and then enclosing the text in parentheses. A typical comment would look like this:

```
* (This is a comment)
```

Comments can be any length and can be on the same line as code. For example:

```
SET VARIABLE ABC TO 17  * (17 is the number of employees)
```

You might also want to use a technique known as *flower boxing* to store your comments. At the beginning of a program, you might have several lines of comments enclosed in a flower box. For example:

```
*(********************)
*(                    )
*(     MAIN MODULE    )
*(     SYSTEM ABCD    )
*(                    )
*(********************)
```

By commenting your code when you write it, you will save a lot of time and aggravation later on.

SET Statements

The first lines of code in any command file are the OPEN command to tell R:base what database you want to use and then one or more SET commands.

SET commands set your environment. They control the way the system will run. When you are debugging your program, you will use such commands as:

```
SET MESSAGE ON
SET ERROR MESSAGE ON
SET ERROR VARIABLE varname
SET ECHO ON
```

SET MESSAGE ON will display diagnostic messages as the system runs. Normally this command is set to OFF when you are running your system because you should have taken care of all possible errors.

SET ERROR MESSAGE ON lets you prevent the display of R:base system error messages. Usually this command is also set to OFF during normal execution of your system.

SET ERROR VARIABLE will let you write an error-handling routine. The variable you specify will hold any R:base error codes. R:base sets its internal error code to 0 when a command is performed without error. Otherwise it sets several different error values. By checking for a nonzero error condition, you can trap errors, such as a database being unable to be opened.

When you are having problems debugging your system, you might need to turn on the SET ECHO ON command. This command displays each and every R:base command in your program as it runs. It gets very messy, but can be invaluable in finding logic errors in your program.

Besides the debugging commands, there are many other commands for setting the environment. The remaining commands follow, along with the their default values.

SET AUTOSKIP OFF—Automatically skip to the next entry field.
SET BELL ON—Beep the speaker upon errors.
SET CASE ON—Upper/lowercase distinction.
SET CLEAR ON—Clear internal buffers and write records to disk after each modification.
SET COLOR FOREGRND color—Set the foreground colors that R:base uses.
SET COLOR BACKGRND color—Set the background colors that R:base uses.
SET DATE datefmt—Choose from a variety of formats.
SET ESCAPE ON—Use the <ESC> key to exit command files.
SET LINES number—Set number of lines used for output.
SET NULL -0—-Set the characters used to display null values.
SET REVERSE ON—Set reverse video in data entry fields.
SET RULES ON—Use the data entry rules specified.
SET WIDTH number—Set the width of the columns per screen 39 to 132.

Running Command Files

Once you have created your command files, you generally have only one starting point—the main menu. If you have named the main menu command file Main.cmd, as you might want to do, you would start the system by entering:

```
R>   RUN MAIN.CMD
```

from the main R:base command mode.

VARIABLES

Many new commands that you will be needing to know are contained in the programs in the following chapters. In order to make the explanations easier, this section will briefly review the commands mostly out of context. You will see them put to the ultimate test in the programs themselves.

Creating a Variable

Variables are very necessary to programming because they are used in every aspect of programming. They are used as accumulators in totaling. They are also used in comparisons and in the logical constructs. Variables are used to hold data that is retrieved from tables or that is entered from the keyboard. Variables are used in calculations and as the variable you need when you are picking from a menu.

There are several functions that automatically create variables. Usually you must define most variables you are going to use yourself. There are two things to define: the type of the variable (text, real, dollar, integer, date) and the initial value.

The easiest way to create a variable is with the SET VARIABLE command. First you must define the variable type. Let's define the variable quantity to 25.

```
SET VARIABLE QUANTITY INTEGER
SET VARIABLE QUANTITY TO 25
```

It takes two statements to define a value. First, you must define the data type, just like defining a table. Second, you must define the value of the variable. This is the simplest way to define a variable. You also might want to define a text variable. For example:

```
SET VARIABLE NAME TEXT
SET VARIABLE NAME TO JOHN
```

In addition to this simplistic data definition, you might want to set a variable equal to another variable. To set the variable Name to the variable Person, you would code the following:

```
SET VARIABLE NAME TO .PERSON
```

The period preceding the variable name tells R:base that it is a variable name and not a value. Without the period, R:base would think you want to set the variable Name to the value Person.

You can also set a variable equal to an arithmetic expression or string expression. You can use literals (values) or variables and mix them:

```
SET VARIABLE AMOUNT TO 3.45 X 50
SET VARIABLE AMOUNT TO .PRICE X .QTY
SET VARIABLE AMOUNT TO 3.45 X .QTY

SET VARIABLE NAME TO CARY & PRAGUE
SET VARIABLE NAME TO .FSTNAME & .LSTNAME
SET VARIABLE NAME TO CARY & .LSTNAME
```

Variables can also be set to values from tables:

`SET VARIABLE AMOUNT TO AMOUNT IN SALES WHERE ITEM = A-205`

Notice that the variables Amount and Item do not have a period preceding their names. This is because these variables can only be variables, and therefore there can be no confusion. *SALES* means the table named Sales.

Later you will also see how to use the SET POINTER command to set a variable to a specific value in a row of a table without using the WHERE command.

The COMPUTE command can also be used to set a variable equal to an amount computed from a table of values. The command:

`COMPUTE AVGSALES AS AVE QTY FROM SALES WHERE MONTH = JAN`

creates a variable called Avgsales, which is the average of the values of the Qty (quantity) column from the Sales table where the value of the column Month is Jan. This command means compute the average sales for January.

This variable would then be available for computing trends, percentages, or ratios. The COMPUTE command can use the keywords shown in Table 20-1 to compute different values.

There are other commands that automatically create a variable. They will be seen later in this chapter.

The command SHOW VARIABLES will show all the variables you have defined, their datatype, and their value for all variables that you have defined, as shown in Table 20-2.

Comparison Operators and Logical Connectors

There are a standard set of comparison operators and logical connectors that can be used in complex expressions. These include the ones listed in Tables 20-3 through 20-5.

CLEAR Command

The number of variables you can define is only limited by the amount of memory you have. Still, good programming dictates that you clear your variables from

Table 20-1. COMPUTE Keywords.

Statistic	Description
Ave	Computes the average of a numeric column
Count	Counts how many entries are in a column
Max	Selects the highest number, alphabetically highest Text string, or latest date from a column
Min	Selects smallest number, alphabetically lowest Text string, or earliest date from a column
Rows	Determines how many rows are in a table
Sum	Computes the sum of numeric data in a column
All	Computes all of the above

```
                SHOW VARIABLES

Variable =          Value            Type

-------------------   ----------------------   --------------

NAME                Cary             TEXT
SALARY              $35,500          DOLLAR
QTY                 645              INTEGER
#DATE               3/15/86          DATE
AMOUNT              345.56           REAL
CITY                Los Angeles      TEXT
```

Table 20-2. Using the SHOW VAR Command.

memory as you are through using them. The CLEAR command can help you with this process.

To clear all your variables from memory, you would type:

```
CLEAR ALL VARIABLES
```

This command might cause some problems in a system if you are not careful. When you have a menu that calls other menus, you are probably using a variable to keep the value of your last menu choice. If you clear all your variables in a subsidiary menu or function, you will also clear that value.

You should use separate CLEAR commands to remove each variable from memory. The commands:

```
CLEAR QTY
CLEAR NAME
CLEAR ABC
```

will clear the three variables Qty, Name, and ABC from memory. Later in this book, you will see another tricky way to save yourself from clearing a lot of variables separately when you only want to keep one or two.

Variable Forms

There is more than one type of data input form. The first type, which you have seen extensively in this book, is the normal data entry forms. The form "belongs" to an individual table. You can display any data from that table. When you use the ENTER or EDIT commands with the form name, R:base 5000 will display different menus at the top when the ENTER or EDIT process is run.

Table 20-3. Arithmetic Operators.

Operator	Definition
+	Addition
−	Subtraction
×	Multiplication
/	Division
%	Percent

244

Arithmetic Operators	
Operator	**Definition**
AND	And
OR	or

Table 20-4. Logical Connectors.

This method is probably not acceptable in custom systems. There may be times when you want to display and enter data to more than one table at a time. You might want to enter data to a set of variables that have no corresponding columns in a table. You might want to input data to two half-screen forms on one screen.

Variable forms are the answer. Although they require some simple programming and a lot of data manipulation, they are invaluable to avoiding the top menus that R:base uses with the ENTER and EDIT commands. Variable forms also let you create your own error messages and write to the screen in any way that you want.

When you create a custom system, you should have custom forms. In his system, Fred will create several custom forms.

Creating a variable form is almost the same as creating a regular form as shown in Chapter 13. The only difference is that the form is not associated with any table. You create variables that are placed on the form. By manipulating those variables later, you can display, enter, and change your data.

To create a variable form, you would begin exactly the same way as with a regular form. You start by typing the FORMS command:

```
R> FORMS
Begin R:base FORMS definition
ENTER FORM Name: CUSTVAR
Enter table name (for a variable FORM press [ENTER]):
```

By pressing <Enter>, the form named Custvar will be a variable form. Remember, creating a form involves two steps. The first is placing the text on the screen. The second step is locating the variables.

The first step is exactly the same as for a regular form; the second step, however, is different. Instead of choosing the variables from the list of columns in a table, you create the variables as you go and as you will use them later.

Figure 20-1 shows a variable form being entered. Notice the top of the screen.

Table 20-5. Comparison Operators.

Operator	Symbol	Definition
EQ	=	Equal
NE	< >	Not equal
GT	>	Greater than
GE	> =	Greater than or equal to
LT	<	Less than
LE	< =	Less than or equal to
CONTAINS		Embedded in the Text column

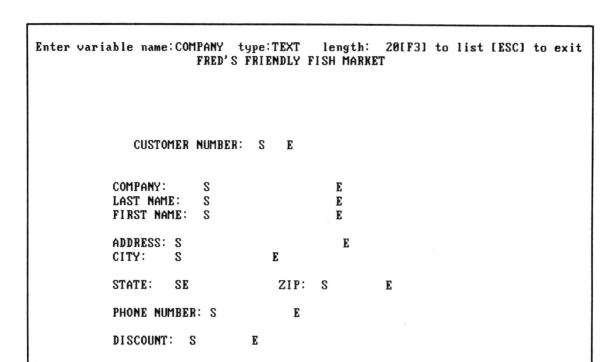

```
Enter variable name:COMPANY  type:TEXT   length:  20[F3] to list [ESC] to exit
                  FRED'S FRIENDLY FISH MARKET




         CUSTOMER NUMBER:  S   E


      COMPANY:      S                    E
      LAST NAME:    S                    E
      FIRST NAME:   S                    E

      ADDRESS: S                      E
      CITY:    S             E

      STATE:   SE            ZIP:  S        E

      PHONE NUMBER: S           E

      DISCOUNT:   S        E
```

Fig. 20-1. Creating a variable form.

Because you are creating the variables as you go, you have to enter a name, type, and length for text variables. Later you will see the commands that are needed to use a variable form, including the DRAW, ENTER VAR, and EDIT VAR commands.

As you will see when Fred creates his system, the variable forms allow complete customization of the screen, including drawing and retrieving anything from the screen.

DATA MANIPULATION COMMANDS

So far you have seen several commands that manipulate variables in memory. There are also several commands that manipulate columns in a table. The first is the AS-SIGN command.

ASSIGN

The ASSIGN command lets you change the value of a column in a table. You can change just one row or all the rows in a table. The simplest form of the AS-SIGN command is the following:

`ASSIGN SALARY TO SALARY X 1.1 IN PAYROLL`

This command multiplies all the salaries in the payroll table by 1.1 to give everyone a 10-percent raise. You can also limit the scope of the ASSIGN command.

```
ASSIGN SALARY TO SALARY X 1.1 IN PAYROLL WHERE NAME = SMITH
```

Now only the people named Smith will receive a raise. You can also have the ASSIGN command use other columns in the table or variables you have created. For example:

```
ASSIGN INVNTRY TO ONHAND + PURCH IN PARTS
```

would add the columns Onhand to Purch in the Parts file and change the value of Invntry in the Parts table.

You can also use a variable in the ASSIGN statement:

```
ASSIGN PCT TO AMT / .TOTAMT IN PAYROLL
```

This command changes the column Pct in the Payroll table to the value of the column Amt divided by the variable Totamt. The variable Totamt could have been created with the Compute command as the sum of the column Amt in the Payroll table. This method would let you calculate the percentage of each employee's salary to the total payroll. The COMPUTE command would have looked like this:

```
COMPUTE TOTAMT AS AVE AMT FROM PAYROLL
```

The ASSIGN command can even be used to change a single record with the #n clause. Later you will see how to set an individual record pointer with the command SET POINTER TO. You will learn that this command sets one of three pointers: #1, #2, or #3. You can then use this pointer to tell the ASSIGN command to only work with the one record to which the pointer is pointing. This form of the ASSIGN command is:

```
ASSIGN PCT TO AMT / .TOTAMT IN #1
```

The pointer #1 has already been set to a record in some table.

CHANGE

The CHANGE command is similar to the ASSIGN command, but it does things a little differently. First, you can use the CHANGE COLUMN command to change the data type or length of a column. These are database commands and are covered in Section 2 of this book.

The CHANGE command without the COLUMN keyword is used to change the column value in one column in a single table or a column in all the tables in the database.

The other important difference between ASSIGN and CHANGE is that the ASSIGN command can work with expressions—that is, mathematical relationships—while the CHANGE command can only work with literal values or variables. For example:

```
CHANGE NAME TO "Mrs John Smith" WHERE CUSTNO EQ A-103
```

will change the column Name in all tables to Mrs John Smith as long as the customer number was A-103. This command would be useful when a person gets married and changes her name. The reason the name is in quotes is that there are blanks in the name. Without the quotes, R:base would get confused.

To change all occurrences in a single table, you would enter:

```
CHANGE AMT TO 100 IN SALES
```

Every row in Sales would have its amount column changed to 100. You should be very careful with the use of the WHERE clause and the IN *tablename* clause.

LOAD

The LOAD command is used in custom command files to add data to tables. Generally, you will set variables equal to the values of a table. You can do so with FILLIN commands or a variable form. Somehow you have to get the data from the variables to the table. The easiest way is to use the noninteractive form of the LOAD command.

Suppose you have a table named Payroll and three variables, Name, Hours, and Payrate. You could load the Payroll table like this:

```
LOAD PAYROLL
.NAME .HOURS .PAYRATE
END
```

The LOAD command will load the values of the variables into the first three columns in the table. The column names of the table do not have to match the variable names, but the relative positioning must match. The first column in the table will receive the value of the Name, the second, Hours, and the third, Payrate. If there are more than three columns in the table, the rest of the columns will be a null value for that row.

MOVE

The MOVE command is used to move text from one text variable to another. This command also lets you move substrings of text variables that don't necessarily have to start with the first character.

Let's look at a nine-digit zip code with a dash between the sections.

```
06074-3546
```

The MOVE command can create two variables from the nine-digit zip code, moving each part of the zip code to separate variables.

```
SET VARIABLE ZIP TEXT
SET VARIABLE DIGI5 TEXT
SET VARIABLE DIGI4 TEXT
SET VARIABLE ZIP TO 06074-3546


MOVE 5 FROM ZIP AT 1 TO DIGI5 AT 1
MOVE 4 FROM ZIP AT 7 TO DIGI4 AT 1
```

248

This sequence of commands moves five characters from Zip starting at the first position of Zip to the first character of Digi5. It also moves four characters from Zip starting at the seventh position of Zip to the first character of Digi4.

The variable Digi5 now contains 06074, while the variable Digi4 now contains 3546. The dash was not moved. The original variable Zip still contains the original text, 06074-3546.

The MOVE command can also be used to create an edit mask. Assume that a telephone number is entered with only the numbers—2035558675. It is hard to recognize this as a telephone number. The MOVE command can move it into a more familiar view.

```
SET VAR PHONE TO 2035558675
SET VAR SPECIAL TEXT
SET VAR SPECIAL TO ()-
SET VAR PHONE TEXT
SET VAR NEWPHONE TEXT

MOVE 1 FROM SPECIAL AT 1 TO NEWPHONE AT 1
MOVE 3 FROM PHONE   AT 1 TO NEWPHONE AT 2
MOVE 1 FROM SPECIAL AT 2 TO NEWPHONE AT 5
MOVE 3 FROM PHONE   AT 4 TO NEWPHONE AT 6
MOVE 1 FROM SPECIAL AT 3 TO NEWPHONE AT 9
MOVE 4 FROM PHONE   AT 7 TO NEWPHONE AT 10
```

The variable Newphone now contains the value (203) 555-8675 and now can be used with the SHOW VAR command to appear in that form on a report.

If you don't know the exact length for some of your moves, you can use variables in the MOVE command. This command is a must to add to your programming library.

INPUT COMMANDS

FILLIN

The FILLIN command is used to allow the entry of a single value from the keyboard. You can display a message and then accept input from the keyboard. The FILLIN command is used extensively in command files to make interactive decisions.

When the command:

```
FILLIN CHOICE USING "Enter a disk drive specification: " +
AT 3 20
```

is run, the screen displays the following at row 3, column 20:

```
Enter a disk drive specification: __
```

You can then enter a disk drive specification. Your answer is set to the variable Choice, or whatever variable you use in the FILLIN command. You do not have to define the variable you use in advance. The data type of whatever you enter will be used as the data type of the variable created. If you want a specific data type such as Text and you know you will be entering a set of numbers, then you would have to predefine the variable before you use it.

You can now use the variable Choice in any expression or statement that allows variables. It will exist until it is cleared or its value is changed.

The FILLIN command is sometimes used in conjunction with a DISPLAY or TYPE command as a substitute for a menu. The DISPLAY command is run first, displaying text that gives menu choices. The FILLIN command is then used to get the choice. The code might look like the following:

```
DISPLAY MENSCRN
FILLIN MENC USING "Enter your menu selection: "  +
AT 20 20
```

and might produce a screen like this:

```
FRED'S FISH MARKET MAIN MENU

1 - Customer System
2 - Employee System
3 - Order System
4 - Inventory System

Enter your menu selection: __
```

The top part of the screen would be found in the Menscrn file and displayed with the DISPLAY command. The bottom entry line is displayed with the FILLIN command.

CHOOSE

The CHOOSE command displays a standard R:base menu and retrieves the choice that the user makes. A sample command might be:

```
CHOOSE MENC FROM MENSCRN
```

This command would display the menu named Menscrn in a procedure block or DOS file named Menscrn. Menscrn would have to be a normal menu file in R:base 5000 that is either a vertical or horizontal menu. The variable Menc is created and will hold the value of the choice made from the menu.

DRAW

The DRAW command is used with a variable form to place it on a screen. Unlike the regular form, the variable form doesn't just pop up ready for data input. You must maintain a much higher degree of control over the screen. You can DRAW the screen without allowing any data entry or editing.

For this example, look at the screen in Fig. 20-1. The DRAW command by itself will display the text on the screen.

```
DRAW CUSTVAR
```

will draw the text of the CUSTVAR screen just as it appears in Fig. 20-1.

If you want to see the present values of the variables, you must use a different form of the DRAW command.

DRAW CUSTVAR WITH ALL

will display the screen and the current value of all the variables in the screen. This command can assist Fred in creating his display function. Later you will see other ways to perform this function.

To limit the variables displayed on the form, such as only displaying the customer's address, the command could be entered like this:

DRAW CUSTVAR WITH ADDRESS CITY STATE ZIP

You can display up to five different variable forms at the same time on one screen as long as you don't use any NEWPAGE commands. You can place the forms on the screen by using the AT clause, like this:

DRAW CUSTVAR WITH ALL AT 10

Notice there is only a row specified. Because the form uses the entire screen width, only the row needs to be entered.

The DRAW command by itself can only display the text and the values of the variables. To enter or change data, you must use the ENTER VAR and EDIT VAR commands.

ENTER/ENTER VARIABLE

The ENTER command is used to enter data into the simple data entry forms. The ENTER VARIABLE command lets you enter data into a variable form.

The ENTER command, which uses regular data entry forms, has the following syntax:

ENTER CUSTFORM

or

ENTER CUSTFORM FOR 50 ROWS

With the FOR *number* ROWS clause, you can limit how many rows can be entered into the form.

When you are using a variable form, the ENTER VARIABLE command is appropriate. The simplest form is:

ENTER VARIABLE USING CUSTVAR

This command allows you to enter all the variables that have been defined on the screen in the CUSTVAR variable form. You can also limit the variables that can be entered by specifying the variables to be entered.

```
ENTER VARIABLE COMPANY FSTNAME LSTNAME PHONE USING CUSTVAR
```

would limit the data entry to the name and telephone number information on the screen. You can also specify what keys can be pressed to leave a data entry form. Normally the <ESC> key completes a data entry session. By using the form of the command:

```
ENTER VARIABLE USING CUSTVAR RETURN ENTER
```

will tell R:base to complete the data entry only when the <Return> key has been pressed. Other keys that can be entered include <ESC>, <PGUP>, and <PGDN>. You can specify from zero to four of those keys.

EDIT USING/EDIT VARIABLE

The EDIT USING and EDIT VARIABLE commands are functionally equivalent to their corresponding ENTER commands. EDIT USING displays a top menu above the standard entry menu that lets you skip from record to record changing the records you want and even deleting records.

The EDIT VARIABLE command lets you use the values that are already displayed in the screen or change the value to anything else.

The syntax for both these commands are exactly the same as for their ENTER counterparts.

OUTPUT COMMANDS

NEWPAGE

The NEWPAGE command is used to clear the screen or issue a page eject to the printer. The command NEWPAGE can appear anywhere in a command file and will clear the screen and make it ready for new output commands.

The NEWPAGE command can be used by itself. It can also be coupled with an IF clause in a command file.

WRITE

WRITE is the simplest of all the output commands to use. This command will write a single line to the screen at any screen location.

A sample WRITE command is:

```
WRITE "This is a screen message" AT 20 15
```

This command will write the message **This is a screen message** on the screen at row 20, column 15. This is about the bottom left side of the screen.

A screen has 24 rows and 80 columns. The top left corner is 0, 0. The top right corner is 0, 79. The bottom left corner is 23, 0, while the bottom right corner is 23, 79.

PAUSE

The PAUSE command stops processing temporarily. It is used as a way to cease the command file until a key is pressed. Accompanied by a WRITE command it can be a valuable command:

```
WRITE "Press any key to continue" AT 10 20
PAUSE
```

DISPLAY

The DISPLAY command is used to display a screenful of text from an external file or an R:base $SCREEN screen file. An external file would be displayed like this:

```
DISPLAY MYSCRN.TXT
```

The DOS file Myscrn.txt will be displayed on the screen. If there are more than 24 lines, there will be a message to press any key to see the rest of the text.

If you want to display a screen from an R:base procedure file, you might enter:

```
DISPLAY MYSCRN IN SALARY.PRC
```

This command would display the screen block named Myscrn in the R:base procedure file called Salary.prc.

If you enter:

```
DISPLAY MYSCRN
```

R:base will search for the screen block Myscrn on the most recently used procedure file. If it doesn't find the block on the procedure file, it will search the disk for the file name Myscrn.

TYPE

The TYPE command is very similar to the DISPLAY command, except that it can only display the contents of an ASCII file. It is used to display menu text, help screens, or even external files that may need to be incorporated into a system. The DISPLAY command is used in most cases.

SHOW VARIABLES

The SHOW VARIABLES command (SHOW VAR) is also a very important command. It is the only way to write variables to the screen or printer. It is, therefore, the command that makes customized reports possible for those few times when the R:base 5000 REPORTS command is not adequate.

Just as the WRITE command can write a message to the screen, SHOW VAR command can write the value of a variable to the screen or printer. To use the SHOW VARIABLES command, you must have variables active. The command SHOW VAR used by itself will show all the variables you have defined, their datatype, and their value. (See Table 20-2.)

When the command is used with a variable, you can control exact placement on the screen or printout. To display the variable Salary on the screen, you might type:

```
SHOW VARIABLES SALARY AT 10 15
```

The value of Salary would be displayed on the screen at row 10, column 15. You can also control the output width of a line. The command:

```
SHOW VARIABLES NAME=60 AT 10 15
```

would display the value of the variable Name using a display length of 60 at row 10, column 15. If the output width specified is less than the width of the variable, the variable will be displayed on more than one line.

The MOVE command is used to fill long variables that the SHOW VAR command would then output to the screen. By using these commands together, you can combine several variables and output them together. The SHOW VARIABLES command can only write to one row at a time. Two succeeding SHOW VAR commands on the same row at different column locations will produce output on different rows.

For example:

```
MOVE 20 FROM NAME AT 1 TO PRINTIT AT 1
MOVE 20 FROM ADDRESS AT 1 TO PRINTIT AT 22
MOVE 15 FROM CITY AT 1 TO PRINTIT AT 43
MOVE 2 FROM STATE AT 1 TO PRINTIT AT 59
MOVE 10 FROM ZIP AT 1 TO PRINTIT AT 62
SHOW VAR PRINTIT=75 AT 10 1
```

Would move values from several variables to a variable named Printit. That variable is then displayed on the screen at row 15. It is now at a length of almost 75 characters; so the width specification is included.

Later, Fred will need to use the SHOW VARIABLES command to produce his mailing labels.

OUTPUT

The OUTPUT command is used to direct output to different sources. Normally it is in the form:

```
OUTPUT SCREEN
```

or

```
OUTPUT PRINTER
```

This command directs the output from all commands to the specified device. You can also direct output to a disk file. For example, to direct the output to a disk file named Myfile.txt, you would enter:

```
OUTPUT MYFILE.TXT
```

You can also direct output to more than one source at a time with commands such as:

□ OUTPUT PRINTER WITH SCREEN

☐ OUTPUT PRINTER WITH MYFILE.TXT
☐ OUTPUT MYFILE.TXT WITH BOTH
☐ OUTPUT MYFILE.TXT WITH YOURFILE.TXT

These direct the output to:

☐ The screen and the printer
☐ The printer and the file Myfile.txt
☐ The file Myfile.txt, the screen, and the printer
☐ The file Myfile.txt and the file Yourfile.txt

respectively. Usually the OUTPUT command is used before a PRINT command.

PRINT

The PRINT command is used to run output through a report form. Because R:base features such a powerful reporting interface, you will find that the PRINT command and report forms are used extensively throughout R:base.

There are several forms of the PRINT command. The simplest is simply:

```
PRINT MYREPT
```

which will print the report Myrept with the data in the tables used by Myrept. You can also limit the scope of the print and the order it prints by using the following syntax:

```
PRINT MYREPT SORTED BY CUSTNO WHERE STATE = CT
```

The REPORTS command to create a report form is described in detail in Chapter 15.

WORKING WITH MULTIPLE TABLES

An important part of any database management system is its ability to perform multiple table processes. Table lookup is just one of those types of processes. Using the EXISTS keyword you can check a table to see if a value exists. For example, a customer number must exist on a customer table in order for the customer information to be retrieved. When you are selecting records, you can use the WHERE clause to retrieve all the records that match the WHERE clause.

However, when you need to find the first record in a table that meets your criteria, how do you retrieve the records data and then go on to check other tables for a matching key? That is where the SET POINTER command is invaluable.

Although you can perform table lookup with variables in report forms and SELECT commands with the WHERE clause, you cannot process this data in any reasonable fashion.

SET POINTER

When you are using R:base 5000 as a database manager and are querying your data with commands such as SELECT and EDIT, you are asking R:base 5000 to search for records that meet a certain criterion and then show all of them to you on the screen. When you are using R:base 5000 as a programming language, you will not use those commands too often because they do not give you very much flexibility when you are displaying the records on the screen.

When you are programming, you might want to process your data one record at a time. You might also want to see if a record exists in the table that meets some criteria. If it does exist, you will want to know where it exists. Once you determine the location of a record, you can use standard programming techniques to process the record and display or store it any way you want.

The SET POINTER is one such command to help you to see if a record exists. The SET POINTER command can be used in a sorted or nonsorted mode. When you use the standard SORTED BY clause, you can process the record in any type of sorted order. In the nonsorted mode, you would process the table in the same sequential order that the data exists on the table.

A normal form of the SET POINTER command is:

```
R> SET POINTER #1 CODE FOR CUSTCRDT WHERE STATE = CT
```

This command searches the file looking for the first record from Connecticut. The #1 sets up one of three available pointers that may be used at the same time on three different tables. The other pointers are called #2 and #3.

The variable Code is a variable that you can name in any way you desire. It holds the value returned from the SET POINTER command. If a record is found, it is set to 0; if it is not found it is set to 2406. There are two reasons it would not find a record: there were no records to find, or the pointer reached the end of the file.

SET POINTER will search the file, beginning with the first record that matches the search criterion specified in the WHERE clause. The pointer is then pointing to the record that meets the specified criterion. In this example the records were processed in sequential order as they were entered. If the example had included the clause SORTED BY Amount, the search would have been in the order of ascending Amount records. The search still would have looked for the first Connecticut record, but in the case of multiple records for Connecticut, it would have found a different Connecticut record first if it was searching in a sorted order.

Once the pointer is on a record, you can process it. For example the commands:

```
R> SET VAR AMT TO AMOUNT IN #1
R> SHOW VAR AMT
$21,533.00
R> SET VAR FN TO FSTNAME IN #1
R> SET VAR LN TO LASTNAME IN #1
R> SET VAR NAME TO .FN & .LN
R> SHOW VAR NAME
BILL JONES
```

extract data from the record. The first example sets a variable Amt to the value of Amount from the row in the Custcrdt table at which the pointer was pointing. The clause *IN #1* tells the SET VAR command to look for the variable specified in the TO clause in the row of the table to which the pointer is set. Because the first Connecticut record is the second record in the table, the amount displayed is $21,533.00.

The second command demonstrates using SET VAR to concatenate the values from Fstname and Lastname to form a new variable, Name. You cannot accomplish this task directly to a row; so you must extract both columns from the table with two separate SET VAR statements.

After you set two new variables, FN and LN, to the values of Fstname and Lastname, respectively, you can put them together in a third SET VAR. Remember, when you are dealing with the TO variables in a SET statement, you must use the period preceding the variable names.

The SHOW VAR command confirms the second record's data. Bill Jones is the second record's first and last name columns' value.

If your file is very large, it might take a long time to get to the record you want because R:base must read every record. If your record is on the bottom or not found, you will be in for a long wait.

As you have seen, SET POINTER does not show you the record. If it finds the record, it responds by setting an internal code to 0. If it doesn't find a record or if there are no more records to find, it sets its internal code to 2406. You can check this code after the SET POINTER command is finished.

You can continue the search without returning to the top of the database. As you find a record, the record pointer moves to the record, the code is set to 0, and you can determine and display the columns.

If you issue another SET POINTER command, R:base 5000 will start searching again from the top of the table.

NEXT

There will be many times when you need to find the first record and then continue searching the rest of the table. The NEXT command allows you to keep searching.

Using the NEXT clause, you can then move to each record that meets the specified criteria. This movement continues until you have reached all the records that meet the criteria. When there are no records left to find or no records at all to find, the pointer will reach the end of the file.

The following set of examples illustrates the use of the NEXT command after the initial SET POINTER command.

```
R> NEXT #1 CODE
R> SHOW VAR CODE
                0
R> SET VAR FN TO FSTNAME IN #1
R> SET VAR LN TO LASTNAME IN #1
R> SET VAR NAME TO .FN & .LN
R> SHOW VAR NAME
PHIL ROBERTS
```

The NEXT command uses the pointer number to move the correct pointer, and the code is again the status code that gets set after the search. In this example, Code is 0, meaning that the next record has been found. The Name is Phil Roberts, the second Connecticut name in the file.

The next example shows a different search, one where only one record exists for the state of Michigan.

```
R> SET POINTER #1 CODE FOR CUSTCRDT WHERE STATE = MI
R> SHOW VAR CODE
            0
R> NEXT #1 CODE
End-of-data encountered
R> SHOW VAR CODE
          2406
```

The first (and only) Michigan record is found with the SET POINTER command. When the NEXT command is entered, there are no more Michigan records, and the code of 2406 is returned. R:base 5000 also tells you that the end of the file has been reached.

You can also see an example of a record not being found in the database. The pointer is set to the bottom of the file and no record could be displayed. The return code is set to 2137 if there are no records at all in the table to satisfy the search.

```
R> SET POINTER #1 CODE FOR CUSTCRDT WHERE STATE = HA
-WARNING- No rows satisfy the WHERE clause
R> SHOW VAR CODE
          2137
```

LOGICAL CONSTRUCTS

IF/ENDIF

One of the most used logical constructs is the IF statement. This IF statement enables you to make decisions during the processing of your program.

The logical constructs explained in detail in Section I have various syntax in R:base 5000. The basic constructs—If-Then-Else, Looping, GoTos, and calling subroutines—are shown here.

The If-Then-Else logical construct allows a two-way path of decision making. The IF clause is followed if the expression in the IF clause is true. If it is not and there is an ELSE clause, then control passes to the ELSE clause.

Notice that all IF-THEN-ELSE statements end with an ENDIF and that the THEN clause must be on the same line as the IF.

```
SET VARIABLE X TO DEF
IF X = ABC THEN
    SHOW VARIABLE X
ENDIF
NO OUTPUT

SET VARIABLE X TO ABC
SET VARIABLE Y TO DEF
IF X = ABC THEN
    SHOW VARIABLE X
  ELSE
    SHOW VARIABLE Y
ENDIF
```

```
ABC is output, the THEN clause

SET VARIABLE X TO ABC
SET VARIABLE Y TO DEF
IF X = DEF THEN
    SHOW VARIABLE X
  ELSE
    SHOW VARIABLE Y
 ENDIF

DEF is output, the ELSE clause
```

In the first example, there is only an IF-THEN clause. Since the condition X = ABC is false, there is no output and control passes out of the IF-THEN construct.

The second example is true, and the THEN condition is executed. The final example is false, and control passes to the ELSE for execution.

You may have as many statements inside an IF statement as you want. You may also have IF statements inside of IF statements; these are known as *nested IFs*. You will be seeing the IF statement a lot in Fred's code. Fred makes a lot of decisions!

WHILE/ENDWHILE

Looping is accomplished through a command known as WHILE. The WHILE loop is performed repeatedly until the condition is no longer true.

```
SET VAR COUNTER TO 1
WHILE COUNTER <= 5 THEN
   SHOW VAR COUNTER AT .COUNTER .COUNTER
   SET VAR COUNTER TO .COUNTER + 1
ENDWHILE
1
 2
  3
   4
   5
```

In this example, the variable Counter is initialized to one. The loop is entered and the condition Counter < = 5 is checked to see if it is true. Since it is true, the loop continues. Each pass through the loop adds one to the variable Counter and outputs the value of Counter at screen location *counter,counter*. The first pass puts it at 1,1; the next pass at 2,2; the third pass at 3,3, all the way to 5,5. Notice the diagonal pattern caused by this program in the output.

Any expression can be put in a WHILE loop. It can be a simple comparison, or a complex conditional expression. You can even make the loop last forever— called an *infinite loop*—if you never make the condition being tested false. Each WHILE must have a THEN and end with an ENDWHILE.

```
SET POINTER #1 CKECKER FOR CUSTOMER WHERE CUSTNO EQ 00001
WHILE CUSTNO EQ 00001 AND DATE = 050587 THEN
 SHOW VAR AMOUNT AT 5 10
  NEXT #1
ENDWHILE
```

Here, you can see a complex loop. The NEXT #1 command assumes you are moving through a table with a pointer. There might be hundreds of records for customer number 00001, but this loop will stop when the date is not 050587.

```
SET VAR X TO 1
WHILE X < 5
WRITE 'HELLO' AT 1 1
ENDWHILE
```

This figure shows an infinite loop caused by not incrementing the variable x.

The WIIILE command is one of the most used commands in programs. It is used to control menu displays, error codes and the complete running of most systems. In Fred's coding you will see many loops, including many nested loops.

GOTO/LABEL

Branching in a single command procedure is accomplished with the GOTO command and the LABEL statement. You may place a LABEL statement anywhere in a command procedure, except in the middle of an IF statement or a WHILE statement. The LABEL statement identifies where a GOTO would branch control to.

For example:

```
SET VAR X TO 10
SET VAR Y 10 15
FILLIN NAME USING 'ENTER YOUR NAME:'
FILLIN AGE USING 'ENTER YOUR AGE:'
IF AGE < 21 THEN
     GOTO TEEN
   ELSE
     GOTO ADULT
ENDIF
SET VAR SCAM TO 1  *(This will never be executed)
LABEL TEEN
  SHOW VAR NAME=14 AT 1 1
  WRITE 'IS A TEENAGER' AT 1 15
  LOAD TEENBASE
   .NAME .AGE
  END
  GOTO ENDAPP
LABEL ADULT
  SHOW VAR NAME=14 AT 1 1
  WRITE 'IS AN ADULT' AT 1 15
  LOAD ADLTBASE
   .NAME .AGE
  END
LABEL ENDAPP
```

would ask the user for his name and age. If the age is less than 21, then the next statement executed would be the first statement after the LABEL Teen statement. The statements then would write a message to the screen and load the Teenbase table. There is an additional GOTO in the Teen section to skip over the Adult processing code. If the user's age was 21 or more, processing would branch to the Adult label.

The code has a comment that one statement will never be executed. The reason is that the IF statement will cause a branch either to the Teen statement or the Adult statement.

Remember, a GOTO simply branches to another location in the code. It then processes every statement from that point on.

Subroutines: RUN/RETURN

Subroutines differ from GOTOs because they let you go off to another set of code and then return from exactly where you left off. The calling subroutine is implemented with the RUN command, as shown in Table 20-6.

The command procedure (program) Main.cmd calls the subprocedures Sub1.cmd and Sub2.cmd. These can be programs by themselves, but probably share common options and data with the main program. A subprocedure can call another subprocedure.

The RETURN statement is R:base 5000's way of keeping track of where it is. The RETURN statement immediately returns control to the statement following the statement from which it was called. In the case of the RETURN statement in Sub1.cmd, it returns to the RUN Sub2 command. The RETURN in Sub2.cmd returns to the statement after RUN Sub2 in Main.cmd.

Most main menus are set to call subroutines to perform the processing for each menu choice. By programming with many subroutines, you will make your individual code modules much more manageable.

BREAK

The BREAK command is used to exit from a WHILE-ENDWHILE loop. It is usually part of an IF clause. Its main use is to quickly exit from a loop or a set of nested loops by eliminating the need to follow all the branches of a nested loop.

The BREAK command will exit from WHILE construct, regardless of what is between the BREAK and the ENDWHILE. (See Table 20-7.)

In the first example in Table 20-7, the WHILE construct is performed five times, as specified in the WHILE condition. The words Hello and There keep repeating each time, one character to the right. The second example contains a BREAK command, telling the program that when X = 3 go immediately to the statement following the ENDWHILE; do not perform any of the other statements in the WHILE; do not collect 200 lobsters. As you can see, the statement following the ENDWHILE prints the value of X. In the second example it is 3. The LOOP command caused a premature and immediate end to the WHILE loop.

The main use for the BREAK command is as a quick way out when an error condition is signaled. If you are performing a series of IF statements and an error

Table 20-6. RUN Command Implements the Calling Subroutine.

MAIN.CMD	SUB1.CMD	SUB2.CMD
Housekeeping Menu Commands RUN Sub1 RUN Sub2	Some Statements More Statements RETURN	Some Statements More Statements RETURN

Table 20-7. Programs with and without BREAK.

```
WITHOUT "BREAK"                  WITH "BREAK"
SET VAR X TO 1                   SET VAR X TO 1
WHILE X < = 5 THEN               WHILE X < = 5 THEN
   SET VAR Y TO .X + 6              SET VAR Y TO .X + 6
   WRITE 'HELLO' AT .X .X           WRITE 'HELLO' AT .X .X
   WRITE 'THERE' AT .X .Y        IF X = 3 THEN
   SET VAR X TO .X + 1              BREAK
ENDWHILE                         ENDIF
SHOW VAR X AT .X 20                 WRITE 'THERE' AT .X .Y
                                    SET VAR X TO .X + 1
                                 ENDWHILE
                                 SHOW VAR X AT .X 20


HELLO THERE                      HELLO THERE
 HELLO THERE                      HELLO THERE
  HELLO THERE                      HELLO        3
   HELLO THERE
    HELLO THERE
                 6
```

condition is signaled, it is usually faster to use a BREAK statement than a series of ELSE statements. The BREAK command should only be used sparingly, however, because it is not the most stable statement, and has been known to lose the end of a loop.

Chapter 21

Coding Selection Menus

In this chapter, we will reexamine the design detailed in Section 1 of this book and put to use the various database management and programming statements. You will see Fred as he creates several different parts of his Customer and Order Entry systems. Only selected parts of the system will be programmed here. Appendix B contains the completed set of programs. These can also be ordered on floppy disk from TAB BOOKS Inc.

SETTING THE ENVIRONMENT

In any system, the first instructions you will enter are the environment instructions and a flower box full of good documentation. You should document the system as you go, not when you are finished.

In the last chapter you learned about the different environment commands to tell your system how to perform. For this system, you will accept the defaults except for the MESSAGE commands. Because you will be debugging your system as you test, you should code the commands:

```
SET MESSAGE OFF
SET ERROR MESSAGE OFF
```

When you are ready to test your program, you should turn on these commands. After everything is running perfectly, set them back to off or remove them from your system. Figure 21-1 shows the beginning of Fred's main menu program. Notice the documentation that has been started. The comments inside the flower box

```
*(******************************)
*(        MAIN.CMD             *)
*(      FRED'S FISH MARKET     *)
*(       MAIN MENU PROGRAM     *)
*(   (c) 1986 Cary N. Prague   *)
*(******************************)
SET MESSAGE OFF
OPEN FREDFSH
SET ERROR MESSAGE OFF
```

Fig. 21-1. Fred sets his environment.

identify the name of the file that contains the module, the name of the program and module, and the date and programmer. This should be the minimum documentation you want to add.

THE MAIN MENU

Fred has now started to create his main menu code. He begins by looking at his design. Fred has created a sample of his main menu, a flowchart of his system, and his main menu pseudocode. These are shown in Figs. 21-2 through 21-4.

Fred starts by looking at his menu screen. He wants to display a menu with the title *Fred's Fish Market*. He would also like to identify the name of the menu. Fred wants to display his four choices for each menu item and a choice to exit. Fred thinks for a moment. He checks his flowchart to make sure that all the choices are on the menu; they are. Fred wonders why the Exit option isn't shown on the flowchart, but remembers that this is a module flowchart and not a process flowchart. The Exit function is always assumed to exist. R:base 5000 usually uses the <ESC> key to exit a function or module.

Next, Fred looks at his pseudocode. He sees that he must create a loop. As long as the user doesn't select X, the program will continue to redisplay the menu. If the user enters a number from 1 to 4, Fred will use a series of IF statements to run the correct subroutine. If the user enters an X, the loop should end.

Fred starts to decide how to create his loop. There are several ways he could do so. Fred could use a WHILE-ENDWHILE loop, or he could create a series of GOTOs to implement the loop. Fred decides the best way is with a WHILE loop.

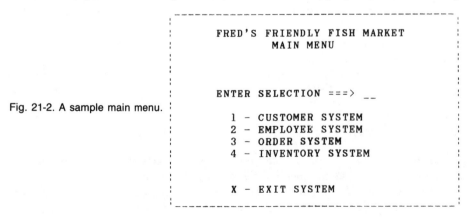

Fig. 21-2. A sample main menu.

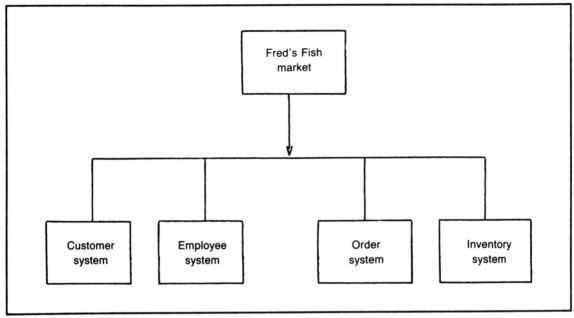

Fig. 21-3. The main menu flowchart.

Fred also thinks about how he will display the menu and let the user enter the choice. Fred knows that he can use a series of WRITE statements to display the menu and then use a FILLIN to capture the user response. He codes the following to display the menu and capture the user response:

```
SET VAR RESP TEXT
SET VAR RESP TO " "
WHILE RESP NE X THEN
   WRITE 'FRED'S FRIENDLY FISH MARKET' AT 1 10
   WRITE '         MAIN MENU          ' AT 2 10
   WRITE ' 1 - CUSTOMER SYSTEM        ' AT 8 10
   WRITE ' 2 - EMPLOYEE SYSTEM        ' AT 9 10
   WRITE ' 3 - ORDER SYSTEM           ' AT 10 10
   WRITE ' 4 - INVENTORY SYSTEM       ' AT 11 10
   WRITE ' X - EXIT SYSTEM            ' AT 14 10
   FILLIN RESP USING 'ENTER SELECTION ===> ' AT 6 10
ENDWHILE
```

Fred thinks for a moment. "OK, this will display the main menu, and as long as the user doesn't enter an X will continue to redisplay and ask for the user to enter a selection."

Fred has created the menu code but has not handled errors or processing—the two most important steps in a menu. Fred next adds an error message:

```
SET VAR RESP TEXT
SET VAR RESP TO " "
WHILE RESP NE X THEN
WRITE 'FRED'S FRIENDLY FISH MARKET' AT 1 10
```

```
MAIN MENU

    SET EXIT TO "N"
    DO WHILE NOT EXIT
      READ SELECTION
      CASE
        WHEN SELECTION = "1"
            PERFORM CUSTOMER SYSTEM
        WHEN SELECTION = "2"
            PERFORM EMPLOYEE SYSTEM
        WHEN SELECTION - "3"
            PERFORM ORDER SYSTEM
        WHEN SELECTION = "4"
            PERFORM INVENTORY SYSTEM
        WHEN SELECTION = "X"
            SET EXIT TO "Y"
        OTHERWISE
            WRITE "INVALID OPTION" ENDCASE
      ENDCASE
    ENDDO
```

Fig. 21-4. The main menu pseudocode.

```
WRITE '          MAIN MENU          ' AT 2 10
WRITE ' 1 - CUSTOMER SYSTEM         ' AT 8 10
WRITE ' 2 - EMPLOYEE SYSTEM         ' AT 9 10
WRITE ' 3 - ORDER SYSTEM            ' AT 10 10
WRITE ' 4 - INVENTORY SYSTEM        ' AT 11 10
WRITE ' X - EXIT SYSTEM             ' AT 14 10
FILLIN RESP USING 'ENTER SELECTION ===> ' AT 6 10
IF RESP NE 1 AND RESP NE 2 AND RESP NE 3 AND   +
   RESP NE 4 AND RESP NE X THEN
   WRITE "INVALID OPTION" AT 4 15
ENDIF
ENDWHILE
```

The Customer and Order Systems

Fred now has his loop and his error message working; now for the processing step. Fred must respond to the data entry with the correct action. He is going to create a Customer system and Order system now. Later he will create the Employee and Inventory systems. Fred codes the following series of IF statements:

```
IF RESP EQ 1 THEN
  RUN CUSTMENU.CMD
ENDIF
IF RESP EQ 2 THEN
ENDIF
IF RESP EQ 3 THEN
  RUN ORDRMENU.CMD
ENDIF
IF RESP EQ 4 THEN
ENDIF
IF RESP EQ X THEN
ENDIF
```

266

Fred has correctly created the code when the value of Resp is 1 or 3. He has designed those systems, but he has left the IF statements uncoded. Fred can leave them out and the error message will be displayed. When the X is entered, the loop will end. Only when the value is 1 or 3 will a subroutine be run. Fred now puts the program together, sits back, and looks at it.

```
SET VAR RESP TEXT
SET VAR RESP TO " "
WHILE RESP NE X THEN
    WRITE 'FRED'S FRIENDLY FISH MARKET' AT 1 10
    WRITE '         MAIN MENU          ' AT 2 10
    WRITE ' 1 - CUSTOMER SYSTEM        ' AT 8 10
    WRITE ' 2 - EMPLOYEE SYSTEM        ' AT 9 10
    WRITE ' 3 - ORDER SYSTEM           ' AT 10 10
    WRITE ' 4 - INVENTORY SYSTEM       ' AT 11 10
    WRITE ' X - EXIT SYSTEM            ' AT 14 10
    FILLIN RESP USING 'ENTER SELECTION ===> ' AT 6 10
    IF RESP EQ 1 THEN
       RUN CUSTMENU.CMD
    ENDIF
    IF RESP EQ 3 THEN
       RUN ORDRMENU.CMD
    ENDIF
    IF RESP NE 1 AND RESP NE 2 AND RESP NE 3 AND   +
       RESP NE 4 AND RESP NE X THEN
          WRITE "INVALID OPTION" AT 4 15
    ENDIF
ENDWHILE
```

Fred thinks, "OK, I've created the menu and all its processing. Now, what's left? I must be missing something!"

Indeed, Fred is. He should be testing his system. If he tested it, he would see that his error message is never erased. You should only display an error message for a short period of time. A good time to erase the statement is after entering the response. The statement:

```
WRITE "                          " AT 4 15
```

should be added after the FILLIN statement to clear the error message. Fred is happy his menu is complete. Now, he reviews his previous learning. He thinks, "I could have used the DISPLAY or TYPE command to display the menu by putting the menu itself in a file. This way when I want to change the menu later, I only have to add a few IF statements."

Using EXPRESS

Just then Myron walks in. Myron says, "Fred, what is this? Is this R:base? Why did you build your own menu code? Why don't you use EXPRESS to generate the code for you for the menu?"

Fred says: "Oh Oh, I forgot." Myron then asks Fred where his help menu is. Fred has blown it. The one place he can use R:base to really save time, he for-

```
MAIN
COLUMN FRED'S FISH MARKET MAIN MENU
CUSTOMER SYSTEM
EMPLOYEE SYSTEM
ORDER SYSTEM
INVENTORY SYSTEM
EXIT SYSTEM
```

Fig. 21-5. The menu code for the main menu.

gets. Myron trades another lobster for the code. Myron also knows that eventually he will own Fred's business; this way it will be easier to change the menus to read:

MYRON'S FRIENDLY FISH MARKET AND COMPUTER CONSULTING

Myron starts by showing Fred how to create a menu file without EXPRESS. Later he will use EXPRESS and then modify the code. Myron creates a file he calls Main.mnu using the R:base word processor (Fig. 21-5).

A menu file consists of the menu name for internal use, the type of menu and title, and the choices. Fred remembers that this file will also automatically handle the display of the menu, the choice of the item, and the error message. Fred remembers the CHOOSE command does all these tasks.

Fred also remembers that he wants a help menu. He moves to the R:base word processor RBEDIT and creates the screen in Fig. 21-6.

Next, Fred must create the code to display this screen when the <F10> key is pressed. Fred grabs some code that EXPRESS created earlier when he used EX-

```
                    MAIN MENU HELP SCREEN
                    ---------------------


    CUSTOMER SYSTEM   - ADD/CHANGE/DELETE CUSTOMER RECORDS

    EMPLOYEE SYSTEM   - MANAGE EMPLOYEE LIST AND PRODUCE PAYROLL

    ORDER SYSTEM      - ADD/CHANGE/DELETE ORDERS FOR CUSTOMERS

    INVENTORY SYSTEM - MANAGE INVENTORY SYSTEM OF SEAFOOD PRODUCTS

    EXIT SYSTEM       - RETURN TO OPERATING SYSTEM



    * Note to Operator - If you have any serious problems call
                    Fred or Frank immediately
```

Fig. 21-6. The help screen for the main menu.

PRESS to create the Customer system. After a few modifications, some testing (and Myron's help), he is finished. The program is shown in Fig. 21-7.

Fred has modified the EXPRESS code well. He started off with his environment statements and opened his database. Fred used labels and GOTOs because that's what EXPRESS used. He thinks it is great that you can implement a program several different ways.

Fred continues examining his code. He sets up a variable called Pick1 to store the choice that the user enters. He creates a label called Startapp to be the top of his "loop." This is not a real loop like the WHILE statement, but it is still a place to execute a repetitive set of statements, which is the definition of a loop.

Fred has also added a NEWPAGE statement to clear the screen. It is of the

```
*(*****************************)
*(          MAIN.CMD          *)
*(       FRED'S FISH MARKET   *)
*(        MAIN MENU PROGRAM   *)
*(   (c) 1986 Cary N. Prague  *)
*(*****************************)
SET MESSAGE OFF
OPEN FREDFSH
SET ERROR MESSAGE OFF
SET VAR PICK1 INT
LABEL STARTAPP
  NEWPAGE
  CHOOSE PICK1 FROM MAIN.MNU
  IF PICK1  EQ -1 THEN
    NEWPAGE
    DISPLAY HELPMAIN.HLP
    WRITE "Press any key to continue "
    PAUSE
    GOTO STARTAPP
  ENDIF
  IF PICK1 EQ 1 THEN
    RUN CUSTMENU.CMD
    GOTO STARTAPP
  ENDIF
  IF PICK1 EQ 2 THEN
    GOTO STARTAPP
  ENDIF
  IF PICK1 EQ 3 THEN
    RUN ORDRMENU.CMD
    GOTO STARTAPP
  ENDIF
  IF PICK1 EQ 4 THEN
    GOTO STARTAPP
  ENDIF
  IF PICK1  EQ 5 THEN
    GOTO ENDAPP
  ENDIF
  GOTO STARTAPP
LABEL ENDAPP
CLEAR PICK1
```

Fig. 21-7. The final code for the main menu screen.

utmost importance that you clear the screen whenever you are changing functions. If you don't, there is no telling what might be left hanging around the screen.

Fred then codes his CHOOSE statement, which will display the main menu choices and wait for a pick. Because the menu only lets you select the choices on the screen, there is no error message. The program will beep at the user until he chooses a valid choice.

Next, Fred codes the help screen display. If the user presses <F10> (PICK = −1), then the program will clear the screen with the NEWPAGE command and display the text in the help screen file (Fig. 21-6). He uses the PAUSE command with a message so the user knows why the machine has stopped. Remember, the PAUSE command will stop processing until any key is pressed.

After displaying the help screen, Fred returns control to the top of the program at the STARTAPP label. In some ways this type of coding is more efficient because the system doesn't have to evaluate all the statements in the loop and then the value of the loop itself to see if the looping condition is still true. The program is told to immediately go to the label.

Lastly, Fred codes the five IF statements. Fred can't leave any of these out because he is not using a loop. He must make the program branch to the top of the program to continue. Fred codes the RUN commands for the choices of 1 or 3 and simply returns to the top of the application for choices 2 and 4. *Choice 5—Exit the system* goes to the bottom of the screen, where the program ends after clearing all the variables defined (all one of them).

It is now time for Fred to test his system. Actually, by reviewing the code he has been testing it all along. It actually took Fred 3 hours to create this menu the first time. He ran the program 50 times until he got it right. Slowly Fred is learning. He has created three files:

☐ Main.mnu—The menu file.
☐ Helpmain.hlp—The help screen.
☐ Main.cmd—The menu program.

He types at the R> prompt:

```
R> RUN MAIN.CMD
```

and the screen in Fig. 21-8 appears.

Fred is happy. The cursor moves up and down. He presses <F10> and the help screen is displayed. He enters a **1** and receives an error message. What is wrong? Fred quickly realizes that the Customer menu Custmenu.cmd doesn't exist yet. Fred makes a copy of his main menu program and creates the Customer menu.

THE CUSTOMER MENU

By copying the main menu code, Fred can get a head start. There are several basic functions in a database system: menus, add, change, delete, display, and print routines. After you create them once, you will only modify copies from then on. Later

```
╔══════════════════FRED'S FISH MARKET MAIN MENU══════════════════╗
║  (1)   CUSTOMER SYSTEM                                          ║
║  (2)   EMPLOYEE SYSTEM                                          ║
║  (3)   ORDER SYSTEM                                             ║
║  (4)   INVENTORY SYSTEM                                         ║
║  (5)   EXIT SYSTEM                                              ║
╚════════════════════════════════════════════════════════════════╝
```

Fig. 21-8. The main menu screen.

you will see that it gets a little harder in multifile systems, but even that is not that difficult.

Fred decides to code the menus for the Customer system next. He is running the Customer system from the main menu. Once he gets to the Customer menu, what does he do?

Fred reexamines the documentation for the Customer menu. He starts by looking at the flowchart for the modules, as shown in Fig. 21-9.

He sees that it is a little more complicated than the main menu. The *Print mailing labels* function has programs of its own. "What do I do about that," Fred wonders. Then he remembers that he will take care of those functions in that module, and he can ignore it for now.

Fred knows that his pseudocode and screen display is exactly the same as the

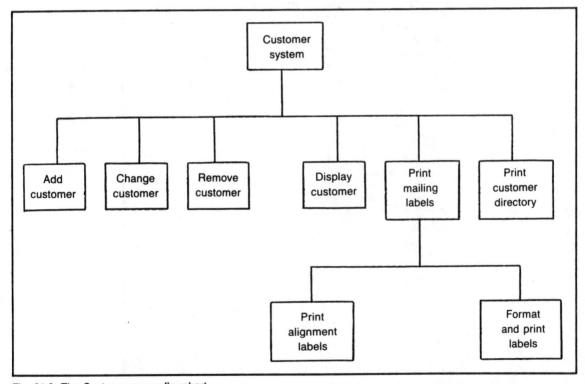

Fig. 21-9. The Customer menu flowchart.

```
CUSTMENU
COLUMN FRED'S FISH MARKET CUSTOMER SYSTEM MENU
ADD CUSTOMER
CHANGE CUSTOMER
REMOVE CUSTOMER
DISPLAY CUSTOMER
PRINT MAILING LABELS
PRINT DIRECTORY
RETURN TO MAIN MENU
EXIT SYSTEM
```

Fig. 21-10. The Customer menu code.

```
*(*****************************)
*(        CUSTMENU.CMD         *)
*(      FRED'S FISH MARKET     *)
*(    CUSTOMER MENU PROGRAM    *)
*(    (c) 1986 Cary N. Prague  *)
*(*****************************)
SET VAR PICK2   INT
SET VAR LEVEL2 INT
SET VAR LEVEL2 TO 0
WHILE LEVEL2 EQ 0   THEN
  NEWPAGE
  CHOOSE PICK2 FROM CUSTMENU.MNU
  IF PICK2   EQ 1 THEN
    RUN CUSTADD.CMD
  ENDIF
  IF PICK2   EQ 2 THEN
    RUN CUSTCHG.CMD
  ENDIF
  IF PICK2   EQ 3 THEN
    RUN CUSTREM.CMD
  ENDIF
  IF PICK2   EQ 4 THEN
    RUN CUSTDIS.CMD
  ENDIF
  IF PICK2   EQ 5 THEN
    RUN CUSTLBL.CMD
  ENDIF
  IF PICK2   EQ 6 THEN
    RUN CUSTDIR.CMD
  ENDIF
  IF PICK2   EQ 7 THEN
    BREAK
  ENDIF
  IF PICK2   EQ 8 THEN
    BREAK
  ENDIF
ENDWHILE
CLEAR LEVEL2
CLEAR PICK2
RETURN
```

Fig. 21-11. The Customer menu program.

main menu system, with just the choices different. Fred creates the Customer menu from a copy of the main menu code. Fred codes the menu as shown in Fig. 21-10.

"It has a few more choices and they are different, but that was easy," thinks Fred. "I should be able to create the same program to display the choices as I create the modules, but I want to use a loop. I really don't like GOTOs." Fred's program is shown in Fig. 21-11.

Fred remembers to document his program again. However, Fred really didn't like the GOTOs in his main menu. Fred decides to write the code with a real loop instead. Fred is getting creative. Fred sets up a variable called Level2 and sets it to 0 to continually display his menu until the choices are 7 or 8 to leave the system. Even then, the loop will never end because Level2 is not 0. Fred uses the BREAK command to leave the loop automatically if the choices are seven or eight.

Fred's loop is a traditional loop that clears the screen at each new pass and displays the menu with the CHOOSE command. A series of IF statements will run the various programs that Fred will create. Fred gives his programs very consistent names. Each name starts with the letters *Cust* followed by a three-letter word that tells what the function does—add (to add), chg (to change), rem (to remove or delete), dis (to display), lbl (for labels), and dir (for directory).

After the ENDWHILE, Fred has cleared the variables he has used and included a RETURN to return to the main menu for another main menu choice.

Fred will code those functions later. Now Fred returns to R:base and types:

```
R> RUN MAIN.CMD
```

Instantly, the main menu appears. Fred chooses **1** for the customer menu and sees the menu as shown in Fig. 21-12.

Fred can't run anything, but the menu seems to work. Later, he will give it a better test. He enters a **7** and returns to the main menu.

THE ORDER MENU

The last menu Fred will create is the Order menu. Once again, Fred looks at the flowchart that he has created to see the various functions his menu will need (Fig. 21-13). By now Fred realizes that he doesn't need to look at the pseudocode or the

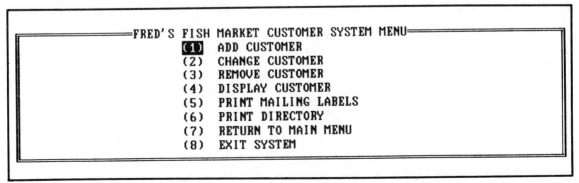

Fig. 21-12. The Customer menu display.

273

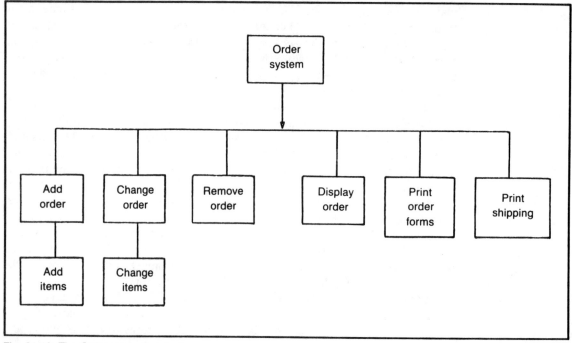

Fig. 21-13. The Order menu flowchart.

menu screen. He has little control over that when he uses the CHOOSE command. Fred's original design called for a space between most of the menu choices and the Exit choice. Fred couldn't do this with CHOOSE but decided it was worth it anyway. He creates the code in a file called Ordrmenu.mnu on his disk.

Fred creates his menu code for the Order menu (Fig. 21-14). It looks very similar to the code for the other two menus and will work just the same.

The last thing Fred does is to copy the Customer menu program, Custmenu.cmd, to a file he calls Ordrmenu.cmd. He then edits that file. He is satisfied with the changes he made in the customer program. He is proud of his WHILE loop. Fred calls Elsa and Fred Jr. over to his desk. He says to Elsa: "Look Elsa, I've created

```
ORDRMENU
COLUMN FRED'S FISH MARKET ORDER SYSTEM MENU
ADD ORDERS
CHANGE ORDER
REMOVE ORDER
DISPLAY ORDER
PRINT ORDER FORMS
PRINT SHIPPING FORMS
RETURN TO MAIN MENU
EXIT SYSTEM
```

Fig. 21-14. The Order menu code.

274

```
*(*****************************)
*(         ORDRMENU.CMD        *)
*(      FRED'S FISH MARKET      *)
*(      ORDER MENU PROGRAM      *)
*(   (c) 1986 Cary N. Prague    *)
*(*****************************)
SET VAR PICK2  INT
SET VAR LEVEL2 INT
SET VAR LEVEL2 TO 0
WHILE LEVEL2 EQ 0   THEN
  NEWPAGE
  CHOOSE PICK2 FROM ORDRMENU.MNU
  IF PICK2 EQ 1 THEN
     RUN ORDRADD.CMD
  ENDIF
  IF PICK2 EQ 2 THEN
     RUN ORDRCHG.CMD
  ENDIF
  IF PICK2 EQ 3 THEN
     RUN ORDRREM.CMD
  ENDIF
  IF PICK2 EQ 4 THEN
     RUN ORDRDIS.CMD
  ENDIF
  IF PICK2 EQ 5 THEN
     RUN ORDRFMS.CMD
  ENDIF
  IF PICK2 EQ 6 THEN
     RUN ORDRSHP.CMD
  ENDIF
  IF PICK2 EQ 7 THEN
     BREAK
  ENDIF
  IF PICK2 EQ 8 THEN
     BREAK
  ENDIF
ENDWHILE
CLEAR LEVEL2
CLEAR PICK2
```

Fig. 21-15. The Order menu program.

a loop. Now it runs over and over again." Elsa says, "That's nice." Fred Jr. says "ga ga."

Fred changes the RUN statements. There are still eight, but numbers 7 and 8 really do the same thing. They will simply leave the loop and return to the main menu. Fred looks at his code (Fig. 21-15) and is satisfied.

Later he will test the menu when he tests the order system. For now Fred is ready to start the data entry process.

Chapter 22

Coding Data
Entry Screens

Fred is ready to create his Add Customer screen. He begins by looking at his design. He gets out his screen diagram and pseudocode (Fig. 22-1).

The screen will let the user enter data into the ten columns of the database. One record at a time will be added. The screen looks fairly simple. Fred's pseudocode shows a simple loop so the operator can enter records until they are finished. Some people might create a custom program that would return to the Customer menu after each entry; not Fred, he knows that would drive an operator crazy. His brother Frank is crazy already. Fred decides that one in the family is enough.

Fred will create the form first. R:base 5000 almost never requires you to write text to the screen and then use FILLINs to capture the data entry.

He could use a simple form to create the form, but as Fred learned with EXPRESS, he doesn't want a menu popping up at the top of the screen asking the operator if he wants to add, edit, reuse, or quit the customer data entry procedure. This is too confusing for Fred. He can use rules to keep the operator from using the same customer number twice, but Fred wants to control his own error messages. He also wants to use the form for adding, changing, deleting, and displaying customers. He doesn't like the fact that using the standard ENTER or EDIT commands places the menu at the top of the screen and also does too much. The EDIT function lets the user change or delete any records. Fred wants the operator to be able to see only one record at a time.

ADDING RECORDS

Fred decides to use a variable form and not connect the form to any one table. Fred

```
         --------------------------------------

                FRED'S FRIENDLY FISH MARKET
                    CUSTOMER ADDITIONS


           CUSTOMER NUMBER: CUSTN

           COMPANY:      COMPANY------------X
           LAST NAME:    LNAME--------------X
           FIRST NAME:   FNAME--------------X

           ADDRESS: ADDRESS----------------X
           CITY:       CITY----------X

           STATE: ST     ZIP: ZIP-----X

           PHONE NUMBER: PHONE-------X

           DISCOUNT: DS

         --------------------------------------


         ADD A CUSTOMER

             ACCESS CUSTOMER FILE
             SET CUSTOMER NUMBER TO NOT BLANK
             DO WHILE CUSTOMER NUMBER NOT BLANK
                DISPLAY SCREEN
                ENTER DATA
                VERIFY CUSTOMER NUMBER
                IF NEW NUMBER
                   THEN
                      ADD CUSTOMER DATA
                      CLEAR DATA FIELDS
                   ELSE
                      WRITE "NUMBER ALREADY ON FILE"
                ENDIF
             ENDDO
```

Fig. 22-1. The Customer screen and pseudocode.

creates the variable form as he has so many times before and examines it as it looks in Fig. 22-2.

Fred has created his variable form. He created ten variables corresponding to the ten columns in the Customer table, for consistency. He could call the variables any name he wanted to, but he preferred to be consistent. It makes it easier to remember them later when you are programming.

Fred created all the variables as text in varying lengths corresponding to the lengths in the Customer table. Later, you will see a form that uses variables from several tables of varying type and length. You can see a list of your defined variables by pressing the <F3> key in the FORMS edit mode.

Now that the form is created, Fred can write the code to use it and to enter

```
┌─────────────────────────────────────────────────────────────────┐
│  ─Edit─Locate─Quit──────────────────────────────────────────     │
│                    FRED'S FRIENDLY FISH MARKET                    │
│                                                                   │
│                                                                   │
│                                                                   │
│          CUSTOMER NUMBER:   S   E                                 │
│                                                                   │
│                                                                   │
│      COMPANY:      S                      E                       │
│      LAST NAME:    S                      E                       │
│      FIRST NAME:   S                      E                       │
│                                                                   │
│      ADDRESS: S                         E                         │
│      CITY:    S                 E                                 │
│                                                                   │
│      STATE:    SE              ZIP:  S          E                 │
│                                                                   │
│      PHONE NUMBER: S              E                               │
│                                                                   │
│      DISCOUNT:   S        E                                       │
│                                                                   │
└─────────────────────────────────────────────────────────────────┘
```

Fig. 22-2. The Customer variable form.

the records into the Customer table. Fred looks back at his pseudocode in Fig. 22-1. Each time Fred runs the loop he will:

☐ Display the screen.
☐ Enter the data.
☐ Verify the customer number.
☐ Enter the record or write an error message.

Fred creates the code, as shown in Fig. 22-3. Fred starts the code by creating a variable named Cont that will control the loop. Fred then starts the loop and clears the screen with the NEWPAGE command.

He than draws the variable form called CUSTVAR with the command:

```
DRAW CUSTVAR
```

This command is stored in the database Fredfsh and was created with the FORMS command. The form is drawn on the screen. Until the ENTER VARIABLE command is executed, there is no data entry. The screen is displayed without any value on the screen. To display the current values of the variables named in the entry screen, Fred would have chosen the command:

```
DRAW CUSTVAR WITH ALL
```

278

After writing some text to the screen to show the name of the screen and a message for the operator to follow, the ENTER VARIABLE command is run to let the operator enter data into all the fields. This form will be used for adding, changing, deleting, and displaying data. The form can remain the same with the title *Fred's Friendly Fish Market* and the data fields, but the name of the actual screen and the message must continually change. This is a good example of *reusable* code. The form can be used for several modules. You will also see some of the same program code again when Fred creates his change, delete, and display functions.

After he enters the data into the form, Fred checks the value of the variable Custno to tell if anything was entered into the variable. Since everything is keyed off of the Customer Number, it is of critical importance that the Customer Number be entered, if nothing else. This program will continue as long as something is entered into the Customer Number field. If it is blank, the module ends.

This is the way Fred will have his operator leave a function. By entering nothing into an important field, you can tell the program that you are through with the function.

```
*(******************************)
*(      1.1-CUSTADD.CMD        *)
*(      FRED'S FISH MARKET     *)
*(      CUSTOMER ADDITIONS     *)
*(   (c) 1986 Cary N. Prague   *)
*(******************************)
SET VAR CONT INTEGER
SET VAR CONT TO 1
WHILE CONT EQ 1 THEN
    NEWPAGE
    DRAW CUSTVAR
    WRITE "  CUSTOMER ADDITIONS SCREEN          " AT 3 25
    WRITE "*** ENTER CUSTOMER RECORD ***        " AT 5 25
    ENTER VARIABLE
    IF CUSTNO FAILS THEN
      BREAK
    ENDIF
    SET POINTER #1 CHECKER FOR CUSTOMER WHERE CUSTNO EQ .CUSTNO
    IF CHECKER EQ 0 THEN
        WRITE "*** CUSTOMER NUMBER ALREADY ON FILE ***" AT 5 20
     ELSE
        LOAD CUSTOMER
        .CUSTNO .COMPANY .FSTNAME .LSTNAME .ADDRESS .CITY .STATE +
        .ZIP .PHONE .DISCOUNT
        END
    ENDIF
ENDWHILE
CLEAR ALL VARIABLES
SET VAR PICK1 INT
SET VAR PICK2 INT
SET VAR LEVEL2 INT
SET VAR LEVEL2 TO 0
RETURN
```

Fig. 22-3. The Customer Additions program.

This procedure, which has been adopted by some programmers, saves you from programming a step to leave the program. The step is easy to program, but requires the operator to answer a question before entering each record, such as:

`Do you want to continue?`

EXPRESS works in this same way by placing a menu at the top of the screen. This confirmation process, although thorough, can cause an operator who must enter a lot of data to become very frustrated with the extra keystrokes that the confirmation message creates.

Because Fred is using a variable form and is not entering the data directly into the table with the standard ENTER USING command, he cannot directly check to see if the Customer Number already exists with rules. Fred must use the SET POINTER command to check the table for the existence of a row that matches some criterion. Fred uses the command:

`SET POINTER #1 CHECKER FOR CUSTOMER WHERE CUSTNO EQ .CUSTNO`

This command places a pointer on a row in the customer file where the value of Custno in the Customer file equals the value of the variable Custno. The variable Custno was used for data entry in the variable form. Naming both the column in the table and the variable Custno is done only for convenience. They can be different, but then you must remember two sets of names.

Just attempting to place the pointer on the row will not tell you if the pointer actually got there. If there are no records or no records that match, the pointer will not be placed on a row. You must check the value of the variable that you specify.

Fred used the name Checker. You can use any name you want after the phrase *SET POINTER #1*. However, the name you use is the name of the variable that is created to hold the completion code of the command. If the code is 0, the record was found and the pointer placed. If the record is anything else, the record was not found.

In this case Fred knows that if the pointer is placed successfully, the Customer Number has already been used and an error message should be displayed. If not, the ELSE clause is executed.

Fred has implemented his duplicate Customer Number check using a simple IF statement. He has made his first right decision.

The ELSE clause means that the Customer Number entered is a new one and the record should be added to the file. Fred could add some other checks, such as that the Address or Name fields must not be blank, but he is not that sophisticated, yet.

Fred uses the LOAD command to add data. He has created ten variables. His Customer file contains ten variables. Fred loads the ten variables by simply listing them in the same order as they appear in the Customer table. The LOAD command specifies the table to load. By creating your variables in the form with the same names as the table, you can easily remember which order in which to place the variables. Notice that the LOAD command ends with an END command.

Fred ends his LOAD command, his IF statement, and his WHILE loop. The last thing to do is to clear the variables. Fred has created a lot of variables. To clear all the variables he has created, he would have to clear 11 variables with 11 separate CLEAR statements. Instead, Fred looks back to the modules that called this Custadd module. They were the Main and the Custmenu modules. He knows the variables that are still active in those modules and their values. It is easier, in this case, to clear all the variables and then recreate the variables and their values from the still open modules that called Custadd.

Now Fred must test his system. Fred runs the main program, chooses the first entry for the Customer system, and then chooses the Customer Add program. His data entry screen appears as shown in Fig. 22-4. Fred enters his record. When he is done entering the record, he presses <Return> again. The cursor bar goes back to the first field on the form. Fred can move anywhere on the screen, but he can't get out of the form. Fred wonders how to get out.

Fred is using R:base 5000. R:base uses the <ESC> key as a standard for leaving. Fred presses the <ESC> key and the record is entered. Fred has learned that, when in doubt, press the <ESC> key.

Fred is finished. His lobsters are clapping their claws. They are proud of Fred. Julie the crab is happy too.

CHANGING RECORDS

Well, Fred can now add records to his system. Now he needs to be able to change records. Fred makes too many mistakes to avoid this module.

```
              FRED'S FRIENDLY FISH MARKET
               CUSTOMER ADDITIONS SCREEN

          *** ENTER CUSTOMER RECORD ***


             CUSTOMER NUMBER:    ██████


          COMPANY:
          LAST NAME:
          FIRST NAME:

          ADDRESS:
          CITY:

          STATE:                 ZIP:

          PHONE NUMBER:

          DISCOUNT:
```

Fig. 22-4. The Customer entry screen.

```
 ---------------------------------
:                                 :
:    FRED'S FRIENDLY FISH MARKET  :
:        CUSTOMER CHANGES         :
:                                 :
:                                 :
:                                 :
:    CUSTOMER NUMBER: CUSTN       :
:                                 :
:                                 :
:                                 :
:                                 :
:                                 :
 ---------------------------------
```

Fig. 22-5. The Customer Changes entry screen.

In the last module you saw how Fred had to check the Customer file to see if the Customer Number he was entering was already on the file. To change a record, Fred will have to check to see if the record exists. You can't change what isn't there.

Fred studies the first screen he has designed (Fig. 22-5). It describes the display of a simple screen that only shows the Customer Number and the title. After the Customer Number is entered and verified, the rest of the screen can be displayed. Fred thinks, "Why build another screen? That is why I created a variable form in the first place. I could display the entire form and let the operator only enter the value of the Customer Number field. If the Customer Number is found on the file, I will display the rest of the fields and let them change the record." Good thinking, Fred!

Fred can use the same screen for all his data manipulation and just enter into different parts of it. Once the Customer Number is entered, the rest of the record will be displayed and the changes can be made. However, the Customer Number cannot be changed because it is the key to the record. In fact, the only way to change a Customer Number is to delete the record and reenter it. That seems like a good control method to Fred.

```
CHANGE A CUSTOMER

      ACCESS CUSTOMER FILE
      SET CUSTOMER NUMBER TO NOT BLANK
      DO WHILE CUSTOMER NUMBER NOT BLANK
        DISPLAY SCREEN
        ENTER CUSTOMER NUMBER
        VERIFY CUSTOMER NUMBER
        IF FOUND
          THEN
             RETRIEVE CUSTOMER DATA
             CHANGE DESIRED FIELDS
             UPDATE RECORD
             CLEAR DATA FIELDS
          ELSE
             WRITE "NUMBER NOT ON FILE"
        ENDIF
      ENDDO
```

Fig. 22-6. The Customer Changes pseudocode.

Fred now looks at the pseuodocode (Fig. 22-6). He knows his screen is exactly the same as for the Add function.

Fred sees that he will set up a loop to enter Customer Numbers. As long as a Customer Number is entered, the loop will continue. Fred then displays the screen

```
*(******************************)
*(        1.2-CUSTCHG.CMD        *)
*(        FRED'S FISH MARKET     *)
*(        CUSTOMER CHANGES       *)
*(   (c) 1986 Cary N. Prague     *)
*(******************************)
SET VAR CONT INTEGER
SET VAR CONT TO 1
WHILE CONT EQ 1 THEN
     NEWPAGE
     DRAW CUSTVAR
     WRITE "   CUSTOMER CHANGES SCREEN              " AT 3 25
     WRITE "*** ENTER CUSTOMER NUMBER ***" AT 5 25
     ENTER VARIABLE CUSTNO
     IF CUSTNO FAILS THEN
        BREAK
     ENDIF
     SET POINTER #1 CHECKER FOR CUSTOMER WHERE CUSTNO EQ .CUSTNO
     IF CHECKER NE 0 THEN
        WRITE "*** CUSTOMER NOT FOUND ***" AT 5 26
      ELSE
        SET VAR COMPANY TO COMPANY IN #1
        SET VAR FSTNAME TO FSTNAME IN #1
        SET VAR LSTNAME TO LSTNAME IN #1
        SET VAR ADDRESS TO ADDRESS IN #1
        SET VAR CITY TO CITY IN #1
        SET VAR STATE TO STATE IN #1
        SET VAR ZIP TO ZIP IN #1
        SET VAR PHONE TO PHONE IN #1
        SET VAR DISCOUNT TO DISCOUNT IN #1
        WRITE "*** CHANGE CUSTOMER RECORD ***" AT 5 25
        EDIT VARIABLE COMPANY FSTNAME LSTNAME ADDRESS CITY STATE ZIP +
                      PHONE DISCOUNT
        CHANGE COMPANY TO .COMPANY IN #1
        CHANGE FSTNAME TO .FSTNAME IN #1
        CHANGE LSTNAME TO .LSTNAME IN #1
        CHANGE ADDRESS TO .ADDRESS IN #1
        CHANGE CITY TO .CITY IN #1
        CHANGE STATE TO .STATE IN #1
        CHANGE ZIP TO .ZIP IN #1
        CHANGE PHONE TO .PHONE IN #1
        CHANGE DISCOUNT TO .DISCOUNT IN #1
     ENDIF
ENDWHILE
CLEAR ALL VARIABLES
SET VAR PICK1 INT
SET VAR PICK2 INT
SET VAR LEVEL2 INT
SET VAR LEVEL2 TO 0
RETURN
```

Fig. 22-7. The Customer Changes program.

and gets the Customer Number. If he finds the Customer Number, he will display the screen with the fields by retrieving the data from the Customer table, update any or all of the fields, and resave the record to the same place from which it was retrieved. Remember, you are changing an existing record, not creating a new one. Finally, you must clear all the data fields so the screen is ready for a new record.

Fred creates his program. The code is shown in Fig. 22-7.

First Fred sets up his loop in exactly the same way as in the Add module. In fact, Fred created this code by starting from the Customer Add program. Fred then clears the screen and draws the Customer form. Fred only allows entry of the Customer Number by specifying a variable name after the ENTER VARIABLE command. The Customer Number variable Custno is first checked to make sure that something was entered. If nothing is entered, then Fred assumes the operator is through changing records.

Once the Customer Number is entered, the pointer is set to see if the record exists. Now Fred wants the value of Checker to be 0, indicating that the record is found. Fred checks to see if the record is not found, and if it is not it will write an error message to the screen.

If the record is found then the record must be retrieved. A record can only be retrieved from a table one column at a time. A special version of the SET VAR command is used. Because there is a pointer pointing to the row in the table that contains the Customer Number, the special pointer notation is used.

For example, the notation to retrieve the company is:

```
SET VAR COMPANY TO COMPANY IN #1
```

There will be as many SET VAR commands as there are variables to retrieve. You don't have to use the same name for your variable as the name of the column, but it makes things easier.

So far you have seen the setting of pointer #1. There can be up to three active pointers at any one time, which lets you track three tables at once.

After he retrieves the data and writes a message to the screen, Fred uses the EDIT VARIABLE command with the remaining nine variables to allow the updating of the screen and the variables. Once the variables are changed on the form, they must be written back to the table. The CHANGE command is used for this purpose. Notice that the CHANGE command requires a period to be used preceding the notation. The CHANGE command also uses the #1 notation because the pointer is still pointing to the correct record.

Fred performs his housekeeping functions and is finished. The program looks like a lot of statements, but it is really just a lot of copying. This type of program requires the use of a word processor other than RBEDIT to be effective.

Fred is ready to test the program. He runs the Customer program from the main menu and chooses **2**. He enters one of the customer numbers, **A-001**, and presses <ESC> (see Fig. 22-8). As soon as he presses <ESC>, the program continues finding the record and displaying the fields so they can be changed. Fred sees his record in Fig. 22-9.

Fred has written his change routine. Now if he could only change Frank.

```
                    FRED'S FRIENDLY FISH MARKET
                      CUSTOMER CHANGES SCREEN

                    *** ENTER CUSTOMER NUMBER ***


                    CUSTOMER NUMBER:   A-001


               COMPANY:
               LAST NAME:
               FIRST NAME:

               ADDRESS:
               CITY:

               STATE:                    ZIP:

               PHONE NUMBER:

               DISCOUNT:
```

Fig. 22-8. Entering the Customer number.

```
                    FRED'S FRIENDLY FISH MARKET
                      CUSTOMER CHANGES SCREEN

                    *** CHANGE CUSTOMER RECORD ***


                    CUSTOMER NUMBER:   A-001


               COMPANY:       LEE SIDE FISHERIES
               LAST NAME:     KAY
               FIRST NAME:    LEE JAY

               ADDRESS: 151 CLEMENS COUTHOUSE
               CITY:    ROCKVILLE

               STATE:   CT              ZIP:   06073

               PHONE NUMBER: (203)555-6134

               DISCOUNT:  5
```

Fig. 22-9. Changing the Customer record.

```
   .-------------------------------------------.
   :                                           :
   :        FRED'S FRIENDLY FISH MARKET        :
   :             CUSTOMER DELETION             :
   :                                           :
   : ENTER "D" TO CONFIRM DELETE ===> __       :
   :                                           :
   : CUSTOMER NUMBER: CUSTN                     :
   :                                           :
   :  COMPANY:     COMPANY------------X         :
   :  LAST NAME:   LNAME-------------X          :
   :  FIRST NAME: FNAME-------------X           :
   :                                           :
   :  ADDRESS: ADDRESS-----------------X        :
   :  CITY:     CITY---------X                  :
   :                                           :
   :  STATE: ST    ZIP: ZIP-----X               :
   :                                           :
   :  PHONE NUMBER: PHONE-------X                :
   :                                           :
   :  DISCOUNT: DS                              :
   :                                           :
   '-------------------------------------------'


            ACCESS CUSTOMER FILE
            SET CUSTOMER NUMBER TO NOT BLANK
            DO WHILE CUSTOMER NUMBER NOT BLANK
               DISPLAY SCREEN
               ENTER CUSTOMER NUMBER
               VERIFY CUSTOMER NUMBER
               IF FOUND
                  THEN
                     RETRIEVE CUSTOMER DATA
                     ENTER DELETE CONFIRMATION
                     IF CONFIRM = "D"
                        THEN
                           DELETE RECORD
                           CLEAR DATA FIELDS
                     ENDIF
                  ELSE
                     WRITE "NUMBER NOT ON FILE"
               ENDIF
            ENDDO
```

Fig. 22-10. The Customer Delete function screen and pseudocode.

REMOVING RECORDS

The next step is to create the Delete or Remove Records function. This function is exactly the same as the Change function with one addition. Instead of displaying and letting the user change the data, the record is displayed and the user asked if he wants to delete the record.

Fred is showing good design here. You never want to delete a record before making sure you are deleting the right record. By entering the Customer Number, then displaying the record and confirming the delete, Fred is adding a margin for safety.

Fred checks his screen and pseudocode as shown in Fig. 22-10. The only difference Fred sees from the Change function is the Delete confirmation instead of the Change code. Fred is ready to start coding. He makes a copy of the Change module code, and in a few seconds he has created the program shown in Fig. 22-11.

```
*(****************************)
*(      1.3-CUSTREM.CMD        *)
*(      FRED'S FISH MARKET     *)
*(      CUSTOMER REMOVALS      *)
*(  (c) 1986 Cary N. Prague    *)
*(****************************)
SET VAR CONT INTEGER
SET VAR CONT TO 1
SET VAR DELCON TEXT
SET VAR CHECKER INTEGER
WHILE CONT EQ 1 THEN
     NEWPAGE
     DRAW CUSTVAR
     WRITE "    CUSTOMER REMOVAL SCREEN              " AT 3 25
     WRITE "*** ENTER CUSTOMER NUMBER ***" AT 5 25
     ENTER VARIABLE CUSTNO
     IF CUSTNO FAILS THEN
       PACK
       BREAK
     ENDIF
     SET POINTER #1 CHECKER FOR CUSTOMER WHERE CUSTNO EQ .CUSTNO
     IF CHECKER NE 0 THEN
        WRITE "*** CUSTOMER NOT FOUND ***" AT 5 26
      ELSE
        SET VAR COMPANY TO COMPANY IN #1
        SET VAR FSTNAME TO FSTNAME IN #1
        SET VAR LSTNAME TO LSTNAME IN #1
        SET VAR ADDRESS TO ADDRESS IN #1
        SET VAR CITY TO CITY IN #1
        SET VAR STATE TO STATE IN #1
        SET VAR ZIP TO ZIP IN #1
        SET VAR PHONE TO PHONE IN #1
        SET VAR DISCOUNT TO DISCOUNT IN #1
        DRAW CUSTVAR WITH ALL
        WRITE "    CUSTOMER REMOVAL SCREEN              " AT 3 25
        FILLIN DELCON USING "ENTER D TO CONFIRM DELETE ===> " AT 5 22
        IF DELCON = D THEN
          DELETE ROWS FROM #1
          WRITE "*** CUSTOMER RECORD DELETED ***          " AT 5 25
        ENDIF
     ENDIF
ENDWHILE
CLEAR ALL VARIABLES
SET VAR PICK1 INT
SET VAR PICK2 INT
SET VAR LEVEL2 INT
SET VAR LEVEL2 TO 0
RETURN
```

Fig. 22-11. The Customer Delete function program.

The program for this function is exactly the same until after the last SET VAR command. Fred doesn't want to enter or edit data; so those commands aren't appropriate here. How does Fred redraw the form and display all the fields? He uses the DRAW CUSTVAR WITH ALL command, which will redisplay the form with all the fields filled in. However, the user will not be able to change the fields. That is exactly what Fred wanted.

After he displays the record and rewrites the customer screen message that is erased when the form is redisplayed, Fred is ready to code the confirmation message.

Fred uses the FILLIN command to get the user's confirmation message. This is the best command for a one-line entry. Fred makes the delete confirmation positive. The user must enter a **D** or the record will not be deleted. A delete message should not let you press <Return> to delete and X to not delete. It's too easy to press <Return> without thinking and the next thing you know, your record is gone.

The command:

```
DELETE ROWS FROM #1
```

is used to delete the record to which the pointer is pointing. The pointer is very important. It controls a lot of functions, especially when you are working with a multifile system.

Notice the PACK command in the IF statement that is executed when the Custno is blank. This is a maintenance command that frees up wasted space caused by deleted records. If your database grows very large, you may want to transfer

```
       FRED'S FRIENDLY FISH MARKET
          CUSTOMER REMOVAL SCREEN

       ENTER D TO CONFIRM DELETE ===>


   CUSTOMER NUMBER:   B-001


   COMPANY:     A PECK OF CHOWDER
   LAST NAME:   HAROLD
   FIRST NAME:  DAVID

   ADDRESS: 23 NEWBORN RD
   CITY:    HARTFORD

   STATE:   CT            ZIP:   06115

   PHONE NUMBER: (203)555-7463

   DISCOUNT:   35.0000
```

Fig. 22-12. The Customer Delete program screen.

```
*(******************************)
*(      1.4-CUSTDIS.CMD         *)
*(      FRED'S FISH MARKET      *)
*(        CUSTOMER DISPLAY      *)
*(   (c) 1986 Cary N. Prague    *)
*(******************************)
SET MESSAGE OFF
OPEN FREDFSH
SET ERROR MESSAGE OFF
SET VAR CONT INTEGER
SET VAR CONT TO 1
SET VAR DELCON TEXT
SET VAR CHECKER INTEGER
WHILE CONT EQ 1 THEN
     NEWPAGE
     DRAW CUSTVAR
     WRITE "    CUSTOMER DISPLAY SCREEN              " AT 3 25
     WRITE "*** ENTER CUSTOMER NUMBER ***" AT 5 25
     ENTER VARIABLE CUSTNO
     IF CUSTNO FAILS THEN
       BREAK
     ENDIF
     SET POINTER #1 CHECKER FOR CUSTOMER WHERE CUSTNO EQ .CUSTNO
     IF CHECKER NE 0 THEN
        WRITE "*** CUSTOMER NOT FOUND ***" AT 5 26
      ELSE
        SET VAR COMPANY TO COMPANY IN #1
        SET VAR FSTNAME TO FSTNAME IN #1
        SET VAR LSTNAME TO LSTNAME IN #1
        SET VAR ADDRESS TO ADDRESS IN #1
        SET VAR CITY TO CITY IN #1
        SET VAR STATE TO STATE IN #1
        SET VAR ZIP TO ZIP IN #1
        SET VAR PHONE TO PHONE IN #1
        SET VAR DISCOUNT TO DISCOUNT IN #1
        DRAW CUSTVAR WITH ALL
        WRITE "     CUSTOMER DISPLAY SCREEN"  AT 5,20
        WRITE "*** PRESS ANY KEY TO CONTINUE *** " AT 5 23
        PAUSE
     ENDIF
ENDWHILE
CLEAR ALL VARIABLES
SET VAR PICK1 INT
SET VAR PICK2 INT
SET VAR LEVEL2 INT
SET VAR LEVEL2 TO 0
RETURN
```

Fig. 22-13. The Customer Display program.

this system to a maintenance choice off the main menu. It could become lengthy as your tables grow in size.

Fred now tests his latest function. He enters his Customer Number, and the record is displayed along with his message, as shown in Fig. 22-12.

Fred only wishes that he could delete Frank just as easily. He is ready for the Display function.

DISPLAYING RECORDS

By now, Fred is getting pretty good with his code. He has already figured that the Display program is his easiest so far. The code is exactly the same as for the Delete function, except that instead of the Delete message he will simply use the PAUSE command to stop the program after the customer record is displayed. The code is displayed in Fig. 22-13.

Fred runs the program to make sure it works; it does. He is ready to produce his reports. That is the reason for the program in the first place.

Chapter 23

Customizing

and Printing Reports

The mailing label program is the first program that Fred will create. It is also a very complicated program. There are many times when the R:base REPORTS command can create an excellent report that saves the need for any programming, except perhaps selecting the records to print.

The one limitation of the REPORT form is the lack of its ability to handle multiple records on the same line in the report. Because Fred has bought three-part mailing labels, he wants to print three records at a time on the mailing labels paper. Fred will create a customer program.

THE MAILING LABEL PROGRAM

Fred starts by checking the design he created. The first thing he looks at is the screen design and label layout, shown in Fig. 23-1.

Fred sees that he will have to create a simple screen that gets a choice of function. There are three functions: print all the mailing labels from all the records of the customer table, print some dummy labels to align the labels in the printer, and exit from the system. Fred remembers his flowchart that he created initially. He will actually create three programs. The first will make the selection and call either the label-alignment print program or the real label print program.

Fred checks his pseudocode for the label choice program (Fig. 23-2). Fred's pseudocode shows that he will display a screen and read a choice. Depending on the choice, he will call the appropriate subroutine. Fred originally designed his pseudocode to retrieve the record and then call a subroutine to print it out. Fred decides that method

```
          --------------------------------------------
          :                                          :
          :         FRED'S FRIENDLY FISH MARKET       :
          :            MAILING LABEL PRINT            :
          :                                          :
          :                                          :
          :                                          :
          :         ENTER "A" FOR ALIGNMENT PRINT,    :
          :             "X" TO EXIT PRINT,            :
          :           OR <cr> TO BEGIN PRINT          :
          :                                          :
          :               ====>  ___                 :
          :                                          :
          :                                          :
          :                                          :
          :                                          :
          :                                          :
          :                                          :
          :                                          :
          :                                          :
          --------------------------------------------


          X-----COMPANY------X
          X------FNAME-------X X------LNAME-------X
          X------ADDRESS---------X
          X----CITY-----X, ST X--ZIP--X
```

Fig. 23-1. The Customer Mailing Labels screen design.

is inefficient. He will call the subroutine and perform all the processing there.

Fred creates the simple code shown in Fig. 23-3. Fred's program clears the screen, writes a simple menu using WRITE commands, and then uses Fred's favorite, the FILLIN command, to get the choice. There is no loop here. Fred will select

```
          PRINT MAILING LABELS

               STORE " " TO CHOICE
               DO WHILE CHOICE NOT "X"
                 DISPLAY SCREEN
                 READ CHOICE
                 IF CHOICE = "X"
                   THEN EXIT
                 ENDIF
                 IF CHOICE = "A"
                   THEN PERFORM "ALIGNMENT PRINT"
                 ENDIF
                 IF CHOICE = "<cr>"
                   ACCESS CUSTOMER FILE
                   READ A CUSTOMER RECORD
                   INITIALIZE RECORD COUNTER
                   PERFORM "LABEL PRINT"
                 ENDIF
               ENDDO
```

Fig. 23-2. The Customer Mailing Labels main pseudocode.

292

```
*(*****************************)
*(        1.5-CUSTLBL.CMD        *)
*(        FRED'S FISH MARKET      *)
*(  CUSTOMER MAILING LABELS      *)
*(   (c) 1986 Cary N. Prague     *)
*(*****************************)
SET VAR PRTCHK TEXT
NEWPAGE
WRITE "FRED'S FRIENDLY FISH MARKET" AT 2 25
WRITE "CUSTOMER MAILING LABEL PRINT              " AT 3 25
WRITE " ENTER <cr> TO BEGIN PRINT" AT 5 25
WRITE "  OR A FOR ALIGNMENT PRINT" AT 6 25
WRITE "  OR X TO EXIT PRINT" AT 7 25
FILLIN PRTCHK USING "====>" AT 9 32
IF PRTCHK EQ A THEN
  RUN CUSTLBLA.CMD
ENDIF
IF PRTCHK FAILS THEN
  RUN CUSTLBLP.CMD
ENDIF
CLEAR PRTCHK
RETURN
```

Fig. 23-3. The Customer Mailing Labels main program.

the function and either print the alignment labels, print the real labels, or do nothing. Two subroutines will take care of everything.

Fred assumes that if the user doesn't enter an X or an A that they want to print the labels. Therefore, Fred uses the FAILS keyword to check the FILLIN variable to see if nothing was entered. Nothing means to print the labels. Be careful, Fred.

Fred checks the pseudocode next for the subroutines. The alignment print is simple: print a row of labels with Xs in every position. The alignment will be set to three sets of labels.

Fred creates a sample of the printout on a typewriter to give him a more accurate assessment of where he wants to place the Xs. This diagram is shown in Fig. 23-4.

Fred can see that each line of the label is different. Each label line will have to be created separately.

Alignment Labels Program

Fred creates the alignment program. Because he doesn't have to retrieve any data from the Customer table to print alignment labels, it is just a lot of text manipulation. The alignment program is shown in Fig. 23-5.

Fred starts the code by displaying a message to turn on and align the printer to the top of the form. It is important to remind the user to align the printer, or the printer might not handle its page break properly.

Next, Fred creates a lot of variables. He creates several variables to keep track of how many labels across he has filled with Xs and how many lines down. He then creates four variables called X1 through X4 to hold the mask of Xs for each line.

```
XXXXXXXXXXXXXXXXXXXX      XXXXXXXXXXXXXXXXXXXX      XXXXXXXXXXXXXXXXXXXX
X. XXXXXXXXXXXXXXXXXXXX    X. XXXXXXXXXXXXXXXXXXXX    X. XXXXXXXXXXXXXXXXXXXX
XXXXXXXXXXXXXXXXXXXXXXXXX  XXXXXXXXXXXXXXXXXXXXXXXXX  XXXXXXXXXXXXXXXXXXXXXXXXX
XXXXXXXXXXXXXXX, XX XXXXX  XXXXXXXXXXXXXXX, XX XXXXX  XXXXXXXXXXXXXXX, XX XXXXX

XXXXXXXXXXXXXXXXXXXX      XXXXXXXXXXXXXXXXXXXX      XXXXXXXXXXXXXXXXXXXX
X. XXXXXXXXXXXXXXXXXXXX    X. XXXXXXXXXXXXXXXXXXXX    X. XXXXXXXXXXXXXXXXXXXX
XXXXXXXXXXXXXXXXXXXXXXXXX  XXXXXXXXXXXXXXXXXXXXXXXXX  XXXXXXXXXXXXXXXXXXXXXXXXX
XXXXXXXXXXXXXXX, XX XXXXX  XXXXXXXXXXXXXXX, XX XXXXX  XXXXXXXXXXXXXXX, XX XXXXX

XXXXXXXXXXXXXXXXXXXX      XXXXXXXXXXXXXXXXXXXX      XXXXXXXXXXXXXXXXXXXX
X. XXXXXXXXXXXXXXXXXXXX    X. XXXXXXXXXXXXXXXXXXXX    X. XXXXXXXXXXXXXXXXXXXX
XXXXXXXXXXXXXXXXXXXXXXXXX  XXXXXXXXXXXXXXXXXXXXXXXXX  XXXXXXXXXXXXXXXXXXXXXXXXX
XXXXXXXXXXXXXXX, XX XXXXX  XXXXXXXXXXXXXXX, XX XXXXX  XXXXXXXXXXXXXXX, XX XXXXX
```

Fig. 23-4. The Customer Mailing Labels Alignment print.

Each mask represents a line from the label. The variables called Line1 through Line4 will be used to hold the Xs.

Fred does this procedure because R:base 5000 has no way to print more than once to any line on the printer. You must print an entire line at once. Fred has learned how to fill an entire line with Xs a label at a time and then print the entire line.

Fred sets the number of labels he will print down the page for the alignment and creates an empty line to print between lines of labels. He is now ready for the hard part—filling the lines with Xs. Fred will use a series of MOVE commands to fill the lines. The MOVE command lets you move any length of text from a variable, starting with any character in that text. You can move that text to any position in another variable.

Fred has created four variables called Line1 through Line4. They will be used to store and then print the lines to the printer. The variables X1 through X4 hold a 25-character line of Xs—one for each label line. The 12 MOVE commands in Fred's program move three sets of Xs from each X variable to the correct position in the Line variable.

The first set of labels start in column 1; the next set start in column 27; while the third set of labels start in column 53. The four lines are filled, and the program is ready to print the lines. When you are filling these lines with Xs, you only have to fill the lines once and then loop through printing the labels. Later, you will see in the real label printing program that you have to format each set of labels in a loop as you have to retrieve the data from the customer table first, then format it, and print it.

After Fred has formatted the four print lines with Xs, he is ready to print them out. Fred first changes the output to the printer with the OUTPUT PRINTER command. Next, Fred creates a loop that will print out as many sets of four lines and a separator line as the value of the variable NUMDOWN.

Although the MOVE command is used to move text from one variable to another, the SHOW command will write a variable to a printer. The SHOW command can only write to the printer one line at a time; so there have to be five separate

```
*(******************************)
*(      1.5.A-CUSTLBLA.CMD      *)
*(        FRED'S FISH MARKET    *)
*(   MAILING LABELS ALIGNMENT   *)
*(    (c) 1986 Cary N. Prague   *)
*(******************************)
WRITE " TURN ON AND ALIGN PRINTER       " AT 5 25
WRITE "   PRESS ANY KEY TO START        " AT 6 25
WRITE "                                 " AT 7 25
WRITE "                                 " AT 9,32
PAUSE
SET VAR COUNTER INTEGER
SET VAR NUMDOWN INTEGER
SET VAR EMPTYLIN TEXT
SET VAR X1 TEXT
SET VAR X2 TEXT
SET VAR X3 TEXT
SET VAR X4 TEXT
SET VAR LINE1 TEXT
SET VAR LINE2 TEXT
SET VAR LINE3 TEXT
SET VAR LINE4 TEXT
SET VAR X1 TO "XXXXXXXXXXXXXXXXXXX       "
SET VAR X2 TO "X. XXXXXXXXXXXXXXXXXXX     "
SET VAR X3 TO "XXXXXXXXXXXXXXXXXXXXXXXXX"
SET VAR X4 TO "XXXXXXXXXXXXXX, XX XXXXX"
SET VAR EMPTYLIN TO " "
SET VAR NUMDOWN TO 3
SET VAR COUNTER TO 1
MOVE 25 FROM X1 AT 1 TO LINE1 AT 1
MOVE 25 FROM X1 AT 1 TO LINE1 AT 27
MOVE 25 FROM X1 AT 1 TO LINE1 AT 53
MOVE 25 FROM X2 AT 1 TO LINE2 AT 1
MOVE 25 FROM X2 AT 1 TO LINE2 AT 27
MOVE 25 FROM X2 AT 1 TO LINE2 AT 53
MOVE 25 FROM X3 AT 1 TO LINE3 AT 1
MOVE 25 FROM X3 AT 1 TO LINE3 AT 27
MOVE 25 FROM X3 AT 1 TO LINE3 AT 53
MOVE 25 FROM X4 AT 1 TO LINE4 AT 1
MOVE 25 FROM X4 AT 1 TO LINE4 AT 27
MOVE 25 FROM X4 AT 1 TO LINE4 AT 53
OUTPUT PRINTER
WHILE COUNTER <= .NUMDOWN THEN
    SET VAR COUNTER TO COUNTER + 1
    SHOW VAR LINE1=80
    SHOW VAR LINE2=80
    SHOW VAR LINE3=80
    SHOW VAR LINE4=80
    SHOW VAR EMPTYLIN
ENDWHILE
OUTPUT SCREEN
RETURN
```

Fig. 23-5. The Customer Mailing Labels Alignment program.

SHOW commands—one to print each type of print line and a separator line. The = *80* clause in the SHOW VAR command tells R:base the print width of the variable.

Once the alignment labels are printed, control returns to the main label program, which returns control to the Customer menu. Fred would then choose labels again to print the actual labels with his Customer table.

Fred decides to leave it that way for now. "Someday," he says, "I should probably come back to the label program to print the labels."

Print Labels Subroutine

Fred now is ready to create the other subroutine to print the labels. Fred begins by checking his pseudocode (Fig. 23-6).

He knows that the program will be roughly the same as the alignment print program, except that he has to retrieve data and place it in the print line instead of the Xs. All of a sudden Fred thinks, "Oh no! What do I do when there isn't exactly three labels on a line? Do I print the last label twice or not at all?" Fred is puzzled. It is time to take a break and have some of Frank's alphabet clam chowder soup.

Fred looks in his bowl. There are letters floating in the soup, but Fred thinks they look strange. F—I—S—H! Why they spell *fish*! But something is wrong. These letters are large and painted on small blocks of hard plastic. Fred checks his computer's keyboard. Fred storms out of the room and dumps the soup on Frank's head. After fixing his keyboard, he is ready to work.

Fred's pseudocode tells him that he must set up variables to hold the data just like with the alignment program. Instead of hardcoding, or setting four variables to the four strings of Xs in the alignment program, he just creates three variables, which he calls *X, Y,* and *Z*. These will be used to retrieve the data and form each print line. He will build one label at a time. The reason he will use X, Y, and Z is

```
ALIGNMENT PRINT

    PRINT ONE ROW OF LABELS WITH X'S IN EVERY PRINT POSITION
    ADVANCE TO NEXT LABEL




LABEL PRINT

    INITIALIZE LABEL HOLDING AREAS
    FIND FIRST RECORD
    WHILE MORE RECORDS
       DECIDE IF FILLING LABEL 1,2 OR 3
       MOVE DATA INTO LABEL POSITION
       READ NEXT RECORD
       IF THREE LABELS FILLED OR NO MORE DATA
          PRINT LABEL SET
          CLEAR HOLDING AREAS
       ENDIF
    ENDWHILE
    CLEAR ALL VARIABLES
```

Fig. 23-6. The Customer Mailing Labels print pseudocode.

to avoid long program lines. The reason there are three variables (and this is the important part) is so that each line can be made at once. In his labels, some lines contain three columns from the table, such as City, State, and Zip. Well, Fred will show you as he programs.

Fred also sees from his pseudocode that he must set up a loop to read each record. The first record will be the first label, the second the second label across, and the third the third label across. After each set of three labels, he will print the line, after which he will clear out the print areas (there are five—the same as in the alignment program) and start over. When he runs out of data, he will print what he has. If there was one label filled only one will print. If none are filled there will be no printing. If two or three are filled then those will print. The last set of labels will be printed with whatever the print line is stuffed. If there is only data in the leftmost label, then that is all that will print.

Fred creates a long program, as shown in Fig. 23-7. First, Fred has set his variables he will later use. You will find that usually you don't know what they are yet, and you create new variables as you go along. That is a perfectly normal procedure. Fred also creates some variables called Coma, which is set to a comma, and Period, which is set to a period. Later you will see why.

Fred sets up a variable called Counter, which will count the number of labels across that have been filled. After the Counter has processed three labels (and the Counter becomes 4), it is time to print a label.

Fred begins by finding the first record. Look at Fred's SET POINTER command. There is no WHERE clause. Fred will process all the records in the order of the Customer Number. This is another use of the SET POINTER command. The variable Fred used in the command, which he called Status, will be 0 as long as there are more records. When it moves beyond (or tries to) the last record, it will be set to a nonzero error code. Fred will know then that he has reached end-of-file.

Fred sets up a loop to check for that end-of-file. As long as the Status code is 0, he will proceed.

His variable counter is used to determine what label he is on. If he is filling the first label of the three across, he sets the variable A (the print position of the beginning of the label) to 1. The variables B and C are actually used to place the Period and Last Name fields and are only used by the first line of each label.

If Counter is 2, then Fred sets his print position to fill to 27, 28, and 30. If Counter is 3, Fred will be writing the data to positions 53, 54, and 56. Fred is really writing all the lines for three labels to some internal memory area. After he has fully created his labels, he sends one set of labels at a time to the printer.

After he decides what label he is working on, Fred begins to retrieve his data from the Customer table. He uses SET VAR commands with the #1 notation to retrieve each field. Because there are ten fields, you will find ten SET VAR statements. Notice that for the first time he is not using the same variable name as the column name. He is using X, Y, and Z. There is nothing wrong with that method in this type of program because as soon as you retrieve it, you move it to a print position and are done with it. The variables X, Y, and Z can then immediately be used for something else.

Let's follow as Fred builds the first line of the first label. He retrieves the com-

```
*(****************************)
*(     1.5.P-CUSTLBLP.CMD      *)
*(      FRED'S FISH MARKET     *)
*(    MAILING LABELS PRINT     *)
*(   (c) 1986 Cary N. Prague   *)
*(****************************)
WRITE " TURN ON AND ALIGN PRINTER      "  AT 5 25
WRITE "   PRESS ANY KEY TO START       "  AT 6 25
WRITE "                                "  AT 7 25
WRITE "                                "  AT 9,32
PAUSE
SET VAR COUNTER INTEGER
SET VAR X TEXT
SET VAR Y TEXT
SET VAR Z TEXT
SET VAR A INTEGER
SET VAR B INTEGER
SET VAR C INTEGER
SET VAR BUILDCSZ TEXT
SET VAR EMPTYLIN TEXT
SET VAR LINE1 TEXT
SET VAR LINE2 TEXT
SET VAR LINE3 TEXT
SET VAR LINE4 TEXT
SET VAR COMA TEXT
SET VAR PERIOD TEXT
SET VAR COMA TO ","
SET VAR PERIOD TO "."
SET VAR EMPTYLIN TO "                                            +
                                        "

SET VAR COUNTER TO 1
SET POINTER #1 STATUS FOR CUSTOMER SORTED BY CUSTNO
WHILE STATUS = 0 THEN
    IF COUNTER = 1 THEN
       SET VAR A TO 1
       SET VAR B TO 2
       SET VAR C TO 4
    ENDIF
    IF COUNTER = 2 THEN
       SET VAR A TO 27
       SET VAR B TO 28
       SET VAR C TO 30
    ENDIF
    IF COUNTER = 3 THEN
       SET VAR A TO 53
       SET VAR B TO 54
       SET VAR C TO 56
    ENDIF
    SET VAR X TO COMPANY IN #1
    MOVE 20 FROM X AT 1 TO LINE1 AT .A
    SET VAR X TO FSTNAME IN #1
    MOVE  1 FROM X AT 1 TO LINE2 AT .A
    MOVE  1 FROM PERIOD AT 1 TO LINE2 AT .B
    SET VAR Y TO LSTNAME IN #1
    MOVE 20 FROM Y AT 1 TO LINE2 AT .C
    SET VAR X TO ADDRESS IN #1
    MOVE 25 FROM X AT 1 TO LINE3 AT .A
    SET VAR X TO CITY IN #1
```

Fig. 23-7. The Customer Mailing Labels print program.

```
              SET VAR Y TO STATE IN #1
              SET VAR Z TO ZIP  IN #1
              SET VAR BUILDCSZ TO .X + .COMA
              SET VAR BUILDCSZ TO .BUILDCSZ & .Y
              SET VAR BUILDCSZ TO .BUILDCSZ & .Z
              MOVE 25 FROM BUILDCSZ AT 1 TO LINE4 AT .A
              NEXT #1 STATUS
              SET VAR COUNTER TO .COUNTER + 1
              IF STATUS NE 0 OR COUNTER = 4 THEN
                  SET VAR COUNTER TO 1
                  OUTPUT PRINTER
                  SHOW VAR LINE1=80
                  SHOW VAR LINE2=80
                  SHOW VAR LINE3=80
                  SHOW VAR LINE4=80
                  SHOW VAR EMPTYLIN
                  MOVE 80 FROM EMPTYLIN AT 1 TO LINE1 AT 1
                  MOVE 80 FROM EMPTYLIN AT 1 TO LINE2 AT 1
                  MOVE 80 FROM EMPTYLIN AT 1 TO LINE3 AT 1
                  MOVE 80 FROM EMPTYLIN AT 1 TO LINE4 AT 1
              ENDIF
          ENDWHILE
          OUTPUT SCREEN
          RETURN
```

Fig. 23-7. The Customer Mailing Labels print program. (Continued from page 298.)

pany from the table and moves those 20 characters to the variable Line1 at print position A, which is currently set at 1. Next he retrieves the first name and only moves the first letter of the name to the second line of the label and the period to the right of the first letter of the name. He then retrieves the last name and writes all of it to print position C, which is 4. This procedure builds the name in the form of first initial, period, space, last name. Next Fred retrieves the address and writes it to the third line of the first label. Finally he retrieves city, state, and zip from the Customer table. He creates a variable called Buildcsz and builds the fourth line into it. This line will be the city followed without a space by a comma. Then, a space and the state, and a space and the zip code. Fred places a comma at the end of the city, then leaves a space and places the state, and again, adds the zip code after leaving a space. Fred can then move the fourth line to the print variable Line4.

The NEXT#1 command checks for the next record. If there is one and the last label across filled wasn't a third label, processing returns up top to fill the next label across. If it was the third label or there are no more records, the print line is sent

Fig. 23-8. The Customer Mailing Labels main screen.

```
FRED'S FRIENDLY FISH MARKET
CUSTOMER MAILING LABEL PRINT

ENTER <cr> TO BEGIN PRINT
 OR A FOR ALIGNMENT PRINT
 OR X TO EXIT PRINT

        ====>
```

```
FRED'S FRIENDLY FISH MARKET
CUSTOMER MAILING LABEL PRINT

TURN ON AND ALIGN PRINTER
PRESS ANY KEY TO START
```

Fig. 23-9. The Customer Mailing Labels print screen.

to the printer with five SHOW VAR commands. The print lines are then emptied out to clear the remains of the labels and the loop starts again.

Fred is getting good. He checks his program. He runs the main label program. The screen appears as shown in Fig. 23-8.

Fred presses a carriage return and the screen changes as shown in Fig. 23-9. With only four records in the Customer table, Fred will not expect much. He turns on his printer and much to his (and Frank's) amazement, his labels appear (Fig. 23-10). Fred sticks a label on Julie, their pet crab, and continues.

USING THE REPORT FORM—A DIRECTORY PROGRAM

Fred is almost done with the Customer system. He now must create his Directory program using R:base. He doesn't have to program this report! Fred creates his report form using the REPORTS command (Fig. 23-11).

Fred has created a simple form. The Customer Number will be displayed first after a small report header. If the report goes for many pages, there will still be only one header. If Fred wanted a page header, he would have marked the header lines **HP** instead of **HR**. The rest of his report is detail lines. He has left several blank detail lines to add some blank spaces in the report between each entry. If he didn't have any blank detail lines, the records would run together.

Fred has created several items that have no text. That is perfectly fine as long as you remember what they are. The unmarked items include name (more about that one), company, address, and citystzp (more about that one too!). Finally the phone and discount are marked. This will be Fred's report.

Fred has his Name and Citystzp fields defined by the Define process in the REPORTS command. By pressing <F3> Fred can see the definitions he created (Fig. 23-12).

```
LEE SIDE FISHERIES        SYLVIA'S SMOKE HOUSE      CARYS FISH PLACE
L. KAY                    E. ZARSKY                 C. PRAGUE
151 CLEMENS COUTHOUSE     1534 WETERSFIELD AVE      12 LOBSTER CT
ROCKVILLE, CT 06073       WIN-SAL, NC 27410-2535    WESTBROOK, CA 95733

A PECK OF CHOWDER
D. HAROLD
23 NEWBORN RD
HARTFORD, CT 06115
```

Fig. 23-10. The Customer Mailing Labels printout.

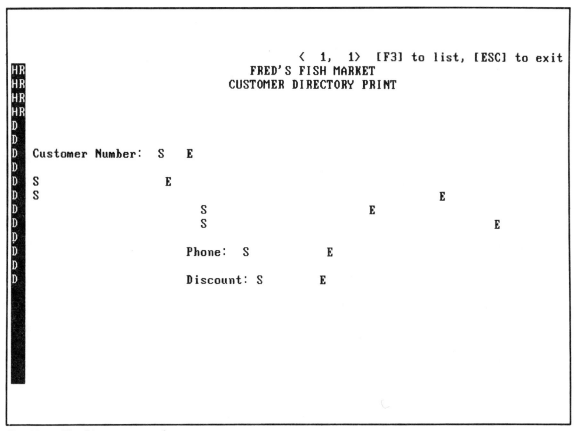

Fig. 23-11. The Directory report form.

Fred first created the Name field. He wants the report to show the last name, a comma, and the first name. The first three items define that scenario. The last three items combine city with a comma and no space, the state to that, and then the zip code. This is exactly the same thing Fred did in the mailing labels program, except now he does it with Define statements.

Fred writes a short program to use this form, as shown in Fig. 23-13. This program is very simple and will just display a message to the screen and wait for a <Return> to begin printing. Fred uses the OUTPUT PRINTER command to direct the output to the printer and uses the PRINT command with the SORTED BY clause to print the report in a sorted order. When Fred is done, he sets the output back to the screen and returns to the Label menu after clearing his variables. Control actually passes through the Label program directly to the Customer menu because there is nothing left to do in the main Label program but a RETURN statement, which returns you to the statement following the RUN command that called the subroutine.

Fred is ready for more. First he runs the program. His directory prints out as shown in Fig. 23-14.

```
                                                           [F3] to list, [ESC] to exit
Expression:

   1:TEXT    : COMMA    = ","
   2:TEXT    : LSNM     = LSTNAME   + COMMA
   3:TEXT    : NAME     = LSNM      & FSTNAME
   4:TEXT    : CITCOM   = CITY      + COMMA
   5:TEXT    : CITST    = CITCOM    & STATE
   6:TEXT    : CITSTZP  = CITST     & ZIP
```

Fig. 23-12. The Directory report define variables.

```
          *(*******************************)
          *(      1.6-CUSTDIR.CMD        *)
          *(      FRED'S FISH MARKET     *)
          *(      CUSTOMER DIRECTORY     *)
          *(   (c) 1986 Cary N. Prague   *)
          *(*******************************)
          SET VAR PRTCHK TEXT
          NEWPAGE
              WRITE "FRED'S FRIENDLY FISH MARKET" AT 2 25
              WRITE "   CUSTOMER DIRECTORY PRINT          " AT 3 25
              WRITE " ENTER <cr> TO BEGIN PRINT" AT 5 25
              WRITE "    OR X TO EXIT PRINT" AT 6 25
              FILLIN PRTCHK USING "====>" AT 8 32
              IF PRTCHK EQ X THEN
                 BREAK
              ENDIF
              WRITE " TURN ON AND ALIGN PRINTER       " AT 5 25
              WRITE "   PRESS ANY KEY TO START        " AT 6 25
              WRITE "                                 " AT 8,32
              PAUSE
              OUTPUT PRINTER
              PRINT CUSTDIR SORTED BY CUSTNO
              OUTPUT SCREEN
          CLEAR ALL VARIABLES
          SET VAR PICK1 INT
          SET VAR PICK2 INT
          SET VAR LEVEL2 INT
          SET VAR LEVEL2 TO 0
          RETURN
```

Fig. 23-13. The Directory report program.

```
                         FRED'S FISH MARKET
                      CUSTOMER DIRECTORY PRINT



      Customer Number:   A-001

      LEE SIDE FISHERIES
      KAY, LEE JAY
                              151 CLEMENS COUTHOUSE
                              ROCKVILLE, CT 06073

                              Phone:  (203)555-6134

                              Discount:    5.00000



      Customer Number:   A-003

      SYLVIA'S SMOKE HOUSE
      ZARSKY, EDITH
                              1534 WETERSFIELD AVE
                              WIN-SAL, NC 27410-2535

                              Phone:  (243)555-3546

                              Discount:    12.5000



      Customer Number:   A-004

      CARYS FISH PLACE
      PRAGUE, CARY
                              12 LOBSTER CT
                              WESTBROOK, CA 95733

                              Phone:  (415)555-6746

                              Discount:    10.0000



      Customer Number:   B-001

      A PECK OF CHOWDER
      HAROLD, DAVID
                              23 NEWBORN RD
                              HARTFORD, CT 06115

                              Phone:  (203)555-7463

                              Discount:    35.0000
```

Fig. 23-14. The Directory report output.

Chapter 24

Adding Records
in a Two-File System

It is time for Fred to start his Order program. Fred is ready to attack more than one table at a time. So far Fred has shown excellent design techniques in his coding. He has ensured that his data will be good. Remember, garbage in, garbage out.

Fred is really moving now. In the last two chapters of this book you will see Fred code two different types of modules. This chapter will explain how Fred coded the Additions module of the Order program. Chapter 25 will discuss a report that Fred did which does some calculating and totaling. The complete design for all programs in Fred's system can be found in Appendix A. The R:base 5000 code for the Customer and Order systems are found in their entirety in Appendix B.

THE MAIN RECORD

Fred designed his Order system using a two-file approach. As explained in Chapter 10 of this book, the Order file is actually made up of two files: the main record and the item records. In the main file, there will only be one record for each order number. In the Order Item file, there will be as many records for each order as there are items.

This is very typical for a relational database system. Each record in the Order Item file represents one item of the total order. This way there are not limits to the number of records that can appear in an order.

Now it is time to watch Fred create the Add function using more than one file. The SET POINTER command gets a lot of use in this area.

Fred begins by looking at the screens for the Order Additions program main record (Fig. 24-1). Fred will display the entire screen, but he will only let the user enter the Order Number and customer. His screen has been created using a variable form in the FORMS command.

Fred has created his variable screen (Fig. 24-2) and reviews it. Why has Fred created a screen that contains the customer information? Fred only needs to enter the Order Number and the Customer Number. However, what if Fred enters the wrong Order Number, possibly one that was already entered? The system would hopefully catch that situation. If, however, Fred entered Customer Number **A-001** when the customer he really wanted was **A-011**, would Fred catch that? Not if he thought the customer he wanted was A-011.

Whenever you enter a code to another table, you should display some of the information from that table to let the user know that he has entered the right code. Just telling the user that the code was found on the table isn't enough.

Fred reviews his pseudocode as shown in Fig. 24-3. Fred plans to have the user enter the Order Number and Customer Number. As long as the Order Number is entered, he proceeds. The Customer Number verification can be checked at the same time the Customer Number file is checked. If the Customer Number is not entered, it will be blank and will fail verification when matched against the Customer file.

Here is where Fred has created a good design. If the Customer Number is found, Fred will retrieve some information from the Customer file and display it so he can verify that he has entered the right customer. Fred's customers get pretty angry when they are billed for merchandise they didn't order. They also get mad when

Fig. 24-1. The main Order record screens.

```
-----------------------------------------------
|                                             |
|        FRED'S FRIENDLY FISH MARKET          |
|              ORDER ADDITIONS                |
|                                             |
|     ORDER NUMBER:       ORDRN               |
|                                             |
|     CUSTOMER NUMBER:    CUSTN               |
|                                             |
-----------------------------------------------
```

```
-----------------------------------------------
|                                             |
|        FRED'S FRIENDLY FISH MARKET          |
|              ORDER ADDITIONS                |
|                                             |
|     ORDER NUMBER:       ORDRN               |
|                                             |
|     CUSTOMER NUMBER:    CUSTN               |
|                                             |
|     COMPANY:       COMPANY------------X     |
|     LAST   NAME:   LNAME--------------X     |
|     FIRST NAME:    FNAME--------------X     |
|                                             |
|                                             |
|     DATE ORDERED:  MM/DD/YY                 |
-----------------------------------------------
```

─Locate─Quit─────────────────────────────────
                    FRED'S FRIENDLY FISH MARKET

        ORDER NUMBER: S   E

        CUSTOMER NUMBER: S   E

        COMPANY: S   E
        LAST   NAME: S   E
        FIRST NAME: S   E

        DATE ORDERED: S   E

Fig. 24-2. The main Order record form.

```
ADD AN ORDER

ACCESS ORDER FILE
SET ORDER NUMBER TO NOT BLANK
DO WHILE ORDER NUMBER NOT BLANK
  DISPLAY SCREEN
  ENTER ORDER NUMBER AND CUSTOMER NUMBER
  IF ORDER NUMBER NOT BLANK
    VERIFY ORDER NUMBER
    IF NEW NUMBER
      THEN
        ACCESS CUSTOMER FILE
        VERIFY CUSTOMER NUMBER
        IF FOUND
          THEN
            DISPLAY CUSTOMER DATA
            ENTER DATE FIELD
            ADD TO ORDER FILE
            PERFORM "ADD ITEMS"
          ELSE
            WRITE "CUSTOMER NUMBER NOT FOUND"
        ENDIF
      ELSE
        WRITE "ORDER NUMBER ALREADY ON FILE"
    ENDIF
  ENDIF
ENDDO
```

Fig. 24-3. The main Order Additions pseudocode.

they are shipped the wrong items. The lobsters also get mad when they have to walk back to Fred's.

After displaying the customer data, the user is prompted to enter the date, and then the program calls the Add Items module to add the actual items to the order.

If there are any errors, Fred will display the appropriate message and loop back to the top of the program. Fred is now ready to code this module.

Fred develops and debugs the code as shown in Fig. 24-4. Fred begins by creat-

```
*(*****************************)
*(      3.1-ORDRADD.CMD        *)
*(      FRED'S FISH MARKET      *)
*(        ORDER ADDITIONS       *)
*(   (c) 1986 Cary N. Prague    *)
*(*****************************)
SET VAR CONT INTEGER
SET VAR CONT TO 1
WHILE CONT EQ 1 THEN
    NEWPAGE
    DRAW ORDERS
    WRITE "      ORDER ADDITIONS SCREEN          " AT 3 25
    WRITE "    *** ENTER ORDER RECORD ***        " AT 5 25
    ENTER VARIABLE ORDNO CUSTNO
    IF ORDNO FAILS THEN
      BREAK
    ENDIF
    SET POINTER #1 CHECKO FOR ORDER WHERE ORDNO EQ .ORDNO
    SET POINTER #2 CHECKC FOR CUSTOMER WHERE CUSTNO EQ .CUSTNO
    IF CHECKO EQ 0 THEN
        WRITE "   *** ORDER NUMBER ALREADY ON FILE ***" AT 5 20
    ELSE
      IF CHECKC NE 0 THEN
          WRITE "    *** CUSTOMER NUMBER NOT FOUND ***" AT 5 20
        ELSE
          SET VAR COMPANY TO COMPANY IN #2
          SET VAR FSTNAME TO FSTNAME IN #2
          SET VAR LSTNAME TO LSTNAME IN #2
          SHOW VAR COMPANY AT 11 22
          SHOW VAR LSTNAME AT 12 22
          SHOW VAR FSTNAME AT 13 22
          WRITE "    *** ENTER ORDER DATE ***          " AT 5 25
          ENTER VARIABLE ORDDATE
          LOAD ORDER
           .ORDNO .CUSTNO .ORDDATE
          END
          RUN ORDRADI.CMD
      ENDIF
    ENDIF
ENDWHILE
CLEAR ALL VARIABLES
SET VAR PICK1 INT
SET VAR PICK2 INT
SET VAR LEVEL2 INT
SET VAR LEVEL2 TO 0
RETURN
```

Fig. 24-4. The main Order Additions program.

ing his usual variables to control his loop. Next he clears the screen and draws the variable form. He writes his initial prompting messages as he had with the Customer system. He then uses the ENTER VARIABLE command to get the Order Number and Customer Number from the user.

Fred then checks the Order Number to make sure it was entered and then proceeds. Now Fred is entering new territory. So far Fred has only accessed one file

```
--------------------------------------------------
    FRED'S FRIENDLY FISH MARKET
        ORDER ITEM ADDITIONS


  ORDER NUMBER:        ORDRN

  COMPANY:      COMPANY-------------X
  LAST   NAME: LNAME---------------X
  FIRST NAME:  FNAME---------------X

     #   QUANTITY   ITEM NUMBER

     1      QTY        ITEMN
     2      QTY        ITEMN
     3      QTY        ITEMN
    ...     QTY        ITEMN
    10      QTY        ITEMN
--------------------------------------------------


    ADD ITEMS

        ACCESS ORDER FILE
        ACCESS ORDER ITEM FILE
        SET ITEMCOUNT TO 1
        SET QUANTITY TO NOT BLANK
        DO WHILE QUANTITY NOT BLANK
          DISPLAY SCREEN AND EXISTING ITEM NUMBERS
          ENTER QUANTITY AND ITEM NUMBER
          IF QUANTITY NOT BLANK
            VERIFY ITEM NUMBER
            IF FOUND
              THEN
                RETRIEVE PRICE
                WRITE RECORD TO ORDER ITEM FILE
                INCREMENT ITEMCOUNT BY 1
              ELSE
                WRITE "ITEM NUMBER NOT ON FILE"
            ENDIF
          ENDIF
          IF ITEMCOUNT IS A MULTIPLE OF 10
            THEN REDISPLAY ITEM SCREEN
          ENDIF
        ENDDO
```

Fig. 24-5. The Order Items screen and pseudocode.

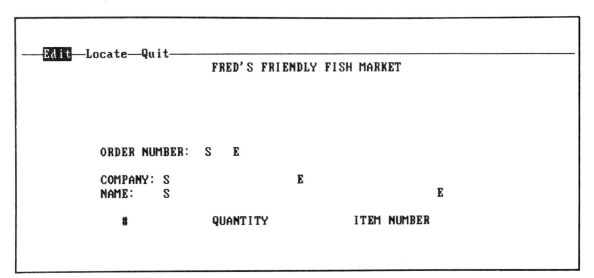

Fig. 24-6. The Order Items form.

at a time—the Customer file. This time he must access the Customer file and the Order file at the same time.

He sets the first pointer to the location of the Order Number in the Order file. Fred is really checking to make sure that the order doesn't already exist on the file. Later he will check the return code in the variable Checko. Next he sets a second pointer (there are three) to the location in the Customer file.

Fred first checks the value of Checko to make sure that the Order Number didn't already exist. If the Order Number exists, he writes an error message, and the IF statement will take control to the bottom of the program and then to the top of the loop.

If the Customer Number is not found, Fred writes an error message and the loop recycles. If the Order Number is not found and the Customer Number is found, everything is all right.

Now processing can begin. First the company name, first name, and last name of the client is retrieved from the file and displayed on the screen. A message is displayed so the user can enter the order date. Then the data is loaded to the Order table. The only data that resides on the table is Order Number, Customer Number, and the Order Date. The LOAD command enters that data. This program is very similar to the Customer Add function except for the extra step to check and display the Customer file data.

After loading the data, Fred's program will run the Order Item Additions program to add the order items.

THE SUBSIDIARY RECORD

Now Fred must create the program that enters the order items. Fred has designed the system. He reviews the screen and pseudocode in Fig. 24-5.

Fred's plan is to display the screen. He will show the variables from the main Order screen to remind the operator which order he is entering. Then Fred will al-

```
*(*****************************)
*(      3.1.I-ORDRADI.CMD      *)
*(       FRED'S FISH MARKET    *)
*(     ORDER ITEM ADDITIONS    *)
*(   (c) 1986 Cary N. Prague   *)
*(*****************************)
SET VAR ITEM# INTEGER
SET VAR ITEM# TO 1
SET VAR ITEMNO TEXT
SET VAR NAME TEXT
SET VAR NAME TO .FSTNAME & .LSTNAME
SET VAR PRICE DOLLAR
SET VAR ROWPTR INTEGER
SET VAR ROWPTR TO 14
NEWPAGE
DRAW ORDERITM WITH VARIABLE ORDNO COMPANY NAME
WRITE "    ORDER ITEM ADDITIONS SCREEN                " AT 3 25
WRITE "      *** ENTER ORDER ITEMS ***              " AT 5 25
WHILE ITEM# LE 20 THEN
  SHOW VAR ITEM# AT .ROWPTR 1
  WRITE "                                          " AT .ROWPTR 20
  FILLIN QTY USING " " AT .ROWPTR 29
  IF QTY FAILS THEN
    BREAK
  ENDIF
  FILLIN ITEMNO USING " " AT .ROWPTR 50
  IF ITEMNO FAILS THEN
      WRITE "*** ITEM NUMBER MUST BE ENTERED - REENTER RECORD *** " AT 5 15
  ELSE
      SET POINTER #3 CHECKI FOR ITEM WHERE ITEMNO EQ .ITEMNO
      IF CHECKI NE 0 THEN
          WRITE "*** ITEM NUMBER NOT ON FILE - REENTER RECORD *** " AT 5 15
        ELSE
          SET VAR PRICE TO PRICE IN #3
          LOAD ORDERITM
            .ORDNO .ITEMNO .QTY .PRICE
          END
        SET VAR ITEM# TO .ITEM# + 1
        SET VAR ROWPTR TO .ROWPTR + 1
        WRITE "               *** ENTER ORDER ITEMS ***                " +
              AT 5 15
        IF ITEM# = 11 THEN
          SET VAR ROWPTR TO 14
        ENDIF
      ENDIF
  ENDIF
ENDWHILE
RETURN
```

Fig. 24-7. The Order Item Additions program.

low the operator to enter each quantity and item number right on the screen in the
position they will occupy under the column labels. As the operator enters an item,
the cursor will move to the next number. As each quantity is entered, it is verified
that it is not blank. Only then will the item number be entered. The item number

is verified to make sure that it is in the Item file, and after it is found the price is retrieved.

Fred designed his system to place the current price on the Order file. Prices in the fish business change daily, and if Fred fills an order today but bills it tomorrow, he doesn't want to bill at an old price which could be higher or lower.

After the operator has entered his tenth order, the display will repeat from the first item. This way he can always see the last 10 items he entered. If you are entering item 15, you would be able to see items 6 through 15.

Next, Fred creates the form. He examines the variable form in Fig. 24-6. Fred can really only create fields for order number, company, and name. The rest of the fields will be displayed as they are entered.

Fred then codes the program as shown in Fig. 24-7. First, Fred sets up some variables. The first will hold the Item Number that Fred will display in the first column and track the number of items he has entered. He also creates a variable called Name, which will be the first and last name. In this way, he will save a line on the display that Fred might need. Fred also creates a variable called Price that he will use to retrieve the price from the Item table.

The last variable Fred creates is the variable Rowptr. This is the row on which the cursor will start. It is set to 14, the first row in the form that will be used for the ten-item display.

Fred clears the screen and draws the form displaying the variables Ordno, Company, and Name. The first two variables are left over from the Order Additions main program. As long as the CLEAR ALL VARIABLES command hasn't been run, the variables are still active.

Fred now sets up a loop that will continue until the twentieth item has been entered. Fred sets up 20 items as the maximum because his order form only has 20 spaces.

The Item Number is displayed in the first column at the present row pointer

```
            FRED'S FRIENDLY FISH MARKET
               ORDER ADDITIONS SCREEN

            *** ENTER ORDER RECORD ***

  ORDER NUMBER:        ██████

  CUSTOMER NUMBER:

  COMPANY:
  LAST  NAME:
  FIRST NAME:


  DATE ORDERED:
```

Fig. 24-8. The Order Item Additions main record screen without data.

```
            FRED'S FRIENDLY FISH MARKET
             ORDER ADDITIONS SCREEN

            *** ENTER ORDER DATE ***

    ORDER NUMBER:      453

    CUSTOMER NUMBER:   A-001

    COMPANY:     LEE SIDE FISHERIES
    LAST  NAME:  KAY
    FIRST NAME:  LEE JAY


    DATE ORDERED: 12/15/86
```

Fig. 24-9. The Order Item Additions main record screen after data entry.

variable, Rowptr. The WRITE command will clear any leftover quantities or item numbers, which is important because you enter the item numbers 11 through 20 in the same areas where the first 10 items were entered.

Fred then uses the FILLIN command to get the quantity. He makes sure the quantity is entered and if not assumes that the data entry session is over and returns the processing to the main Order program to start another order.

After he gets a nonblank quantity, Fred uses another FILLIN command to get the Item Number from the user. Notice that Fred has coded the FILLIN command with the USING clause blank. Fred doesn't want a message displayed on that part of the screen. The message is already being displayed at the top of the screen.

```
            FRED'S FRIENDLY FISH MARKET
             ORDER ITEM ADDITIONS SCREEN

            *** ENTER ORDER ITEMS ***


    ORDER NUMBER:  453

    COMPANY: LEE SIDE FISHERIES
    NAME:    LEE JAY KAY

      #          QUANTITY          ITEM NUMBER
      1
```

Fig. 24-10. Order Item Additions Screen.

Fred first has the program check to make sure the Item Number was entered. If not, a message is displayed and the record must be reentered. This procedure lets you change the quantity if you have made a mistake before it actually gets entered.

Once the Item Number is entered, it must be checked to make sure it exists in the file and to get the present price. The SET POINTER command is used to check the Item Number. The third pointer is used because the first two are already in use. In this case, there is no reason not to reuse the first or second pointer. In some cases you must keep the value of the older pointers.

After the pointer is set, the Item Number is checked. If the Item Number doesn't exist, then the record is reentered from the Quantity. Once the Item Number is verified, processing can continue.

The Price is retrieved from the Item file. Then the record is added to the table Orderitm. The columns added are Order Number, Item Number, Quantity, and Price.

Once an item and quantity pass the tests and are added to the table, the Item# and Rowptr variables are incremented by one. A new message is then displayed at the top of the screen to enter a new set of order items. This message will also clear any error messages that might have been previously displayed.

The last IF statement will check to see if the tenth record has been entered. If it has, the variable Item# would be equal to 11. The variable Rowptr is set back to 14 so the next entry will be at the top of the entry area.

Fred is done. He has coded an interesting program with one simple loop and several nested IF statements. By creating your logical constructs first, you can see the various paths the program might take and then fill in the processing steps to make it work.

```
              FRED'S FRIENDLY FISH MARKET
              ORDER ITEM ADDITIONS SCREEN

                  *** ENTER ORDER ITEMS ***


          ORDER NUMBER:   453

          COMPANY: LEE SIDE FISHERIES
          NAME:    LEE JAY KAY

              #              QUANTITY          ITEM NUMBER
              1                25                00001
              2                32                00003
              3               104                00010
              4                 6                00004
              5              1000                00006
              6
```

Fig. 24-11. Order Item Additions Screen after several items have been entered.

Fred is ready to test his program. He chooses the Order System choice from the main menu screen and presses **1** from the Order menu to add orders. The screen in Fig. 24-8 appears. Fred enters the Order Number and Customer Number. The customer information is retrieved and Fred enters the date (Fig. 24-9).

Next, the screen changes so Fred can enter his order items, as shown in Fig. 24-10. Fred enters several items and looks at his monitor (Fig. 24-11). Fred is very happy with his program. It seems to work quickly and accurately. He has used simple programming techniques and has accomplished a lot.

Fred will finish the final chapter by producing a report using the report form and several tables. He will save his other modules for later.

Chapter 25

Producing Reports
in a Multifile System

In Chapter 23, you saw how Fred created reports both with programming statements and with a report form. Now Fred will create a report without programming statements that access all four of his tables at once.

REEXAMINING THE DESIGN

Fred is ready to create a very complicated report. He first looks at the design of the output report he created earlier in this book (Fig. 25-1).

When you are creating a report, the detail lines always dictate to what table the form will belong. Fred knows that his detail lines in this report come from the Orderitm table. Fred also sees that various pieces of information will come from other tables. The Order Number will come from the Orderitm table but will reference back to the Order table to retrieve the Date and the Customer Number. The Customer Number will be used to retrieve the customer information and the customer's discount. The Item Number also comes from the Orderitm file and is used to retrieve the item's description.

CREATING THE REPORT FORM

Fred wonders how many variables he will need. He creates his variables shown in Fig. 25-2.

Fred knows that because the form is tied to the Orderitm table, each record will be processed in the Orderitm file in the order the PRINT statement specifies. Fred, therefore, knows that when he creates the variables in the *Define* function,

```
        Order Number: ORDRN

        X------FNAME-------X X------LNAME-------X
        X-----COMPANY-----X
        X--------ADDRESS--------X
        X-----CITY----X, ST
        X--ZIP--X

        Order Date: MM/DD/YY

    Quantity        Description           Price Each        Amount

      QTN     X---------DESC----------X      999.99        $99,999.99
      QTN     X---------DESC----------X      999.99        $99,999.99
      QTN     X---------DESC----------X      999.99        $99,999.99
      QTN     X---------DESC----------X      999.99        $99,999.99
      QTN     X---------DESC----------X      999.99        $99,999.99
      QTN     X---------DESC----------X      999.99        $99,999.99
      QTN     X---------DESC----------X      999.99        $99,999.99
      QTN     X---------DESC----------X      999.99        $99,999.99
                                                          ----------
                                        Total Amount:     $999,999.99

                                        Discount:        ($ 99,999.99)
                                                          ------------
                                        Amount Due:       $999,999.99
                                                          ============
```

Fig. 25-1. Fred's Order form report design.

```
                                          [F3] to list, [ESC] to exit
   Expression:

    1:TEXT    : CUSTNO   = CUSTNO   IN ORDER    WHERE ORDNO = ORDNO
    2:TEXT    : FSTNAME  = FSTNAME  IN CUSTOMER WHERE CUSTNO EQ CUSTNO
    3:TEXT    : LSTNAME  = LSTNAME  IN CUSTOMER WHERE CUSTNO EQ CUSTNO
    4:TEXT    : COMPANY  = COMPANY  IN CUSTOMER WHERE CUSTNO EQ CUSTNO
    5:TEXT    : ADDRESS  = ADDRESS  IN CUSTOMER WHERE CUSTNO EQ CUSTNO
    6:TEXT    : CITY     = CITY     IN CUSTOMER WHERE CUSTNO EQ CUSTNO
    7:TEXT    : STATE    = STATE    IN CUSTOMER WHERE CUSTNO EQ CUSTNO
    8:TEXT    : ZIP      = ZIP      IN CUSTOMER WHERE CUSTNO EQ CUSTNO
    9:DATE    : ORDDATE  = ORDDATE  IN ORDER    WHERE ORDNO = ORDNO
   10:TEXT    : ITEM     = ITEM     IN ITEM     WHERE ITEMNO EQ ITEMNO
   11:DOLLAR  : AMOUNT   = QTY      X PRICE
   12:REAL    : DISCOUNT = DISCOUNT IN CUSTOMER WHERE CUSTNO EQ CUSTNO
   13:DOLLAR  : TOTAMT   = SUM      OF AMOUNT
   14:REAL    : DISC     = DISCOUNT / 100
   15:DOLLAR  : DISCDISP = TOTAMT   X DISC
   16:DOLLAR  : AMTDUE   = TOTAMT   - DISCDISP
   17:TEXT    : NAME     = FSTNAME  & LSTNAME
   18:TEXT    : CITYST   = CITY     & STATE
```

Fig. 25-2. Fred's Order form variables.

316

they must be in the correct logical order. They are equivalent to retrieving a record from the Orderitm file and then running a series of SET VAR statements. If you think of it that way, it is easy to code.

Fred also remembers that you can only tie tables together which have common keys unless you create another tie. Fred starts by creating a variable called Custno, which will be a tie to the Customer table. This is the Customer Number from the main Order table that has the same Order Number as the Orderitm table. Once this tie is established, you can use the Custno variable to retrieve all the information from the Customer table. Fred creates eight variables from the Customer table, which stores the names, address information, and even the discount.

Next Fred retrieves the date from the Order file to use in the report. Next, Fred retrieves the Item description called *Item* from the Item table by using the Itemno as a tie from the Orderitm table. Fred has now retrieved all the information he needs from all four tables. The rest is calculation.

Fred calculates Amount by multiplying the Quantity times the Price. Next Fred sets up a totaling variable called *Totamt* by adding up all the Amounts as the rows are processed. The discount is divided by 100 to become a fraction instead of the whole number that was entered.

A variable called Discdisp is set to the multiplication of Totamt times Disc. The Amtdue variable is set to a simple mathematical equation to subtract the Discount

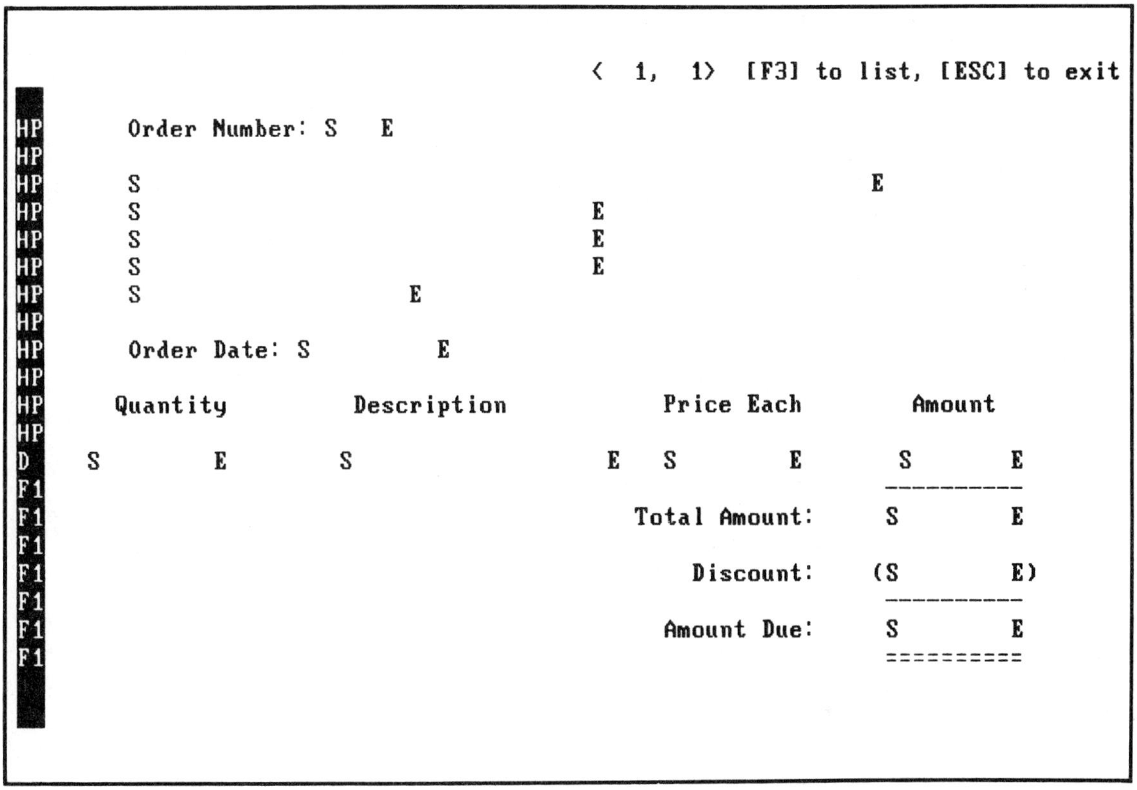

Fig. 25-3. Fred's Order report form.

from the Total Amount. Finally Name is created from concatenating the First and Last Names, and Cityst is created from City and State.

Fred is ready to create his form, shown in Fig. 25-3. Fred enters a small amount of text on the screen. He creates the Order Number, all the Name and Address information, the order Date, and the column headers as a page header. There is one detail line that comes from the Orderitm file directly. Finally, at the end of each order number is a break footer to print the Total Amount, the Discount, and the Amount Due.

Fred creates the simple program shown in Fig. 25-4 to ask the user what Order Number he wants to print and then tells him to align the printer.

PRODUCING THE REPORT

Fred is now ready to run the report. He runs the program and enters the Order Number 17. Fred sees his report in Fig. 25-5.

Fred has completed the hardest parts of his system. He is ready for a vacation.

```
*(*****************************)
*(       3.6-ORDRSHP.CMD         *)
*(      FRED'S FISH MARKET        *)
*( ORDER SHIPPING FORMS PRINT *)
*(    (c) 1986 Cary N. Prague     *)
*(*****************************)
SET VAR CONT INTEGER
SET VAR CONT TO 1
WHILE CONT EQ 1 THEN
   NEWPAGE
   DRAW ORDERS
   WRITE "        ORDER PRINT SCREEN              " AT 3 25
   WRITE "   *** PRINT ORDER RECORD ***           " AT 5 25
   ENTER VARIABLE ORDNO
     IF ORDNO FAILS THEN
        BREAK
     ENDIF
   SET POINTER #1 CHECKO FOR ORDER WHERE ORDNO EQ .ORDNO
   IF CHECKO NE 0 THEN
        WRITE "     *** ORDER NUMBER NOT ON FILE ***" AT 5 20
     ELSE
        WRITE "  TURN ON AND ALIGN PRINTER       " AT 5 25
        WRITE "   PRESS ANY KEY TO START       "   " AT 6 25
        WRITE "                                "   " AT 8 32
        PAUSE
        OUTPUT PRINTER
        PRINT ORDERSHP WHERE ORDNO EQ .ORDNO
        OUTPUT SCREEN
     ENDIF
ENDWHILE
CLEAR ALL VARIABLES
SET VAR PICK1 INT
SET VAR PICK2 INT
SET VAR LEVEL2 INT
SET VAR LEVEL2 TO 0
RETURN
```

Fig. 25-4. Fred's Order program.

```
Order Number: 17

LEE JAY KAY
LEE SIDE FISHERIES
151 CLEMENS COUTHOUSE
ROCKVILLE CT
06073

Order Date: 01/31/86

Quantity          Description          Price Each          Amount

    1             HALIBUT                 $2.34              $2.34
    7             SWORDFISH              $12.45             $87.15
   13             TUNA FISH             $23.54            $306.02
   14             SHRIMP - LARGE        $17.45            $244.30
   12             CLAMS                  $7.56             $90.72
   23             SCALLOPS              $14.56            $334.88
    1             CLAMS                  $7.56              $7.56
   15             SCALLOPS              $14.56            $218.40
   12             TUNA FISH             $23.54            $282.48
    5             LOBSTER                $6.59             $32.95
    5             TUNA FISH             $23.54            $117.70
   10             SCALLOPS              $14.56            $145.60
                                                        ----------
                          Total Amount:              $1,870.10

                              Discount:        (     $93.51)
                                                        ----------
                            Amount Due:              $1,776.59
                                                        ==========
```

Fig. 25-5. Fred's Order report.

SUMMARY

In this book, you have been given the tools to produce basic programs using R:base 5000. (That's basic as in simple, not the language BASIC; that's not used when you know R:base 5000.) Whether you are a novice or seasoned professional, this book, hopefully, has shown you tricks and techniques for contemporary program design for the eighties.

You may wish to review each section as you begin to code in R:base 5000. A complete list of the designs for the Customer and Order systems are found in Appendix A. A complete list of all the programs can be found in Appendix B. Good luck in all your data processing endeavors, and . . . may the Fred be with you.

Appendices

Appendix A

The System Design

This appendix shows all the steps Fred followed in designing his system.

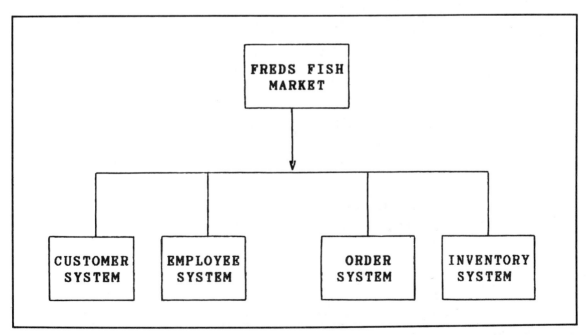

Fig. A-1. The main system hierarchy.

```
        FRED'S FRIENDLY FISH MARKET
                MAIN MENU



        ENTER SELECTION ===>  __

            1 - CUSTOMER SYSTEM
            2 - EMPLOYEE SYSTEM
            3 - ORDER SYSTEM
            4 - INVENTORY SYSTEM


            X - EXIT SYSTEM
```

Fig. A-2. The main system menu.

```
MAIN MENU

 SET EXIT TO "N"
 DO WHILE NOT EXIT
   READ SELECTION
   CASE
     WHEN SELECTION = "1"
         PERFORM CUSTOMER SYSTEM
     WHEN SELECTION = "2"
         PERFORM EMPLOYEE SYSTEM
     WHEN SELECTION = "3"
         PERFORM ORDER SYSTEM
     WHEN SELECTION = "4"
         PERFORM INVENTORY SYSTEM
     WHEN SELECTION = "X"
         SET EXIT TO "Y"
     OTHERWISE
         WRITE "INVALID OPTION" ENDCASE
   ENDCASE
 ENDDO
```

Fig. A-3. The main system pseudocode.

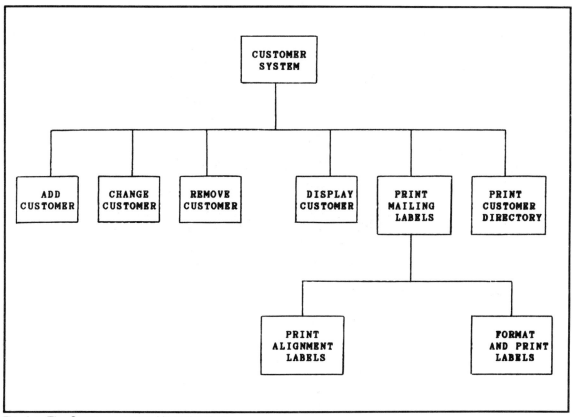

Fig. A-4. The Customer system hierarchy chart.

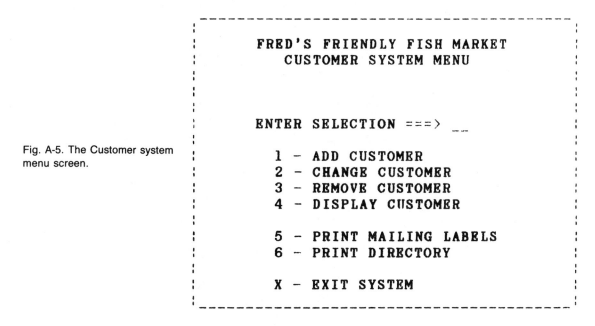

Fig. A-5. The Customer system menu screen.

```
SET EXIT TO "N"
DISPLAY MENU SCREEN
DOWHILE EXIT = "N"
  READ OPTION
  CASE
    WHEN OPTION = 1 PERFORM "ADD CUSTOMER"
    WHEN OPTION = 2 PERFORM "CHANGE CUSTOMER"
    WHEN OPTION = 3 PERFORM "REMOVE CUSTOMER"
    WHEN OPTION = 4 PERFORM "DISPLAY CUSTOMER"
    WHEN OPTION = 5 PERFORM "PRINT MAILING LABELS"
    WHEN OPTION = 6 PERFORM "PRINT DIRECTORY"
    WHEN OPTION = X SET EXIT TO "Y"
    OTHERWISE WRITE "INVALID OPTION"
  ENDCASE
ENDDO
```

Fig. A-6. The Customer system menu pseudocode.

Fig. A-7. The Customer Additions screen.

```
FRED'S FRIENDLY FISH MARKET
      CUSTOMER ADDITIONS


CUSTOMER NUMBER: CUSTN

COMPANY:      COMPANY-----------X
LAST NAME:    LNAME-------------X
FIRST NAME:   FNAME-------------X

ADDRESS: ADDRESS----------------X
CITY:    CITY---------X

STATE: ST    ZIP: ZIP-----X

PHONE NUMBER: PHONE-------X

DISCOUNT: DS
```

```
ADD A CUSTOMER

   ACCESS CUSTOMER FILE
   SET CUSTOMER NUMBER TO NOT BLANK
   DO WHILE CUSTOMER NUMBER NOT BLANK
      DISPLAY SCREEN
      ENTER DATA
      VERIFY CUSTOMER NUMBER
      IF NEW NUMBER
         THEN
            ADD CUSTOMER DATA
            CLEAR DATA FIELDS
         ELSE
            WRITE "NUMBER ALREADY ON FILE"
      ENDIF
   ENDDO
```

Fig. A-8. The Customer Additions pseudocode.

```
FRED'S FRIENDLY FISH MARKET
         CUSTOMER CHANGES




   CUSTOMER NUMBER: CUSTN
```

Fig. A-9. The Customer Changes preliminary screen.

```
   FRED'S FRIENDLY FISH MARKET
         CUSTOMER CHANGES


CUSTOMER NUMBER: CUSTN

COMPANY:      COMPANY------------X
LAST NAME:    LNAME--------------X
FIRST NAME:   FNAME--------------X

ADDRESS: ADDRESS----------------X
CITY:      CITY----------X

STATE: ST    ZIP: ZIP-----X

PHONE NUMBER: PHONE-------X

DISCOUNT: DS
```

Fig. A-10. The Customer Changes data entry screen.

```
        CHANGE A CUSTOMER

                ACCESS CUSTOMER FILE
                SET CUSTOMER NUMBER TO NOT BLANK
                DO WHILE CUSTOMER NUMBER NOT BLANK
                   DISPLAY SCREEN
                   ENTER CUSTOMER NUMBER
                   VERIFY CUSTOMER NUMBER
                   IF FOUND
                      THEN
                         RETRIEVE CUSTOMER DATA
                         CHANGE DESIRED FIELDS
                         UPDATE RECORD
                         CLEAR DATA FIELDS
                      ELSE
                         WRITE "NUMBER NOT ON FILE"
                   ENDIF
                ENDDO
```

Fig. A-11. The Customer Changes pseudocode.

```
------------------------------------------
|        FRED'S FRIENDLY FISH MARKET       |
|              CUSTOMER DELETION           |
|                                          |
|  ENTER "D" TO CONFIRM DELETE ===>  __     |
|                                          |
|     CUSTOMER NUMBER: CUSTN                |
|                                          |
|     COMPANY:     COMPANY-------------X    |
|     LAST NAME:   LNAME--------------X     |
|     FIRST NAME:  FNAME--------------X     |
|                                          |
|     ADDRESS: ADDRESS------------------X   |
|     CITY:     CITY----------X             |
|                                          |
|     STATE: ST    ZIP: ZIP-----X           |
|                                          |
|     PHONE NUMBER: PHONE-------X           |
|                                          |
|     DISCOUNT: DS                          |
|                                          |
------------------------------------------
```

Fig. A-12. The Customer Removal screen.

```
ACCESS CUSTOMER FILE
SET CUSTOMER NUMBER TO NOT BLANK
DO WHILE CUSTOMER NUMBER NOT BLANK
   DISPLAY SCREEN
   ENTER CUSTOMER NUMBER
   VERIFY CUSTOMER NUMBER
   IF FOUND
     THEN
        RETRIEVE CUSTOMER DATA
        ENTER DELETE CONFIRMATION
        IF CONFIRM = "D"
           THEN
              DELETE RECORD
              CLEAR DATA FIELDS
        ENDIF
     ELSE
        WRITE "NUMBER NOT ON FILE"
   ENDIF
ENDDO
```

Fig. A-13. The Customer Removal pseudocode.

Fig. A-14. The Customer Display screen.

```
------------------------------------------------
:          FRED'S FRIENDLY FISH MARKET          :
:                CUSTOMER DISPLAY               :
:                                               :
:                                               :
:      CUSTOMER NUMBER: CUSTN                    :
:                                               :
:      COMPANY:     COMPANY-------------X        :
:      LAST NAME:   LNAME---------------X        :
:      FIRST NAME:  FNAME---------------X        :
:                                               :
:      ADDRESS: ADDRESS-----------------X       :
:      CITY:        CITY----------X              :
:                                               :
:      STATE: ST    ZIP: ZIP-----X               :
:                                               :
:      PHONE NUMBER: PHONE-------X               :
:                                               :
:      DISCOUNT: DS                              :
:                                               :
------------------------------------------------
```

```
ACCESS CUSTOMER FILE
SET CUSTOMER NUMBER TO NOT BLANK
DO WHILE CUSTOMER NUMBER NOT BLANK
   DISPLAY SCREEN
   ENTER CUSTOMER NUMBER
   VERIFY CUSTOMER NUMBER
   IF FOUND
      THEN
         RETRIEVE CUSTOMER DATA
         DISPLAY INFORMATION
      ELSE
         WRITE "CUSTOMER NUMBER NOT ON FILE"
   ENDIF
ENDDO
```

Fig. A-15. The Customer Display pseudocode.

```
            FRED'S FRIENDLY FISH MARKET
                MAILING LABEL PRINT



        ENTER "A" FOR ALIGNMENT PRINT,
             "X" TO EXIT PRINT,
          OR <cr> TO BEGIN PRINT

               ====>  ___
```

Fig. A-16. The Customer Mailing Label printout.

```
    X------COMPANY------X
    X------FNAME-------X X------LNAME-------X
    X------ADDRESS----------X
    X----CITY-----X, ST X--ZIP--X
```

Fig. A-17. The Customer Mailing Label Print layout.

```
            PRINT MAILING LABELS

                STORE " " TO CHOICE
                DO WHILE CHOICE NOT "X"
                  DISPLAY SCREEN
                  READ CHOICE
                  IF CHOICE = "X"
                    THEN EXIT
                  ENDIF
                  IF CHOICE = "A"
                    THEN PERFORM "ALIGNMENT PRINT"
                  ENDIF
                  IF CHOICE = "<cr>"
                    ACCESS CUSTOMER FILE
                    READ A CUSTOMER RECORD
                    INITIALIZE RECORD COUNTER
                    PERFORM "LABEL PRINT"
                  ENDIF
                ENDDO
```

Fig. A-18. The Customer Mailing Label Print pseudocode.

```
ALIGNMENT PRINT

    PRINT ONE ROW OF LABELS WITH X'S IN EVERY PRINT POSITION
    ADVANCE TO NEXT LABEL
```

Fig. A-19. The Customer Mailing Label Alignment pseudocode.

```
            LABEL PRINT

                INITIALIZE LABEL HOLDING AREAS
                FIND FIRST RECORD
                WHILE MORE RECORDS
                  DECIDE IF FILLING LABEL 1,2 OR 3
                  MOVE DATA INTO LABEL POSITION
                  READ NEXT RECORD
                  IF THREE LABELS FILLED OR NO MORE DATA
                    PRINT LABEL SET
                    CLEAR HOLDING AREAS
                  ENDIF
                ENDWHILE
                CLEAR ALL VARIABLES
```

Fig. A-20. The Customer Mailing Label Format pseudocode.

```
--------------------------------------------------------
:                                                        :
:            FRED'S FRIENDLY FISH MARKET                 :
:            CUSTOMER DIRECTORY PRINT                    :
:                                                        :
:                                                        :
:                                                        :
:          ENTER <cr> TO BEGIN PRINT                     :
:            OR "X" TO EXIT PRINT                        :
:                                                        :
:                 ====> ___                              :
:                                                        :
--------------------------------------------------------
```

Fig. A-21. The Customer Directory Print screen.

```
Customer Number: CUSTN

X------COMPANY------X
X------LNAME-------X, X------FNAME-------X
                       X------ADDRESS----------X
                       X----CITY-----X, ST X--ZIP--X

                       Phone: (AAA)NNN-NNNN

                       Discount: XX%
```

Fig. A-22. The Customer Directory Print layout.

```
PRINT MAILING LIST

   READ CHOICE
   IF CHOICE = 'X'
      THEN EXIT
   ENDIF
   IF CHOICE = "<cr>"
      THEN
         ACCESS CUSTOMER FILE
         READ CUSTOMER RECORD
         SET LINECOUNT TO 1
         DO WHILE MORE RECORDS
            IF LINECOUNT = 1 OR = 56
               THEN
                  PRINT HEADER
                  SET LINECOUNT TO 4
            ENDIF
            PRINT DIRECTORY ENTRY
            UPDATE LINECOUNT
            READ NEXT RECORD
         ENDDO
   ENDIF
```

Fig. A-23. The Customer Directory Print pseudocode.

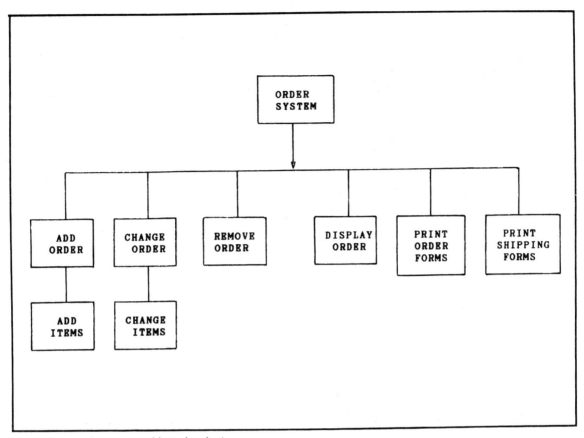

Fig. A-24. The Order system hierarchy chart.

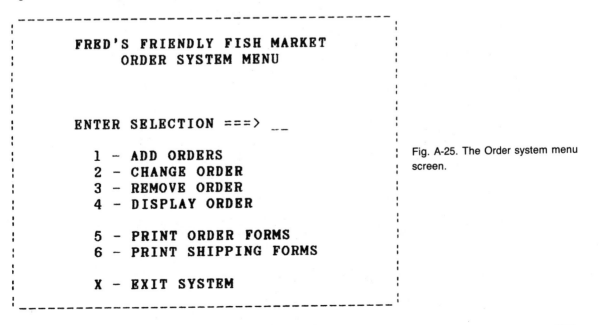

Fig. A-25. The Order system menu screen.

```
      SET EXIT TO "N"
      DISPLAY MENU SCREEN
      DOWHILE EXIT = "N"
        READ OPTION
        CASE
          WHEN OPTION = 1 PERFORM "ADD ORDERS"
          WHEN OPTION = 2 PERFORM "CHANGE ORDER"
          WHEN OPTION = 3 PERFORM "REMOVE ORDER"
          WHEN OPTION = 4 PERFORM "DISPLAY ORDER"
          WHEN OPTION = 5 PERFORM "PRINT ORDER FORMS"
          WHEN OPTION = 6 PERFORM "PRINT SHIPPING FORMS"
          WHEN OPTION = X SET EXIT TO "Y"
          OTHERWISE WRITE "INVALID OPTION"
        ENDCASE
      ENDDO
```

Fig. A-26. The Order system menu pseudocode.

```
          FRED'S FRIENDLY FISH MARKET
                ORDER ADDITIONS



      ORDER NUMBER:        ORDRN

      CUSTOMER NUMBER:     CUSTN
```

Fig. A-27. The Order Additions preliminary screen.

```
          FRED'S FRIENDLY FISH MARKET
                ORDER ADDITIONS


      ORDER NUMBER:        ORDRN

      CUSTOMER NUMBER:     CUSTN

      COMPANY:      COMPANY------------X
      LAST   NAME:  LNAME--------------X
      FIRST NAME:   FNAME--------------X


      DATE ORDERED: MM/DD/YY
```

Fig. A-28. The Order Additions screen.

334

```
        FRED'S FRIENDLY FISH MARKET
           ORDER ITEM ADDITIONS

    ORDER NUMBER:        ORDRN

    COMPANY:        COMPANY------------X
    LAST   NAME:  LNAME--------------X
    FIRST  NAME:  FNAME--------------X

       #    QUANTITY    ITEM NUMBER

       1       QTY         ITEMN
       2       QTY         ITEMN
       3       QTY         ITEMN
      ...      QTY         ITEMN
      10       QTY         ITEMN
```

Fig. A-29. The Order Item Additions screen.

```
ADD AN ORDER

    ACCESS ORDER FILE
    SET ORDER NUMBER TO NOT BLANK
    DO WHILE ORDER NUMBER NOT BLANK
       DISPLAY SCREEN
       ENTER ORDER NUMBER AND CUSTOMER NUMBER
       IF ORDER NUMBER NOT BLANK
          VERIFY ORDER NUMBER
          IF NEW NUMBER
             THEN
                ACCESS CUSTOMER FILE
                VERIFY CUSTOMER NUMBER
                IF FOUND
                   THEN
                      DISPLAY CUSTOMER DATA
                      ENTER DATE FIELD
                      ADD TO ORDER FILE
                      PERFORM "ADD ITEMS"
                   ELSE
                      WRITE "CUSTOMER NUMBER NOT FOUND"
                ENDIF
             ELSE
                WRITE "ORDER NUMBER ALREADY ON FILE"
          ENDIF
       ENDIF
    ENDDO
```

Fig. A-30. The Order Additions pseudocode.

```
ADD ITEMS

    ACCESS ORDER FILE
    ACCESS ORDER ITEM FILE
    SET ITEMCOUNT TO 1
    SET QUANTITY TO NOT BLANK
    DO WHILE QUANTITY NOT BLANK
       DISPLAY SCREEN AND EXISTING ITEM NUMBERS
       ENTER QUANTITY AND ITEM NUMBER
       IF QUANTITY NOT BLANK
         VERIFY ITEM NUMBER
         IF FOUND
            THEN
               RETRIEVE PRICE
               WRITE RECORD TO ORDER ITEM FILE
               INCREMENT ITEMCOUNT BY 1
            ELSE
               WRITE "ITEM NUMBER NOT ON FILE"
         ENDIF
       ENDIF
       IF ITEMCOUNT IS A MULTIPLE OF 10
         THEN REDISPLAY ITEM SCREEN
       ENDIF
    ENDDO
```

Fig. A-31. The Order Item Additions pseudocode.

Fig. A-32. The Order Changes preliminary screen.

```
FRED'S FRIENDLY FISH MARKET
          ORDER CHANGES


    ORDER NUMBER:      ORDRN
```

```
        FRED'S FRIENDLY FISH MARKET
              ORDER CHANGES

        CHANGE ITEMS? ===>  __
      ENTER <cr> TO CONTINUE, X TO ABORT

      ORDER NUMBER:        ORDRN

      CUSTOMER NUMBER:  CUSTN

      COMPANY:      COMPANY-------------X
      LAST  NAME: LNAME--------------X
      FIRST NAME: FNAME--------------X

      DATE ORDERED: MM/DD/YY
```

Fig. A-33. The Order Changes screen.

```
CHANGE AN ORDER

    ACCESS ORDER FILE
    SET ORDER NUMBER TO NOT BLANK
    DO WHILE ORDER NUMBER NOT BLANK
       DISPLAY SCREEN
       ENTER ORDER NUMBER
       IF ORDER NUMBER NOT BLANK
          VERIFY ORDER NUMBER
          IF FOUND
             THEN
                ACCESS CUSTOMER FILE
                RETRIEVE CUSTOMER INFORMATION
                DISPLAY "CHANGE ITEMS" MESSAGE
                READ CHOICE
                IF CHOICE NOT X
                   THEN PERFORM "CHANGE ITEMS MENU"
                ENDIF
             ELSE WRITE "ORDER NUMBER NOT FOUND"
          ENDIF
       ENDIF
    ENDDO
```

Fig. A-34. The Order Changes pseudocode.

```
FRED'S FRIENDLY FISH MARKET
      ORDER ITEM CHANGES

   ENTER SELECTION ===> __
   C/CHANGE,S/SCROLL,X/EXIT

ORDER NUMBER:      ORDRN

COMPANY:      COMPANY------------X
LAST   NAME: LNAME--------------X
FIRST  NAME: FNAME--------------X

   #   QUANTITY   ITEM NUMBER

   1     QTY        ITEMN
   2     QTY        ITEMN
   3     QTY        ITEMN
  ...    QTY        ITEMN
  10     QTY        ITEMN
```

Fig. A-35. The Order Item Changes screen.

Fig. A-36. The second Order Item Changes screen.

```
FRED'S FRIENDLY FISH MARKET
      ORDER ITEM CHANGES

   RECORD NUMBER ==> __
ENTER RECORD NUMBER TO BE CHANGED

ORDER NUMBER:      ORDRN

COMPANY:      COMPANY------------X
LAST   NAME: LNAME--------------X
FIRST  NAME: FNAME--------------X

   #   QUANTITY   ITEM NUMBER

   1     QTY        ITEMN
   2     QTY        ITEMN
   3     QTY        ITEMN
  ...    QTY        ITEMN
  10     QTY        ITEMN
```

```
                  FRED'S FRIENDLY FISH MARKET
                    ·ORDER ITEM CHANGES

              QUANTITY: QTY   ITEM NUMBER: ITEMN
                        ENTER CHANGES

                ORDER NUMBER:      ORDRN

                COMPANY:     COMPANY-------------X
                LAST   NAME: LNAME---------------X
                FIRST  NAME: FNAME--------------X

                    #   QUANTITY   ITEM NUMBER

                    1     QTY         ITEMN
                    2     QTY         ITEMN
                    3     QTY         ITEMN
                   ...    QTY         ITEMN
                   10     QTY         ITEMN
```

Fig. A-37. The third Order Item Changes screen.

```
            FRED'S FRIENDLY FISH MARKET
              ORDER ITEM CHANGES

           RECORD NUMBER ==>  __
       ENTER RECORD NUMBER TO BE CHANGED

        ORDER NUMBER:      ORDRN

        COMPANY:     COMPANY-------------X
        LAST   NAME: LNAME---------------X
        FIRST  NAME: FNAME---------------X

           #   QUANTITY   ITEM NUMBER

          11     QTY         ITEMN
          12     QTY         ITEMN
           3     QTY         ITEMN
          ...    QTY         ITEMN
          20     QTY         ITEMN
```

Fig. A-38. The Order Items scroll screen.

```
CHANGE ITEMS

 SET EXIT TO 'N'
 DISPLAY MENU SCREEN
 DOWHILE EXIT = 'N'
    DISPLAY ITEMS
    DISPLAY SELECTION
    READ SELECTION
    CASE
       WHEN SELECTION = 'X'
          SET EXIT TO 'Y'
       WHEN SELECTION = 'C'
          ACCESS ORDER ITEM FILE
          SET RECORD NUMBER TO NOT BLANK
          SET SCROLL COUNTER TO 10
          DO WHILE RECORD NUMBER NOT BLANK
             DISPLAY SCREEN
             ENTER RECORD NUMBER
             IF RECORD NUMBER NOT BLANK
               THEN
                  VERIFY RECORD NUMBER IN THE 10 DISPLAYED
                  IF IN THE 10
                    THEN
                       RETRIEVE RECORD
                       DISPLAY QTY AND ITEMN
                       IF BLANK
                         THEN
                            DISPLAY ADD MESSAGE
                       ENDIF
                       ENTER CHANGES
                       IF QTY AND ITEMN NOT BLANK
                         THEN                          /* ADD RECORD */
                            IF OLD QUANTITY BLANK
                              THEN
                                 VERIFY ITEM NUMBER
                                 IF FOUND
                                   THEN
                                      RETRIEVE PRICE
                                      WRITE RECORD TO ORDER ITEM FILE
                                   ELSE
                                      WRITE "ITEM NUMBER NOT ON FILE"
                                 ENDIF
                            ENDIF
```

Fig. A-39. The Order Item Changes pseudocode.

```
                        IF QTY OR ITEM NUMBER DIFFERENT THEN ORIGINAL
                           THEN                        /* DELETE RECORD */
                             IF QTY = 0
                                THEN
                                   REMOVE RECORD FROM ORDER ITEM FILE
                                ELSE                   /* CHANGE RECORD */
                                   VERIFY ITEM NUMBER
                                   IF FOUND
                                      THEN
                                         RETRIEVE PRICE
                                         WRITE RECORD TO ORDER ITEM FILE
                                      ELSE
                                         WRITE "ITEM NUMBER NOT ON FILE"
                                   ENDIF
                             ENDIF
                          ENDIF
                       ELSE
                          WRITE "RECORD NUMBER NOT ON DISPLAY"
                    ENDIF
                 ENDIF
              ENDDO
           WHEN SELECTION = 'S'
              ADD 10 TO SCROLL COUNTER
        ENDCASE
ENDDO
```

Fig. A-39. The Order Item Changes pseudocode. (Continued from page 340.)

Fig. A-40. The preliminary Order Removal screen.

```
-------------------------------------------------
        FRED'S FRIENDLY FISH MARKET
               ORDER REMOVAL


     ORDER NUMBER:        ORDRN


-------------------------------------------------
```

```
---------------------------------------------------
|                                                 |
|         FRED'S FRIENDLY FISH MARKET             |
|              ORDER REMOVAL                      |
|                                                 |
|    ENTER D TO CONFIRM DELETE ==>  __            |
|                                                 |
|                                                 |
|     ORDER NUMBER:      ORDRN                     |
|                                                 |
|     COMPANY:      COMPANY-------------X          |
|     LAST   NAME:  LNAME---------------X          |
|     FIRST  NAME:  FNAME---------------X          |
|                                                 |
|     DATE ORDERED: MM/DD/YY                       |
|                                                 |
|       #   QUANTITY   ITEM NUMBER                 |
|                                                 |
|       1     QTY         ITEMN                    |
|       2     QTY         ITEMN                    |
|       3     QTY         ITEMN                    |
|      ...    QTY         ITEMN                    |
|      10     QTY         ITEMN                    |
|                                                 |
|                                                 |
---------------------------------------------------
```

Fig. A-41. The Order Removal screen.

```
REMOVE ORDERS
        ACCESS ORDER FILE
        SET ORDER NUMBER TO NOT BLANK
        DO WHILE ORDER NUMBER NOT BLANK
           DISPLAY SCREEN
           ENTER ORDER NUMBER
           IF ORDER NUMBER NOT BLANK
              VERIFY ORDER NUMBER
              IF FOUND
                THEN
                    RETRIEVE ORDER
                    ACCESS CUSTOMER FILE
                    RETRIEVE CUSTOMER INFORMATION
                    DISPLAY ORDER
                    ACCESS ORDER ITEMS FILE
                    DISPLAY 1ST 10 ITEMS
                    ENTER DELETE CONFITMATION
                    IF CONFIRM = D
                       THEN
```

Fig. A-42. The Order Removal pseudocode.

```
                DELETE MAIN ORDER RECORD
                DELETE ALL ITEM RECORDS
            ENDIF
        ELSE
            WRITE "ORDER NOT ON FILE"
        ENDIF
    ENDIF
ENDDO
```

Fig. A-42. The Order Removal pseudocode. (Continued from page 342.)

Fig. A-43. The preliminary Order Display screen.

```
--------------------------------------------------
|                                                |
|         FRED'S FRIENDLY FISH MARKET            |
|              ORDER DISPLAY                     |
|                                                |
|                                                |
|     ORDER NUMBER:        ORDRN                 |
|                                                |
--------------------------------------------------
```

Fig. A-44. The Order Display screen.

```
--------------------------------------------------
|                                                |
|         FRED'S FRIENDLY FISH MARKET            |
|              ORDER DISPLAY                     |
|                                                |
|           ENTER <cr> TO CONTINUE               |
|                                                |
|     ORDER NUMBER:        ORDRN                 |
|                                                |
|     CUSTOMER NUMBER:   CUSTN                   |
|                                                |
|     COMPANY:      COMPANY--------------X       |
|     LAST   NAME:  LNAME---------------X        |
|     FIRST NAME:   FNAME---------------X        |
|                                                |
|     DATE ORDERED: MM/DD/YY                     |
|                                                |
|                                                |
|        #  QUANTITY   ITEM NUMBER               |
|                                                |
|        1    QTY         ITEMN                  |
|        2    QTY         ITEMN                  |
|        3    QTY         ITEMN                  |
|       ...   QTY         ITEMN                  |
|       10    QTY         ITEMN                  |
|                                                |
--------------------------------------------------
```

```
DISPLAY ORDERS

    ACCESS ORDER FILE
    SET ORDER NUMBER TO NOT BLANK
    DO WHILE ORDER NUMBER NOT BLANK
       DISPLAY SCREEN
       ENTER ORDER NUMBER
       IF ORDER NUMBER NOT BLANK
          VERIFY ORDER NUMBER
          IF FOUND
             THEN
                 RETRIEVE ORDER
                 ACCESS CUSTOMER FILE
                 RETRIEVE CUSTOMER INFORMATION
                 DISPLAY ORDER
                 ACCESS ITEM FILE
                 DO WHILE MORE RECORDS
                    DISPLAY 10 ITEMS
                    ENTER CONTINUE CONFIRMATION
                 ENDIF
             ELSE
                 WRITE "ORDER NOT ON FILE"
          ENDIF
       ENDIF
    ENDDO
```

Fig. A-45. The Order Display pseudocode.

Fig. A-46. The Print Order Forms screen.

```
FRED'S FRIENDLY FISH MARKET
     ORDER FORMS PRINT


ORDER NUMBER:      ORDRN
```

```
        Order Number: ORDRN

        X-----COMPANY------X
        X------FNAME-------X X------LNAME-------X

        Order Date: MM/DD/YY

ITEM #      QUANTITY      ITEM NUMBER       DESCRIPTION
   1          QTN           ITEMN       X----------DESC---------X
   2          QTN           ITEMN       X----------DESC---------X
   3          QTN           ITEMN       X----------DESC---------X
   4          QTN           ITEMN       X----------DESC---------X
   5          QTN           ITEMN       X----------DESC---------X
   6          QTN           ITEMN       X----------DESC---------X
   7          QTN           ITEMN       X----------DESC---------X
   8          QTN           ITEMN       X----------DESC---------X
```

Fig. A-47. The Print Order Form layout.

```
    PRINT ORDER FORM

        STORE BLANK TO ORDER NUMBER
        DO WHILE ORDER NUMBER NOT BLANK
           DISPLAY SCREEN
           ENTER ORDER NUMBER
           IF ORDER NUMBER NOT BLANK
              ACCESS ORDER FILE
              VERIFY ORDER NUMBER
              IF FOUND
                 THEN
                    PRINT HEADER OF ORDER
                    ACCESS CUSTOMER FILE
                    RETRIEVE CUSTOMER INFORMATION
                    DISPLAY ORDER INFORMATION
                    ACCESS ORDER ITEM FILE
                    DO WHILE MORE RECORDS
                       RETRIEVE QUANTITY AND ITEM NUMBER
                       ACCESS ITEM FILE
                       RETRIEVE DESCRIPTION
                       PRINT RECORD
                    ENDDO
                 ELSE
                    WRITE "ORDER NUMBER NOT ON FILE"
              ENDIF
           ENDIF
        ENDDO
```

Fig. A-48. The Print Order Form pseudocode.

```
  ---------------------------------------------
 |                                             |
 |        FRED'S FRIENDLY FISH MARKET          |
 |          SHIPPING FORMS PRINT               |
 |                                             |
 |                                             |
 |      ORDER NUMBER:       ORDRN              |
 |                                             |
 |                                             |
  ---------------------------------------------
```

Fig. A-49. The Print Shipping Forms screen.

```
       Order Number: ORDRN

       X-------FNAME-------X X------LNAME------X
       X-----COMPANY------X
       X--------ADDRESS--------X
       X-----CITY----X, ST
       X--ZIP--X

       Order Date: MM/DD/YY

Quantity           Description          Price Each          Amount

   QTN   X---------DESC----------X      999.99         $99,999.99
   QTN   X---------DESC----------X      999.99         $99,999.99
   QTN   X---------DESC----------X      999.99         $99,999.99
   QTN   X---------DESC----------X      999.99         $99,999.99
   QTN   X---------DESC----------X      999.99         $99,999.99
   QTN   X---------DESC----------X      999.99         $99,999.99
   QTN   X---------DESC----------X      999.99         $99,999.99
   QTN   X---------DESC----------X      999.99         $99,999.99
                                                       ----------
                                  Total Amount:      $999,999.99

                                  Discount: (xx%)   ($ 99,999.99)
                                                       ----------
                                  Amount Due:        $999,999.99
                                                     ============
```

Fig. A-50. The Print Shipping Forms layout.

```
PRINT SHIPPING FORM

    STORE BLANK TO ORDER NUMBER
    DO WHILE ORDER NUMBER NOT BLANK
       DISPLAY SCREEN
       ENTER ORDER NUMBER
       IF ORDER NUMBER NOT BLANK
          ACCESS ORDER FILE
          VERIFY ORDER NUMBER
          IF FOUND
             THEN
                 PRINT HEADER OF ORDER
                 ACCESS CUSTOMER FILE
                 RETRIEVE CUSTOMER INFORMATION
                 PRINT ORDER INFORMATION
                 ACCESS ORDER ITEM FILE
                 SET TOTAL TO 0
                 DO WHILE MORE RECORDS
                    RETRIEVE QUANTITY AND ITEM NUMBER
                    ACCESS ITEM FILE
                    RETRIEVE DESCRIPTION AND PRICE
                    AMOUNT = QUANTITY X PRICE
                    ADD AMOUNT TO TOTAL
                    PRINT RECORD
                 ENDDO
                 WRITE TOTAL
                 DISCOUNT AMOUNT = DISCOUNT/100 X TOTAL
                 WRITE DISCOUNT
                 SUBTRACT DISCOUNT FROM TOTAL
                 WRITE AMOUNT DUE
             ELSE
                 WRITE "ORDER NUMBER NOT ON FILE"
          ENDIF
       ENDIF
    ENDDO
```

Fig. A-51. The Print Order Shipping Forms pseudocode.

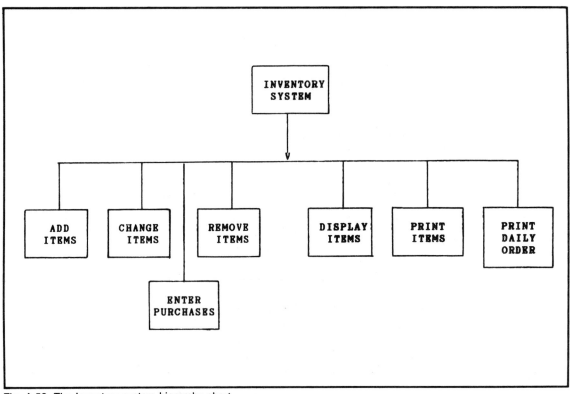

Fig. A-52. The Inventory system hierarchy chart.

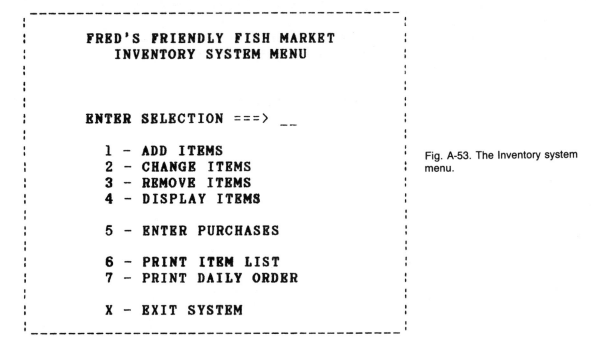

Fig. A-53. The Inventory system menu.

Appendix B

The Complete Programs

The complete programs Fred will use for his Friendly Fish Market are listed here.

```
Table: CUSTOMER
Read Password: NO
Modify Password: NO

Column definitions
 # Name      Type     Length         Key
 1 CUSTNO    TEXT      5 characters  yes
 2 COMPANY   TEXT     20 characters
 3 FSTNAME   TEXT     20 characters
 4 LSTNAME   TEXT     20 characters
 5 ADDRESS   TEXT     25 characters
 6 CITY      TEXT     15 characters
 7 STATE     TEXT      2 characters
 8 ZIP       TEXT     10 characters
 9 PHONE     TEXT     13 characters
10 DISCOUNT  REAL      1 value(s)

Current number of rows:       0

Table: ORDER
Read Password: NO
Modify Password: NO

Column definitions
 # Name      Type     Length         Key
 1 ORDNO     TEXT      5 characters  yes
 2 CUSTNO    TEXT      5 characters  yes
 3 ORDDATE   DATE      1 value(s)
Current number of rows:       0
```

Fig. B-1. Fred's Fish Market tables.

```
              Table: ORDERITM
              Read Password: NO
              Modify Password: NO

              Column definitions
              # Name      Type      Length          Key
              1 ORDNO     TEXT       5 characters   yes
              2 ITEMNO    TEXT       5 characters   yes
              3 QTY       INTEGER    1 value(s)
              4 PRICE     DOLLAR     1 value(s)

              Current number of rows:        0

              Table: ITEM
              Read Password: NO
              Modify Password: NO

              Column definitions
              # Name      Type      Length          Key
              1 ITEMNO    TEXT       5 characters   yes
              2 ITEM      TEXT      25 characters
              3 PRICE     DOLLAR     1 value(s)
              4 ONHAND    INTEGER    1 value(s)
              5 STOCKLVL  INTEGER    1 value(s)
              6 ORDAMT    INTEGER    1 value(s)
              7 ORDFLAG   TEXT       1 characters

              Current number of rows:        0
```

Fig. B-1. Fred's Fish Market tables. (Continued from page 349.)

```
              MAIN
              COLUMN FRED'S FISH MARKET MAIN MENU
              CUSTOMER SYSTEM
              EMPLOYEE SYSTEM
              ORDER SYSTEM
              INVENTORY SYSTEM
              EXIT SYSTEM
              CUSTMENU
              COLUMN FRED'S FISH MARKET CUSTOMER SYSTEM MENU
              ADD CUSTOMER
              CHANGE CUSTOMER
              REMOVE CUSTOMER
              DISPLAY CUSTOMER
              PRINT MAILING LABELS
              PRINT DIRECTORY
              RETURN TO MAIN MENU
              EXIT SYSTEM
              ORDRMENU
              COLUMN FRED'S FISH MARKET ORDER SYSTEM MENU
              ADD ORDERS
              CHANGE ORDER
              REMOVE ORDER
              DISPLAY ORDER
              PRINT ORDER FORMS
              PRINT SHIPPING FORMS
              RETURN TO MAIN MENU
              EXIT SYSTEM
```

Fig. B-2. The menu files.

```
               MAIN MENU HELP SCREEN
               ---------------------


    CUSTOMER SYSTEM   - ADD/CHANGE/DELETE CUSTOMER RECORDS

    EMPLOYEE SYSTEM   - MANAGE EMPLOYEE LIST AND PRODUCE PAYROLL

    ORDER SYSTEM      - ADD/CHANGE/DELETE ORDERS FOR CUSTOMERS

    INVENTORY SYSTEM  - MANAGE INVENTORY SYSTEM OF SEAFOOD PRODUCTS

    EXIT SYSTEM       - RETURN TO OPERATING SYSTEM

  * Note to Operator - If you have any serious problems call
                    Fred or Frank immediately
```

Fig. B-3. The main menu help screen.

Fig. B-4. The main menu program.

```
*(*******************************)
*(            MAIN.CMD          *)
*(       FRED'S FISH MARKET     *)
*(        MAIN MENU PROGRAM     *)
*(   (c) 1986 Cary N. Prague    *)
*(*******************************)
SET MESSAGE OFF
OPEN FREDFSH
SET ERROR MESSAGE OFF
SET VAR PICK1 INT
LABEL STARTAPP
  NEWPAGE
  CHOOSE PICK1 FROM MAIN.MNU
  IF PICK1  EQ -1 THEN
    NEWPAGE
    DISPLAY HELPMAIN.HLP
    WRITE "Press any key to continue "
    PAUSE
    GOTO STARTAPP
  ENDIF
  IF PICK1 EQ 1 THEN
    RUN CUSTMENU.CMD
    GOTO STARTAPP
  ENDIF
  IF PICK1 EQ 2 THEN
    GOTO STARTAPP
  ENDIF
  IF PICK1 EQ 3 THEN
    RUN ORDRMENU.CMD
    GOTO STARTAPP
  ENDIF
  IF PICK1 EQ 4 THEN
    GOTO STARTAPP
  ENDIF
  IF PICK1  EQ 5 THEN
    GOTO ENDAPP
  ENDIF
  GOTO STARTAPP
LABEL ENDAPP
CLEAR PICK1
```

```
*(*****************************)
*(        CUSTMENU.CMD          *)
*(       FRED'S FISH MARKET     *)
*(    CUSTOMER MENU PROGRAM     *)
*(   (c) 1986 Cary N. Prague    *)
*(*****************************)
SET VAR PICK2  INT
SET VAR LEVEL2 INT
SET VAR LEVEL2 TO 0
WHILE LEVEL2 EQ 0   THEN
  NEWPAGE
  CHOOSE PICK2 FROM CUSTMENU.MNU
  IF PICK2  EQ 1 THEN
    RUN CUSTADD.CMD
  ENDIF
  IF PICK2  EQ 2 THEN
    RUN CUSTCHG.CMD
  ENDIF
  IF PICK2  EQ 3 THEN
    RUN CUSTREM.CMD
  ENDIF
  IF PICK2  EQ 4 THEN
    RUN CUSTDIS.CMD
  ENDIF
  IF PICK2  EQ 5 THEN
    RUN CUSTLBL.CMD
  ENDIF
  IF PICK2  EQ 6 THEN
    RUN CUSTDIR.CMD
  ENDIF
  IF PICK2  EQ 7 THEN
    BREAK
  ENDIF
  IF PICK2  EQ 8 THEN
    BREAK
  ENDIF
ENDWHILE
CLEAR LEVEL2
CLEAR PICK2
RETURN
```

Fig. B-5. The Customer menu program.

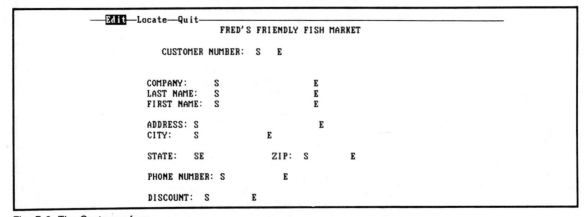

Fig. B-6. The Customer form.

```
*(******************************)
*(       1.1-CUSTADD.CMD          *)
*(       FRED'S FISH MARKET       *)
*(       CUSTOMER ADDITIONS       *)
*(    (c) 1986 Cary N. Prague     *)
*(******************************)
SET VAR CONT INTEGER
SET VAR CONT TO 1
WHILE CONT EQ 1 THEN
     NEWPAGE
     DRAW CUSTVAR
     WRITE "  CUSTOMER ADDITIONS SCREEN            " AT 3 25
     WRITE "*** ENTER CUSTOMER RECORD ***          " AT 5 25
     ENTER VARIABLE
     IF CUSTNO FAILS THEN
       BREAK
     ENDIF
     SET POINTER #1 CHECKER FOR CUSTOMER WHERE CUSTNO EQ .CUSTNO
     IF CHECKER EQ 0 THEN
        WRITE "*** CUSTOMER NUMBER ALREADY ON FILE ***" AT 5 20
      ELSE
        LOAD CUSTOMER
         .CUSTNO .COMPANY .FSTNAME .LSTNAME .ADDRESS .CITY .STATE +
         .ZIP .PHONE .DISCOUNT
        END
     ENDIF
ENDWHILE
CLEAR ALL VARIABLES
SET VAR PICK1 INT
SET VAR PICK2 INT
SET VAR LEVEL2 INT
SET VAR LEVEL2 TO 0
RETURN
```

Fig. B-7. The Customer Additions program.

```
*(******************************)
*(       1.2-CUSTCHG.CMD          *)
*(       FRED'S FISH MARKET       *)
*(       CUSTOMER CHANGES         *)
*(    (c) 1986 Cary N. Prague     *)
*(******************************)
SET VAR CONT INTEGER
SET VAR CONT TO 1
WHILE CONT EQ 1 THEN
     NEWPAGE
     DRAW CUSTVAR
     WRITE "   CUSTOMER CHANGES SCREEN            " AT 3 25
     WRITE "*** ENTER CUSTOMER NUMBER ***" AT 5 25
     ENTER VARIABLE CUSTNO
     IF CUSTNO FAILS THEN
       BREAK
     ENDIF
     SET POINTER #1 CHECKER FOR CUSTOMER WHERE CUSTNO EQ .CUSTNO
     IF CHECKER NE 0 THEN
        WRITE "*** CUSTOMER NOT FOUND ***" AT 5 26
      ELSE
        SET VAR COMPANY TO COMPANY IN #1
        SET VAR FSTNAME TO FSTNAME IN #1
        SET VAR LSTNAME TO LSTNAME IN #1
```

Fig. B-8. The Customer Changes program.

```
                    SET VAR ADDRESS TO ADDRESS IN #1
                    SET VAR CITY TO CITY IN #1
                    SET VAR STATE TO STATE IN #1
                    SET VAR ZIP TO ZIP IN #1
                    SET VAR PHONE TO PHONE IN #1
                    SET VAR DISCOUNT TO DISCOUNT IN #1
                    WRITE "*** CHANGE CUSTOMER RECORD ***" AT 5 25
                    EDIT VARIABLE COMPANY FSTNAME LSTNAME ADDRESS CITY STATE ZIP +
                                       PHONE DISCOUNT
                    CHANGE COMPANY TO .COMPANY IN #1
                    CHANGE FSTNAME TO .FSTNAME IN #1
                    CHANGE LSTNAME TO .LSTNAME IN #1
                    CHANGE ADDRESS TO .ADDRESS IN #1
                    CHANGE CITY TO .CITY IN #1
                    CHANGE STATE TO .STATE IN #1
                    CHANGE ZIP TO .ZIP IN #1
                    CHANGE PHONE TO .PHONE IN #1
                    CHANGE DISCOUNT TO .DISCOUNT IN #1
              ENDIF
        ENDWHILE
        CLEAR ALL VARIABLES
        SET VAR PICK1 INT
        SET VAR PICK2 INT
        SET VAR LEVEL2 INT
        SET VAR LEVEL2 TO 0
        RETURN
```

Fig. B-8. The Customer Changes program. (Continued from page 353.)

```
        *(*****************************)
        *(        1.3-CUSTREM.CMD      *)
        *(       FRED'S FISH MARKET    *)
        *(       CUSTOMER REMOVALS     *)
        *(   (c) 1986 Cary N. Prague   *)
        *(*****************************)
        SET VAR CONT INTEGER
        SET VAR CONT TO 1
        SET VAR DELCON TEXT
        SET VAR CHECKER INTEGER
        WHILE CONT EQ 1 THEN
              NEWPAGE
              DRAW CUSTVAR
              WRITE "   CUSTOMER REMOVAL SCREEN             " AT 3 25
              WRITE "*** ENTER CUSTOMER NUMBER ***" AT 5 25
              ENTER VARIABLE CUSTNO
              IF CUSTNO FAILS THEN
                PACK
                BREAK
              ENDIF
              SET POINTER #1 CHECKER FOR CUSTOMER WHERE CUSTNO EQ .CUSTNO
              IF CHECKER NE 0 THEN
                 WRITE "*** CUSTOMER NOT FOUND ***" AT 5 26
               ELSE
                 SET VAR COMPANY TO COMPANY IN #1
                 SET VAR FSTNAME TO FSTNAME IN #1
                 SET VAR LSTNAME TO LSTNAME IN #1
                 SET VAR ADDRESS TO ADDRESS IN #1
                 SET VAR CITY TO CITY IN #1
                 SET VAR STATE TO STATE IN #1
                 SET VAR ZIP TO ZIP IN #1
```

Fig. B-9. The Customer Removal program.

```
                    SET VAR PHONE TO PHONE IN #1
                    SET VAR DISCOUNT TO DISCOUNT IN #1
                    DRAW CUSTVAR WITH ALL
                    WRITE "   CUSTOMER REMOVAL SCREEN                " AT 3 25
                    FILLIN DELCON USING "ENTER D TO CONFIRM DELETE ===> " AT 5 22
                    IF DELCON = D THEN
                       DELETE ROWS FROM #1
                       WRITE "*** CUSTOMER RECORD DELETED ***          " AT 5 25
                    ENDIF
                 ENDIF
          ENDWHILE
          CLEAR ALL VARIABLES
          SET VAR PICK1 INT
          SET VAR PICK2 INT
          SET VAR LEVEL2 INT
          SET VAR LEVEL2 TO 0
          RETURN
```

Fig. B-9. The Customer Removal program. (Continued from page 354.)

```
          *(*****************************)
          *(      1.4-CUSTDIS.CMD        *)
          *(      FRED'S FISH MARKET     *)
          *(       CUSTOMER DISPLAY      *)
          *(   (c) 1986 Cary N. Prague   *)
          *(*****************************)
          SET MESSAGE OFF
          OPEN FREDFSH
          SET ERROR MESSAGE OFF
          SET VAR CONT INTEGER
          SET VAR CONT TO 1
          SET VAR DELCON TEXT
          SET VAR CHECKER INTEGER
          WHILE CONT EQ 1 THEN
              NEWPAGE
              DRAW CUSTVAR
              WRITE "   CUSTOMER DISPLAY SCREEN            " AT 3 25
              WRITE "*** ENTER CUSTOMER NUMBER ***" AT 5 25
              ENTER VARIABLE CUSTNO
              IF CUSTNO FAILS THEN
                 BREAK
              ENDIF
              SET POINTER #1 CHECKER FOR CUSTOMER WHERE CUSTNO EQ .CUSTNO
              IF CHECKER NE 0 THEN
                 WRITE "*** CUSTOMER NOT FOUND ***" AT 5 26
               ELSE
                 SET VAR COMPANY TO COMPANY IN #1
                 SET VAR FSTNAME TO FSTNAME IN #1
                 SET VAR LSTNAME TO LSTNAME IN #1
                 SET VAR ADDRESS TO ADDRESS IN #1
                 SET VAR CITY TO CITY IN #1
                 SET VAR STATE TO STATE IN #1
                 SET VAR ZIP TO ZIP IN #1
                 SET VAR PHONE TO PHONE IN #1
                 SET VAR DISCOUNT TO DISCOUNT IN #1
                 DRAW CUSTVAR WITH ALL
                 WRITE "    CUSTOMER DISPLAY SCREEN"  AT 5,20
                 WRITE "*** PRESS ANY KEY TO CONTINUE *** " AT 5 23
                 PAUSE
              ENDIF
```

Fig. B-10. The Customer Display program.

```
ENDWHILE
CLEAR ALL VARIABLES
SET VAR PICK1 INT
SET VAR PICK2 INT
SET VAR LEVEL2 INT
SET VAR LEVEL2 TO 0
RETURN
```

Fig. B-10. The Customer Display program. (Continued from page 355.)

```
*(*****************************)
*(      1.5-CUSTLBL.CMD        *)
*(      FRED'S FISH MARKET     *)
*(   CUSTOMER MAILING LABELS   *)
*(   (c) 1986 Cary N. Prague   *)
*(*****************************)
SET VAR PRTCHK TEXT
NEWPAGE
WRITE "FRED'S FRIENDLY FISH MARKET" AT 2 25
WRITE "CUSTOMER MAILING LABEL PRINT           " AT 3 25
WRITE " ENTER <cr> TO BEGIN PRINT" AT 5 25
WRITE "   OR A FOR ALIGNMENT PRINT" AT 6 25
WRITE "   OR X TO EXIT PRINT" AT 7 25
FILLIN PRTCHK USING "====>" AT 9 32
IF PRTCHK EQ A THEN
  RUN CUSTLBLA.CMD
ENDIF
IF PRTCHK FAILS THEN
  RUN CUSTLBLP.CMD
ENDIF
CLEAR PRTCHK
RETURN
```

Fig. B-11. The Customer Label program.

```
*(*****************************)
*(      1.5.A-CUSTLBLA.CMD     *)
*(      FRED'S FISH MARKET     *)
*(   MAILING LABELS ALIGNMENT  *)
*(   (c) 1986 Cary N. Prague   *)
*(*****************************)
WRITE " TURN ON AND ALIGN PRINTER   "  AT 5 25
WRITE "   PRESS ANY KEY TO START    "  AT 6 25
WRITE "                             "  AT 7 25
WRITE "                             "  AT 9,32
PAUSE
SET VAR COUNTER INTEGER
SET VAR NUMDOWN INTEGER
SET VAR EMPTYLIN TEXT
SET VAR X1 TEXT
SET VAR X2 TEXT
SET VAR X3 TEXT
SET VAR X4 TEXT
SET VAR LINE1 TEXT
SET VAR LINE2 TEXT
SET VAR LINE3 TEXT
```

Fig. B-12. The Customer Label Alignment program.

356

```
                SET VAR LINE4 TEXT
                SET VAR X1 TO "XXXXXXXXXXXXXXXXXXXXX       "
                SET VAR X2 TO "X. XXXXXXXXXXXXXXXXXXX     "
                SET VAR X3 TO "XXXXXXXXXXXXXXXXXXXXXXXXX"
                SET VAR X4 TO "XXXXXXXXXXXXXX, XX XXXXX"
                SET VAR EMPTYLIN TO " "
                SET VAR NUMDOWN TO 3
                SET VAR COUNTER TO 1
                MOVE 25 FROM X1 AT 1 TO LINE1 AT 1
                MOVE 25 FROM X1 AT 1 TO LINE1 AT 27
                MOVE 25 FROM X1 AT 1 TO LINE1 AT 53
                MOVE 25 FROM X2 AT 1 TO LINE2 AT 1
                MOVE 25 FROM X2 AT 1 TO LINE2 AT 27
                MOVE 25 FROM X2 AT 1 TO LINE2 AT 53
                MOVE 25 FROM X3 AT 1 TO LINE3 AT 1
                MOVE 25 FROM X3 AT 1 TO LINE3 AT 27
                MOVE 25 FROM X3 AT 1 TO LINE3 AT 53
                MOVE 25 FROM X4 AT 1 TO LINE4 AT 1
                MOVE 25 FROM X4 AT 1 TO LINE4 AT 27
                MOVE 25 FROM X4 AT 1 TO LINE4 AT 53
                OUTPUT PRINTER
                WHILE COUNTER <= .NUMDOWN THEN
                    SET VAR COUNTER TO COUNTER + 1
                    SHOW VAR LINE1=80
                    SHOW VAR LINE2=80
                    SHOW VAR LINE3=80
                    SHOW VAR LINE4=80
                    SHOW VAR EMPTYLIN
                ENDWHILE
                OUTPUT SCREEN
                CLEAR ALL VARIABLES
                SET VAR PICK1 INT
                SET VAR PICK2 INT
                SET VAR LEVEL2 INT
                SET VAR LEVEL2 TO 0
                SET VAR PRTCHK TEXT
                SET VAR PRTCHK TO A
                RETURN
```

Fig. B-12. The Customer Label Alignment program. (Continued from page 356.)

```
                *(******************************)
                *(      1.5.P-CUSTLBLP.CMD       *)
                *(        FRED'S FISH MARKET     *)
                *(     MAILING LABELS PRINT      *)
                *(    (c) 1986 Cary N. Prague    *)
                *(******************************)
                WRITE " TURN ON AND ALIGN PRINTER      "  AT 5 25
                WRITE "   PRESS ANY KEY TO START       "  AT 6 25
                WRITE "                                "  AT 7 25
                WRITE "                                "  AT 9,32
                PAUSE
                SET VAR COUNTER INTEGER
                SET VAR X TEXT
                SET VAR Y TEXT
                SET VAR Z TEXT
                SET VAR A INTEGER
                SET VAR B INTEGER
                SET VAR C INTEGER
```

Fig. B-13. The Customer Label print program.

```
                SET VAR BUILDCSZ TEXT
                SET VAR EMPTYLIN TEXT
                SET VAR LINEl TEXT
                SET VAR LINE2 TEXT
                SET VAR LINE3 TEXT
                SET VAR LINE4 TEXT
                SET VAR COMA TEXT
                SET VAR PERIOD TEXT
                SET VAR COMA TO ","
                SET VAR PERIOD TO "."
                SET VAR EMPTYLIN TO "                                              +
                                                                                   "

                SET VAR COUNTER TO 1
                SET POINTER #1 STATUS FOR CUSTOMER SORTED BY CUSTNO
                WHILE STATUS = 0 THEN
                     IF COUNTER = 1 THEN
                        SET VAR A TO 1
                        SET VAR B TO 2
                        SET VAR C TO 4
                     ENDIF
                     IF COUNTER = 2 THEN
                        SET VAR A TO 27
                        SET VAR B TO 28
                        SET VAR C TO 30
                     ENDIF
                     IF COUNTER = 3 THEN
                        SET VAR A TO 53
                        SET VAR B TO 54
                        SET VAR C TO 56
                     ENDIF
                     SET VAR X TO COMPANY IN #1
                     MOVE 20 FROM X AT 1 TO LINEl AT .A
                     SET VAR X TO FSTNAME IN #1
                     MOVE  1 FROM X AT 1 TO LINE2 AT .A
                     MOVE  1 FROM PERIOD AT 1 TO LINE2 AT .B
                     SET VAR Y TO LSTNAME IN #1
                     MOVE 20 FROM Y AT 1 TO LINE2 AT .C
                     SET VAR X TO ADDRESS IN #1
                     MOVE 25 FROM X AT 1 TO LINE3 AT .A
                     SET VAR X TO CITY IN #1
                     SET VAR Y TO STATE IN #1
                     SET VAR Z TO ZIP  IN #1
                     SET VAR BUILDCSZ TO .X + .COMA
                     SET VAR BUILDCSZ TO .BUILDCSZ & .Y
                     SET VAR BUILDCSZ TO .BUILDCSZ & .Z
                     MOVE 25 FROM BUILDCSZ AT 1 TO LINE4 AT .A
                     NEXT #1 STATUS
                     SET VAR COUNTER TO .COUNTER + 1
                     IF STATUS NE 0 OR COUNTER = 4 THEN
                        SET VAR COUNTER TO 1
                        OUTPUT PRINTER
                        SHOW VAR LINEl=80
                        SHOW VAR LINE2=80
                        SHOW VAR LINE3=80
                        SHOW VAR LINE4=80
                        SHOW VAR EMPTYLIN
                        MOVE 80 FROM EMPTYLIN AT 1 TO LINEl AT 1
                        MOVE 80 FROM EMPTYLIN AT 1 TO LINE2 AT 1
                        MOVE 80 FROM EMPTYLIN AT 1 TO LINE3 AT 1
                        MOVE 80 FROM EMPTYLIN AT 1 TO LINE4 AT 1
                     ENDIF
```

Fig. B-13. The Customer Label print program. (Continued from page 357.)

```
      ENDWHILE
      OUTPUT SCREEN
      CLEAR ALL VARIABLES
      SET VAR PICK1 INT
      SET VAR PICK2 INT
      SET VAR LEVEL2 INT
      SET VAR LEVEL2 TO 0
      SET VAR PRTCHK TEXT
      RETURN
```

Fig. B-13. The Customer Label print program. (Continued from page 358.)

```
      *(*****************************)
      *(        1.6-CUSTDIR.CMD      *)
      *(       FRED'S FISH MARKET    *)
      *(       CUSTOMER DIRECTORY    *)
      *(   (c) 1986 Cary N. Prague   *)
      *(*****************************)
      SET VAR PRTCHK TEXT
      NEWPAGE
          WRITE "FRED'S FRIENDLY FISH MARKET" AT 2 25
          WRITE "   CUSTOMER DIRECTORY PRINT           " AT 3 25
          WRITE " ENTER <cr> TO BEGIN PRINT" AT 5 25
          WRITE "    OR X TO EXIT PRINT" AT 6 25
          FILLIN PRTCHK USING "====>" AT 8 32
          IF PRTCHK EQ X THEN
             BREAK
          ENDIF
          WRITE " TURN ON AND ALIGN PRINTER      "  AT 5 25
          WRITE "   PRESS ANY KEY TO START       "  AT 6 25
          WRITE "                                "  AT 8,32
          PAUSE
          OUTPUT PRINTER
          PRINT CUSTDIR SORTED BY CUSTNO
          OUTPUT SCREEN
      CLEAR ALL VARIABLES
      SET VAR PICK1 INT
      SET VAR PICK2 INT
      SET VAR LEVEL2 INT
      SET VAR LEVEL2 TO 0
      RETURN
```

Fig. B-14. The Customer Directory program.

```
                                          [F3] to list, [ESC] to exit
Expression:

1:TEXT    : COMMA    = ","
2:TEXT    : LSNM     = LSTNAME   + COMMA
3:TEXT    : NAME     = LSNM      & FSTNAME
4:TEXT    : CITCOM   = CITY      + COMMA
5:TEXT    : CITST    = CITCOM    & STATE
6:TEXT    : CITSTZP  = CITST     & ZIP
```

Fig. B-15. The Customer Directory report variables.

FRED'S FISH MARKET
CUSTOMER DIRECTORY PRINT

Customer Number: S   E

S   E
S   E
              S   E
              S   E

          Phone: S   E

          Discount: S   E

Fig. B-16. The Customer Directory report form.

```
*(******************************)
*(        ORDRMENU.CMD          *)
*(      FRED'S FISH MARKET      *)
*(      ORDER MENU PROGRAM      *)
*(   (c) 1986 Cary N. Prague    *)
*(******************************)
SET VAR PICK2  INT
SET VAR LEVEL2 INT
SET VAR LEVEL2 TO 0
WHILE LEVEL2 EQ 0   THEN
  NEWPAGE
  CHOOSE PICK2 FROM ORDRMENU.MNU
  IF PICK2 EQ 1 THEN
    RUN ORDRADD.CMD
  ENDIF
  IF PICK2 EQ 2 THEN
    RUN ORDRCHG.CMD
  ENDIF
  IF PICK2 EQ 3 THEN
    RUN ORDRREM.CMD
  ENDIF
  IF PICK2 EQ 4 THEN
    RUN ORDRDIS.CMD
  ENDIF
  IF PICK2 EQ 5 THEN
    RUN ORDRFMS.CMD
  ENDIF
```

Fig. B-17. The Order menu program.

```
      IF PICK2 EQ 6 THEN
         RUN ORDRSHP.CMD
      ENDIF
      IF PICK2 EQ 7 THEN
        BREAK
      ENDIF
      IF PICK2 EQ 8 THEN
        BREAK
      ENDIF
   ENDWHILE
   CLEAR LEVEL2
   CLEAR PICK2
```

Fig. B-17. The Order menu program. (Continued from page 360.)

```
      *(******************************)
      *(       3.1-ORDRADD.CMD        *)
      *(       FRED'S FISH MARKET     *)
      *(         ORDER ADDITIONS      *)
      *(   (c) 1986 Cary N. Prague    *)
      *(******************************)
      SET VAR CONT INTEGER
      SET VAR CONT TO 1
      WHILE CONT EQ 1 THEN
          NEWPAGE
          DRAW ORDERS
          WRITE "      ORDER ADDITIONS SCREEN          " AT 3 25
          WRITE "   *** ENTER ORDER RECORD ***         " AT 5 25
          ENTER VARIABLE ORDNO CUSTNO
          IF ORDNO FAILS THEN
            BREAK
          ENDIF
          SET POINTER #1 CHECKO FOR ORDER WHERE ORDNO EQ .ORDNO
          SET POINTER #2 CHECKC FOR CUSTOMER WHERE CUSTNO EQ .CUSTNO
          IF CHECKO EQ 0 THEN
            WRITE "   *** ORDER NUMBER ALREADY ON FILE ***" AT 5 20
           ELSE
            IF CHECKC NE 0 THEN
                WRITE "    *** CUSTOMER NUMBER NOT FOUND ***" AT 5 20
              ELSE
                SET VAR COMPANY TO COMPANY IN #2
                SET VAR FSTNAME TO FSTNAME IN #2
                SET VAR LSTNAME TO LSTNAME IN #2
                SHOW VAR COMPANY AT 11 22
                SHOW VAR LSTNAME AT 12 22
                SHOW VAR FSTNAME AT 13 22
                WRITE "    *** ENTER ORDER DATE ***          " AT 5 25
                ENTER VARIABLE ORDDATE
                LOAD ORDER
                 .ORDNO .CUSTNO .ORDDATE
                END
                RUN ORDRADI.CMD
            ENDIF
          ENDIF
      ENDWHILE
      CLEAR ALL VARIABLES
      SET VAR PICK1 INT
      SET VAR PICK2 INT
      SET VAR LEVEL2 INT
      SET VAR LEVEL2 TO 0
      RETURN
```

Fig. B-18. The Order Additions main program.

```
 ┌─Edit─Locate─Quit───────────────────────────────────────────┐
 │                    FRED'S FRIENDLY FISH MARKET              │
 │                                                            │
 │                                                            │
 │       ORDER NUMBER:       S   E                            │
 │                                                            │
 │       CUSTOMER NUMBER:    S   E                            │
 │                                                            │
 │       COMPANY:    S                    E                   │
 │       LAST  NAME: S                    E                   │
 │       FIRST NAME: S                    E                   │
 │                                                            │
 │                                                            │
 │       DATE ORDERED: S      E                               │
 │                                                            │
 └────────────────────────────────────────────────────────────┘
```

Fig. B-19. The main order form.

```
*(*****************************)
*(      3.1.I-ORDRADI.CMD     *)
*(        FRED'S FISH MARKET  *)
*(     ORDER ITEM ADDITIONS   *)
*(    (c) 1986 Cary N. Prague  *)
*(*****************************)
SET VAR ITEM# INTEGER
SET VAR ITEM# TO 1
SET VAR ITEMNO TEXT
SET VAR NAME TEXT
SET VAR NAME TO .FSTNAME & .LSTNAME
SET VAR PRICE DOLLAR
SET VAR ROWPTR INTEGER
SET VAR ROWPTR TO 14
NEWPAGE
DRAW ORDERITM WITH VARIABLE ORDNO COMPANY NAME
WRITE "   ORDER ITEM ADDITIONS SCREEN          " AT 3 25
WRITE "     *** ENTER ORDER ITEMS ***          " AT 5 25
WHILE ITEM# LE 20 THEN
  SHOW VAR ITEM# AT .ROWPTR 1
  WRITE "                              " AT .ROWPTR 20
  FILLIN QTY USING " " AT .ROWPTR 29
  IF QTY FAILS THEN
    BREAK
  ENDIF
```

Fig. B-20. The Order Item Additions program.

```
        FILLIN ITEMNO USING " " AT .ROWPTR 50
    IF ITEMNO FAILS THEN
        WRITE "*** ITEM NUMBER MUST BE ENTERED - REENTER RECORD *** " AT 5 15
    ELSE
        SET POINTER #3 CHECKI FOR ITEM WHERE ITEMNO EQ .ITEMNO
        IF CHECKI NE 0 THEN
            WRITE "*** ITEM NUMBER NOT ON FILE - REENTER RECORD *** " AT 5 15
        ELSE
            SET VAR PRICE TO PRICE IN #3
            LOAD ORDERITM
              .ORDNO .ITEMNO .QTY .PRICE
            END
            SET VAR ITEM# TO .ITEM# + 1
            SET VAR ROWPTR TO .ROWPTR + 1
            WRITE "                *** ENTER ORDER ITEMS ***              " +
                    AT 5 15
            IF ITEM# = 11 THEN
              SET VAR ROWPTR TO 14
            ENDIF
        ENDIF
    ENDIF
ENDWHILE
RETURN
```

Fig. B-20. The Order Item Additions program. (Continued from page 362.)

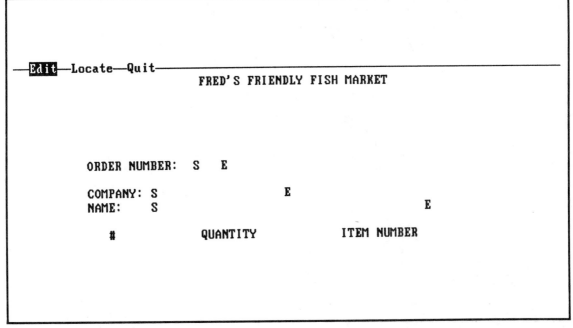

Fig. B-21. The Item order form.

```
*(*****************************)
*(       3.2-ORDRCHG.CMD       *)
*(      FRED'S FISH MARKET      *)
*(         ORDER CHANGES        *)
*(  (c) 1986 Cary N. Prague    *)
*(*****************************)
SET VAR CONT INTEGER
SET VAR CUSTNO TEXT
SET VAR ORDDATE DATE
SET VAR CONT TO 1
WHILE CONT EQ 1 THEN
    NEWPAGE
    DRAW ORDERS
    WRITE "        ORDER CHANGES SCREEN              " AT 3 25
    WRITE "    *** CHANGE ORDER RECORD ***           " AT 5 25
    ENTER VARIABLE ORDNO
    IF ORDNO FAILS THEN
      BREAK
    ENDIF
    SET POINTER #1 CHECKO FOR ORDER WHERE ORDNO EQ .ORDNO
    IF CHECKO NE 0 THEN
      WRITE "      *** ORDER NUMBER NOT ON FILE ***" AT 5 20
     ELSE
      SET VAR CUSTNO TO CUSTNO IN #1
      SET VAR ORDDATE TO ORDDATE IN #1
      SET POINTER #2 CHECKC FOR CUSTOMER WHERE CUSTNO EQ .CUSTNO
      SHOW VAR CUSTNO AT 9 28
      SET VAR COMPANY TO COMPANY IN #2
      SET VAR FSTNAME TO FSTNAME IN #2
      SET VAR LSTNAME TO LSTNAME IN #2
      SHOW VAR COMPANY AT 11 22
      SHOW VAR LSTNAME AT 12 22
      SHOW VAR FSTNAME AT 13 22
      WRITE " *** CHANGE CUSTOMER NUMBER OR DATE ***     " AT 5 20
      EDIT VARIABLE CUSTNO ORDDATE
      SET POINTER #2 CHECKC FOR CUSTOMER WHERE CUSTNO EQ .CUSTNO
      IF CHECKC NE 0 THEN
         WRITE "     *** CUSTOMER NUMBER NOT FOUND ***" AT 5 20
        ELSE
         SET VAR COMPANY TO COMPANY IN #2
         SET VAR FSTNAME TO FSTNAME IN #2
         SET VAR LSTNAME TO LSTNAME IN #2
         SHOW VAR COMPANY AT 11 22
         SHOW VAR LSTNAME AT 12 22
         SHOW VAR FSTNAME AT 13 22
         CHANGE CUSTNO TO .CUSTNO IN #1
         CHANGE ORDDATE TO .ORDDATE IN #1
         RUN ORDRCHI.CMD
       ENDIF
     ENDIF
ENDWHILE
CLEAR ALL VARIABLES
SET VAR PICK1 INT
SET VAR PICK2 INT
SET VAR LEVEL2 INT
SET VAR LEVEL2 TO 0
RETURN
```

Fig. B-22. The Order Changes main program.

```
*(*****************************)
*(     3.2.I-ORDRCHI.CMD      *)
*(     FRED'S FISH MARKET     *)
*(      ORDER ITEM CHANGES    *)
*(  (c) 1986 Cary N. Prague   *)
*(*****************************)
SET VAR ITEM# INTEGER
SET VAR ITEM# TO 1
SET VAR CHOICE TEXT
SET VAR CHOICE TO " "
SET VAR NAME TEXT
SET VAR NAME TO .FSTNAME & .LSTNAME
SET VAR PRICE DOLLAR
SET VAR ROWPTR INTEGER
SET VAR ROWPTR TO 14
SET VAR RECS INTEGER
SET VAR MAXRECS INTEGER
SET VAR RECHANGE TEXT
SET VAR ITEMCTR INTEGER
COMPUTE MAXRECS AS COUNT ORDNO FROM ORDERITM WHERE ORDNO = .ORDNO
NEWPAGE
DRAW ORDERITM WITH VARIABLE ORDNO COMPANY NAME
WRITE "    ORDER ITEM CHANGES SCREEN              " AT 3 26
IF MAXRECS >= 10 THEN
    SET VAR RECS TO 10
  ELSE
    SET VAR RECS TO .MAXRECS
ENDIF
SET POINTER #1 CHECKI FOR ORDERITM WHERE ORDNO EQ .ORDNO
WHILE ITEM# <= .RECS THEN
  SET VAR QTY TO QTY IN #1
  SET VAR ITEMNO TO ITEMNO IN #1
  SHOW VAR ITEM# AT .ROWPTR 1
  SHOW VAR QTY AT .ROWPTR 19
  SHOW VAR ITEMNO AT .ROWPTR 51
  SET VAR ROWPTR TO .ROWPTR + 1
  SET VAR ITEM# TO .ITEM# + 1
  NEXT #1 CHECKI
ENDWHILE
SET VAR ITEM# TO .ITEM# - 1
WHILE CHOICE NE X THEN
  WRITE "                                              " AT 5 20
  WRITE "                                              " AT 6 20
  WRITE "     C/CHANGE,S/SCROLL,X/EXIT" AT   6 25
  FILLIN CHOICE USING "ENTER SELECTION ===> " AT 5 30
  WRITE "                  " AT 4 15
  IF CHOICE FAILS OR CHOICE EQ X THEN
    BREAK
  ENDIF
  IF CHOICE EQ C THEN
    WRITE "                                              " AT 5 20
    WRITE "                                              " AT 6 20
    WRITE "  ENTER RECORD NUMBER TO BE CHANGED" AT   6 23
    FILLIN RECNO USING "RECORD NUMBER ===> " AT 5 30
    IF RECNO EXISTS AND RECNO > 0 THEN
      SET VAR RECHANGE TO Y
      WHILE RECHANGE = Y THEN
        IF RECNO > 20 THEN
          WRITE " *** ILLEGAL RECORD NUMBER - REENTER *** " AT 4 20
          BREAK
        ENDIF
```

Fig. B-23. The Order Item Changes program.

```
            IF ITEM# < 10 THEN
              IF RECNO > 10 THEN
                WRITE " *** ILLEGAL RECORD NUMBER - REENTER *** " AT 4 20
                BREAK
              ENDIF
            ENDIF
            IF ITEM# = 10 THEN
              IF MAXRECS = 10 THEN
                IF RECNO > 11 THEN
                   WRITE " *** ILLEGAL RECORD NUMBER - SCROLL *** " AT 4 20
                   BREAK
                ENDIF
                ELSE
                  IF RECNO >= 11 THEN
                    WRITE " *** ILLEGAL RECORD NUMBER - SCROLL *** " AT 4 20
                    BREAK
                  ENDIF
              ENDIF
            ENDIF
            IF ITEM# > 10 THEN
              IF RECNO <= 10 THEN
              WRITE " *** ILLEGAL RECORD NUMBER - SCROLL *** " AT 4 20
              BREAK
            ENDIF
          ENDIF
          IF ITEM# > 10 THEN
            SET VAR MAXRECS TO .MAXRECS + 1
            IF RECNO > .MAXRECS THEN
                WRITE " *** ILLEGAL RECORD NUMBER - REENTER *** " AT 4 20
                SET VAR MAXRECS TO .MAXRECS - 1
                BREAK
              ELSE
                SET VAR MAXRECS TO .MAXRECS - 1
            ENDIF
          ENDIF
          IF RECNO <= .MAXRECS THEN
              WRITE "                                          " AT 4 15
              WRITE "                                          " AT 5 20
              WRITE "                    ENTER CHANGES          " AT 6 20
              SET POINTER #1 CHECKI FOR ORDERITM WHERE ORDNO EQ .ORDNO
              SET VAR ITEMCTR TO 1
              WHILE ITEMCTR < .RECNO THEN
                NEXT #1 CHECKI
                SET VAR ITEMCTR TO .ITEMCTR + 1
              ENDWHILE
              WRITE "ITEM NUMBER:" AT 5 41
              FILLIN QTY USING "QUANTITY: " AT 5 26
              IF QTY NE 0 THEN
                  FILLIN ITEMNO USING " " AT 5 53
                  IF ITEMNO EXISTS THEN
                      SET POINTER #2 CHECKI FOR ITEM WHERE ITEMNO EQ .ITEMNO
                      IF CHECKI EQ 0 THEN
                          SET VAR PRICE TO PRICE IN #2
                          CHANGE QTY TO .QTY IN #1
                          CHANGE ITEMNO TO .ITEMNO IN #1
                          CHANGE PRICE TO .PRICE IN #1
                          IF RECNO > 10 THEN
                              SET VAR ROWPTR TO .RECNO + 3
                            ELSE
                              SET VAR ROWPTR TO .RECNO + 13
                          ENDIF
```

Fig. B-23. The Order Item Changes program. (Continued from page 365.)

```
                    SHOW VAR QTY AT .ROWPTR 19
                    SHOW VAR ITEMNO AT .ROWPTR 51
                    SET VAR RECHANGE TO N
                ELSE
                    WRITE "       *** ITEM NUMBER NOT ON FILE ***" AT 4 20
              ENDIF
            ELSE
              WRITE " *** ITEM NUMBER MUST BE ENTERED ***    " AT 4 20
          ENDIF
        ELSE
          DELETE ROWS FROM #1
          SET VAR MAXRECS TO .MAXRECS - 1
          SET VAR RECHANGE TO N
          SET POINTER #1 CHECKI FOR ORDERITM WHERE ORDNO EQ .ORDNO
          SET VAR ITEM# TO 1
          IF RECNO = 11 AND MAXRECS = 10 THEN
            SET VAR RECNO TO 10
          ENDIF
          IF RECNO >= 11 AND MAXRECS >= 10 THEN
            WHILE ITEM# <= 10 THEN
              NEXT #1 CHECKI
              SET VAR ITEM# TO .ITEM# + 1
            ENDWHILE
          ENDIF
          SET VAR ROWPTR TO 14
          WHILE ITEM# <= .MAXRECS THEN
            SET VAR QTY TO QTY IN #1
            SET VAR ITEMNO TO ITEMNO IN #1
            SHOW VAR ITEM# AT .ROWPTR 1
            SHOW VAR QTY AT .ROWPTR 19
            SHOW VAR ITEMNO AT .ROWPTR 51
            SET VAR ROWPTR TO .ROWPTR + 1
            SET VAR ITEM# TO .ITEM# + 1
            NEXT #1 CHECKI
          ENDWHILE
          SET VAR ITEM# TO .ITEM# - 1
          WHILE ROWPTR <= 23 THEN
            WRITE "                            " AT .ROWPTR 1
            WRITE "                            " AT .ROWPTR 40
            SET VAR ROWPTR TO .ROWPTR + 1
          ENDWHILE
      ENDIF
    ELSE
      WRITE "                                        " AT 4 15
      WRITE "                                        " AT 5 30
      WRITE "                 ENTER NEW RECORD       " AT  6 20
      WRITE "ITEM NUMBER:" AT 5 41
      FILLIN QTY USING "QUANTITY: " AT 5 26
      IF QTY NE 0 THEN
          FILLIN ITEMNO USING " " AT 5 53
          IF ITEMNO EXISTS THEN
              SET POINTER #2 CHECKI FOR ITEM WHERE ITEMNO EQ .ITEMNO
              IF CHECKI EQ 0 THEN
                  SET VAR PRICE TO PRICE IN #2
                  LOAD ORDERITM
                    .ORDNO .ITEMNO .QTY .PRICE
                  END
                  IF RECNO > 10 THEN
                      SET VAR ROWPTR TO .RECNO + 3
                  ELSE
                      SET VAR ROWPTR TO .RECNO + 13
```

Fig. B-23. The Order Item Changes program. (Continued from page 366.)

```
                            ENDIF
                            IF ITEM# NE 10 THEN
                               SET VAR ITEM# TO .ITEM# + 1
                            ENDIF
                            IF RECNO NE 11 THEN
                               SHOW VAR ITEM# AT .ROWPTR 1
                               SHOW VAR QTY AT .ROWPTR 19
                               SHOW VAR ITEMNO AT .ROWPTR 51
                            ENDIF
                            SET VAR MAXRECS TO .MAXRECS + 1
                            SET VAR RECHANGE TO N
                         ELSE
                            WRITE "      *** ITEM NUMBER NOT ON FILE ***" AT 4 20
                       ENDIF
                     ELSE
                       WRITE "  *** ITEM NUMBER MUST BE ENTERED ***      " AT 4 20
                  ENDIF
               ELSE
                  WRITE "  *** QUANTITY MUST NOT BE 0 ***          " AT 4 25
               ENDIF
         ENDIF
       ENDWHILE
   ENDIF
ENDIF
IF CHOICE EQ S THEN
   IF ITEM# <= 10 THEN
      IF MAXRECS <= 10 THEN
         WRITE " *** THERE ARE NO RECORDS TO SCROLL ***" AT 4 23
       ELSE
         SET POINTER #1 CHECKI FOR ORDERITM WHERE ORDNO EQ .ORDNO
         SET VAR ITEM# TO 1
         WHILE ITEM# <= 10 THEN
            NEXT #1 CHECKI
            SET VAR ITEM# TO .ITEM# + 1
         ENDWHILE
         SET VAR ROWPTR TO 14
         WHILE ITEM# <= .MAXRECS THEN
            SET VAR QTY TO QTY IN #1
            SET VAR ITEMNO TO ITEMNO IN #1
            SHOW VAR ITEM# AT .ROWPTR 1
            SHOW VAR QTY AT .ROWPTR 19
            SHOW VAR ITEMNO AT .ROWPTR 51
            SET VAR ROWPTR TO .ROWPTR + 1
            SET VAR ITEM# TO .ITEM# + 1
            NEXT #1 CHECKI
         ENDWHILE
         SET VAR ITEM# TO .ITEM# - 1
         WHILE ROWPTR <= 23 THEN
            WRITE "                                          " AT .ROWPTR 14
            SET VAR ROWPTR TO .ROWPTR + 1
         ENDWHILE
      ENDIF
    ELSE
      SET VAR ROWPTR TO 14
      SET VAR ITEM# TO 1
      IF MAXRECS >= 10 THEN
         SET VAR RECS TO 10
       ELSE
         SET VAR RECS TO .MAXRECS
      ENDIF
      SET POINTER #1 CHECKI FOR ORDERITM WHERE ORDNO EQ .ORDNO
```

Fig. B-23. The Order Item Changes program. (Continued from page 367.)

```
              WHILE ITEM# <= .RECS THEN
                SET VAR QTY TO QTY IN #1
                SET VAR ITEMNO TO ITEMNO IN #1
                SHOW VAR ITEM# AT .ROWPTR 1
                SHOW VAR QTY AT .ROWPTR 19
                SHOW VAR ITEMNO AT .ROWPTR 51
                SET VAR ROWPTR TO .ROWPTR + 1
                SET VAR ITEM# TO .ITEM# + 1
                NEXT #1 CHECKI
              ENDWHILE
              SET VAR ITEM# TO .ITEM# - 1
              WHILE ROWPTR <= 23 THEN
                WRITE "
                SET VAR ROWPTR TO .ROWPTR + 1
              ENDWHILE
          ENDIF
       ENDIF
    ENDWHILE
    RETURN
```

Fig. B-23. The Order Item Changes program. (Continued from page 368.)

```
*(******************************)
*(        3.3-ORDRREM.CMD        *)
*(       FRED'S FISH MARKET      *)
*(          ORDER REMOVALS       *)
*(    (c) 1986 Cary N. Prague    *)
*(******************************)
SET VAR CONT INTEGER
SET VAR ORDDATE DATE
SET VAR CUSTNO TEXT
SET VAR CONT TO 1
SET VAR RECS INTEGER
SET VAR MAXRECS INTEGER
SET VAR ITEM# INTEGER
SET VAR ROWPTR INTEGER
WHILE CONT EQ 1 THEN
  SET VAR ITEM# TO 1
  SET VAR ROWPTR TO 14
  NEWPAGE
  DRAW ORDERITM
  WRITE "       ORDER REMOVAL SCREEN             " AT 3 25
  WRITE "    *** REMOVE ORDER RECORD ***         " AT 5 25
  WRITE " DATE ORDERED:                " AT 9 11
  ENTER VARIABLE ORDNO
    IF ORDNO FAILS THEN
      BREAK
    ENDIF
    SET POINTER #1 CHECKO FOR ORDER WHERE ORDNO EQ .ORDNO
    IF CHECKO NE 0 THEN
      WRITE "      *** ORDER NUMBER NOT ON FILE ***" AT 5 20
    ELSE
      COMPUTE MAXRECS AS COUNT ORDNO FROM ORDERITM WHERE ORDNO EQ .ORDNO
      SET VAR CUSTNO TO CUSTNO IN #1
      SET VAR ORDDATE TO ORDDATE IN #1
      SET POINTER #2 CHECKC FOR CUSTOMER WHERE CUSTNO EQ .CUSTNO
      SET VAR COMPANY TO COMPANY IN #2
      SET VAR FSTNAME TO FSTNAME IN #2
      SET VAR LSTNAME TO LSTNAME IN #2
```

Fig. B-24. The Order Removal program.

369

```
                SET VAR NAME TEXT
                SET VAR NAME TO .FSTNAME & .LSTNAME
                SHOW VAR COMPANY AT 10 27
                SHOW VAR NAME AT 11 27
                SHOW VAR ORDDATE AT 9 27
                IF MAXRECS >= 10 THEN
                    SET VAR RECS TO 10
                  ELSE
                    SET VAR RECS TO .MAXRECS
                ENDIF
                SET POINTER #1 CHECKI FOR ORDERITM WHERE ORDNO EQ .ORDNO
                WHILE ITEM# <= .RECS THEN
                  SET VAR QTY TO QTY IN #1
                  SET VAR ITEMNO TO ITEMNO IN #1
                  SHOW VAR ITEM# AT .ROWPTR 1
                  SHOW VAR QTY AT .ROWPTR 19
                  SHOW VAR ITEMNO AT .ROWPTR 51
                  SET VAR ROWPTR TO .ROWPTR + 1
                  SET VAR ITEM# TO .ITEM# + 1
                  NEXT #1 CHECKI
                ENDWHILE
                FILLIN DELCON USING "ENTER D TO CONFIRM DELETE ===>    " AT 5 22
                IF DELCON = D THEN
                  DELETE ROWS FROM ORDER WHER ORDNO EQ .ORDNO
                  DELETE ROWS FROM ORDERITM WHERE ORDNO EQ .ORDNO
                  WRITE "*** CUSTOMER RECORD DELETED ***          " AT 5 25
                ENDIF
          ENDIF
      ENDWHILE
      CLEAR ALL VARIABLES
      SET VAR PICK1 INT
      SET VAR PICK2 INT
      SET VAR LEVEL2 INT
      SET VAR LEVEL2 TO 0
      RETURN
```

Fig. B-24. The Order Removal program. (Continued from page 369.)

```
      *(*****************************)
      *(        3.4-ORDRDIS.CMD        *)
      *(      FRED'S FISH MARKET       *)
      *(        ORDER DISPLAY          *)
      *(   (c) 1986 Cary N. Prague     *)
      *(*****************************)
      SET VAR CONT INTEGER
      SET VAR ORDDATE DATE
      SET VAR CUSTNO TEXT
      SET VAR CONT TO 1
      SET VAR RECS INTEGER
      SET VAR MAXRECS INTEGER
      SET VAR ITEM# INTEGER
      SET VAR ROWPTR INTEGER
      WHILE CONT EQ 1 THEN
        SET VAR ITEM# TO 1
        SET VAR ROWPTR TO 14
        NEWPAGE
        DRAW ORDERITM
        WRITE "      ORDER DISPLAY SCREEN            " AT 3 25
        WRITE "   *** DISPLAY ORDER RECORD ***       " AT 5 25
        WRITE " DATE ORDERED:              " AT 9 11
```

Fig. B-25. The Order Display program.

```
  ENTER VARIABLE ORDNO
    IF ORDNO FAILS THEN
  BREAK
ENDIF
SET POINTER #1 CHECKO FOR ORDER WHERE ORDNO EQ .ORDNO
IF CHECKO NE 0 THEN
    WRITE "      *** ORDER NUMBER NOT ON FILE ***" AT 5 20
  ELSE
    COMPUTE MAXRECS AS COUNT ORDNO FROM ORDERITM WHERE ORDNO EQ .ORDNO
    SET VAR CUSTNO TO CUSTNO IN #1
    SET VAR ORDDATE TO ORDDATE IN #1
    SET POINTER #2 CHECKC FOR CUSTOMER WHERE CUSTNO EQ .CUSTNO
    SET VAR COMPANY TO COMPANY IN #2
    SET VAR FSTNAME TO FSTNAME IN #2
    SET VAR LSTNAME TO LSTNAME IN #2
    SET VAR NAME TEXT
    SET VAR NAME TO .FSTNAME & .LSTNAME
    SHOW VAR COMPANY AT 10 27
    SHOW VAR NAME AT 11 27
    SHOW VAR ORDDATE AT 9 27

    IF MAXRECS >= 10 THEN
        SET VAR RECS TO 10
      ELSE
        SET VAR RECS TO .MAXRECS
    ENDIF
    SET POINTER #1 CHECKI FOR ORDERITM WHERE ORDNO EQ .ORDNO
    WHILE ITEM# <= .RECS THEN
      SET VAR QTY TO QTY IN #1
      SET VAR ITEMNO TO ITEMNO IN #1
      SHOW VAR ITEM# AT .ROWPTR 1
      SHOW VAR QTY AT .ROWPTR 19
      SHOW VAR ITEMNO AT .ROWPTR 51
      SET VAR ROWPTR TO .ROWPTR + 1
      SET VAR ITEM# TO .ITEM# + 1
      NEXT #1 CHECKI
    ENDWHILE
    IF MAXRECS > 10 THEN
        WRITE " *** PRESS ANY KEY TO SEE MORE RECORDS ***      " AT 5 18
        PAUSE
        SET VAR ROWPTR TO 14
        WHILE ITEM# <= .MAXRECS THEN
          SET VAR QTY TO QTY IN #1
          SET VAR ITEMNO TO ITEMNO IN #1
          SHOW VAR ITEM# AT .ROWPTR 1
          SHOW VAR QTY AT .ROWPTR 19
          SHOW VAR ITEMNO AT .ROWPTR 51
          SET VAR ROWPTR TO .ROWPTR + 1
          SET VAR ITEM# TO .ITEM# + 1
          NEXT #1 CHECKI
        ENDWHILE
        WHILE ROWPTR <= 23 THEN
          WRITE "                                            " AT .ROWPTR 1
          WRITE "                                            " AT .ROWPTR 50
          SET VAR ROWPTR TO .ROWPTR + 1
        ENDWHILE
        WRITE "        *** PRESS ANY KEY TO CONTINUE ***        " AT 5 18
        PAUSE
      ELSE
        WRITE "        *** PRESS ANY KEY TO CONTINUE ***        " AT 5 18
```

Fig. B-25. The Order Display program. (Continued from page 370.)

```
        PAUSE
    ENDIF
ENDIF
ENDWHILE
CLEAR ALL VARIABLES
SET VAR PICK1 INT
SET VAR PICK2 INT
SET VAR LEVEL2 INT
SET VAR LEVEL2 TO 0
RETURN
```

Fig. B-25. The Order Display program. (Continued from page 371.)

```
        *(******************************)
        *(        3.5-ORDRFMS.CMD         *)
        *(        FRED'S FISH MARKET       *)
        *(        ORDER FORMS PRINT        *)
        *(    (c) 1986 Cary N. Prague     *)
        *(******************************)
        SET VAR CONT INTEGER
        SET VAR CONT TO 1
        WHILE CONT EQ 1 THEN
          NEWPAGE
          DRAW ORDERS
          WRITE "         ORDER PRINT SCREEN              " AT 3 25
          WRITE "    *** PRINT ORDER RECORD ***          " AT 5 25
          ENTER VARIABLE ORDNO
            IF ORDNO FAILS THEN
              BREAK
            ENDIF
            SET POINTER #1 CHECKO FOR ORDER WHERE ORDNO EQ .ORDNO
            IF CHECKO NE 0 THEN
               WRITE "      *** ORDER NUMBER NOT ON FILE ***" AT 5 20
             ELSE
               WRITE "  TURN ON AND ALIGN PRINTER     " AT 5 25
               WRITE "    PRESS ANY KEY TO START      " AT 6 25
               WRITE "                                " AT 8 32
               PAUSE
               OUTPUT PRINTER
               PRINT ORDERFMS WHERE ORDNO EQ .ORDNO
               OUTPUT SCREEN
            ENDIF
        ENDWHILE
        CLEAR ALL VARIABLES
        SET VAR PICK1 INT
        SET VAR PICK2 INT
        SET VAR LEVEL2 INT
        SET VAR LEVEL2 TO 0
        RETURN
```

Fig. B-26. The Order Forms program.

```
                                            [F3] to list, [ESC] to exit
Expression:

  1:TEXT   : CUSTNO   = CUSTNO   IN ORDER    WHERE ORDNO = ORDNO
  2:TEXT   : FSTNAME  = FSTNAME  IN CUSTOMER WHERE CUSTNO EQ CUSTNO
  3:TEXT   : LSTNAME  = LSTNAME  IN CUSTOMER WHERE CUSTNO EQ CUSTNO
  4:TEXT   : COMPANY  = COMPANY  IN CUSTOMER WHERE CUSTNO EQ CUSTNO
  5:DATE   : ORDDATE  = ORDDATE  IN ORDER    WHERE ORDNO = ORDNO
  6:TEXT   : ITEM     = ITEM     IN ITEM     WHERE ITEMNO EQ ITEMNO
  7:TEXT   : NAME     = FSTNAME  & LSTNAME
```

Fig. B-27. The Order Forms report variables.

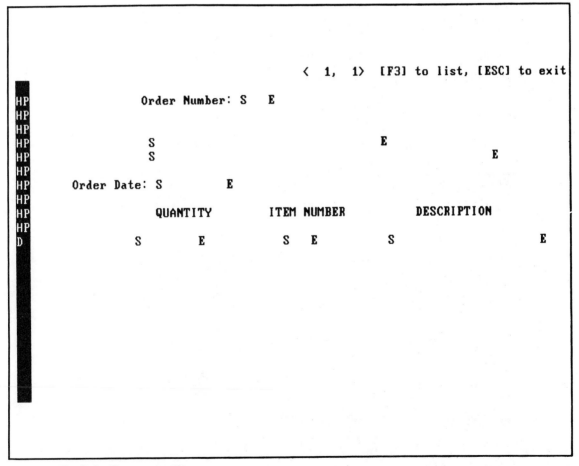

Fig. B-28. The Order Forms report form.

373

```
*(*****************************)
*(      3.6-ORDRSHP.CMD      *)
*(      FRED'S FISH MARKET   *)
*( ORDER SHIPPING FORMS PRINT *)
*(   (c) 1986 Cary N. Prague  *)
*(*****************************)
SET VAR CONT INTEGER
SET VAR CONT TO 1
WHILE CONT EQ 1 THEN
  NEWPAGE
  DRAW ORDERS
  WRITE "        ORDER PRINT SCREEN           " AT 3 25
  WRITE "    *** PRINT ORDER RECORD ***       " AT 5 25
  ENTER VARIABLE ORDNO
    IF ORDNO FAILS THEN
      BREAK
    ENDIF
    SET POINTER #1 CHECKO FOR ORDER WHERE ORDNO EQ .ORDNO
    IF CHECKO NE 0 THEN
      WRITE "      *** ORDER NUMBER NOT ON FILE ***" AT 5 20
    ELSE
      WRITE "   TURN ON AND ALIGN PRINTER       " AT 5 25
      WRITE "     PRESS ANY KEY TO START        " AT 6 25
      WRITE "                                   " AT 8 32
      PAUSE
      OUTPUT PRINTER
      PRINT ORDERSHP WHERE ORDNO EQ .ORDNO
      OUTPUT SCREEN
    ENDIF
ENDWHILE
CLEAR ALL VARIABLES
SET VAR PICK1 INT
SET VAR PICK2 INT
SET VAR LEVEL2 INT
SET VAR LEVEL2 TO 0
RETURN
```

Fig. B-29. The Order Shipping Forms program.

```
                                      [F3] to list, [ESC] to exit
   Expression:

    1:TEXT   : CUSTNO   = CUSTNO   IN ORDER    WHERE ORDNO = ORDNO
    2:TEXT   : FSTNAME  = FSTNAME  IN CUSTOMER WHERE CUSTNO EQ CUSTNO
    3:TEXT   : LSTNAME  = LSTNAME  IN CUSTOMER WHERE CUSTNO EQ CUSTNO
    4:TEXT   : COMPANY  = COMPANY  IN CUSTOMER WHERE CUSTNO EQ CUSTNO
    5:TEXT   : ADDRESS  = ADDRESS  IN CUSTOMER WHERE CUSTNO EQ CUSTNO
    6:TEXT   : CITY     = CITY     IN CUSTOMER WHERE CUSTNO EQ CUSTNO
    7:TEXT   : STATE    = STATE    IN CUSTOMER WHERE CUSTNO EQ CUSTNO
    8:TEXT   : ZIP      = ZIP      IN CUSTOMER WHERE CUSTNO EQ CUSTNO
    9:DATE   : ORDDATE  = ORDDATE  IN ORDER    WHERE ORDNO = ORDNO
   10:TEXT   : ITEM     = ITEM     IN ITEM     WHERE ITEMNO EQ ITEMNO
   11:DOLLAR : AMOUNT   = QTY      X PRICE
   12:REAL   : DISCOUNT = DISCOUNT IN CUSTOMER WHERE CUSTNO EQ CUSTNO
   13:DOLLAR : TOTAMT   = SUM      OF AMOUNT
   14:REAL   : DISC     = DISCOUNT / 100
   15:DOLLAR : DISCDISP = TOTAMT   X DISC
   16:DOLLAR : AMTDUE   = TOTAMT   - DISCDISP
   17:TEXT   : NAME     = FSTNAME  & LSTNAME
   18:TEXT   : CITYST   = CITY     & STATE
```

Fig. B-30. The Order Shipping Forms report variables.

```
                              < 1, 1>  [F3] to list, [ESC] to exit
HP
HP        Order Number: S   E
HP        S                                          E
HP        S                        E
HP        S                        E
HP        S                        E
HP        S                 E
HP
HP        Order Date: S          E
HP
HP        Quantity         Description         Price Each      Amount
HP
D    S        E        S            E   S        E    S        E
F1                                                   ----------
F1                                      Total Amount:   S        E
F1
F1                                         Discount:  (S        E)
F1                                                   ----------
F1                                      Amount Due:    S        E
F1                                                   ==========
```

Fig. B-31. The Order Shipping Forms report form.

Appendix C

Compiling Programs

Fred created his system to have almost 20 programs. If you count the screen and menu files, there are several more. Although using many programs is easier to maintain because you will always be working with "smaller pieces of the puzzle," it will make your system run considerably slower. One solution is to compile each command file to translate the program you have coded into a program that is more readily understood to your computer. R:base can process it faster, and, therefore, it will run faster.

To use the R:base compiler requires typing the command:

```
R> RCOMPILE
```

The screen in Fig. C-1 appears.

You can use the first choice to translate your program into a special type of file known as a *binary command file*. This is your compiled program. When you run your programs you will see them execute faster.

If you want to take all 23 of your program, menu, and screen files and put them together, you can. A file combining these kinds of files is called an *application file*. The keyword $COMMAND must precede each command file, along with the name of the command. Menus are preceded by the keyword $MENU and the menu name, while the help screens would be preceded by the keyword $SCREEN.

After you put all of your files together, you can use selection 5 to convert the application file into a large binary compiled file. There is one thing to remember.

```
                                    RCOMPILE
           Copyright (c) 1985 by Microrim, Inc. (Uer. 1.01 PC-DOS)

    ╔══════════════════════════Select an option══════════════════════════╗
    ║  (1)  Convert an ASCII command file to a binary command file         ║
    ║  (2)  Add an ASCII command file to a procedure file                  ║
    ║  (3)  Add an ASCII screen file to a procedure file                   ║
    ║  (4)  Add an ASCII menu file to a procedure file                     ║
    ║  (5)  Convert an ASCII application file to a binary application file ║
    ║  (6)  Display directory                                              ║
    ║  (7)  Display the contents of an ASCII file                          ║
    ║  (8)  Exit                                                           ║
    ╚═════════════════════════════════════════════════════════════════════╝
```

Fig. C-1. The R:base RCompile screen.

Your CHOOSE and RUN commands must specifically identify the application file as the source of the input.

Compiled files will save you time and effort when you are running the programs. Remember, however, that to make changes you would have to use the original uncompiled file.

Appendix D

Database Commands
Used in This Book

DATABASE STRUCTURE COMMANDS

DEFINE
TABLES
COLUMNS
RULES
BUILD KEY
OPEN
CLOSE
OWNER
PASSWORDS

DATABASE RECORD COLUMNS

ASSIGN
CHANGE
CHANGE COLUMN
DELETE
END
ENTER
LOAD
MOVE

DATABASE DISPLAY COMMANDS

SELECT
EDIT
COMPUTE
TALLY
PRINT
FORMS
REPORTS

Appendix E

Programming Commands Used in This Book

HOUSEKEEPING

SET MESSAGE ON
SET ERROR MESSAGE ON
SET ERROR VARIABLE
SET ECHO ON
SET AUTOSKIP OFF
SET BELL ON
SET CASE ON
SET CLEAR ON
SET COLOR FOREGRND color
SET COLOR BACKGRND color
SET DATE datefmt
SET ESCAPE ON
SET LINES number
SET NULL -0-
SET REVERSE ON
SET RULES ON
SET WIDTH number
CLEAR

INPUT

FILLIN
CHOOSE
ENTER/ENTER VARIABLES
EDIT/EDIT VARIABLES

OUTPUT

DRAW
NEWPAGE
WRITE
PAUSE
DISPLAY
TYPE
SHOW VARIABLES
OUTPUT
PRINT

RELATIONAL COMMANDS

SET POINTER
NEXT

LOGICAL CONSTRUCTS

IF-THEN-ELSE-ENDIF
WHILE-ENDWHILE
GOTO
LABEL
RUN
RETURN
BREAK

Index

Other Bestsellers From TAB

Other Bestsellers From TAB

Programming with R:base® 5000

If you are intrigued with the possibilities of the programs included in *Programming with R:base® 5000* (TAB Book No. 2666), you should definitely consider having the ready-to-run disk containing the software applications. This software is guaranteed free of manufacturer's defects. (If you have any problems, return the disk within 30 days, and we'll send you a new one.) Not only will you save the time and effort of typing the programs, the disk eliminates the possibility of errors that can prevent the programs from functioning. Interested?

Available on disk for the IBM PC 512K at $24.95 for each disk plus $1.00 each shipping and handling.